Brazil in the world

MANCHESTER
1824

Manchester University Press

Brazil in the world

The international relations of a
South American giant

Sean W. Burges

Manchester University Press

Published by Manchester University Press
Altrincham Street, Manchester M1 7JA

www.manchesteruniversitypress.co.uk

British Library Cataloguing-in-Publication Data
A catalogue record for this book is available from the British Library

Library of Congress Cataloging-in-Publication Data applied for

ISBN 978 1 5261 0739 8 hardback

ISBN 978 1 5261 0740 4 paperback

First published 2017

Typeset in Sabon and Gill Sans by
Servis Filmsetting Ltd, Stockport, Cheshire
Printed in Great Britain by
TJ International Ltd, Padstow

Contents

Lists of figures and tables   vi
Acknowledgements   viii
List of abbreviations   x

1   Thinking about Brazil in the world   1
2   The domestic foreign policy context   25
3   O jeito brasileiro... the Brazilian way   48
4   Brazil's multilateralist impulse   64
5   Trade policy   86
6   Brazil Inc.   110
7   Security policy   134
8   Brazil and Latin America   153
9   Brazil and the Global South   174
10 Brazil and the United States   197
11 Brazil and China   222
12 Conclusions and future possibilities   241

References   251
Index   278

Figures and tables

Figures

5.1 Machinery, electrical and transportation as % of exports,
1992–2000   91

8.1 Mercosul country exports to Brazil as % of total exports,
1991–2013   162

8.2 Exports to Brazil as % of total exports, non-Mercosul
countries, 1991–2013   163

10.1 Brazilian exports to the US and the world, 1989–2014   205

10.2 Brazilian exports to the US in nominal and % of total,
1989–2014   206

11.1 Brazilian and Chinese share of South American
manufactured imports, 1995–2013   229

11.2 Brazilian exports to China, 1995–2013   230

11.3 Brazilian imports from China, 1986–2013   231

Tables

5.1 Brazil trade with Mercosul (USD millions), 1992–1998   90

5.2 Brazilian trade with Mercosul (USD millions), 1998–2003   94

5.3 Selected Brazilian agricultural commodity exports by
volume (tonnes), 1996–2006   96

5.4 Percentage of total exports to selected regions, 2007–2012   106

5.5 Percentage of exports by value aggregation, 2007–2012   107

6.1 Brazilian outward FDI (USD millions), 1990–2012   120

6.2 Brazilian outward equity FDI by sector (USD millions),
2006–2012   121

6.3 Brazilian FDI flows to South America (USD millions),
2006–2012   128

7.1   Military expenditure by country as % of GDP, 2000–2014   137
7.2   Military expenditure by country as % of government
        spending, 2000–2014   137
7.3   Percentage of South American military expenditure,
        2000–2014   138
8.1   Percentage of total Brazilian exports, 1991–1998   158
8.2   Manufactureds as % of Brazilian exports, 1991–1998   158
10.1 FDI inflows (USD millions) and % of total FDI stocks held
        in Brazil, 2001–2012   208
10.2 Brazilian FDI stocks abroad (USD millions) and % of total
        FDI stocks held abroad, 2001–2012   209
11.1 Brazilian bilateral trade with China (USD 000s),
        2003–2013   227

Acknowledgements

This book would not have been possible without the encouragement and assistance of a great many people. Jean Daudelin was instrumental in my decision to complete this project in its current format. The extended discussions about Brazilian foreign policy in our small 'para-network' helped shape the research agenda behind the book. Towards the end of the project Fabrício Chagas Bastos was an invaluable sounding board and boundless source of energy searching out the final details. Shelter from unexpected turbulence was provided at critical times by John Ravenhill, John Minns and Andrew Banfield in their respective leadership positions at the Australian National University, all of whom intervened at key points to keep the project going forward. Ravenhill and Minns, as well as Carlos Pio, Zuleika Arashiro, Guy Emerson, Tom Chodor, and many of my other colleagues in the School of Politics and International Relations and the Australian National Centre for Latin American Studies, added to the intellectual stimulation driving the book with their constant willingness to help me sort through a series of conceptual conundrums during the research and writing.

Outside of the ANU a long list of people contributed to my understanding of and thinking about Brazilian foreign policy and South–South relations with their ongoing conversations and penetrating commentaries on ideas critical to the book: Adriana Abdenur, Leslie Elliott Armijo, Sandra Borda, Stephen Brown, Barry Carr, Miguel Carter, Mahrukh Doctor, Carlos Aurélio Pimenta de Faria, Nicholas Firman, Daniel Flemes, Lucinda Foote-Short, Rosario Santa Gadea, Gian Luca Gardini, Randal Germain, Adrian Hearn, Monica Herz, Kathy Hochstetler, Andrew Hurrell, Kai Kenkel, Peter Kingstone, Tom Legler, Charmain Levy, Dawisson Belém Lopes, Andrés Malamud, Joseph Marques, Laura Gómez-Mera, Carlos Milani, Al Montero, Amâncio Jorge de Oliveira,

Lorena Oyarzun, Nicola Phillips, Leticia Pinheiro, Tim Power, Antonio Jorge Ramalho, Carmen Robledo, Roberto Russell, Marcelo Saguier, Pedro Seabra, Paulo Sotero, Anthony Spanakos, Matias Spektor, Marco Antonio Vieira, and Eduardo Viola. There are also a large number of individuals at various international organizations, governments and multinational corporations not named on this list who generously gave up their time to answer my questions about Brazil in the world on condition of anonymity. In this respect I would like to give particular thanks to the Brazilian foreign ministry. For me it stands as a mark of the professionalism at Itamaraty that Brazilian diplomats would consistently provide me with assistance not only through the interviews they granted, but also with critical logistical and networking issues despite my certainty that the analyses I was publishing did not always find favour within the Palace's halls. The impression I continue to have is that Brazilian diplomats are eager to help any attempt to seriously understand their country and build linkages abroad, something that is consistent with the foreign policy logic outlined in this book.

The financial support to pursue the project came through Australian Research Council Discovery Early Career Research Award number DE120100401. Supplementary financial assistance was provided by the Research School of Social Sciences in the College of Arts and Social Sciences at the Australian National University. The bulk of chapter three is drawn directly from Sean W. Burges, 'Strategies and Tactics for Global Change: Democratic Brazil in Comparative Perspective', *Global Society* 26 (3) (July, 2012): 351–368 [www.tandfonline.com/doi/full/10.1080/13600826.2012.682272], and is reproduced with the gracious permission of Taylor and Francis.

Finally I want to thank Shelley Kennedy for her patience, support, and understanding not just for the disruptions caused by this book, but for the generalized chaos I have brought into her life. For William I offer my apologies that the book took me away so often, but would also point to the overflowing basket of toy cars and t-shirts from around the world as perhaps being a small measure of compensation.

Abbreviations

ABC	Agência Brasileira de Cooperação (Brazilian Cooperation Agency)
ALADI	Asociación Latinoamericana de Integración (Latin American Integration Association)
ASEAN	Association of Southeast Asian Nations
BNDES	Banco Nacional de Desenvolvimento Econômico e Social (National Bank of Economic and Social Development)
BRICS	Brazil, Russia, India, China, South Africa
CAMEX	Câmara de Comércio Exterior (Foreign Trade Council)
CASA	Comunidade de Nacões Sulamerica (Community of South American Nations)
CDS	Conselho de Defesa Sul-Americano (South American Defense Council)
CELAC	Comunidade de Estados Latino-Americanos e Caribenhos (Community of Latin American and Caribbean States)
COSBAN	Comissão Sino-Brasileira de Alto Nível de Concertação e Cooperação (High Level Sino-Brazilian Coordination and Cooperation Commission)
CPLP	Comunidade dos Países de Língua Portuguesa (Community of Portuguese-Speaking Nations)
CSR	Corporate Social Responsibility
FAO	Food and Agricultural Organization
FDI	foreign direct investment
FIESP	Federação de Indústrias Estadual de São Paulo (São Paulo Federation of Industrial Enterprises)
FTAA	Free Trade Area of the Americas
GATT	General Agreement on Tarrifs and Trade

GDP	gross domestic product
IAEA	International Atomic Energy Agency
IBSA	India-Brazil-South Africa Dialogue Forum
ICONE	Instituto de Estudos do Comércio e Negociações Internacioanais (Institute for International Trade Negotiations)
IIRSA	Iniciativa para la Integración de la Infraestructura Regional Suramericana (Initiative for the Integration of the Regional Infrastructure of South America)
IMF	International Monetary Fund
MDIC	Ministério do Desenvolvimento, Indústria e Comércio Exterior (Ministry of Development, Industry and Foreign Trade)
Mercosul	Mercado Comum do Sul (Common Market of the South; Mercosur in Spanish)
NAFTA	North American Free Trade Agreement
NGO	non-governmental organization
NPT	Nuclear Non-Proliferation Treaty
OAS	Organization of American States
OECD-DAC	Organization of Economic Cooperation and Development Development Assistance Committee
PICE	Programa de Integración y Cooperación Económica Argentina-Brasil (Argentina-Brazil Integration and Economics Cooperation Program)
PSDB	Partido da Social Democracia Brasileira
PT	Partido dos Trabalhadores (Workers' Party)
UNASUL	União de Nações Sul-Americanas (Union of South American Nations; UNASUR in Spanish)
UNSC	United Nations Security Council
WTO	World Trade Organization
ZOPACAS	Zona de Paz e Cooperação do Atlântico Sul (Zone of Peace and Cooperation of the South Atlantic)

1

Thinking about Brazil in the world

A long-standing, self-deprecating joke in Brazil runs as follows: 'Brazil is the country of the future, and always will be.' Although ambitions of global importance and international influence are not new to Brazilian foreign policy, the capacity and credibility to realize these dreams have until recently been absent. Whether it be Brazil's relative geographic isolation from the main US–Europe axis of power, a lack of industrial capacity in the first half of the twentieth century, financial disaster in the 1980s and 1990s, or a generalized lack of military force-projection capacity, Brazil has long been seen externally as a capable negotiator, but not a country that is of great significance when it comes to concrete regional or international action. At the start of the twenty-first century, the reality is different. For Brazil the future has seemingly arrived. Brazil's counsel is sought at global governance decision tables, and Brazilian investment, trade and economic cooperation have become important goods for countries across Latin America and the Global South. As the authors of two recent books put it, Brazil is on the rise and has become the 'New' Brazil (Roett, 2010; Rohter, 2010).

The reality of Brazil's rapid rise in the 2000s also brings up another salient quip for policy makers, namely the bosa nova musician Tom Jobim's observation that 'Brazil is not for beginners.' Nowhere is this more typified than in quick analyses of Brazil's emergence focusing on the country as a potential problem seeking to resist US hegemony and overturn the world order. As this book will argue, the reality was considerably more complicated. Brazilian foreign policy makers focused on a subtler morphing of the structures of regional and global politics and economics to create more space for their country to pursue its interests. Often this ocurred in symphony with the foreign policy agendas of established major international actors, although there were inevitable divergences. Part of the reason why this theme has been overlooked is the nature of scholarship and coverage of Brazil. A common theme to the more popularized English-language books published on contemporary Brazil is an attempt to provide insight into how this enormously complex country operates. Emphasis in these books ranges from the academic and more economically focused (Brainard and Martinez-Diaz, 2009; Montero, 2014) through to historical tracings of change and continuity (Fishlow, 2011; Roett, 2010), to the more journalistic and anecdotally illustrative (Reid, 2014; Rohter, 2010) or grounded in major events such as the FIFA World Cup and the Olympic Games (Zirin, 2014). Other volumes have taken a more targeted approach by examining Brazil's political pop star, Luiz Inácio Lula da Silva, and what the rise of his Workers' Party (PT – Partido dos Trabalhadores) and its national electoral victories starting in 2002 tell us about how the country has changed and where it is going (Bourne, 2008; Hunter, 2010). Each of these books and the many others published in recent years provides an introduction and exploration of various elements of the complex realities that drive Brazilian politics, society and economy, and thus start to offer a way past Jobim's warning. What remains particularly notable in all of these books is that the treatment of foreign policy is an addition, not a central theme despite the critical role that Brazil plays in South America, its leading role across the Global South and its persistent appearance as a player of note in global governance frameworks. In part this may because newcomers to Brazil are seeking to understand what makes the country tick. A repeated point made in the following pages is that foreign policy is an important and often overloooked aspect of domestic policies.

Until recently there was little call outside of Brazil for a more detailed understanding of the country's foreign policy ambitions and actions. Indeed, even within Brazil the attention given to foreign policy has generally been minimal outside a group of specialists. True, over the last decade there has been an increasingly vibrant debate in the newspapers of record such as O Estado de São Paulo (circulation of 234,863), Folha de São Paulo (294,811), Valor Econômico (58,920), and O Globo (379,278) and a minor flourishing of internet sites and Facebook pages concentrating on Brazil's foreign affairs (Belém Lopes and Faria, 2014). But despite the large number of column inches now devoted to foreign policy questions, we need to remember discussion of issues such as the expansion of Mercosul (Mercado Comum do Sul), the Southern turn in foreign policy, and the management of relations with China and the US, is taking place in newspapers read by a relatively small elite. Circulation numbers for each newspaper as recorded in the Dow Jones Factiva news database are listed after the titles, creating a total daily readership of just under a million, which compares to Brazil's national population of just over 200 million. Perhaps a more accurate indication of the salience of foreign policy to wider Brazil comes from the 2014 televised presidential election debates, which comprehensively bypassed this public policy area.

Domestically, the lack of interest in foreign policy is partially attributable to the many serious social, economic and political challenges confronting the Brazilian people. On an international level the lack of interest in Brazilian foreign policy stems from a certain degree of historical marginality to the North Atlantic-dominated world of 'high politics'. For the most part Brazil was just another actor in the room, albeit one usually trying to get a seat at the main negotiating table. Political transition in the 1980s, economic consolidation in the 1990s and then commodity-boom fueled rapid growth in the 2000s have changed the situation, allowing Brazil to develop the capabilities that finally match its ambitions as a significant global power. The result has been a sudden desire by scholars and policy makers to understand what Brazilian diplomats are trying to achieve and why. This reactive quest for understanding is complicated not only by the need to at least read Portuguese in order to grapple with much of what drives Brazil's international interactions, but also by the shift in emphases in Brazilian foreign policy stemming from a sustained sense of structural exclusion within the global system. This latter aspect is magnified by a key domestic public policy difference that sets Brazil apart from its Northern counterparts. Where socio-economic development and poverty eradication are niche areas relegated to international development agencies in North America and Europe, these remain the overriding public policy priorities impacting almost every decision made in Brasília. The drive for national development is consequently central to the ambitions underlying much of Brazil's foreign policy planning and execution. In what will emerge as a the central argument in this book, Brazilian foreign policy often appears to be confusing to Northern countries because it is not predicated on the same jostling for relative position that has marked the European and North American arena. As one scholar has perceptively argued, Brazil looks for the power 'to do' and not power 'over' others (Gardini, 2016). Brazil's diplomats have been engaging in a structural game over the last two decades, which is all the more confusing for the North because the ambition is not to tear down the existing system in rebellion against injustice, but rather to shift some of the frames of reference and in many cases reinforce core principles such as rule of law and liberal economics, albeit with a Southern orientation that preferably puts Brazil near the centre of attention.

Theorizing Brazil's foreign policy

Despite Brazil's position as the seventh largest economy in the world and seat-holder at almost every major global and regional governance table from 2005 to 2015, only four of the books amidst the flurry of English-language texts focus exclusively on foreign policy. Each was written with more of an academic than popular audience in mind. Christina Stolte's 2015 book on Brazil in Africa tries to explain the turn to the South, arguing that Lula 'went East' as part of a strategy of building national prestige and establishing Brazil's bona fides as a legitimate potential great power. While elements of Stolte's prestige argument can certainly be extracted from the following pages, her concentration on role theory overlooks the depth of the economic opportunity found in the turn to Africa as well as how it fits into the wider structural game I argue drives Brazil's foreign policy. The 2015 volume edited by Oliver Stuenkel and Matthew Taylor provides less of a unified overarching theoretical model for Brazilian foreign policy, but does an admirable job of explaining the historical trajectory and identity-based grounding of recent developments in Brazilian foreign policy that has led to an international approach focused on questions of structural power. The two other major book-length works on Brazilian foreign policy pre-date the inauguration of the Dilma presidency in 2011, but remain highly instructive as explanatory tools for those seeking to understand Brazil in the world.

Tullo Vigevani's and Gabriel Cepaluni's important 2009 book argues Brazilian foreign policy is, above all, dominated by a quest to maintain domestic policy autonomy. While this has taken various forms since the 1985 transition to democracy and is applied with different strategic imperatives and styles in mind, the overriding factor is that Brazilian foreign policy is singularly dedicated to vouchsafing the country's autonomy and ensuring it is free to pursue those policies, both foreign and domestic, it sees as necessary to advance national development. Of course, this is a common ambition of nearly every country. What sets the Brazilian case apart is the consistency of its strategy to this end and the subtlety with which the goal is pursued. The autonomy through engagement argument about Brazil's active participation in international forums as a technique for retarding attempts to limit Brasília's room for action is therefore an important building block in understanding Brazilian foreign policy, and a theme that recurs in the pages presented here. But it only presents part of the picture of what is going on and why.

The final major book-length study in English of Brazil's post-democratization foreign policy is my 2009 volume focusing on leadership in South America. Like Vigevani's and Cepaluni's text, it addresses only part of the story, unpacking the techniques developed predominantly during the Cardoso presidency to establish Brazil as a regional leader. Mainstream approaches to understanding international relations are heavily moderated with a critical political economy approach drawing on Susan Strange's (1994) ideas of structural power and Coxian as well as neo-Gramscian thinking to develop the notion of consensual hegemony, which will be sketched out a bit later in this chapter. What matters at this point is that consensual hegemony is an operational device, a way of understanding how foreign policy is coordinated to gain leadership over other states without having to expend significant economic, security or political resources. It is the pursuit of consensual hegemony, not its full attainment that is ultimately important because the encompassed actions work to disseminate an ideational approach that, when effective, quietly embeds Brazilian interests in institutions and other countries. In this respect it offers a way of partially explaining how Brazil has gone about pursuing the autonomist foreign policy agenda outlined by Vigevani and Cepaluni. Consensual hegemony does not, however, provide an integrated understanding of why a foreign policy is pursued. It also offers little insight into how domestic pressures impact external policies and how institutional structures channel, advance or block the internal/external dynamics influencing decision makers (Allison, 1969; Fonseca, 2004; Lafer, 2001a; Putnam, 1988).

Comprehensive attempts to grandly theorize Brazilian foreign policy fare little better if we turn our attention to the Portuguese-language oeuvre. Generational change within Itamaraty, as the foreign ministry is widely known, has resulted in a series of memoires and reflections from central practitioners that shed considerable light on what was going on at a given moment (Amorim, 2011a; 2013; 2015; Barbosa, 2011; Cardoso, 2006; 2015; Cardoso with Winter, 2006; Lampreia, 1999a; 2009). A series of impressive single-authored scholarly books published in Brazil have also contributed to a deeper understanding of Brazilian foreign policy as a whole, but not in the direction of a clear, unified theory that can be consistently used to explain what has happened and what may occur going forward (Almeida, 2012; 2014; N. Amorim, 2012; Belém Lopes, 2013a; 2015; Fonseca, 2004; Oliveira, 2005; Souza, 2009; Spektor, 2014; Vizentini, 2003a). Adding to these works are many edited collections and journal articles, which will be repeatedly referenced throughout the text, but which again do not provide a clear theoretical modelling of Brazilian foreign policy.

To be fair, expectations that scholars can construct grand theories about Brazilian foreign policy likely overreach what is reasonably possible. We can subject the conduct of Brazil's foreign affairs to any one of a number of well-established theoretical lenses and come up with a different story each time. While intellectually stimulating, this does not necessarily help us understand why Brazil has acted as it has and what it will do in the future. To delve into this territory we need to shift gears and instead engage with what sometimes appears to be the poor cousin of international relations, namely the practice of foreign policy analysis. Even here we need to exercise some caution that we do not become overly anchored in a specific approach, be it the rational actor model, bureaucratic politics, identity-focused analysis, structural accounts, or interpretations anchored too firmly on the persona of the national leader. As scholars are now increasingly pointing out, we need a more holistic approach to the art of foreign policy analysis to search out how factors on an individual, national and structural level interact to shape foreign policy planning and reactions (Alden and Aran, 2012; Hudson, 2007; Mintz and DeRouen, 2010; Neack, 2008).

With these analytical and theoretical qualifications in mind, the goal of this book is to contribute to the construction of an integrated analysis of Brazilian foreign policy by focusing on the country's insertion into both the regional and global system over the roughly twenty-five years through to the end of Dilma's first term as president in 2014. A political economy approach to foreign policy analysis will be used to explore how domestic and international factors in the realms of politics, economics and security have interacted to shape Brazil's approach to the international environment across a number of different areas. Set at a largely macro-level of analysis, each of the chapters unpacks different aspects of the structural power game that the book argues Brazil is playing. In some cases this involves an exploration of a specific issue area while in others it will look at bilateral or regional relationships.

As will be sketched out throughout the book, one of the key characteristics of this is continuity and change, which sees the broad outlines of foreign policy developed in the 1990s taking stronger and more expansive shape throughout the 2000s as the economic situation improved and, possibly more significantly, as the country's striking social transformations 'trickled up' via the PT to change conceptions of what was considered possible and appropriate. Although there will inevitably be overlap between chapters, an attempt has been made to order the discussion through exploration of a series of themes, which are further broken down into key component parts. The first section presents the context, with chapters on institutional structures and the tactical behaviours exhibited by the country's diplomacy, which will be used to guide the analysis in subsequent chapters. The second section focuses on issues, taking in trade, the rise of Brazilian foreign direct investment (FDI), security policy and multilateralism. Key relationships are covered in the final section, encompassing Latin America, the Global South, the US and China.

The scope of the book is admittedly vast and each chapter deserving of at least a full-length book in its own right. Indeed, many of the chapters are the subject of extensive bibliographies – much of which is referenced in the text – particularly from the Brazil-based scholars and practitioners who are rapidly generating a massive and high quality literature in Portuguese. There are arguably also significant gaps in the coverage provided in the following pages, most notably environmental policy and the regionally important relationship with Argentina, to begin what could be a long list of issue areas and bilateral relationships. Rather than claiming to be a comprehensive and definitive treatise on the entirety of Brazilian foreign policy, the ambition of this book is instead to provide the reader with a wide-ranging introduction to the topic by focusing on key questions and relationships. For the engaged student of Brazilian foreign policy the chapters will hopefully introduce new ideas and provocations to advance debate and stimulate new research. Readers just turning to an examination of Brazilian foreign policy should find a solid primer on the broad subject in the following pages that will offer a good 'feel' for what Brazil is about in the international arena, providing the grounding for asking new questions or for finding answers to existing queries. To this end the book draws on the large body of research materials the author has compiled over the last fifteen years in addition to new research specific to this project. Central sources include statistics on the investment, trade and military capabilities, quadrilingual (Portuguese, English, Spanish and French) surveys of the secondary literature, government statements, speeches by political figures and officials, congressional testimony, media reports and organization reports. Significant portions of the text are developed from over 70 interviews conducted in Brazil, Angola, Australia, Britain, Canada, Mozambique, Switzerland and the US with policy makers and officials from across a wide range of international bodies, organizations, governments, civil society and industry. Many of the interview subjects have been kept anonymous due to the sensitivity of the material and the interview subject's position. While the research focus is primarily on qualitative sources, descriptive statistics and charts will be deployed to support the arguments in the book.

A (non)theory of Brazilian foreign policy

Rather than trying to develop a complex theory of Brazilian foreign policy, the approach taken here is that foreign policy analysis remains something of an art. While specialists fall back on narrower and more specific models and theories, one of the contentions running through the background to these pages is that theories of international relations developed in the North Atlantic do not always provide the expected insight when applied to emerging power countries such as Brazil, despite the fact that until recently the Brazilian academy has been dominated by Western theorization. Some scholars and analysts assume states behave like utility-maximizing rational individuals, which then allows inferences to be made about how a country will act and react in the global and regional system. According to realists the dominant factor is the anarchic nature of global order, which lacks an overarching authority to police state action and thus forces countries to rely on self-help and concentrate on how much power they have relative to other states. Liberals focus on challenges like global warming or long-term economic stability, which overwhelm the capacity of individual states and emphasize their interdependence, encouraging them to build institutions to collectively tackle those challenges. Neoliberals build on this to argue that when interdependence is very asymmetric the extent of such joint actions and the autonomy of supra-national institutions are constrained because smaller states fear the likely loss of autonomy to stronger actors. Constructivists, meanwhile, shift focus to how states mutually define one another as well as their environment, concluding that the absence of effective governance at the international level is not a given, but rather the result of certain social interpretations and behaviours. As the title of a central constructivist article succinctly puts it, 'anarchy is what states make of it' (Wendt, 1992: 391).

The problem with applying any single school of theory to the Brazilian case is that it quickly breaks down and starts to raise more questions than it answers (Lima, 2015). Indeed, a pattern that will emerge in the text is the mixed signals emerging from policies apparently stemming from a simultaneous application of myriad theories to understand a particular situation or strategic imperative. Although diplomats within the Brazilian foreign ministry are certainly well versed in the canonical literature – Itamaraty had several of the key texts from the realist and liberal traditions translated into Portuguese in the 1990s – the application of the precepts in these approaches builds upon a fundamentally different understanding of world order, and the challenges that states face, than is found in the North. While the questions of relational power that dominate Northern thinking do matter to the architects of Brazil's foreign policy, the evidence presented in this book repeatedly suggests that structural issues are more pressing and provide a better lens for understanding what is done and why. Thus, rather than attempting to develop a predictive theory, the book is instead built around an under-standing that sees structural realities as limiting what is possible and foreign policy practice guided by the sorts of behaviours consistent with consensual hegemony with a view to morphing, not destroying, key governing regimes, beliefs and practices in global politics. With these two markers in place the book becomes about the tensions created by a series of recurring themes and contradictions.

Power, autonomy and consensual hegemony

As mentioned above, one of the most influential approaches to thinking about Brazilian foreign policy is to look at the subject as a sustained quest for autonomy (Fonseca, 2004). This stands distinct from the idea of sovereignty, focusing more on retaining the ability to set domestic and foreign policy to advance national development goals than a strict observation of the concept of sovereignty that excludes outsiders from internal affairs. In their book, Vigevani and Cepaluni (2009) highlight three foreign policy strategies that Brazil has used to protect its autonomy, namely 'autonomy through distance', 'autonomy through participation' and 'autonomy through diversification'. In each case the challenge for policy makers is how policy autonomy can be maintained in the face of international pressures, most notably those from the US. In the first option the proposal is that a country separate itself from Northern centres and pursue an autonomist approach. Although Brazil never moved beyond observer status, the Non-Aligned Movement stands as an example of this strategy. The two authors attribute 'autonomy through participation' to the Cardoso period when serious efforts were made to join international organizations with a view to influencing global norms and practices. From the Lula years they develop the 'autonomy through diversification' model, which saw an expansion of South–South linkages as part of a strategy to increase Brazil's global influence and generate alternatives to existing global governance frameworks. In one respect this book can be interpreted as a validation of the three approaches to seeking autonomy set out by Vigevani and Cepaluni, which at its core is essentially a defensive analytical frame that allows for some skirting around the overt question of power and its accrual, preservation and application. Indeed, their categorizations provide some valuable high-level sign posts for starting an examination of Brazil's foreign policy, but less detail on successes and failures, as well as questions about why decision makers have chosen to pursue particular approaches to various bilateral, multilateral and sectoral relationships and issues.

Implicit in the discussion of autonomy is the question of power and having enough of it to maintain the desired degree of independence. Andrew Hurrell focuses on the interplay between power and autonomy in contemporary Brazilian foreign policy in the preface he wrote for the 2013 publication of his 1986 doctoral thesis, which is now available through Itamaraty's Fundação Alexandre Gusmão website. At the outset of his thesis, *The Quest for Autonomy: The Evolution of Brazil's Role in the International System, 1964–1985,* Hurrell (2013: 42–44) directs the reader towards the importance of power when thinking about Brazilian foreign policy, reminding us not only that power and the ability to wield it is embedded in a pattern of historical relationships, but also that analysing a country's power must account for its intentions, objective and values. His preface reiterates the point he made twenty-seven years earlier by observing that Brazil is a difficult case for the power analysis approaches of mainstream schools of international relations because the country has had extended periods where power has deliberately not been developed and others where it has studiously not been deployed in the hard power-projection sense associated with realist analyses. The important reminder he gives us is that power, soft power and their relevant dimensions are not necessarily quantifiable in a material sense, but may in fact have more significance as social phenomena that allow a country to accumulate and wield influence in a subtler manner.

The utility of social power as characterized by Hurrell becomes immediately apparent if you talk with ranking Brazilian diplomats about leadership and their country's bilateral relations. Comments are studiously phrased in the conditional tense and great effort is devoted to clarifying that while Brazil may lead, it does not wish to impose, coerce or engage in material pressure to cause others to follow it. The emphasis is instead upon the power of ideas and the generation of consensus around different conceptualizations of order and regional and international organization and collaboration. This avoidance of classical power projection presents a challenge for the mainstream international relations approaches to hegemony and leadership, which prompted my development of the idea of consensual hegemony to explain Brazil's increasingly active intra-South American foreign policy from the outset of the Cardoso era (Burges, 2008; 2009). Turning for inspiration to the Gramscian adaptations of Robert W. Cox (1987), consensual hegemony begins with the observation that for hegemony to be effective and lasting it must account for the interests and ambitions of those it encompasses (Gramsci, 1957: 154–155) and that it is another level of power a state achieves when it is able to frame its vision of the system in a way others see as being in the universal interest (Arrighi, 1993: 149–150). It is presented as something akin to an ideationally based order that exists through a broad measure of consent offering some satisfaction to all encompassed by it (Cox, 1987: 7). Consensual hegemony thus becomes an ideationally based type of order because it grows from a generated consensus about how affairs should be ordered and managed, embedding the core interests of the predominant actor in the system's structure (Burges, 2008: 71).

The consensual hegemony understanding is a useful analytical tool when combined with Hurrell's focus on social power because it opens space for actively examining an ideas-based leadership where the 'hegemon' can marshal agreement around the form of the proposed order without having to underwrite the associated costs of forcibly imposing it. Unlike the dominant approaches to hegemony in the North American international relations cannon, the inclusive nature of consensual hegemony means gains come as much from its pursuit as its achievement; the continuous dialogue explicit in the attempt to form the ideational consensus provides recurring opportunities to implant the would-be hegemon's ambitions and world-view in the subconscious of the other actors. This is particularly useful if we think about Hurrell's conundrum for realists studying Brazilian foreign policy and their difficulty in explaining Brazil's failure to either exploit opportunities to develop material power or project it. Consent, a fundamentally social phenomenon, becomes critical for the consensual hegemony, and its substance comes from the cooptive and inclusive nature of its underlying ideas, which sees other states subscribing to it autonomously and self-interestedly adopting and advocating policies that advance the agenda and interests of the hegemon. In its fullest expression absorption of the hegemony extends beyond an idea of 'buy-in' to a set of ideas to become a subconscious rewiring of ways of thinking and conceptualizing what is possible and what is desired. If the would-be hegemon is successful in inculcating a consensual hegemony it consequently finds itself in a position where much of the costs of the hegemonic project are borne by the other actors encompassed by it.

The significance of the consensual hegemony for discussion of Brazil's autonomy-protecting foreign policy lies in the concept's Gramscian roots. Where the various realist, liberal institutionalist and constructivist approaches to international relations typically view hegemony in terms of the relational power of domination, variants of the Gramscian tradition view hegemony in structural terms. Susan Strange's (1994) work on structural power provides a useful shortcut for isolating the importance of this difference. In her framework, structural power is the ability to set the overarching rules of the game in which various relational contests take place. Significantly, she argues that if a given actor has set the rules of the game it no longer matters if it has all-domineering power because the structure of the system ensures the actor's core interests are absorbed by all, and that future shifts and modifications of the structure remain only marginal and, more importantly, continue to privilege the interests of its original architect. Structure thus becomes a crucial factor setting limits on what is even imaginable for policy planners, which Hurrell (2013: 28) clearly identifies as a central aspect of power in general along with the more commonly examined relational aspects of power.

Hurrell's brief discussion of power in the preface to the book version of his thesis is a quietly invaluable reminder for those engaged in the analysis of Brazilian foreign policy. In addition to highlighting the centrality of relational and structural power he also points out that the context within which power is exercised and the motives and values behind its use are of paramount importance. Approached differently, we can frame the point as a question: where are the limits to a state's power and influence and to what extent do intentions impact its ability to successfully lead and get its own way in the international or regional system? In analytical terms these elements combine to form what the following chapters identify as the central problematique recurring in contemporary Brazilian foreign policy. It also points the way forward for understanding why other countries, particularly Northern countries well staffed with diplomats trained in conventional approaches to international relations, frequently struggle to discern what Brazil is doing and why.

In blunt terms, Brazilian foreign policy is not fundamentally focused on contests of relational power. After all, these might bring conflict and the need to draw on overtly coercive options, something Brazilian diplomacy has studiously long-avoided in both a regional and global context. Far from being an altruistic policy position, this approach to international relations finds its roots in the structural power aspects of the drive for autonomy: by avoiding the overt and forceful exertion of power, which would likely require a violation of a neighbouring country's sovereignty, Brazil seeks to prevent the creation of precedents that might later be used to curtail its own freedom and autonomy. Viewed from this angle, Brazilian foreign policy is fundamentally about questions of structural power, be it through the obstruction of institutions and norms that might impinge autonomy, or through the development and support of new patterns of bilateral and multilateral relations that weaken the embedded Northern structural power. In a South American context the emphasis is not so much on forcing the US out, a country with which Brazil quite fruitfully collaborates, but rather with getting neighbours to find new options by looking in, which conveniently almost necessitates an implicit central role for Brazil. On a global level we see an attempt to open new opportunities for Brazil by encouraging a rise of South–South political, cultural and economic collaboration and coordination. This can be seen in a variety of forms ranging from coalition building within the WTO (World Trade Organization), calls for a new international economic geography, or quiet efforts to dampen the reinvigoration of norms and institutions that continue to embed a Northern focus across the South. The emphasis is not on tearing down existing structures and norms, but rather on either opening them up or encouraging the rise of new options so that space is created for the advancement of Brazilian objectives and developmental priorities within the existing global structural framework.

In many respects the fundamental thing that Brazilian diplomacy is trying to achieve is more aptly captured by the word 'influence', which intuitively comes with connotations of discussion and collaboration, than 'power', which suggests a more muscular avenue for getting one's way. For the consensual hegemony approach to work Brazil must be able to convince others to join its projects, and exert positive influence that causes other states to see the new options as being in their own interests. The benefit for Brazil to this approach is that it becomes relatively cost free in terms of fungible resources, although political capital does need to be carefully managed. How Brazilian diplomacy makes this work is also where we find one of the quirks that can so confuse Northern analysts. Foreign policy becomes fundamentally about managing relationships, which is not quite the same thing as exerting power to keep relationships on track. In practice, considerations of relational power are left in the background and, particularly with other Southern countries, quietly shelved as an inconvenient reality by an ostensibly magnanimous Brazil. Attention is instead turned to advancing the idea of inclusiveness, of pan-Southern solidarity, all with the aim of creating new patterns of relations, norms and institutions that supplement existing structures to build space for the new opportunities across the South, which policy planners see as essential for Brazil's national development.

For scholars and analysts steeped in mainstream theoretical traditions the result is a confusing blend of realism and idealism, all spun through a web of constructivism. There is no shortage of examples in the following pages of Brazil acting quite firmly to squarely advance its own national interests in a manner that would be familiar to most realists. Yet, in many instances this activity is carefully cloaked in the language of idealism, particularly notions of pan-Southern solidarity and aspirations for collective global development in the face of Northern-erected structural challenges. Space emerges for missteps in Brazilian foreign policy when the realist backbone softens and idealism or ideology is allowed to derail analyses and lead to poor appraisals of the power balance as well as the relative significance and opportunity of bilateral relationships. This is particularly evident in relations with China where assumptions about shared structural ambitions subjugated more pointed analyses of the nature of Sino-Brazilian collaboration and cooperation.

By looking to the regional and pan-Southern context with this blended theoretical presentation we also find the challenge created by the structural focus of an autonomy-protecting foreign policy. Regional and multilateral mechanisms are central to the consensual hegemonic mechanisms leveraged by Brazilian diplomacy. Yet, a reliance on ideas can only take a foreign policy so far. Eventually decisions have to be made, leadership goods furnished, and actions taken, which may result in a need to impinge upon another country's sovereignty in order to maintain the collective project or engage in a deliberate ceding of some autonomy to the collective to strengthen the new structure. This, as will be argued with particular reference to the South American context, is where the structural focus of Brazil's autonomist priority sometimes trips up the larger foreign policy project. Concrete action is avoided, resulting in a weakening of the project being advanced by Brazil or a grumbling from partners that helps drive their attention in a different direction. Where the bureaucratic momentum of the structurally focused autonomist tradition in Brazilian foreign policy has been overcome to build regional or pan-Southern initiatives we find clear domestic political leadership, most often in the form of presidential diplomacy. The catch, as this book will demonstrate, is that such leadership is not always present or clear-headed.

Brazil's structural context

One way of applying the theoretical discussion of autonomy and power in a foreign policy analysis approach is to think about the constraints and freedoms impacting a state's room for manoeuver in the world and the pressures brought to bear upon decision makers. In practical terms foreign policy is simply another area of public policy conditioned by institutional structures and practices reacting to the possibilities and limitations inherent in the domestic and international political, economic, security and social context (Belém Lopes, 2013a; Patriota, 2013a). Actions relevant to foreign policy are carried out within and outside the country, conducted not only by agents of the state such as the foreign ministry, presidency, diplomatic corps, and military, but also by new arrivals on the scene such as the finance ministry, development ministry, state banks, major national corporations and other actors outside of the president's direct control with international interests to advance and protect (Belém Lopes, 2015: chapter one; Pinheiro and Milani, 2012). The range of fields of action with foreign policy implications and the actors involved is rapidly growing beyond the military, trade, security and international political issues that have traditionally occupied diplomats. Even seemingly innocuous policy decisions about the promotion of national culture, the development of health protocols, or investigations into specialist areas such as phytosannitary regulations and digital television standards can quietly impact a country's 'soft power' and bring influence to bear upon other international actors.

The first structural factor impacting Brazilian foreign policy is geography. Brazilians often refer to their country's 'continental dimension' and indeed, Brazil's large physical size matters a lot for its foreign relations. With the fifth largest landmass in the world, it easily dominates South America and sticks out on any map. Importantly, although the Amazon is a vast and complicated geographical feature in the heart of the country, Brazil is not only devoid of the frozen or arid expanses marking other geographical giants, but also lacks towering mountains that might complicate logistics. The country is instead blessed with huge reserves of water and arable land, including some 22 million hectares of suitable land currently not under production (Deininger et al., 2011: 85). A coastline extending some 7,500 km also provides opportunities, not least through the 200-mile economic zone, which encompasses the massive 'pre-salt' oil fields discovered off the coasts of Rio de Janeiro and São Paulo states in the mid-2000s. The productive potential of these natural assets, combined with Brazil's large population of 200 million people, has the potential to create a massive internal market for domestic industry and FDI that many observers thought was in place during the Lula years. Even before we turn our attention to the technical, creative and scientific capabilities that can be found in Brazil's public and private universities, as well as state-run and private corporations and institutes, it is clear that the country satisfies some of the key power potential requisites in international relations theory, particularly those of a realist variant (Morgenthau, 1967: chapter nine).

Brazil's geographic location offers another major structural advantage to its foreign policy planners. Its position in the Southern Atlantic is far from the tensions that afflicted the North for much of the twentieth century, distancing Brazil from global security flashpoints. Brazil can thus absent itself from major international security questions should it so choose, but conversely has to work harder to make a case for its involvement when it does choose to become engaged, which was a sustained challenge during the Lula era. The national security benefits stemming from this accident of geography are magnified by the existence of something approximating a regional security community in South America and the wider area of Latin America. While the formal structures to this end are weak and the prospects of next generation security threats spilling over borders increasing, the reality remains that the region is marked by the absence of armed inter-state conflict and a general unwillingness of governments to seriously consider war as a viable dispute resolution mechanism (Hurrell, 1998). When combined with the amicable settling of all ten of Brazil's borders over a century ago, policy makers in Brasília find themselves in the luxurious position of not having to be excessively concerned with armed aggression against the territory under their care. The benefits gained from these regional realities are amplified by the protection afforded by the US strategic umbrella, which has sheltered the Americas from external intervention for at least the last century. Brazil is consequently able to safely continue relatively low levels of military investment, which leaves the country as a non-threat to other Southern countries and thus an appealing partner seemingly unlikely to bring the imperial tendencies found in Europe and North America. As the discussion of security policy will show, despite a recent flurry of planned investments Brazil has been remarkably laid back in that field and its investments in military hardware appear to be driven more by preoccupations with technology transfer and industrialization than security qualms.

Another structural factor easing the way for Brazilian diplomats, and one often overlooked by conventional foreign policy analysis, is national identity. A defining aspect of Brazilian foreign policy is the amount of time and energy given to thinking through how the internal and external interact to form the national identity and how this in turn is consciously used to define the parameters and practice of the country's foreign relations. There is perhaps no better illustration of the extent to which this permeates official diplomatic thinking than twice-Foreign Minister Celso Lafer's authoring of a book entitled *A Identidade Internacional do Brasil e a Política Externa Brasileira* (The International Identity of Brazil and Brazilian Foreign Policy). Brazil is a racially mixed society where you can find large diasporas from virtually every corner of the globe, although this is not reflected in the racial make up of the diplomatic corps, which is almost totally white. Mixed with this is a cultural tradition of talking – possibly the worst thing you can do to a Brazilian is refuse to speak to them – and negotiating to find mutually beneficial outcomes in almost every situation. The result is a remarkable level of comfort in a wide range of cultural and geographic contexts that couples with a genuine desire to understand and engage with the local context. In diplomatic terms this translates into a proclivity to talk issues through rather than attempting to impose resolutions, which creates a culture of inclusion that many countries, particularly those across the Global South, find somewhat refreshing. Brazilian diplomats consequently usually find that the door is usually open to them in most venues, which at least gives them a chance to put their country's position forward and attempt to shift the debate on a wide range of issues. The self-confidence to take these opportunities is underpinned by a quiet, but deeply held belief that Brazil should be at central decision making tables and is a constructive actor (Maia and Taylor, 2015).

Internal economic and social factors have traditionally served as major restraint on Brazil's international ambitions, with a lack of industrial capacity initially forestalling foreign policy ambitions through the 1970s, followed thereafter by rolling economic crises in the 1980s and 1990s that still cast a shadow over political debate and macroeconomic policy. Although Brazil was suffering a severe recession as this book was being finished, the situation was still considerably different, ableit not as economically healthy and self-confident as during the Lula years. Responding to the ideological drive of the Lula and Dilma PT presidencies and the possibilities opened by the global commodities boom Brazil has recently been moving away from its traditional hemispheric 'insertion', diversifying its relations and adopting a much more global outlook. As a result, the relevant points of reference to assess its strategic situation have changed and the relative position of the country in the world as a whole now matters much more than before. Trade volumes and values have flourished and, as will be discussed in the Brazil Inc chapter, the country's multinationals are emerging as important foreign direct investors in Latin America, Africa and beyond, reflecting the enormous economic changes that have taken place since sweeping macroeconomic and structural reforms were launched in the early 1990s. Depending on the measure chosen, Brazil now ranks seventh or eighth in the world in terms of GDP (gross domestic product) and has moved from being a net external debtor to creditor, including a ten billion dollar 'loan' to the International Monetary Fund (IMF) in 2009. Despite this new room for manoeuver, different constraints are emerging in the form of competition for position in the invigorated markets of the Global South. Brazil's 'emergence' is just part of the 'emerging markets' story and is taking place at a time when many new players are also gaining ground, not least of which are China and India.

Although space for a more assertive foreign policy has been growing at the regional and global level over the last twenty years, wider political and societal interest in the possibilities and significance of international affairs has not kept pace. Part of the issue is the enormous complexity of Brazil's domestic political system, which is marked by a coalitional congressional system with a single party-affiliated national president. In other words, although Cardoso, Lula and Dilma were each elected as the presidential candidate for their respective parties (PSDB, PT and PT), none had a majority in Congress and thus had to form a coalition amongst the twenty or so parties in order to get enough support to pass legislation. Matters are further complicated by the fragmentation of the parties into interest or region-specific 'bancadas', a Brazilian version of the different 'caucuses' found in the US Congress. The result is a complex political game requiring the president to distribute 'pork' and cabinet positions in order to build the congressional coalition necessary to govern (Raile, Pereira and Power, 2010). For rent-seeking members of congress the foreign ministry is a uniquely unappealing portfolio because it has a relatively small budget and almost no regulatory power of interest to economic interest group, both of which matter for the onward transfer of pay-offs and articulation of a personalized political machine.

Further reducing the appeal of the foreign ministry is the sense that it is a specialist preserve and one operating in an environment of strategic tranquility thanks to the pacific nature of intra-regional relations. Widespread interest in foreign affairs is consequently minimal except in times of crisis or wounded Brazilian pride. The general attitude in congress is neatly summarized by a 2005 complaint from Senator Pedro Simon, member of the Senate Commission for Foreign Relations and National Defense: 'Our Committee is very timid... In other countries, such as Argentina where I was a guest discussing Mercosul, the foreign affairs committee has significant weight and provides guidance for the country's international decisions. In Brazil neither the Chamber of Deputies nor the Senate do this. We are here to approve. We ratify everything' (Senado, 2005: 255). Although Congress is markedly uninterested in foreign affairs, partly because the country's electoral procedures mitigate against the accumulation of the necessary expertise in the political class, the negotiating skills necessary to manage the passage of legislation and ensure the ability of a president to govern have had an important effect on foreign affairs. With power widely dispersed between the presidency, a coalitional congress, powerful state governors and municipalities there is as much need for diplomatic skill within Brazil as without. The public policy context is thus well suited to preparing Brazilian officials for the patient approach to negotiation and 'consensus generation' that have become the hallmark of the country's foreign policy.

Consistent themes and contradictions

A central contradiction that will recur throughout this book is the clear sense that Brazilian foreign policy makers want to position their country as leader, but are almost pathologically averse to explicitly stating this role or accepting the implicit responsibilities. Language such as 'not wanting to impose' or 'respect of national sovereignty' is the oft-used deflection, which to a certain extent should be given some credence at face value. A more penetrating reading, however, quickly becomes grounded in questions of risk management and the worry that an inability to consistently meet the expectations of followers will undercut Brazil's ability to lead and result in even greater material and political costs. Worse, this would destroy Brazil's constructed reputation as a reliable, impartial partner focused on peace and development before the naked pursuit of the national interest.

Brazilian policy planners are able to take a slower approach to developing foreign relations because of the country's notable lack of existential security threats or crises. Sustained patterns of dialogue, negotiation and consensus creation are possible and provide a cost-effective method for spreading the Brazilian vision of regional and global order as well as distributing the costs amongst the partners pulled into the associated ventures. As some of the diplomats interviewed for this book observed about their Brazilian counterparts, they are wonderful conversationalists, but extremely difficult to pin down to a clear statement on many issues. In part this is attributable to a belief within Itamaraty that there must be consistency in the country's foreign policy, which means any commitment must be very carefully considered and situated within longer-term traditions and ambitions. How to do this points to another contradiction grounded in in the structural focus of foreign policy thinking, namely a vague sense that while Brazil has very high-level goals – i.e., maintaining autonomy and national development – there nevertheless remains a lack of clarity about what these actually mean in terms of a tangible set of policies for regional and global order. Phrased differently, while Brazilian foreign policy makers devote a considerable amount of energy to decrying injustices and inequalities in global order and global governance institutions, it is not clear what alternative they are advocating other than to gain a seat at the main decision making table. There is thus sometimes a feeling that Brazilian foreign policy is acting like the Italian revolutionaries in Giuseppe Tomasi di Lampedusa's classic novel

The Leopard, seeking to change everything so that it can remain more or less the same.

In part the lack of specificity about what Brazil would do with a new global or regional order can be understood because it is a second order challenge that can only begin to be addressed once the first challenge is overcome: systemic exclusion from global order and decision making. The danger for Brazilian diplomats, and one that does creep through in the discussions in this book on South–South relations and multilateralism, is that Brazil might find itself in a decision making position without a clear sense of where to go next, which could negatively impact its credibility and ability to strategically allocate resources to maintain its international position. This potential risk is highlighted by the consistent theme in Brazilian diplomatic statements over the last twenty-five years that the global order needs to be 'democratized', that global governance institutions need to include all voices, not just a subset of rich countries. Again, this relates back to the Brazilian desire to win a seat for itself at the main global governance decision making tables like the UNSC (United Nations Security Council). But it also sheds important light on why Brazil takes such a critical voice in so many forums and pushes seemingly counter-systemic ideas such as a new economic geography and enhanced South–South relations. For many policy makers and analysts in the North and even Brazil the rise of a Southward focus in Brazilian foreign policy from the start of the PT era appears unremittingly ideological and deliberately anti-American or anti-European (Almeida, 2003). The stumbling blocks for Brazil's strategic foreign policy thinkers are the questions of 'what next' and 'what is your alternative'?

While there is some truth to the politicization charge, which is elaborated in chapter ten, it is too simple an answer and overlooks the larger process at work. Insight comes from Lula's speech to the United Nations General Assembly in 2004 when he quoted Frantz Fanon, a leader of the African anti-colonial movement and an important figure in post-colonial theory. Lula's reference to Fanon was designed to shift thinking in the Global South away from reliance upon the North for solutions and assistance, bringing attention to the possibilities of intra-Southern collaboration and cooperation. In a significant break with the New International Economic Order ideas of the 1970s, no intimation was made that the South should delink from the North. Rather, the idea his foreign policy pushed over the next decade was that expanded intra-Southern interaction would increase opportunities and bring to the table new ways of addressing existing challenges. Far from advocating a destruction of the global system, Lula was in effect seeking to expand and strengthen the existing order, albeit in a manner that would almost certainly result in a more prominent position for Brazil. Questions of relational power were notable for their absence, replaced instead by a clear focus on issues linked to structural power and the implicit restrictions they placed on developing and emerging market states.

A related aspect to Lula's call for expanded South–South interaction is the role that foreign policy plays in Brazil's national development plans. The idea that foreign policy can advance national economic interests is not new and indeed sits as a fundamental precursor to many major international conflicts (Hirschman, 1945; Kindleberger, 1973). The difference is that in the Brazilian case attention is given to more than just trade flows and market penetration. On a governmental level effort is devoted to using the international context as a training ground to improve public policy capacity. The corporate sector has turned to global markets not only for capital, but also to gain access to new technology and management techniques. An additional layer is added through South–South diplomacy and technical cooperation, which in part seeks to build new markets for Brazilian goods and services from the ground up in Latin America and Africa. Moreover, the vision extends beyond trade to actively encompass investment flows and opportunities. As will be discussed later in the book, the attitude driving policy is one that sees Brazilian growth and socio-economic development as being dependent on parallel improvements throughout the South. Brazilian exploitation of poorer countries does exist within this framework, but not to the same extent as seen with traditional colonial relationships or modern North–South economic relations or even some aspects of Chinese economic expansionism. At times this distinction results in foreign policy decisions that seem to make little overt sense or have scant connection to larger national ambitions. The theme encapsulating this disjuncture from Northern practices is the use of foreign policy ventures to create long-term conditions to advance Brazilian interests and ambitions at the expense of interest maximization in the short-term, a sort of 'buy and hold' political investment strategy looking to sustained profitability, not short-run booms followed by busts.

Underlying this longer-term view in Brazilian foreign policy are a number of significant structural changes within Brazil. The first is the rise and consolidation of presidential diplomacy (Belém Lopes, 2015; Cason and Power, 2009; Danese, 1999; Malamud, 2005). Since the early 1990s the president has taken an increasingly forceful role in setting the direction for Brazil's foreign policy, consciously using the country's pattern of international insertion as a device for advancing domestic policy plans as well as opening new opportunities for Brazilian entrepreneurs and civil society. The Lula era was perhaps the apex of presidential diplomacy as he displayed a remarkable intuitive ability to build international relationships and firmly establish Brazil as a highly credible international actor. His successes, particularly in the internationalization of the Brazilian economy throughout the Global South and North further advanced a second important change in foreign policy making, further democratizing the process by dramatically increasing the number of actors and interests looking and acting outside of the country. For Itamaraty this represented a direct assault on their institutional autonomy, which has long sought to wall off foreign policy as something best left to the 'experts' (Belém Lopes, 2013a). In matters of traditional high diplomacy this may still be the case, but in a situation seen in nearly every other country increasingly the foreign ministry's authority and capability on a whole range of issues is being challenged. While this has not created a collapse in Brazilian foreign policy capacity, it has put the policy formulation and implementation process into a state of flux and transition, which is part of the story running through these pages.

To a certain degree contemporary Brazilian foreign policy is marked by a struggle to maintain continuity in an environment of rapid change. On a policy planning level the domestic political pressures at play are rapidly changing, although not yet to the point where foreign policy becomes an electoral issue. This is being driven by changes in Brazil's hard and soft power capabilities, which grew in part due to the sixteen years of very active international engagement during the Cardoso and Lula years. The result is a recurrent theme in this book, namely rising confusion about what Brazil's international identity is, what it should be, and what this means Brazil can and should do. Diplomats will naturally dispute this claim, but disjuncture in Brazilian rhetoric and action in areas as widely diversified as international development, regional crisis management, international peace and security, trade, investment, and global governance all point to a period of uncertainty masked under reliance upon traditional positions and processes.

The institutional changes sketched out above play a role in this as the number of actors engaging in foreign affairs multiply and, in a pattern seen in other countries, increasingly begin their own autonomous actions (Daudelin, 2005; Pinheiro and Milani, 2012). Added to this is a process of generational change, which created its own turbulence during the Lula years as successive senior diplomats retired with parting shots across the PT's bow decrying the damage it was doing to the institution of Itamaraty and the misguided concentration on South–South relations. In a sense the changes were foreign policy manifestations of wider transformations taking place in Brazilian society. Some scholars refer to

Itamaraty as the last bastion of nobility in Brazil (Belém Lopes, 2013), focused as it is on high politics, courtly protocol, and being involved in affairs in European and North American capitals. As important as these functions are, the logic and ambience that goes with them are alien to the majority of Brazilians, many of whom have experienced remarkable improvements in their personal situations since 2002 due to focused anti-poverty programmes and assistance with massive micro-economic growth initiatives. Part of the 'magic' of Lula's poverty reduction miracle was his government's ability to see opportunities amongst the lower socio-economic classes in Brazil that were invisible to the traditional ruling elite. As will become clearer through the trade and investment chapters as well as the discussions about the Global South and Latin America, the turn to South–South foreign policy was in many ways a replication of this domestic mentality shift on an international level, which is in turn being reflected in the evolving composition and operation of Itamaraty.

The turbulence created by institutional flux, generational change and increased globalization of the Brazilian economy and society has in some respects increased the pressure for clear political leadership, particularly from the president. In the following pages much of the innovation and creativity will be located within the Cardoso and Lula presidencies, with the first Dilma's presidency appearing as one running more on momentum than active engagement. The theme emerging from this discontinuity is a clear clash between tradition and renovation, which means the inclusion and engagement of economic and civil society actor in the foreign policy process depends heavily on sustained pressure from the Planalto Presidential Palace, not internal Itamaraty decisions to democratize foreign policy planning. Absent the clear pressure to push this inclusiveness forward seen during the Cardoso and Lula years, the tendency at Itamaraty has been to take on a defensive posture on both a domestic and international level. Bureaucratic turf fights are quietly fought on the Esplanada in Brasília. Externally the default strategy in bargaining terms often seems to be one of 'blocking' or taking what Odell (2000) might characterize as a distributive or value-claiming strategic view that sees a limited pool of goods as being available for contending interests. The default to defensive value-claiming strategies increases as new types of issues arise in the international arena, contributing to the sense that Brazil can be more obstructionist than facilitative in global governance forum. This, however, is not a foregone conclusion, but rather relies upon the extent to which there is clear political engagement in the issues and direction for Itamaraty's corps of diplomats. In short, political leadership remains very important for the formulation and implementation of Brazilian foreign policy despite the enormous technocratic resources and experience in the Itamaraty Palace complex.

The top-level themes which consequently permeate the book are continuity and change, and the struggle for policy makers and practitioners to manage the concomitant uncertainty and seize the resultant opportunities. Historically foreign policy has played a minor role in the lives of Brazilians, but this is changing even if it still not immediately available in the face of the country's still-serious social policy challenges. As the economy has internationalized, society has become wealthier and begun to travel, and communications advances have ensured a greater international insertion of all Brazilians into global society, the foreign context increasingly matters. The result is a process of learning and adaption by a large number of actors as well as varying levels of interest and engagement in international questions as Brazil continues to move steadily forth into the world.

2

The domestic foreign policy context

In some important respects Brazil is a lot like the US. Both countries are geographically vast with immense national populations that can produce a great deal of what is consumed domestically. The outside world matters, but in an abstracted sense that is not normally felt by the average citizen on a day-to-day basis. In the Brazilian case this element of exceptionalism and inward focus has historically been reinforced by struggles with national debt, hyper-inflation and poverty which meant there were few opportunities for most Brazilians to travel internationally, leaving a vacation in Rio de Janeiro or Carnaval in Salvador as the annual break. Put more prosaically, just as English is a near-necessity for easy travel by a foreigner in the US, life in Brazil without some basic Portuguese can be almost impossible – Spanish is not a substitute. It is thus not too surprising to find that until recently foreign policy has remained something of an esoteric pursuit undertaken by an isolated group of specialists, most of whom could be found inside the Itamaraty Palace. Indeed, the 2014 presidential election debates in Brazil were marked by the almost total absence of discussion about foreign policy by the candidates, with the subject being restricted to a single throwaway line about security and drug smuggling. The scant discussion of Brazilian foreign policy was all the more surprising given its increasing importance to a wide range of economic interests as well as the succession of managerial crises afflicting Itamaraty as it sought to adapt to an increasingly democratized process with an absence of clear political guidance and support. Apart from the occasional rant against US imperialism or complaints about Argentine protectionism, foreign affairs has simply had no public profile and, more significantly, was definitely not something around which a flourishing political career might be built.

Outside of the political arena academic study of international relations has historically been restricted to a small group of very capable scholars working largely from those documents the government chose to release from its archives. Until the early 2000s think tanks and lobbies such as those found in the US and Europe were virtually non-existent, and the first major private institute to be established – the Centro Brasileiro de Relações Internacionais – was set up by a group of retired diplomats. This situation changed rapidly over the subsequent decade with the launch of high quality academic programmes at a number of public and private universities, and not just in Brasília, Rio de Janeiro and São Paulo, but also in cities such as Belo Horizonte, Florianopolis and Porto Alegre. Where previously a handful of students were trained annually in international relations the numbers are now well into the thousands, many moving into careers in business and the various levels of government. For its part the mainstream media has responded to the internationalization of Brazilian economy and society by increasing coverage of foreign affairs and, more tellingly, adding significant bite to its analysis and questioning of Brazilian foreign policy. Like their counterpart in academia, journalists are no longer relying on the official word from Itamaraty or Planalto, but are searching out new sources of information and engaging in integrated analyses that reveal much about what foreign policy makers are trying to achieve and where efforts are falling short of the mark.

For the Brazilian foreign ministry, commonly known as Itamaraty after the name of the palace that originally housed it in Rio de Janeiro, this has proven highly unsettling, feeding a degree of institutional crisis about not only the process, but also the content and ambitions of policies. An important part of the story of Brazil in the world is consequently the 'crisis' or challenge of institutional transformation facing Itamaraty as it seeks to adjust to the accelerating democratization of foreign policy formulation (Belém Lopes, 2013a). For its part, the foreign ministry has quietly but assiduously worked to encourage an attitude that privileges its position as the experts, the apolitical representatives of Brazil abroad who advance policies of state, not policies of government. The systems established by the founding father of modern Brazilian diplomacy, José Maria da Silva Paranhos Junior, the Baron of Rio Branco positioned Itamaraty as a consistent bastion of professionalism relatively free from the problems of patronage politics, something further reinforced by the perception that the external was not particularly fertile ground for illicit personal enrichment. For their part, diplomats presented themselves as having a uniquely comprehensive view of the reality in Brazil, garnered from a combination of their need to understand the totality of their country to represent it abroad and the sense of slightly detached observation that comes from spending extended periods of time away from one's home. As late as the end of the twentieth century some Brazilian diplomats still maintained that there was no capacity in their country outside of Itamaraty to grapple with international affairs. Perhaps seeing change coming, they applauded the increase in the number of international relations students and tried to take some credit for the rising profile of foreign affairs in Brazil, including through the translation of key theoretical texts into Portuguese and their free distribution online. The reality, as this chapter and the wider book will set out, was somewhat different. Itamaraty effectively had its doors forced open by new voices and actors seeking a more dynamic and variegated foreign policy that reflected Brazil's increasingly complicated and intricate insertion into the regional and global political economy. As subsequent chapters will explain, this in turn has impacted how Brazilian foreign policy contests the global structural power game, opening new avenues for engagement grounded in 'low' politics fields such as trade, investment and development.

The story in this chapter is how Itamaraty's iron grip on foreign policy formulation and decision making has been eroded over the twenty-five years since the completion of the Brazil's democratic transition. Building on the historical traditions and trends outlined in the previous chapter, the tale begins with an explanation of the function and operation of Itamaraty, Brazil's highly professionalized foreign service. As will be explained, becoming a diplomat in Brazil is no mean feat, requiring passage not only through a highly competitive and lengthy examination system, but also completion of a rigorous preparation and indoctrination programme at the Rio Branco Institute. The result is an extremely strong esprit de corps amongst Brazil's diplomats and one of the largest concentrations of technocratic professionalism in the Brazilian state, which in the past allowed the bureaucratic system to effectively ring-fence foreign policy as an area only for the experts (Belém Lopes, 2013a; Mourão, 2013). With this context in place, the second section of the chapter will set out how factors such as the rise of presidential diplomacy and the increasing internationalization of Brazilian business and government have emerged as new pressures in the foreign policy debate across the Cardoso, Lula and Dilma presidencies, culminating in the sense of institutional crisis surrounding Itamaraty at the end of Dilma's first term. Attention will also be given to how Itamaraty has worked to manage this debate and incorporate these disparate voices in the foreign policy process in a manner that still leaves final decision making power within the Palace walls. The chapter will conclude by setting out the emerging politics of foreign policy making in Brazil.

Inside Itamaraty

The lack of political interest in foreign policy finds its roots in the technocratic norms Rio Branco constructed around the field in 1902. His essential point was that international affairs is an area of state policy, not governmental policy, meaning that it requires a continuity and structure that extends beyond the short-term partisan political struggle (Faria, 2008; Ricupero, 2000). This is broadly reflected in the 1988 Constitution, which devotes only minor attention to external policy. Article 49 grants the National Congress the exclusive competence to decide on international treaties and approve presidential decisions to declare war, make peace, or allow foreign forces to transit Brazilian territory. This is supported by Article 84, which gives the president of the Republic the exclusive power to 'conclude international treaties, conventions and acts' and to 'decree the state of defense and the state of siege'. Itamaraty retains the power and responsibility for presenting international initiatives to the president, a charge that it tends to interpret fairly broadly.The need to obtain congressional approval for any treaty or agreement negotiated by the president should drive the sort of consultative approach to foreign affairs seen in the US through the 'fast-track' process. In practical terms these provisions result in a delegation of authority from Congress to the Executive in the field of foreign affairs (Forjaz, 2011). The Executive is left to get on with the job and Itamaraty given a sometimes controlling degree of input into strategic as well as tactical decision making.

Itamaraty in effect holds a privileged position in the foreign policy making framework that draws on the notion of a 'state policy' to at times almost place ministerial thinking above that of the day's government (Belém Lopes, 2013a; 2015; Cheibub, 1984; 1989), leaving diplomats remarkably isolated from the pressures exerted by other interest groups such as civil society, business and political interests. In part this slight of hand is accepted because of the clear qualifications and professionalism of Brazil's diplomats. Entry to the foreign service is through highly competitive examination – in 2014 over 4,000 individuals contested 18 positions – which begins with written examinations on the history of Brazil, geography, international politics, public and international law, English and Portuguese. Candidates successful at this stage proceed to a series of interviews with ranking diplomats in Brasília. Most aspiring diplomats spend at least a year preparing for the exams and interviews, where they are also judged on deportment, personal presentation and the quality of their spoken Portuguese. Indeed, it is not uncommon to see embassies in Brasília seeking contract employees by presenting their jobs as ideal for candidates preparing for the Itamaraty entrance exams. Many take the exam multiple times, reaching the interview stage in some years and falling short in others. Those that are successful proceed to what is effectively a professional masters degree in diplomacy at Itamaraty's training academy, the Rio Branco Institute, where they are acculturated and professionalized into the traditions, practices and process of the foreign ministry. The result is a corps of exceptionally bright and capable public servants able to handle the intricacies of public policy with the light touch of a diplomat and thus smooth potentially fractious bureaucratic relations.

As one young diplomat explained while walking through the corridors of the Itamaraty Palace complex in Brasília, 'the price of having this wonderful job is working in a building designed by Oscar Niemeyer'. This new entrant to the Itamaraty career structure unwittingly delivered a very apt metaphor for life in Brazil's foreign service. Like a Niemeyer building, Brazilian diplomacy is wonderfully elegant and carries tremendous domestic and international prestige, not least from the pay, which in 2014 began at BRZ 185,800 (comfortably over USD 70,000 at the time). The other similarity to the Brazilian architect's oeuvre is that life in Itamaraty is defined by clear hierarchies and structures, remaining fundamentally dependent on the 'physics' of these policy processes to retain its integrity and solidity. No decision on a policy position is taken without extensive consultation of the Itamaraty archives to ensure long-running consistency is maintained or breaks with tradition merited. Even when the issue in question stems from new factors in foreign affairs, such as the growing importance of intellectual property, the Brazilian stance is constructed in direct reference to prior positions in other areas that guide the overarching tenor of the country's foreign policy. Change comes slowly and carefully to Brazil's foreign policy. Even when there appear to be big changes, such as the Lula administration's turn to Africa or Cardoso's launch of the South American geopolitical approach, these new directions are often presented as amplification of past practices, not departures from the norm. Moreover, great pains are taken to post facto ground these new directions in Brazil's foreign policy traditions, often through the holding of seminars linking the new idea to Rio Branco's legacy or through the extensive catalogue of quasi-academic works written by the country's diplomats and published by the Fundação Alexandre Gusmão (Lima, 2014; Pinheiro, 2007).

The centrality of Itamaraty to the foreign policy process in Brazil is inescapable. A clear sense of responsibility and tutelary privilege is instilled in Brazilian diplomats from the first days of their training at the Rio Branco Institute. Explicit socialization into an elite cadre is enhanced by briefings from the most senior officials from other departments as well as the foreign minister – Celso Amorim published his 'conversations with young diplomats' in 2011, noting that he tried to take a less formal approach to the discussions in order to explain not just what Brazil was doing, but how decisions were being made in Brasilia and abroad (p. 13). Membership in the policy elite is further reinforced by a ritualized formal ceremony at the end of the two-year course where the president of the Republic invests Rio Branco Institute graduates in the Order of Rio Branco and thus as Brazilian diplomats (Moura, 2007).

All of this combines to instill three central characteristics in Brazilian diplomats. First, from their earliest days in the training institute they become accustomed to being in the presence of powerful decision makers and thus have little trouble filling key advisory roles to high officials throughout the Brazilian government. The surety that diplomats should take this role is underpinned by the second characteristic, which is a belief that only diplomats have the high-level macro view of Brazil which is necessary to understand the cross-cutting needs of the country and thus escape capture by the specific interests of individual ministries or political prerogatives. Further gravity is added to this belief by the frequent secondment of diplomats to the *gabinete* (Minister's office) in other departments, particularly major ministries such as Finance, Defence and the Presidency. The final characteristic is a belief that only the diplomats in Itamaraty have the preparation, and personal and institutional experience necessary to engage with the outside world. Questions of technical expertise and issue-specific knowledge take second place to the primacy Itamaraty places on the discourse and praxis of foreign relations.

Cracking the Palace walls

This last characteristic can drive officials in other ministries to distraction and leads to procedural quirks where trade negotiations are undertaken by Itamaraty, not the Ministry of Development and International Trade (MDIC); technical officials in ministries such as Agriculture, as well as Rural Development, complain they are ignored in the formulation of Brazil's position in forums such as the World Trade Organization. This has also created serious tensions between the diplomatic corps and the Planalto Palace in recent years. Cardoso and Lula actively engaged in direct presidential diplomacy and gave clear support to their foreign ministers, which resulted in extensive deployment of the skills at Itamaraty abroad and at home. This was not particularly evident during Dilma's first term, which saw her expectations focus tightly on technocratic deliverables and the application of expertise to the domestic context, not the more ethereal, but still-important business of diplomacy. To this end in 2012 she effectively castigated newly minted diplomats for being the generalists required of their jobs and not the experts in specific concrete fields such as science, engineering and technology, which she felt were critical for Brazil's advancement (Belém Lopes, 2013b: 80). While she tacitly recognized the unfairness of her criticism by pointing out diplomats had to generalize and have a working-level understanding of specific technical subjects, her pointed advice got to the heart of the challenge Itamaraty had been confronting during the PT presidencies of Lula and Dilma as the technocracy of 'low' politics assumed ever-more importance than the 'high' politics issues that had traditionally been the foreign policy focus of diplomats.

For Itamaraty the challenge has been the depth and strength of its institutional identity and surety of its preeminence in the Brazilian state, none of which was seriously challenged prior to the return to full democracy with Fernando Collor's inauguration in 1990. The process of Argentina–Brazil economic approximation driven by the 1986 Programa de Integración y Cooperación Económica Argentina-Brasil (PICE) was accelerated with Collor's decision to pursue tighter sub-regional integration, leading to the Treaty of Asunción in 1991 and the launch of Mercosul. Collor's turn to the regional context was in part driven by the changes in the global system that came with the end of the Cold War. The resultant increase in economic exchange with neighbouring Argentina, Paraguay and Uruguay rapidly raised the importance of trade as a critical issue for Itamaraty. In 1986 Brazilian exports to the other Mercosul countries stood at USD 1.176 billion, climbing to USD 4.127 billion in 1992 and USD 9.043 billion in 1997. Value-added products, especially manufactured goods involving a wide range of industries and companies, dominated these rising exports, which opened a space for foreign affairs to have a new resonance in domestic politics. This was amplified during the Fernando Henrique Cardoso era, when the management of regional relations and positive international insertion became critical elements of the larger plan to establish Brazil as a credible country and not just a perennial economic basket case. Foreign affairs became something that was too important to be left to the technocratic experts and the bureaucratic traditions of the foreign ministry.

A key shift that emerged from Collor's brief period in the Planalto Palace was the return of presidential diplomacy (Danese, 1999) as the force of the president's full attention on the issue of regional integration with Argentina emerged as a crucial element in redirecting Brazilian foreign policy and overcoming institutional opposition to the plan (Malamud, 2005). Under the presidential diplomacy model there is almost an expansion of roles that place the president in the position of foreign minister as key visionary and instigator of foreign policy ideas, shifting the actual minister into a more technocratic space of managing implementation of the new policy direction. The various elements within the foreign ministry then become the instruments for coordinating other governmental areas to push the given policy forward. When points of crisis or blockage are encountered, internal or external, the president again steps forward and exerts authority to resolve the impasse and hopefully give the policy initiative the impetus needed to keep it moving forward. The key point to remember in the Brazilian case is that the president has not been raised – 'formed', in Brazilian terminology – by Itamaraty and is thus not constrained by the traditions, beliefs and attitudes impressed upon the diplomatic corps through their training and career progression. New departures and major reinterpretations of existing foreign policy positions become possible with presidential diplomacy, although this is not to say that Itamaraty as an institution does not subtly resist ideas it sees as excessive or ill-considered.

Although Collor started the move to presidential diplomacy with his push to establish Mercosul, it was Cardoso who took it to new heights and set the stage for Lula's expansive dynamism. Having served briefly as foreign minister less than two years prior to his inauguration as president, he was keenly aware of Itamaraty's limitations, particularly with respect to dealing with the rapidly changing international environment as well as the new role that regional relations were taking in backstopping Brazilian economic stability and reform. Unease with his political intervention in state policy rather than remaining restricted to government policy was mollified by the genuine respect diplomats felt for him as well as his decision to appoint senior diplomats to several of the main presidential advisory positions. This left Itamaraty with the institutional security that they were still central to directing the nation's foreign policy even if the decisions were now actively driven in the Planalto Palace. First, Foreign Minister Luiz Felipe Lampreia and then Celso Lafer, who had also served as MDIC Minister, were effectively given hybrid roles of implementing the initiatives Cardoso launched himself during a bevy of international trips and summits.

The issue Cardoso (2015: 44) was seeking to manage was Itamaraty's inherent conservativeness, something which he wanted to disrupt from the first moments of his presidency when seeking a foreign minister 'from outside who could dinamize Itamaraty'. Although the long-view taken in the Palace resulted in a remarkable degree of foreign policy consistency and the avoidance of costly rash decisions, such a measured approach was only possible because foreign policy decisions taken at Itamaraty had remarkably small consequences for Brazil's larger political and economic situation, although negotiations conducted by the Finance Ministry and Central Bank with the Bretton Woods Institution remained very important. By the mid-1990s the situation had changed, with trade-related economic issues vaulting to the fore as Mercosul-driven exchange boomed and the ability to manage and bring stability to the Southern Cone became a prerequisite for establishing Brazil as a credible country and safe destination for the FDI and financial capital investment needed to resuscitate the national economy. The challenge for Itamaraty was that this pulled the actual conduct of meaningful diplomacy away from the ritualized courtliness of high politics towards the earthier approaches found in Track II and Track III diplomacy, with the latter being particularly important as Cardoso simultaneously sought to assuage a vast range of non-governmental actors ranging from financial market makers through to foreign non-governmental environmental advocates.

After being inaugurated president in 1995, Cardoso wasted little time in driving through this change. In April 1995 he informed his ambassador he would receive representatives from environmental and indigenous rights non-governmental organizations (NGOs) during a visit to Washington, DC. As Cardoso recalls, the tenor of discussions at the resultant meeting were almost too much for ambassador Paulo Tarso Flecha de Lima, who was close to leaving the room in protest at what he saw as the insulting manner in which the NGO representatives were questioning his president. Cardoso was more sanguine, recognizing that the NGOs were not immersed in the protocol-filled world of traditional diplomacy, but operating in a more dynamic and direct style of issue politics that sidestepped the sort of state–society divisions carefully guarded through the formalities shepherded by Itamaraty (Cardoso, 2007). Although relatively minor, this incident neatly illustrates the clash in styles, cultures and praxis facing Itamaraty. Inside the foreign ministry the traditional culture was absolutely against this kind of direct interaction between non-state agents and the president, operating according to an ancient model deliberately placing diplomats between external voices and the president to avoid accidental statements leading to new and potential harmful lines of policy. For Cardoso, an internationally oriented non-diplomat who was also deeply embedded in the academic study of democracy, these sorts of meetings were essential to establishing Brazilian credibility in the amorphous, but now critical world of soft power diplomacy supplanting old-world European practices of formal diplomatic protocol.

A related challenge facing Cardoso was an absence of the specialist expertise within Itamaraty to deal with the technicalities of the country's foreign economic agenda that were becoming the heart of its foreign policy. Near the beginning of his period as foreign minister he attended an ALADI (Asociación Latinoamericana de Integración) trade grouping meeting where he discovered Itamaraty had a limited ability to deal with technocratic arcana being discussed and its wider implications for Brazil. Upon his return to Brasília he pushed Itamaraty into forming an interministerial working group to ensure that proper technical positions were prepared and that the considerable diplomatic skills of the country's diplomats operated from an equally strong technocratic base (Cardoso, 2007). Although this did at least open up lines of communication, other government ministries remained frustrated with Itamaraty and the difficulty of getting it to take on board the implications of underlying technical issues that did not align with the larger trajectories associated with foreign policy (Cason and Power, 2009; Deitos, 2012; Faria, 2012; Hopewell, 2013).

The underlying reality of the Cardoso years was Itamaraty's sustained belief that foreign policy remained a policy of state, not of governmental politics, and thus something that should remain within the Ministry's walls. Despite the centrality of 'Cardoso the president' to Brazil's rise as a credible nation in the 1990s – something bolstered by the extensive presidential diplomacy of 92 foreign trips during his eight years in office – Itamaraty still sought to control innovation and new directions in foreign policy. It was thus through direct presidential command, not diplomatic initiative that Itamaraty convened the 2000 Brasília Summit of South American Presidents and shifted Brazil's regional orientation away from a tight concentration on Mercosul and Latin America towards the new concept of South America as a geopolitical space. Perhaps more significantly, the approach taken to this project broke with the political and trade focus of diplomatic endeavours to focus on physical infrastructure as the precursor for expanded economic and political linkages. Although modeled on the somewhat successful *Avança Brasil* project of linking the different regions of Brazil, the continental infrastructure axes approach advanced at the Brasília Summit was seriously questioned by Itamaraty. To keep the project on track Cardoso recruited Celso Lafer, a former and future foreign minister, and Hélio Jaguaribe, one of Brazil's leading international relations scholars, to convene a conference at Itamaraty on regional infrastructure integration. The proceedings from the event were released in a volume entitled *Rio Branco, A América do Sul e a Modernização do Brasil*, bluntly emphasizing to diplomats that the new direction was not to be questioned by unambiguously linking it to the timeless priorities established by the patron saint of Brazilian foreign policy.

Wedging the Palace doors open

By the end of the Cardoso presidency foreign policy had become something of direct concern to vocal segments of the national economy. This was reflected in a consistent stream of editorials in the newspaper *Folha de São Paulo* calling for a more democratized approach to foreign policy, particularly one that would allow greater input by regionally and internationally oriented business actors (Deitos, 2012; Vieira de Jesus, 2009–2010). Pressures caused by a unipolar international system as well as the rise of internationalization of important segments of Brazil's economy suddenly made the external context important to more than the denizens of Itamaraty, creating a substantial change from the pattern that had dominated the previous 100 years of foreign policy thinking (Hirst and Soares de Lima, 2002). Moreover, the interests being articulated by these rising domestic voices focused on very specific economic, trade and legal questions set within complicated scientific, social and geographical contexts requiring specialization, not the sort of generalist approach found at Itamaraty (Pinheiro and Milani, 2012).

During the Cardoso years the shift had been towards presidential diplomacy, with the president not only setting the foreign policy agenda, but also using the symbolism of the office to directly negotiate new arrangements and agreements with foreign counterparts (Danese, 1999; Lins da Silva, 2002). Summit meetings became critical avenues for not only establishing Brazil as an internationally credible country, but also for integrating Brazilian actors into international political, economic and trade networks. Part of the domestic underpinning for Cardoso's presidential diplomacy was the economic and state reform process that extended beyond the privatization of vast swathes of the state-controlled economy to include encouragement of the rise of agro-industry and the positioning of state institutions such as the Banco Nacional de Desenvolvimento Econômico e Social (BNDES) as support structures for Brazil's internationalization. As the hard editorial line in newspapers such as *Folha de São Paulo* and *Valor Econômico* in 2001 and 2002 highlighted, this strategy worked and resulted in the rise of a new sector of internationally oriented businesses discussed in chapter five and chapter six. The problem faced by these new economic interests was that they remained largely shut out of the foreign policy formulation process.

The election of Lula in October 2002 proved critical for the further broadening of voices contributing to the debate on trade policy and other international questions. Lula's personal history as a leftist labour leader raised immediate concerns he would adopt policy positions inimical to business interests and might actively seek to exclude industry from the policy making process. To assuage these concerns Lula effectively bifurcated policy in his government between the serious business of protecting the nation's economic health and fuzzier areas such as symbolic, but low cost policy initiatives and departments. This game of continuing the liberal economic policies of the Cardoso regime while simultaneously maintaining the support of the PT by giving them some policy areas as near-playgrounds had an immediate impact on Itamaraty and the formulation of foreign policy in Brazil. The Palace doors were wedged wide open and the conduct of foreign policy divided into three areas titularly headed by Itamaraty: trade policy, South American policy, and South–South relations. While the North–South relationships that had historically been the main focus of Itamaraty's work were effectively downgraded, though far from discarded in the centrality of presidentially guided thinking, new avenues across the Global South were opened. Although far more forthrightly packaged and presented, the underlying idea to Lula's foreign policy and engagement opening was an extension of the Cardoso-era's approach to deliberately inserting Brazil into the world rather than waiting to be inserted (Cardoso, 2001; Hurrell, 2010). The overt shift, which became increasingly explicit throughout the Lula era, was to turn foreign policy into an almost explicit instrument of national development by extending existing regionalization processes throughout the continent and encouraging the spread of Brazilian trade and investment across the Global South as well as the North.

Celso Amorim, Lula's foreign minister, managed the trade file and issues of North–South relations. The South–South initiative fell under the guidance of Samuel Pinheiro Guimarães, who was appointed secretary general of foreign affairs, the number two job at Itamaraty and the position from which issues such as institutional structure and reform were driven. Samuel Pinheiro's appointment was very controversial because not only had he yet to be appointed to the rank of ambassador, a near-prerequisite for the secretary-general post, but he was also seen as a staunch leftist ideologue explicitly hostile to the North. The final member of the troika fitted neatly into this ideological predisposition. Marco Aurélio Garcia was Lula's chief foreign affairs advisor and directed the strategic level of Brazil's turn towards South America from his office in the Planalto Palace, a job he retained with the transition to Dilma. Cuban trained while in exile during the military dictatorship, he quietly collaborated behind the scenes with PT backroom operator José Dirceu in an attempt to corral the mercurial regional leftist voices of leaders such as Hugo Chávez and Evo Morales behind the Lulista vision of South American solidarity (interview with Brazilian diplomats, 2007). Although the rise of this troika was resisted strongly by a sizeable constituency within Itamaraty, with early accounts suggesting Samuel Pinheiro would be sent abroad as an ambassador for a period of 'rehabilitation', presidential authority was firmly exerted and the troika put in place. Foreign policy making in Brazil was launched into a process of pluralization that brought it more closely in line with the wider democratization processes that had been ongoing since 1985. Indeed, the naming of Amorim and Samuel Pinheiro – two diplomats deeply immersed in international trade issues at the global and regional level – to the top of Itamaraty clearly signaled keen attention on the economic possibilities of foreign policy.

The trade file

One of the first steps Lula took in his strategy of reassuring domestic business and foreign investors was to make a number of key cabinet appointments beyond his vice president, José Alencar, who was a major player in the Brazilian textile industry. For central bank president he chose Henrique Meirelles, former president of global banking for FleetBoston Financial. The ministry of development and international trade (MDIC) went to Luiz Fernando Furlan, head of the food conglomerate Sadia, and Agriculture went to Roberto Rodrigues, an agricultural engineer who would later run the agricultural trade unit at the São Paulo Federation of Industrial Enterprises (FIESP). Appointment of Furlan and Rodrigues was important because they provided a direct communication channel between the increasingly important agro-industrial sector and the highest levels of policy making. These two cabinet stars were also instrumental in widening the number of voices at the discussion table when Itamaraty was working to formulate trade negotiation positions, which proved a bit discombobulating for diplomats because the two ministers actively pulled in external expertise to assist with the formation of their ministry's positions heading towards the 2003 WTO ministerial meeting.

One increasingly vocal sector demanding inclusion in discussions about trade policy was the growing export-oriented agricultural industry, which saw surging export numbers in terms of both volume and value (see chapter five). By 2001 the market reforms of the Cardoso years had begun to reveal their full impact and producers of commodities ranging from soya through citrus fruits and sugar to proteins such as beef, chicken and pork were becoming increasingly impatient with what they saw as governmental ineptitude. This shift in the economic structure of Brazil was accompanied by the return to Brazil of Marcos Jank, a talented agricultural economist who had been working in the Washington, DC-based multilateral development institutions. Jank worked with a number of important agro-industrial voices in the São Paulo region, most notably Furlan and Rodrigues to found the think tank, the Instituto de Estudos do Comércio e Negociações Internacioanais (ICONE) in 2003. In a significant break from past practice in the Brazilian polity, a consortium of peak business groups in the agricultural sector provided financial backing for ICONE's research agenda without attempting to transform it into a partisan political lobbying campaign, relying instead on its imbedded liberal trading ideology to advance their interests. The last year of Cardoso's tenure and the beginning of the Lula regime saw an increasingly forceful stream of opinion editorials and technical papers from Jank and ICONE critiquing the government's approach to trade policy. While guided by a clear belief in free trade and market economics, the analysis provided by ICONE was consistently technical and independent.

Of particular note was the close, but informal relationship between Rodrigues and Jank (interview with Brazilian diplomats, 2007). Itamaraty's proclivity to draw on its considerable negotiating capacity to maintain preeminence in the formulation of negotiating positions was directly assaulted by the detailed technical papers provided to Rodrigues and Furlan by ICONE. For its part ICONE was sanguine about its role, insisting that it existed solely to provide analysis and background information on an independent basis. With this in mind the Institute assiduously avoided taking any money from the Brazilian government (interview with ICONE official, 2007). This raised two significant points for Itamaraty. First, ICONE closely ascribed to the apolitical precepts laid down by Rio Branco and firmly established itself as an institute operating outside the daily political fray. The second point it highlighted was the lack of internal technical expertise and resources at Itamaraty, let alone the Ministry of Agriculture (interview with Ministry of Agriculture officials, 2007), which in turn created a push for reform of the career structure at the institution, as well as an expansion in the number of diplomats from 997 to 1,400. As part of this reform there was a clear indication that greater attention needed to be given to hiring individuals with the requisite economic and legal skills necessary to understand and debate the sort of material prepared by groups such as ICONE.

The idea that Itamaraty might create an in-house advanced econometric analysis function appears never to have been seriously entertained. Arguably the focus on the ability to understand the external analyses and integrate it into negotiating positions was a more appropriate use of scarce resource. Added heft was given to this approach as ICONE's international credibility grew and the impact of its technocratic approach was noted by other Brazilian industry groups who set up their own analysis divisions. It soon became common practice for ICONE-funded analysts to be included in Brazilian WTO negotiating delegations, with these independent voices even on occasion presenting Brazil's position to international meetings (interview with Ministry of Agriculture officials, 2007). Indeed, as the Lula years progressed the agricultural lobby as a whole proved particularly adept at working with Itamaraty to exploit the opportunities available through the WTO system at both the negotiating table and in the dispute resolution body (Hopewell, 2013; Jatkar and McFarlene, 2013). Other organizations such as FIESP tell stories of Amorim stepping out of talks in Geneva to personally call their analysts in order to get instant analysis on the implications for Brazil of technical positions suggested by other countries (interview with FIESP trade analyst, 2007).

Similar efforts to maintain Itamaraty privilege by co-opting intra-governmental expertise could be found in efforts to retain control over the trade negotiating position formation process. Furlan and Rodrigues used their ministerial positions to aggressively push the role of the Câmara de Comércio Exterior (CAMEX) in MDIC as a central forum for settling negotiating positions. Within the ambit of CAMEX three separate coordinating forums were established to broker state–society discussions about policy positions on Mercosul, the Free Trade Area of the Americas (FTAA), the EU and the WTO. A further unit of CAMEX brought more opportunity for business input through its second-highest organ, the Consultative Council of the Private Sector, CONEX. Although CAMEX and its subsidiary councils were chaired by MDIC and not Itamaraty, the final formulation, coordination and implementation of Brazilian trade policy still remained in the hands of Itamaraty despite business sector desires that it be transferred to MDIC (Cason and Power, 2009: 121). This continued to create frustration on the Esplanada dos Ministerios in Brasília through the 2000s, with international affairs officials in other ministries with major trade interests freely expressing exasperation with their colleagues at Itamaraty; industry groups in São Paulo had similar complaints.

More startling were suggestions from diplomats in neighbouring countries that Brazilian industrial and agricultural interest groups were approaching them to press Itamaraty to change its policies. An additional complaint from the agro-industrial sector was that government officials did not understand the technical issues being negotiated, with a particular problem being the granting of technical advisory positions in fields such as phytosanitary controls to unqualified individuals as rewards for political support. Symptomatic of this resistance by Itamaraty to what it viewed as incursions into its domain was the length of time it took to create agricultural counsellor positions in Brazil's foreign missions. Despite the clear need for these specialized officers to protect Brazil's considerable agricultural interests abroad, Itamaraty quietly blocked the Agriculture Ministry's efforts to establish the posts until the presidential palace commanded the diplomats to comply (Faria, 2012).

Trading politics

Lula faced a major challenge when he was inaugurated president. He had to continue the liberal economic policies of the Cardoso presidency, but his leftist support base in the PT and other left-wing congressional factions were demanding major redistributional changes. One of the strategies Lula employed to retain support was to hand the political dimension of foreign policy to the left, giving individuals such as Marco Aurélio Garcia and Samuel Pinheiro Guimarães major control over the strategic direction that Itamaraty would take. The result was a rapid change in course to orient Brazilian foreign policy towards South America and the Global South, which exposed a deep schism within Itamaraty. Traditionalist factions in the Palace were quick to speak up about the dangers of politicizing matters of state such as foreign policy (Marin, 2004). Roberto Abdenur, Brazil's ambassador in Washington, retired with a bang by giving a pointed interview to the news magazine *Veja* where he savaged the Lula administration for ignoring and even damaging the still important relationship with the US. As the title of the article suggested, not even during the most nationalist days of the dictatorship were Brazilian government attitudes towards Washington so hostile (Cabral, 2007). Although the tenor of his subsequent remarks to a special meeting of the Senate Foreign Affairs and National Defense Committee were more measured, the theme of concern about opportunities lost due to wandering attention in Planalto remained.

Abdenur's blast was echoed by a number of other former diplomats of his generation who were highly critical of the Lula administration's intervention in the foreign policy arena to orient Brazil towards the South.

While there was certainly a strong element of truth in their accusation that Brazil was being launched on a pattern of Third Worldist adventurism to satisfy the ego of a globe trotting president and the ideological dreams of his advisors and partisan political supporters, the actual picture was more complicated and reflected the extent to which foreign policy was being mobilized for wider national developmental goals and to pursue new avenues for contesting patterns of structural power in the global system (FUNAG, 2007; Scolese and Nossa, 2006). Figures outside of Itamaraty, such as Marco Aurélio Garcia and José Dirceu, were definitely pushing Brazil to look South in order to develop a leadership position from which it could attain a stronger international position and a seat a the main global decision making tables. What remained unclear to many observers was to what end, other than national prestige and a desire to partake in the business of high politics, Brazil engaged in a Southern engagement push with its foreign policy between 'end' and 'other' (Stolte, 2015). On the economic front major voices around the cabinet table saw opportunity in the Southern turn, particularly those with links to industries such as construction and civil engineering busy moving into African and Latin American markets. Viewed with a little more detachment, the new policy direction amounted to a continuation of the economic and trade diversification programme that Itamaraty had pushed from the mid-1980s, only focusing on developing, not developed markets. Rodrigues and Furlan both pushed to include business leaders in presidential delegations travelling abroad. Lula himself turned to a vigorous programme of presidential diplomacy to use his personal charisma to open doors and launch agreements that he and his advisors believed would create opportunities for Brazil.

The result during Lula's first term was a flurry of Brazil/South America presidential summits with leaders from Africa, the Middle East, and virtually any other grouping of countries that appeared to fit the agenda. New South–South initiatives such as the India-Brazil-South Africa (IBSA) Dialogue Forum were launched in an attempt to give substance to Lula's vision of a new international economic geography and alternatives to organization bypassing Northern capitals. When the BRICS (Brazil, Russia, India, China, South Africa) concept captured the international imagination the presidential palace was quick to jump on the bandwagon and join Russia in organizing a series of summits (Stuenkel, 2015). On a continental level the regional infrastructure integration process launched by Cardoso was reaffirmed, but also repackaged in a new political skin to create the Comunidade de Nacões Sulamerica (CASA) and given a quiet focus on energy (interview with Brazilian diplomats, 2007). When CASA appeared to be moribund it was reinvented as the Union of South American Nations (UNASUL), replete with propositions for cooperation in previously highly sensitive areas such as defence. All of this presented a considerable challenge for Itamaraty because a central driving force was Lula's personal desire and the ideological guidance of his personal advisors and not what appeared to be the accepted long-running policy logic at Itamaraty (for a sampling, see Almeida, 2014; Gonçalves, 2013; Lafer, 2013a; Ricupero, 2013; Sotero, 2011–2012). Although Lula was responding partially to society and business pressures for greater internationalization, there was still at times a tendency for ambition to exceed grasp. Amorim was thus frequently left with the challenge of reigning in expectations that came in the wake of his president's optimistic, but frequently ill-advised public musings, such as conversion of IBSA or the trade G20 coalition into a pan-Southern regional grouping.

Internal changes in Itamaraty did not help Amorim with his post-facto policy management tasks. One of the major changes Samuel Pinheiro brought in through a series of structural shifts at Itamaraty was a sense of politicization within the Palace. Diplomats were required to read a selection of books set by the secretary general and there was a growing sense that positions were being filled based on ideological congruence, not merit (Marin, 2004; OESP, 2004). Although the internal factional politics at Itamaraty had long been vicious, professionalism had remained the paramount skill, with the ability to deliver sage advice and penetrating analysis to senior officials and political figures being the hallmark of diplomats at all levels (Almeida, 2001). The perception in Itamaraty early in the Lula years was that this had definitively changed, prompting some individuals to radically depart from protocol and secretly record discussions at events such as Mercosul meetings in order to have proof that they were adhering to the new political tone (OESP, 2003). On the positive side Celso Amorim and Samuel Pinheiro were able to pair these changes with remarkable skill at the inter-ministerial bureaucratic game on the Esplanada, which resulted in major increases in Itamaraty funding, including a rapid expansion of diplomatic staff and a flurry of mission openings throughout Africa and the Caribbean.

Brokering palaces

By 2005 the confusion and discontent that had marked Lula's forcing open of Brazilian foreign policy to new directions and approaches was coming under some measure of control, with an apparent accommodation between Amorim and Lula's advisors that kept the political direction of the PT in place. A series of changes in key Itamaraty leadership positions were quietly announced, placing diplomats more closely linked to Amorim's measured style in important policy and implementation posts (Marin, 2005). Credibility for the traditionalists would only grow over the next year as Venezuela's Hugo Chávez leadership ambitions grew in parallel to rising oil prices, resulting in a direct challenge to Brazilian continental leadership ambitions. Most notable in this respect was Chávez's encouragement of Bolivian Evo Morales' shock nationalization of Petrobras gas assets on 1 May 2006, threatening Brazil with the loss of a critical energy source for the São Paulo-Rio de Janeiro industrial heartland. This latter event suddenly brought home to Brazilians that events in other countries had implications for their daily lives and that regional leftist 'allies' might not be the best of friends (interviews with Brazilian diplomats, 2007). It also placed enormous pressure on the political architects of Lula's Southern-oriented foreign policy to bring matters quickly under control lest it cost him victory in the October presidential election. The charge floating at the time was that ideology had trumped interests and directly resulted in material harm to Brazil.

By the end of the first Lula presidency the shiny veneer of solidarity and fraternity that appeared to drive intra-continental relations took on a rougher edge. The longer-term implication of the Bolivian gas nationalization crisis was not a change in the new trajectory set by Lula's advisors, but rather a shift in its conduct and tone. Lula's coterie of advisors remained in place, but became less visible and found a more cooperative style of working with Itamaraty to implement the South–South policies (interviews with Brazilian diplomats, 2007). They also worked to control some of the bombast that had marked the president's foreign policy statements. More significantly, ideological affinity was directly drawn upon through back channels to send key Lula advisors such as Marco Aurélio Garcia and José Dirceu on shuttle diplomacy missions to the Bolivarian capitals to quietly reassert Brazil's leadership in South America. As will be set out in later chapters, this was married with a strategic willingness to use a variety of avenues of pressure to quietly bring the Chávez axis countries into line, most notably through subtle financial pressures via access to central bank currency swaps as well as careful review of accounts receivables. Above all Lula drew on the size of his country's economy and the success his social policies were having to take on something akin to the guiding role of an elder brother, counselling, not chastising his counterparts. Direct presidential interaction was ramped up and in the Venezuelan case regularized and strategically used as a central forum to ensure that niggles in the bilateral relationship, including payment of invoices from Brazilian firms, were settled 'mano-a-mano em portuñol'.

While domestic political risk management played a role in this approximation between the Planalto and Itamaraty palaces, perhaps of greater significance were the new voices outside of government quietly supporting continuation of the South American and African engagement initiatives. Efforts by Furlan and Rodrigues to include business actors in Lula's international travels dovetailed nicely with rising global commodity prices and the growth of the Brazilian resource extraction and construction sectors to create a new dynamic in the Brazilian economy discussed in chapter six: the foreign expansion of Brazilian firms. Creative financing through state institutions such as the BNDES, Banco do Brasil and Caixa Econômica were allowing Brazilian construction firms to win major infrastructure contracts not only throughout South America, but also in Africa and parts of Europe. These engineering firms found that they were particularly successful in growing Southern markets because of similarities in underlying cultural norms and their understanding of how to manage and benefit from the social pressures found in countries marked by high poverty rates. Mining companies such as Vale and Petrobras were able to draw on similar levels of Southern-specific contextual awareness as well as the personal charisma of Lula to gain entry into new markets. Outward flows of Brazilian FDI were also welcomed by neighbouring countries and actively sought, not least because of the involved firms' proclivity for trying to employ as many local professionals and laborers as possible. This in turn reinforced the Cardoso/Lula nod to Cepalista thinking, feeding an ambition of internationalizing the Brazilian economy to bring the benefits of opportunities throughout the world back to advance national development in a manner similar to that seen in Europe, North America and Japan (Ocampo and Martin, 2003).

Luckily for Lula the large, wealthy and influential construction and agricultural industries added economic impetus to what had originally been seen by many as a mistaken and ideologically driven foreign policy shift. Their massive campaign finance contributions to the three leading political parties in Brazil – to say nothing of off-the-books illegal payments – also helped keep their internationalization priorities on the agenda (Boulos, 2014). The idea that the Global South represented an opportunity for Brazil was also clearly evident in the thinking of a number of Lula's chief advisors, not least of whom was Samuel Pinheiro Guimarães, but there was no certainty that the gamble would pay-off. Indeed, the unexpected global rise of commodity prices in the 2000s is arguably the glue that held the strategy together. Outside of government the construction companies were thankful that the foreign policy framework had finally been used to open international markets, but there was also a clear sense that this was a fortuitous alignment of interests, not a conscious response by policy makers to their calls for assistance. To this end they highlight the extent to which Brazil's growing official development assistance agenda has been used to generate political relations across the South without being integrated into a clear policy designed to explicitly advance Brazil's commercial interests as an ancillary benefit consistent with Lula's assertions that the South must grow together if poverty is to be eradicated (Amorim, 2015b).

The underlying suggestion that direct presidential pressure played a critical role in sustaining the South–South foreign policy trajectory became clear during the first Dilma presidency and pointed to what may emerge in the coming years as a key bureaucratic weakness of Itamaraty. For Dilma the business of diplomacy was just so much flimflammery offering specious and certainly not tangible results. Her first term was thus marked by a slashing of almost 50% off Itamaraty's budget and sustained attempts to wrest policy areas away from the foreign ministry. In particular she focused her attention on the need to develop more markets and increase Brazilian trade flows, prompting a 2013 proposition that development cooperation policy be moved from Itamaraty to the MDIC to form something approximating an 'Africa Agenda' prioritizing her country's economic interests (Rossi, 2013). A further push on Itamaraty came late in 2014 with word that its trade promotion arm was likely to be collapsed and the responsibilities moved to other ministries, which would post commercial officers in embassies abroad. Meanwhile, there was a sense in the countries Lula had opened up, most notably the Portuguese-speaking African nations, that Brazil was quietly disappearing as a sustained and reliable presence. While this was not manifest in Brazil's profile in major international institutions such as the UN, business actors and diplomats noted it was becoming increasingly difficult to keep Dilma engaged with Africa and that her participation in events surrounding the African Union's fiftieth anniversary celebrations was largely a result of major pressure from Lula.

Conclusion

The lesson made apparent by Dilma's first term, and which will repeat as a theme throughout this book, is that presidential leadership in the form of strong political direction and support plays an essential role in Brazilian foreign policy despite the mythology that international affairs should be a policy of state managed by professionals and held apart from the partisan political fray. Indeed, one of the most interesting aspects of the security chapter later in this text is the extent to which military engagement appeared to take the lead in building South–South bilateral relationships during the Dilma years at the same moment that diplomatic attention seemed to wane. Attempts at ring-fencing aside, foreign policy remains an area of public policy and Itamaraty a bureaucracy, albeit one staffed with immensely capable professionals. This latter aspect is critical for understanding the foreign policy process, emphasizing that the foreign ministry is subservient to the presidency in democratic Brazil and that we should have very limited expectations of or desire for diplomatic creativity by the professionals at Itamaraty without clear political direction (Belém Lopes, 2013c). Indeed, Itamaraty does not have the legal licence to autonomously 'create' Brazil's foreign policy, something diplomats are keenly aware of to their great credit. The result is a reliance on past precedent and attempts at consistency when political direction and support is lacking. Unfortunately, this is also a comfortable stance to take and results in the inherent conservativeness of Itamaraty's approach to foreign policy, a preference for caution found in virtually any large and established bureaucracy. The response from other ministries and even other levels of government has been to go it alone or to seek ways of engaging internationally that bypass the foreign ministry (Candeas, 2012; Kleiman, 2012; Lessa et al., 2012; Salomón, 2012; Souza, 2012; Tavares, 2013).

One of the greatest challenges facing Brazilian foreign policy thus has little to do with its regional and global insertion, questions of global structural power, or Brazil's actual or latent power capabilities. Rather, it is the capacity to get public and political attention focused on the international questions that are increasingly impacting domestic Brazilian interests and developments. While Itamaraty has already taken some important steps towards building greater public engagement, most notably through the public consultations it held in March, 2014 with a view to releasing a foreign policy White Paper, and the advancement of internal thinking on foreign policy and democracy (Mourão, 2013; Patriota, 2013a), these are episodic arrangements intermediated by bureaucratic structures that almost reflexively delimit the space open for debate. Indeed, as the book was going to press in 2016 there was general skepticism that the White Paper would ever be released, if in fact it had been drafted in the first place. A lack of deep and sustained congressional engagement with foreign policy can join with weak presidential leadership to ensure that little changes, and that core conceptual issues remain unchallenged, thus risking failure to reflect the interests, ethical and identity understandings Brazilians hold about themselves, their country, and its place in the region and world. In a democracy one of the key functions of elected representatives is to reflect the interests, ethics and identity of a country in its highest decision making institutions.

As apt as Itamaraty has proven at discerning these key foreign policy inputs over the years, which makes diplomats invaluable participants in the discussion, members of the foreign service are not elected officials and arguably not particularly representative of large parts of the wider Brazilian population. In this sense there is at times a strong indication that the greatest strength in Brazil's foreign policy – Itamaraty – can also be a distinct weakness in a world of increasingly diverse and technically complicated questions.

3

O jeito brasileiro… the Brazilian way

One of the central organizing features of Brazilian life, and something that often leaves North Americans flummoxed, is the *jeito*, or in its diminutive, the *jeitinho*. At its simplest, to make a *jeitinho* – *faz um jeitinho* – is to find a way 'around' something that is preventing you from achieving an objective. In an intensely legalistic society with myriad layers of rules and regulations that can impact everything from the purchase of a coffee in the morning to the awarding of a contract to construct a new soccer stadium, making a *jeitinho* becomes a critical skill. To be clear, this does not mean opening the path with an unmarked envelope containing a wad of high denomination bills, although a number of politicians have been caught on tape doing just this, and the Dilma government and the PT was facing serious corruption charges as this book was being written. Rather, it means slowing down just a bit and having a conversation, asking what everybody wants from a given situation, then looking to see where a mutually satisfying accommodation might be reached. The emphasis is squarely on relationships and mutual assistance over an extended period of time requiring a level of empathy with others, and an understanding of their position and priorities. It can also lead to the rise of parallel informal institutions and practices, which quietly step around obstacles with the slick dexterity of a striker streaking towards goal on the soccer pitch (Matta, 1984).

A basic understanding of the *jeitinho* is an important building block for grappling with the practical realities of Brazilian diplomacy and foreign policy as it engages in its agenda of challenging structural power realities in international affairs. Just as avoiding direct confrontation and conflict is central to successful execution of a *jeitinho*, avoiding discord and disharmony stands as a central facet of Brazilian diplomatic practice. Rarely will Brazilians utter a direct 'no', preferring instead

extensive use of the conditional tense or a call for further consideration and reflection. In short, there is an ingrained belief that a way can
be found, and if there is no avenue forward, it is still desirable to avoid
direct confrontation or overt disappointment. What is left unsaid in
the context of foreign policy is that the challenge is often to find a way
around two directly competing interests, with Itamaraty taking the
unstated view that clearly the point to the *jeitinho* is to bring about successful implementation of the Brazilian approach. The result is a focus
on what the diplomats in Itamaraty call 'creating consensus', which
in terms of the theory of international relations aligns neatly with the
concept of consensual hegemony (Burges, 2008): convincing others that
they are the owners of ideas you originally proposed.

To flesh out *o jeito brasileiro*, or the Brazilian way, this chapter will
set out the three essential building blocks of any essential *jeitinho*.
First, it will put forward the Brazilian outlook on the world, one that
at times is simultaneously realist and idealist. This makes the tenor
of Brazilian foreign policy remarkably similar to that of the US and
France, two countries who have definite views of their ideal version of
the world and total confidence about what is their rightful place in it.
While Brazil shares this confidence, it is a bit more circumspect about
asserting it, which reflects the bureaucratic factors outlined in the previous chapter. The second section of this chapter will set out the broad
strategies employed by Brazil to achieve its foreign policy goals. Long-
running historical analyses feature large in a strategic approach that
works through what might be described as consensual hegemony to
make long-term bets with very small wagers. In other words, Brazil risks
little and whenever possible tries to pursue its policies in the company
of others. This is evident in the seven tactics outlined, which focus on
a preference for multilateralism with weak institutionalization and a
carefully constructed identity as a supporter of Southern solidarity who
simultaneously adopts a remarkably tough negotiating attitude to all-
comers. As will become apparent later in the book as specific issues and
bilateral relationships are discussed, these tactics encapsulate the central
techniques employed by Brazilian foreign policy in an attempt to build
international support for its structural power reform agenda.

The world according to Brazil

To really grapple with how Brazil approaches international affairs it
helps to start with a quick detour to sociology and the work of Berger
and Luckman (1966) on the creation of social norms. The point these
two sociologists make is that what an individual thinks and how an

individual is likely to act or react is deeply conditioned by what society considers normal or expected behaviour. Although these norms are not legally codified and take generations to become embedded in the collective psyche, once in place they are very difficult to dislodge and circumscribe the sort of actions seen as a possible. For example, the social norm that seats at the front of the bus are for the elderly and infirm is so strong in Western society that most people won't even consider sitting in them no matter how empty a bus might be. This sense of behaviour and expectations being collectively delimited through socialization processes is also found in international relations, most particularly with respect to expected and accepted norms of conduct on both a national and global level. It is in this very process that we find the actual substance of structural power and the practices and instruments contested by Brazilian foreign policy.

In the Brazilian foreign policy context the relevant socially constructed norm is the tradition of non-aggression. The last intra-continental war fought by Brazil was a response to Paraguayan aggression, which resulted in the War of the Triple Alliance from 1864–1870. War and participation in external armed conflicts has subsequently been a comparative rarity for Brazil, marked most recently by a significant, but still adjunct role with the Allies in World War Two (Espach, 2015). This combines with the pride Brazilians take in having settled their national boundaries without armed conflict, creating a self-imposed policy norm that military aggression towards neighbouring countries is unimaginable. Moreover, the centrality of international legal mechanisms in the fixing of Brazil's borders blends into the Brazilian role in erecting international institutions, such as the United Nations, the General Agreement on Tarrifs and Trade (GATT) and the Organization of American States (OAS), to create an outlook that privileges international law and a deep commitment to multilateralism, albeit with the weak institutionalization discussed in chapter four.

Brazil emerges as something of a gentle giant that has consistently declined to use its size or economic capacity in an attempt to militarize and project force regionally or globally. As a result Brazil has no real enemies, particularly in the Americas, because it poses no real existential threat. The corollary of this is that Brazil also has few real friends, in part because its traditions of non-aggression mean the country might prove an unreliable partner in a mutual defence arrangement. A lack of real friends in the international arena also stems from the Brazilian normative approach to the founding precepts of multilateralism, namely a rigid approach to the respect of national sovereignty. This highlights the apparent contradiction in Brazil's approach to foreign affairs. Its diplomats are seemingly unwilling to directly or unilaterally impose a position on others or take an outwardly obstructionist stance in international talk shops and negotiations, yet they remain unbending in pursuit of their own national interests.

In terms of the structural power transformation argument set out in this book, on an international level Brazil is in effect resisting the sort of social norm construction process outlined by Berger and Luckman. Most approaches to global governance imply some sort of pooling of elements of sovereignty through the acceptance of an international authority to arbitrate or coordinate in a particular issue area. While Brazil outwardly accepts this, it does so with an important normative emphasis on the sanctity of sovereignty that can drive negotiators from other countries to distraction. The result is Brazil will sign onto international protocols and agreements, but in a manner that effectively undermines them if they are considered to impinge on the autonomist aspects of sovereignty as the pre-eminent normative principle in foreign affairs. Preservation of sovereignty and national policy autonomy is one of the constants in Brazilian foreign policy because it not only reflects the country's embedded non-aggressiveness, but also provides a shield to ward off external interventions that the country would be unable to prevent militarily. This is particularly important if we consider the extent to which the rest of the world pressures Brazil to preserve and protect the Amazon, a vast wilderness area that the Brazilian state is barely able to monitor, let alone patrol and actively protect. Similar issues have arisen historically with respect to the protection of human rights in Brazil, all of which has contributed to an underlying fear in the Brazilian security community that external actors are looking for a pretext to place vast swathes of the national territory under an international protectorate and radically curtail governmental policy autonomy to pursue national socio-economic development (Martins Filho and Zirker, 2000).

The result is an almost schizophrenic approach to global governance and international law, more than a little in keeping with the idea of the *jeito brasileiro* and strongly redolent of the saying attributed to Getulio Vargas: 'For my friends, anything; for my enemies, the law.' Diplomats hold up the United Nations and international legal frameworks as binding rules that states must follow while simultaneously looking for ways to ensure that these global governance mechanisms do not impinge on national autonomy or denude substantive sovereignty. Framed in terms of the foreign policy challenge to global structural power argued in this book, at issue is the genesis of the normative framework that is governing international affairs, with Brazilian diplomats consistently maintaining that the dominant approach to international law is constructed in a manner that maintains existing power asymmetries in the global system and ensures developing countries such as Brazil are kept on the margins (Lampreia, 1999a: 383–389; Rousseff, 2014a). As Amorim (2011a: 273) noted about his country's changed position in the global system: 'Brazil has overcome the false paradigm challenge that our foreign policy should be guided by the notion of 'limits of power'.

Disquiet with the ideational underpinning of the Western-created normative framework might look like a desire to tear down the system and create a new one except that Brazil has done exceedingly well under the existing rules. Global trade regimes have facilitated the most recent commodity boom, and international understandings of security have left Brazil on the margins of major inter-state conflict and afforded it the luxury of not engaging in major military expenditures. Consequently, the last thing Brazil wants to do is actually dismantle the existing inter-national global governance system. Instead, Brazilian foreign policy is dedicated to shifting the normative frame of the global governance system, and resetting the nature and application of structural power in the international economic system. The fortunate thing for Brazilian diplomats is that the very nature of their domestic context imbues them with an intrinsic understanding of how to undertake this task. Conflict is something to be avoided in Brazilian society, with subtle codes of recognition, incorporation and exclusion playing a far more important role than in Northern countries such as the US or UK (Matta, 1984; O'Donnell, 1999). Fractious congressional political parties, regional divisions between the country's northeast and south, cities with more economic clout than some states, and islands of super-rich surrounded by seas of poverty all combine to create an environment where the art of negotiation is key and politics is about trying to reconcile competing interests grounded in monumental contradictions of wealth, power and position (Cardoso, 2006a).

Seven tactics in foreign affairs

The 'Brazilian way' thus becomes one of avoiding conflict, of seeking a common point from which to move forward, of being seen to be positive and contributing to what is sold as a desired outcome. Above all else, the 'Brazilian way' is about negotiating, patiently talking through the issue rather than engaging in rumbustious debate. In applied terms this can be captured in seven different patterns of behaviour exhibited by Brazil in international affairs: avoiding mindless opposition, collectivization, consensus creation, technocratic speak, building new organizations, propagating new thinking, and principled presidential righteousness.

Tactic #1: avoid mindless opposition

Under this tactic Itamaraty negotiators concentrate their attention and criticism on the micro-level details with a macro-level rhetoric suggesting to their counterparts that if they could just iron out these pesky wrinkles then this much needed and wanted agreement could be signed. The message broadcast by Brazil through this defensive tactic is particularly effective because it gives off an implicit signal that Brazil wants things to 'progress', that Brazil is a positive and constructive player uninterested in zero-sum games. More importantly, the explicit signals and demonstrated effort of Brazilian diplomats in the form of alternate language and proposals positions Brazil as an actor committed to a successful resolution of talks, which in turn creates a strong logic for including Brazil as a mediating voice in the small 'executive councils' that generally hammer out the nuts and bolts of international agreements.

This tactic was in clear display during the FTAA negotiations and the early stages of the WTO's Doha development round. While it is doubtful that policy makers in Itamaraty ever had any intention of recommending to their president that Brazil sign on to the FTAA (Lampreia, 2010: 255–256), public governmental criticisms of a free trade deal with the US were few and far between. Diplomats of the period opted for a moderate language of opposition, with Itamaraty secretary general Osmar Chohfi noting in 2002 that Brazil and other regional countries were interested in the idea of an FTAA, but not simply as an extension of the North American Free Trade Agreement (NAFTA). Chohfi's comments simply mirrored in a more elaborate speech given by Celso Lafer in 2001, where he forcefully reasserted Brazil's commitment to being a global trader and then implicitly sidelined the entire FTAA process as simply one option that could be pursued on the way to a larger global trade deal through the WTO. Lafer (2001b) concluded by noting that simply rejecting the FTAA idea was overly risky, but this did not mean that Brazil should simply accept what was put on offer. Amorim continued this approach during the Lula presidency, taking the view that careful analysis was necessary and that a patient approach to exhaustive negotiating could cause the talks to quietly implode (Amorim, 2013: chapter 3).

Such careful analysis lay at the heart of the position Celso Amorim advanced as Brazil's foreign minister at the 2003 Cancun and 2005 Hong Kong WTO ministerial negotiating sessions. While Brazil did say no to the agreement that US and EU trade negotiators had presented as a *fait accompli* in Cancun, it was a qualified no. The trans-Atlantic position was instead taken as an opening gambit for negotiations to which Brazil, through the G20, presented alternate language and interpretations. Robert Zoellick (2003), the chief US trade negotiator, attempted to resurrect the sort of strong-arm tactics traditionally used to keep developing countries in line at global trade talks by accusing Brazil of being willfully obstructionist. Although repeated by powerful US political figures such as Senate Finance Committee chair Charles Grassly (Sotero, 2003), the charge failed to stick in part because the principles and ambitions of global trade liberalization were embraced by the Brazilian position, which explicitly advanced a valid alternate way to a greatly liberalized world trading system (Hurrell and Narlikar, 2008; Narlikar and Tussie, 2004; Narlikar and Wilkinson, 2004).

A subset of this tactic is to stretch out an issue until all parties loose interest or decide that the opportunity costs of continuing talks is not worth the effort. Clinton's original intent with the FTAA was to sign the deal at the 1994 Miami Summit of the Americas (Magalhães, 1999). A decade later officials around the hemisphere effectively gave up when they came to realize that the US as much as Brazil were drawing irreconcilable lines in the sand (Arashiro, 2011). Nevertheless, the negotiations have yet to be declared formally dead. The negotiating groups just do not meet anymore and officials rarely talk about it. The WTO is not quite in the same state, but there are also clear indications that Brazil is much more positively inclined to a successful conclusion of the Doha round, not least due to the tremendous personal energy put into the talks by Amorim, changes brought by global commodity price rises, and the 2013 election of Brazilian diplomat Roberto Azevêdo as director general of the WTO.

Tactic #2: collectivize
One of the interesting characteristics of Brazilian efforts to shape international negotiations and regimes is the extent to which their position is presented as a shared approach or articulated by another country or institution as the shared view. The tactic at play here is to collectivize what Brazil wants to do or say. This brings three important factors into play. First, it deflects direct attention and accountability for the position away from Brazil. For example, the US was advancing an aggressive interpretation of the OAS's Democratic Charter at the 2005 OAS General Assembly that would have effectively turned the organization into a sort of political policeman for the Americas. In keeping with a long tradition of opposing such efforts, Brazil organized behind the scenes to quash Washington's proposal. In a rather bizarre turn of events, the dormant Latin American trade grouping ALADI was awakened in order to release a completely political document that tied the OAS General Assembly up to the point that where there was no agreed

final declaration when the majority of participants left after the scheduled conclusion of the assembly.

A second aspect of the collectivization approach is that it introduces an element of plausible deniability. Brazilian negotiators can express sympathy with the position of their interlocutors, but still disagree by claiming their hands are tied by the agreed position of the collective. This is one of the characteristics that marked Brazil's management of the Doha round of WTO talks. By working very hard to keep the WTO G20 coalition of developing nations together Brazil was able to consistently advance ideas that pushed the boundaries of what the EU and US would have liked to see. It also allowed Brazil to stall and ensure there was ample time to refine negotiating positions and work on recalcitrant members of its own coalition (Veiga, 2005).

A final and critical aspect is that collectivization greatly expands Brazil's international gravitas. Irrespective of the vaunted technical expertise of Brazilian negotiators, the mere ability to construct negotiating positions with intricate econometric models would not have been sufficient to earn Brazil a position as one of the 'new quad' of core countries in the WTO negotiating process. A significant part of the reason the US and EU chose Brazil and India as critical negotiating partners after Cancun was the perception that these two countries represented – and could deliver – the Global South that had proven so difficult in Seattle in 1998 and Cancun in 2003. Brazil thus gained credibility due to its role as a representative for a larger group of nations, a status amplified by the strenuous efforts of Brazilian diplomats to preach patience to the Global South and encourage the continued engagement of groups such as the G90 through the trade G20 rather than as an independent voice in trade talks (Amorim, 2004a; 2011a: chapter 14; 2013: chapter 4).

Tactic #3: consensus creation
One phrase frequently used by Brazilian diplomats is 'we work to create consensus'. The nuance of this phrase is important because they speak of 'creating', not 'reaching' consensus, suggesting there is a preferred Brazilian option. Within the context of the FTAA negotiations, one Brazilian negotiator explained that if Brazil was dubious about the prospect of a sudden launch of a hemispheric free trade zone, then others likely were as well. In his view Brazil was one of the countries best prepared to deal with the US, but still at a point where Itamaraty considered Brazil too weak for outright opposition. The trick, therefore, was to bring other countries around to Brazil's point of view, which was achieved through a detailed and patient process of discussions seeking to bring others to commonalities and shared positions (Magalhães, 1999).

The same tactic was repeated within the WTO in the lead up to and after the 2003 Cancun ministerial meeting. Significantly, efforts to build and strengthen this consensus continued as the Doha round dragged on, with weekly strategy and analysis sessions being hosted at the Brazilian mission in Geneva. The process was, as one participating trade G20 diplomat observed in 2007 with more than a bit of ennui, very comprehensive, lengthy, consultative and ultimately constructed around a Brazilian-led vision of where the talks should go. For Itamaraty the pay-off has been to position Brazil as a good faith negotiator who can bring disparate interests to the table whilst ensuring that Brazil's central ambitions are included by all as core considerations. At regional and global meetings this does not translate into instant trust that Brazil is acting in a disinterested, munificent manner – indeed, the other South American countries are wary of the self-interested, distributive tendency in Brazil's negotiating strategy – but it does create confidence that Brazilian diplomats will continue patiently talking rather than attempting the sort of strong-arm tactics sometimes deployed by the traditional major powers (Jawara and Kwa, 2004). This gives Brazil a great deal of traction at international negotiating tables because it becomes a country that can prevent the collapse of talks and get some clarity on where resolution might eventually lie.

Tactic #4: technocratic-speak

There are a limited number of countries able to attack a question with the at times exclusionary language of econometric modelling and economic theory (Teivaninen, 2002). As was briefly sketched out in the previous chapter, Brazil has developed the endogenous skills to play the technocratic game in global economic forums. Nowhere has the Brazilian mastery of technocratic language been more evident than the WTO, where Celso Amorim was perhaps one of a handful of people in the world who fully understood the entirety of the Doha round talks. The ability to stymie the 2003 US/EU Cancun deal in large part came down to Itamaraty's ability to attack the technocratic merit of the proposal, not the morality of the proposition on the table. A similar example of challenging the structural power of international affairs can be found in the Brazilian response to the HIV/AIDS crisis that confronted the country in the 1980s and 1990s. Rather than discarding global norms on patents, Cardoso's government effectively reaffirmed the global intellectual property regime, signing into law strong pharmaceutical patent protection rules closely reflective of the language found in the international agreements on trade related intellectual property rights. The Cardoso government's response to the public health crisis of

HIV/AIDS was thus to invoke these measures, specifically the 'national emergency' clause to compel the major pharmaceutical companies to deliver a massive reduction in the costs of the needed drug cocktail. Similar measures were subsequently pursued or discussed in thirty-one other countries, including South Africa, Namibia, Uganda and Ethiopia (Cohen and Lybecker, 2005).

Brazilian technocratic expertise also helped to shift thinking on global financial governance at the IMF. One of the complaints Cardoso had about the IMF and economic policy during his tenure as finance minister and president was that the Fund consistently questioned the workability of Brazil's approach to financial crises, quietly working to subvert international confidence in the Brazil-grown policies (Cardoso, 2007). In part the problem was that officials at the IMF were far from convinced a developing country such as Brazil possessed the technocratic capacity necessary to independently formulate successful economic policies. The successes of Cardoso's economic policies in preventing a series of complete fiscal collapses in the 1990s laid the groundwork for 2004 proposals during the Lula presidency that the rules for calculating the primary fiscal surplus be altered to exclude capital investment on critical infrastructure and profit-making state enterprises (Sotero, 2004). While both of these developments did not result in a fundamental reshaping of how the IMF operates, they did drive a substantial wedge into the hegemony of Northern economic policy dictates and gave demonstrable substance to the idea that Southern countries were in fact capable of endogenously managing their own economic affairs. This, combined with the dramatic economic improvements under the Lula presidency – which saw Brazil go from owing the IMF $50 billion in 2002 to loaning it $10 billion in 2009 – opened the space for Brazil's legitimate inclusion in key economic governance institutions such as the G20 Finance and the quieter, but possibly more significant Financial Stability Forum (Armijo and Katada, 2014). Indeed, IMF confidence in former Brazilian macroeconomic officials is such that they form a preferred pool of consultants for work in other developing countries, particularly the Portuguese-speaking nations of Africa.

Tactic #5: build new organizations

As was set out earlier in this chapter, Brazil has a slightly different normative view of the world and how global governance institutions should operate. One response from the Itamaraty and the Planalto Presidential Palaces has been to create new organizations reflective of the Brazilian world-view. The idea that existing patterns of international relations were not necessarily framed in a manner conducive to

Brazilian developmental ambitions is one of the many themes carried through from the Cardoso to the Lula and then Dilma presidencies. Prior to early 2015 Brazilian diplomats were not shy about opining that existing talk shops, such as the Organization of Economic Cooperation and Development (OECD), offered little space for inclusion of the policy questions Brazil wanted to address. One resultant analysis within Itamaraty was that India, Brazil and South Africa appeared to have remarkably similar voting behaviours in a number of different international institutions, as well as a shared series of national development challenges. More to the point, each country had successes in different areas, offering opportunities for mutual learning and cooperation. The launch of the IBSA Dialogue Forum in 2003 erupted with a flurry of interest in policy and business circles that quickly collapsed into apathy as the triumvirate failed to launch the sort of bold, globally transformative initiatives that industrialized-country analysts expected from hyper-active Southern countries. But, as in the case of Brazil's larger foreign policy agenda, revolution was never the guiding premise behind IBSA. Rather, finding a stronger insertion into the global system to gain a greater share of the spoils was the dominant external aim of the grouping (Alden and Vieira, 2005).

As one Brazilian diplomat explained about IBSA in 2010, multilateral diplomatic gain was a secondary goal that would naturally come from the main goal. The real ambition was to start and entrench substantive and sustained cross-bureaucracy interaction with a view to greatly expanding all levels of bilateral and trilateral interaction on both a government and private level. None of this, the diplomat pointed out, happens quickly, emerging more as a process of slow accretion than the dramatic surge sought by Western observers. Tellingly, IBSA at the time was also positioned as a more sustainable and useful device than the disposable Goldman Sachs-created BRICS concept because the trilateral initiative was seen to be growing organically through work in areas that are of pressing concern to the three countries, but marginal interest to the OECD members interested in exploring North–South relations. What IBSA explicitly does not attempt to do is to disengage any of its members from the existing global order. Instead it seeks to quietly shift the norms and rules of the international order and, through intra-South cooperation and collective action, carve away some of the power and privilege of the North. This is the same logic that emerged within the BRICS framework during the first Dilma presidency, most notably through the formation of parallel institutions such as the BRICS Development Bank and the Contingency Reserve Agreement, which were designed to complement, not compete, with existing global governance institutions.

Tactic #6: propagate new thinking

Tactic six parallels the fifth, but focuses more on the conceptual and ideational than action. Cardoso's intellectual output during his years as president demonstrated a clear understanding that global governance structures were in need of reform because they codified a fundamentally unequal distribution of power and potential that did not reflect emerging realities. In a sense he was refining the basic argument he scripted with Enzo Faletto in their book *Dependency and Development in Latin Ameirca* (1979), namely that the international system was not so much one of exclusion as marginalization. The challenge was to find a way to shift the normative frame and take advantage of the structure to improve relative position, which in turn could be used to reframe application of the structure itself. While Cardoso was able to get the ball rolling with ideas such as the Comunidade de Países da Linguagem Português (CPLP; Cardoso and Soares, 1998), in substantive terms he could offer little more than inspiring speeches and interesting analyses because of the restraints imposed on his presidency by rolling financial crises and the challenges of establishing Brazil as a serious country. A different situation greeted the Lula presidency, with the business community's calm reaction to election of the leftist leader working to quickly position Brazil as a positive model of left-leaning governance in the face of rather more radical alternatives in countries such as Venezuela.

Lula's foreign policy team hit the heart of the structural questions driving Brazilian foreign policy, asking a series of rather provocative questions, chief of which was why Southern countries had to use Northern intermediaries for their bilateral exchange. Why should we expect improvements in South–South trade and interaction if most exchanges involved transshipment through a Northern port or airport? In response to these questions they floated the idea of a new international economic geography. Distinct from the New International Economic Order of the 1970s, the idea of a new economic geography held more in common with the Cardoso-era South American infrastructure integration project in that the focus was on laying down the physical and emotional infrastructure needed to facilitate direct bilateral commerce and travel. New air routes and shipping lanes opened up the idea that cargo and people could travel in straight lines between Southern destinations. Bolstering this proposition was a revivification of earlier Brazilian ideas of the strategic import substitution model that was used to bolster Mercosul and regional trade through the purchase of Argentine wheat and Bolivian gas.

As Antonio Patriota (2013b: 37) observed at his inauguration as Dilma's first foreign minister, 'we have left behind the time when an accumulation of vulnerabilities limited our room for action'. The point he was making was that successes of the Lula years, such as the work within the WTO framework with the G20 negotiating coalition, had changed global frames of reference and the scope of what Brazil and other developing countries found imaginable. In a sense Brazil helped to shine a light into the dark recesses of the global political economy and demonstrate how to effectively deal with the dragons hiding in the corners. The result was a Southernization of the *auto-estima*, or self-confidence that allowed Brazil not only to elect a street-smart, formally uneducated president, but also to retreat from the precipice of economic disaster and lift over thirty million people from poverty in half a decade (IPEA, 2010a). Knock-on effects of this can be seen internationally and regionally, fed further by the global commodities boom. One example was the emergence of coalitions such as the Small and Landlocked Group of States within the WTO as a technocratically serious grouping, albeit one still fighting against the tide of the dominant trading powers (Oxford Analytica, 2005b). In a South–South context, where African countries were at one point delighted to except Chinese investments and assistance as an attractive alternative to the strictures of the Organization of Economic Cooperation and Development Development Assistance Committee (OECD-DAC), many countries have begun to actively question the terms and conditions proposed by their new patron, showing instead a more hard-edged approach to international negotiation rather than what at times has appeared to be simple gratitude.

Tactic #7: principled presidential righteousness

The more aggressive stances in Brazilian foreign policy have found their greatest success in the political realm and have been most tightly linked to traditional concepts of sovereignty and the new ideal of defending democracy and human rights. The interesting aspect of the transition from the centre-right Cardoso administration to the centre-left Lula presidency was that in areas where we might have expected the left to be stronger, it appears to have proven weaker. Two examples stand out strongest in this respect. First is the defence of democracy. Cardoso took a hard, but nuanced line to democracy in the Americas which amounted to a position that a country could arrange and rearrange its democracy any way it chose provided it stuck to its own duly constituted mechanisms for change. Under Cardoso this at times involved taking a very pointed stance against Canada and the US at the OAS, particularly with respect to the 2000 presidential election in Peru and the 2002 attempted coup against Hugo Chavez in Venezuela. Lula and Dilma proved somewhat more pragmatic and interest-centred, turning a blind eye to the

Franco-American-backed toppling of Jean Bertrand Aristide in Haiti, going so far as to take on direction of the MINUSTAH intervention force sent by the UN. Intervention during the 2009 Honduran crisis was even more direct, with Brazil at times being seen to actively block the operation of domestic institutions to the frustration of other major regional players (Freitas, 2010). On a personal level Lula was far from adverse about expressing his preference for particular presidential candidates in the various contests throughout the region if he felt it would advance his agenda.

On the human rights file the distinction appears to be even starker. While Cardoso's foreign policy never went as far as severing relations or pursuing other punitive reprisals in support of human rights, it did not shy from speaking plain truths with individuals such as Cuba's Fidel Castro. In contrast, the last few years of Lula's period in office and the first Dilma presidency were marked by a succession of incidents fiercely criticized by the international human rights community, including a refusal to address the hunger strike death of a Cuban dissident during a state visit to the island, an unwillingness to criticize the Iranian regime for allowing a woman to be sentenced to death by stoning for adultery, and a sustained reluctance to make any substantive official statement as Venezuelan democracy appeared to teeter on the edge of an authoritarian crisis. The PT foreign policy team provided some justification for these stances by explaining that their public silence allowed them to retain access and influence events from behind the scenes (Carnegie, 2010). Diplomats quietly offered a parallel explanation by suggesting Brazil was taking a 'sociological' approach to political change in Venezuela, working to stabilize the economy and then allow political evolution to take care of itself (interview with Brazilian diplomats, 2010). The concerns expressed by commentators was that while this may have been the case, there were limits to this approach and the PT had exceeded them, which partly explains Dilma's decision to at least rhetorically reverse her patron's policy and take a much harder line on human rights with Iran and in the United Nations Human Rights Council.

A critique of Lula's human rights and democracy positions highlights one of the real challenges of the principled righteousness approach. When Lula rejected the G8 Hellingendam outreach process as demeaning or called on the international community to take global hunger seriously he gained a great deal of international traction because of the inherent 'rightness' of the stance in the face of distortions in global structural power. The difficulty comes when the line between national interest and state position is blurred with the desire to secure a historical legacy or drifts into a nakedly distributive negotiating agenda. Again, the contrast is with Cardoso, who managed to reject participation in the coalition invading Afghanistan without crippling US–Brazil bilateral relations because of the larger threat he felt it raised for international stability, not to mention the sustainability of the policy. Complaints about US post-2001 anti-terror policies were put in technocratic terms, and largely ignored in Washington. Similarly, Cardoso's decision to sign the Nuclear Non-Proliferation Treaty (NPT) treaty but not the additional protocol was grounded in the solid legal logic that additional measures were unnecessary because democratic Brazil's constitution explicitly forbids development of nuclear weapons (Tourinho, 2015: 85–87). When disputes arose over Brazil's refusal to allow International Atomic Energy Agency (IAEA) inspections per the additional protocol, word eventually came from Washington that all was okay because Brazil was manifestly different from a North Korea or Iran and thus not a threat to global peace and security. The challenge for diplomats, and a key reason why this tactic is rarely seen, is that it becomes very difficult to keep the personal political prerogative separate from the national interests. Moreover, overuse erodes the effectiveness of the tactic, as evinced by reactions to the ocassionally perceptive stream of commentaries from leaders such as Hugo Chavez and Fidel Castro.

Conclusion

As one senior Brazilian diplomat remarked shortly before this book was completed, in years past Brazil had to push very hard to gain inclusion in the global governance discussions taking place at the United Nations. By the end of Dilma's first term, largely thanks to the subtlety and consensus-generating capacity of the tactics outlined in this chapter, very few substantive meetings were taking place without Brazilian participation. The seven tactical approaches outlined here are particularly important for Itamaraty because none of them rely upon a preponderance of economic or military might. Instead, they draw upon the same ideational strengths that make consensual hegemony such an apt concept for explaining Brazilian foreign policy, and provide a relatively low-cost, low-risk approach to contesting the application of structural power in the international system.

It would be pushing the point to suggest the tactics outlined here have been explicitly created and inculcated to diplomats by Itamaraty. Rather, they are behaviours which emerge from a macro level view of Brazilian foreign policy, which will become apparent as a range of policy areas and relationships are explored in the rest of the book. What is particularly telling about these seven tactics is that they rise almost organically from the sociological construction of daily life in Brazil. The need to manage sensitive relationships between vastly differing socio-economic classes living closely together in a compressed space has created a pattern of domestic social conduct that works hard to avoid direct confrontation. Wrapped on top of this is the reality of living within a juridical system anchored with distressing strength in Portuguese colonial traditions – it is not a surprise that Brazil consistently ranks, in a good year, 120th on the World Bank's ease of doing business table. The *jeito*, finding a way through, is not so much a quirk of Brazilian culture, but an essential skill for survival.

The combination of these factors often flummoxes diplomats from other countries. Brazilian diplomats remain endearingly affable and pleasant, but notoriously difficult to pin down to a final decision. Dialogue and discussion are prioritized, even if it is just to delay an unwanted decision in the hopes that it will quietly die, as was the case with the FTAA. For Northern capitals this is infuriating. But for the rest of the world it is something of a breath of fresh air, particularly since Brazil has demonstrated a proclivity to at least provide a briefing about what is going on in the main decision making rooms. Ultimately Brazil is just as cutthroat about its interests as the US and EU, a story that will quietly emerge on the following pages. Where Brazil differs is in the process and reliance upon unstated acceptance of leadership rather than sustained exertion and restatement of dominance.

4

Brazil's multilateralist impulse

Perhaps one of the most consistent themes in Brazilian foreign policy over the last century has been the drive for a seat at the main global governance decision making tables. Whether it be the Versailles Palace talks after World War One, the San Francisco discussions leading to the United Nations system or negotiations in countless international forums such as the Food and Agriculture Organization, GATT/WTO, or World Health Organization, Brazilian diplomats have devoted enormous efforts to ensuring they are given space to be active participants. This has recently seen its most visible expression in the Lula era's renewed push for an expanded UN Security Council to give Brazil permanent membership in the political realm and very active engagement with the WTO Doha round in the economic sphere. In short, multilateral groupings, whether they be on a regional or global level, have long been an important strut of Brazilian foreign policy, crucial to efforts to protect national autonomy and, more latterly, work to reshape the realities of structural power in the contemporary global system. Active participation in multilateral frameworks is also central to the application of many of the tactics outlined in chapter three, particularly attempts to collectivize the Brazilian position, create consensus, and avoid direct opposition to initiatives advanced by other countries. It is thus hardly surprising that Brazil has been an active proponent of the multilateralization of global affairs, signing literally hundreds of multilateral agreements and increasingly working to form new multilateral ventures, particularly on the regional and pan-Southern level.

Yet, there is a catch to the expansive diplomatic language of wanting a truly multilateral world order. Since 1989, Brazil has supported multilateralism in principle, but only translated this diplomatic rhetoric into clear and proactive engagement when a multilateral approach or institution has been consistent with narrowly defined national interests. Indeed, the prevailing logic is highly instrumentalist and defensive, often being directly related to conscious efforts ensuring that institutions and frameworks evolve in a manner that does not impinge upon Brazilian autonomy and sovereignty (Fonseca, 2004; Haslam and Barreto, 2009; Vigevani and Cepaluni, 2009). On trade files, multilateralism is encouraged, but only to the extent that Brazil can control discussions, gain immediate benefit from the arrangement, or exercise a veto over new directions that an existing institution might take. None of this is done directly. Coalitions and negotiations are used to mask and collectivize Brazil's ambitions; technocratic language obscures the political game; seeking consensus replaces obstructionism. Similar phenomena are found on the security file, only with Brazil taking a more explicit stand with respect to opposing outside interference in South America and the wider South, which is viewed as its natural sphere of influence. Only in cases where Brazil sees a real prospect of controlling and directing the institution for its own ends can one expect sustained and concentrated attempts to create functioning multilateral structures.

Brazil consequently displays a somewhat rebellious attitude towards existing multilateral arrangements, which has progressively solidified as the country has gained increased international recognition and internal economic stability. In keeping with the focus on questions of structural over relational power, Brazil's approach to multilateralism has followed three broad patterns. One involves a direct challenge to the governance of existing arrangements, denounced as inequitable, undemocratic and consequently illegitimate and ineffective. The second one entails increasingly forceful attempts to carve out whole areas of action to reserve them for regional mechanisms in which Brazil's weight is overwhelming. Finally, Brazilian diplomacy has joined and created weak, poorly institutionalized and under-financed multilateral arrangements, both to coordinate ad-hoc collective action to substitute the existing mechanisms that are being challenged or kept out, and to promote the reform of the latter.

This rebellious multilateralism remains largely confined to the mechanics of global and hemispheric governance, not to the order-generating purposes of these institutions. Indeed, Brazilian rebellion is quite conservative in that the changes sought are ultimately meant to enhance the legitimacy and efficacy of existing global and regional governance. Albeit clearly self-serving in the case of Brazil, this argument is credible and largely consistent with the country's behaviour in the global arena. As a growing power whose economy and interests are increasingly internationalized, Brazil clearly has a vested interest in the stability that only effective multilateral arrangements can provide. The question for Brazil is how these structure-perpetuating institutions operate and what sort of role Brazil has in influencing their future direction and day-to-day operation.

While it would be easy to get the impression that this chapter is setting Brazil up as an obstructive actor in the multilateral frame, such an understanding would be mistaken and takes as given that the approach advanced by established Northern actors of influence is necessarily correct. Brazilian diplomats face a contradictory challenge in their approach to multilateralism. Within Itamaraty there is a clear awareness that existing institutions entrench particular patterns of structural power that not only tend to marginalize Brazil, but also can threaten to actively impinge the country's autonomy and limit its developmental possibilities. International bodies are therefore something to be monitored to prevent transgressions and also engaged to open new policy space (Fonseca, 2002; Vigevani and Cepaluni, 2009). The foreign policy pay-off from this form of engagement extends beyond the protection of Brazilian interests to the strengthening of links with other countries in the South that result in greater support of Brazil in global forums, the sorts of expanded economic opportunities seen in chapters five and six, and a growth in security-enhancing cooperation activities. This also brings expectations that Brazil will provide greater leadership goods and also a sense, particularly in South America, that it would be wise to develop regional institutions that can balance an increasingly powerful Brazil (Flemes and Wehner, 2013; Malamud, 2011), initiatives which Itamaraty quietly resists. Brazil's multilateralist impulse thus emerges as something of a contradiction, demonstrating strong elements of positive active engagement and soft obstructionism.

Why multilateralism?

The fundamental challenge that faced Brazil's foreign policy planners immediately after the Cold War was how they could protect the national interest in an international environment that was becoming increasingly dynamic, multifaceted and diverse in terms of centres of influence and authority. While there was an integrationist imperative to the accelerating globalization of the early 1990s, for a relatively weak, crisis-riven economy on the margins of global attention, the greater risk was one of marginalization and even subjugation.

Drawing on Brazil's long-standing interest in multilateralism, diplomats argued that it was in the national interest to strengthen multilateral rules and frameworks as an avenue for enhancing the country's international insertion (IPRI, 1993). The 1992–1993 foreign policy review underpinning this strategic decision makes specific mention of the need for reform in major multilateral agencies such as the Bretton Woods Institutions, the GATT/WTO system, and the United Nations in order to create more space for Brazil to have a voice in global governance. In a theme that would continue to reverberate particularly loudly during the Lula presidency, the UN was given special emphasis through a clearly stated goal of 'updating' the Security Council so that Brazil could have a permanent seat on the main international conflict resolution body (IPRI, 1993: 27). More broadly, the idea advanced in the forward planning document was to defend multilateralism and a greater opening – democratization, in Brazilian diplomatic parlance – of international decision making bodies to ensure Brazil helped shape the rules, regulations and future direction of bodies Itamaraty saw as crucial to the management of world order.

An internal Itamaraty memorandum written at the same time as the foreign policy review highlights the extent to which the overarching strategic dimension of the multilateralist turn permeated diplomatic planning. After noting the upcoming rotation of the director generalships of the GATT, United Nations Conference on Trade and Development (UNCTAD), United Nations Industrial Development Organization and the IAEA, the memorandum makes a series of recommendations. While the IAEA was ruled out because Brazil was not a signatory to the NPT, a bid for the United Nations Industrial Development Organization and UNCTAD director generalships was suggested because both were scheduled to rotate to a Latin American head (MRE, 1992); the latter eventually went to Brazilian diplomat Rubens Ricupero who occupied the post from 1995 to 2004. Even more telling of the strategic nature of Brazil's approach to multilateral institutions was a marginal note recommending that despite certain failure Brazil should seek the director generalship of the GATT because it would create leverage for obtaining a deputy directorship and a corresponding voice at the core of the body as it transformed into the WTO.

The importance of multilateral engagement for the structural power imperative at the core of contemporary Brazilian foreign policy was captured in 2000 by Celso Lafer, who twice served as foreign minister: 'if the country was previously able to construct [...] autonomy through a relative distancing from the world, then at the turn of the millennium this autonomy [...] can only be achieved through active participation in the elaboration of norms and codes of conduct for the governance of world order'. The principle challenge requiring an active engagement with multilateral institutions was what Cardoso (1996) labelled a homogenization of national and regulatory institutions driven by the pressures of an accelerating process of globalization. On a public policy level this was presented as problematic because it limited the capacity of states to follow different development strategies and forced adoption of orthodox macroeconomic policies of the sort being avoided by Brazil in the 1990s. A central Cardoso strategy was thus to seek change from within, which required rebuilding Brazilian diplomatic credibility – a major factor behind the 1996 decision to sign the NPT – and to actively advance a constructive agenda for reform, which was a central theme of his speeches on global governance reform (Cardoso with Font, 2001: part 7 & 8).

In what can now almost be seen as a foreshadowing of Lula's foreign policy rhetoric of *auto-estima*, Cardoso called upon leaders at the 1999 Iberoamerican Summit in Havana to enhance cooperation and advance a globalization of solidarity that would eliminate the sorts of inequalities in national growth and development that were being seen in the 1990s. What this meant in practical terms, which is critical for understanding the Brazilian approach to multilateralism and the redrafting of the structures of global power, was hinted at by Lampreia in his 1999 speech opening the UN General Assembly: 'With the implantation of democracy, the Latin American countries could assist each other – without undue and unsolicited interference, but with a spirit of solidarity' (1999b). Autonomy from the dictates of the North was being sought, in this instance through the existing global governance institutions and emerging regional bodies. As will be discussed below, while some effort was given to creating alternatives during the Cardoso era, the construction of new organizational forums took off during the Lula years. The common theme across the PSDB and PT presidencies was one of using and manipulating multilateral institutions, whether existing or purpose constructed, as de facto manifestations of the prevailing structural power framework to mitigate and deflect actual and potential attempts by external actors to constrain Brazilian policy autonomy.

Regional multilateralism

The extent to which multilateralism was used to shift orientations of structural power and protect Brazilian autonomy is particularly evident on the regional level of Latin America and even more so on the South American continental level. On trade and economics files Brazil has noisily and forcefully advocated the establishment and consolidation of regional economic groupings such as Mercosul and UNASUL as stepping-stones towards global trade liberalization, as well as avenues for maintaining the country's international credibility. Real action, however, has proven more subdued. Although Mercosul has added Venezuela as a new member and was looking at full inclusion of Bolivia and Ecuador as this book was being written, the bloc as a whole remains woefully under-institutionalized. It has a still-tiny and ineffective administrative secretariat in Montevideo as well as an ineffectual and barely used dispute resolution mechanism (R. Barbosa, 2014; Gonçalves, 2013; Malamud and Dri, 2013). The result is that periodic crises – of which there have been plenty – are invariably resolved through presidential diplomacy, not the strong mechanisms expected of effective multilateralism (Gómez-Mera, 2013). UNASUL, meanwhile, is still a work in progress and is certainly not developing into a significant vehicle for freer trade in the region, although it is offering interesting advances in the technical aspects of policy coordination and mutual learning to advance the regional anti-poverty agenda (Arízaga, 2015; Riggirozzi, 2014).

This is not to argue that Mercosul has failed to deliver significant economic and political gains for Brazil and the region. During the still-tentative years of democratic transition in the 1990s the bloc played an important role in stabilizing the region's representative political regimes (Fournier, 1999; Gardini, 2010). As discussed in chapters five and six, the economic benefits have also been substantial, both in terms of greatly expanding intra-regional trade – intra-bloc trade went from USD 6.6 billion in 1992 to USD 50.6 billion in 2013 – and providing a platform for the internationalization of Brazilian businesses. What is often not discussed is the extent to which Mercosul and more latterly UNASUL have served the larger foreign policy goal of protecting national autonomy by diluting potential extra-regional influences. Brazilian diplomats have studiously worked to derail, delay or reframe every significant initiative to foster hemispheric trade liberalization, arguing – not without reason – that none of these adequately protected their country's interests.

Perhaps the most telling example of this behaviour was the Free Trade Area of the Americas process launched by the Clinton administration at the 1994 Miami Summit of the Americas. Brazil's agreement to any deal was critical because it was access to the large Brazilian and Mercosul markets that were the prize for the US, not the prospect of greater sales to insignificant Ecuador and Honduras or already quite liberalized Colombia or Peru. Itamaraty negotiators were well aware of the bargaining power this created for Brazil during the negotiation process. Although there were clear signs that the policy makers in Itamaraty were against the FTAA from the outset (Lampreia, 2009: 186–192; Magalhães, 1999), the challenge was that Brazil lacked sufficient economic strength and credibility to oppose the deal with the bluntness that was to become typical of the Lula administration's later engagements in global governance discussions. The central challenge facing Brazilian foreign policy makers during both the Cardoso and notably more sceptical Lula presidencies was how to derail the FTAA without engaging in naked obstructionism.

Brazil's multilateralist impulse played an important role in derailing the FTAA, paralleling the technocratic dismantling of US positions by offering a possible continental alternative. As early as 1996 Lampreia used a speech in La Paz to clearly signal the centrality of Mercosul in Brazilian foreign policy as an instrument for expanding continental integration. By 2000 Cardoso was actively using the pulpit of presidential diplomacy to further push the regionalist option, writing on the eve of the Brasília Summit words that could just as easily be attributed to Lula's pan-Southern solidarity rhetoric: 'The South American Countries today are in a condition to take a leap in the quality of their development, following a path on which social justice and economic efficiency are not in conflict, but rather strengthen each other mutually' (Cardoso, 2000). Efforts to expand Mercosul to include Bolivia and Chile that were already running by the time FTAA talks hit full stride quickly grew to include the idea of interregional deals, most notably with the Andean Community, but also with the EU as a counter-balance to the US.

Progress with the continentalist project was hampered in the 1990s by Argentina, which feared a loss of influence within Mercosul and competition from Chile for access to the Brazilian market (Lampreia, 2010: 228). Fed up with an apparent repetition of delays grounded in the economic nationalism that has historically crippled Latin American integration projects, Cardoso elected for an element of subterfuge, eschewing discussions about trade in favour of the process of physical infrastructure integration that he launched at the 2001 Brasília Summit of South American Presidents. His idea was to set up a technocratic multilateral institution – La Iniciativa para la Integración de la Infraestructura Regional Suramericana (IIRSA) – focused on building the transportation energy, and communication linkages between the countries of South America necessary to support a surge in intra-continental trade (Araujo, 2009/2010). Implicit in this soft multilateral institution was a structural reframing embedded in the suggestion that South Americans should look to Brazil for new opportunities, not to the US, an idea that was taken up to a certain extent by some of the Andean countries (Gadea, 2012). The critical point here is that the IIRSA infrastructure integration process was not publicly presented as an alternative to the FTAA, but as a necessary building block to make a possible FTAA work. Implicit in this language was the proposition that the current state of affairs in the hemisphere would only support, at some later stage, an FTAA beneficial to the US and possibly Canada.

Cardoso's technocratic approach also laid the groundwork for the parallel Latin American multilateral arrangements that would be created during the Lula years. Cardoso's IIRSA – which was transformed into COSIPLAN at the 2009 UNASUL Summit – was quickly subsumed by Lula into the short-lived Comunidad Sudamericana de Naciones (CASA), which in turn rapidly morphed into the current União de Nações Sul-Americanas (UNASUL) that is now providing the framework for purported regional infrastructure integration and moves towards expanded South American political and security coordination. Although significant breakthroughs were made on the economic front, most notably in the form of completing Venezuela's full accession to Mercosul in 2012, the broader story is hinted at in chapter eleven where the loss of market share and economic influence to China began to clearly emerge in the second Lula presidency. Indeed, it is arguably on the security and political front that the Lula and Dilma presidencies focused their regional multilateral attention and gained the most traction in broadening the regional appeal of the foreign policy agenda seeking transformations in the structural biases embedded in multilateral institutions in the Americas.

Brazil has been extremely active at building alternative institutional arrangements that notionally would enable the region to effectively take over its own security and political governance. The political framework of UNASUL was extended to the rest of the hemisphere through the formation of the Comunidade dos Estados Latino-Americanos e Caribenhos (CELAC), sometimes referred to as a sort of Organization of American States 'plus one, minus two' for its inclusion of Cuba and exclusion of the US and Canada. Although formally launched at a December 2011 regional meeting in Venezuela, the body was conceived at a Rio Group-Caribbean countries meeting held in late 2008 at Costa de Sauípe, Brazil, which explicitly excluded US and Canadian officials despite repeated requests for observer status. While still lacking substantive institutionalization beyond meetings that function largely as a presidential talk shop, CELAC is significant because it expands upon the Rio Group, which was set up in 1986 and grew out of the Contadora Group's efforts to find a regional solution to the Central American conflicts that were being fed by the US. As was the case with the Rio Group in the 1980s, CELAC was formed with the clear intention of keeping the US and its perceived proxy the OAS out of the management of minor and major crises in Latin America. The utility of CELAC as a device for protecting national autonomy in the Americas was made apparent during the 2014 political protests in Venezuela when communiqués and missions from the new inter-American grouping were used to deflect Northern attempts to intervene in events in Caracas.

Despite the efforts to promote the rise of CELAC, the realities of tight Caribbean linkages to the US and Canada mean that it will never be an especially pliable creature for Brazilian diplomats. UNASUL, on the other hand, brings together a greater commonality of interests, which is further strengthened through ongoing consultative mechanisms such as its military cooperation component, the Conselho de Defesa Sul-Americano (CDS). The CDS was inaugurated at the 2009 Quito UNASUL Summit, bringing member-country defence ministers together in a forum to advance cooperation around security issues with a particular emphasis on fostering confidence-building measures, enhancing collaboration in military industrial production and humanitarian action, and formulating common positions on global security issues. Further efforts in this inward turn for collective support come from the December 2012 launching of a UNASUL electoral monitoring council, which was quietly positioned as a counterweight to similar work performed by the OAS or bodies such as the Carter Center. Perhaps the most fruitful area of intra-continental cooperation has been in the area of health policy (Riggirozzi, 2014), giving the regional project a strong social foundation to compensate for some of the deficiencies on the economic front. In this sense the regional projects pushed by Brazil have been of a new approach to integration, comprising what some are characterizing as 'post-hegemonic' regionalism (Legler, 2013; Riggirozzi and Tussie, 2012).

While Brazil was central to the emergence of both the Rio Group and UNASUL, the two entities, particularly UNASUL, have clearly acquired a life of their own consistent with the structural objectives of Brazilian foreign policy. Each has worked successfully to dramatically reduce the US presence and direct influence in South America. Management of the aftermath of regional tensions has increasingly been taken by UNASUL and not left to traditional multilateral groupings such as the OAS or even UN. Special summits of UNASUL have been called by Chile in 2008 to address concerns about Colombia's continued hosting of US military bases (Colombia Reports, 2008-03-05; Sánchez, 2008). Similarly, Juan Gabriel Valdes, a Chilean diplomat, was named special UNASUL representative to manage the 2008 Pando crisis in Bolivia, and Argentina's Nestor Kircher, as newly minted secretary general of the organization, mediated the August 2010 resolution to the Colombia-Venezuela standoff after Colombian forces bombed a FARC base just over the border in Ecuador (TELAM, 2010-08-11). Significantly, where it was the OAS that played a central role in settling the serious democratic disruptions suffered by Paraguay in the 1990s, it was UNASUL along with Mercosul that handled the crises brought on by the coup-like impeachment of Fernando Lugo in 2012. Repeated crises in Venezuela since the death of Hugo Chávez have also been intermediated by UNASUL-convened delegations, most notably the March 2015 UNASUL foreign ministers' visit to Caracas. In addition to being important contributions to Brazil's efforts to carve out the region as a distinct, independent space, these examples are particularly telling because they demonstrate the extent to which the rest of the continent has joined the project and is acting independently to proactively advance national and regional autonomy. Indeed, OAS secretary general Insulza's complaints about UNASUL's role in Bolivia's Pando crisis (Sánchez, 2008) should be read as testimonies to Brazil's success in this endeavour.

Despite the importance of regional groupings like Mercosul, UNASUL and CELAC as devices to shift structural power frameworks by nudging the US and its perceived proxies like the OAS out of South and Latin America, the abiding reality is that these Brazilian creations are remarkably weak. UNASUL was explicitly founded with a very weak institutional structure that has a rotating *pro tempore* presidency and a double bureaucracy, part in the country that occupies the presidency and the other in the organization's geographical seat in Quito. The South American Defense Council provides an interesting space for exchange of information and confidence building, but little else in terms of institutionalized collaboration. As suggested above, Mercosul is similarly weakened institutionally, with little actual authority being devolved to the secretariat, disputes often escalating to the point where direct presidential intervention is required, and notions of a wider 'Europeanization' to follow the EU model foundering upon the relative irrelevance of the bloc parliament. Above all, these mildly formalized arrangements exist in a context of summit hyperinflation: more than 240 regional and sub-regional summits have taken place since 1987 in the region, i.e. more than ten per year and 1800 agreements have been signed by leaders (Rojas Aravena, 2010), most of which were not followed up in any significant way.

The important point for the argument in this chapter is that the institutional weakness of the regional multilateral arrangements advanced by Planalto and Itamaraty is exactly the outcome sought by Brazilian foreign policy. While any strongly institutionalized and empowered regional body would necessarily be dominated by Brazil, there would nevertheless be significant resistance from Venezuela, Argentina and, perhaps less openly, Colombia. In practical terms this means Brazil would not be able to control an institutionally strong body to ensure its own autonomy remained sacrosanct, something which would be essential because any attempt to build a deep and effective regional grouping redolent of the European or even North American example would require some substantive pooling of sovereignty. The skeptical quip from one Brazilian official during an interview was that no rational person would accept granting Paraguay the power to make decisions binding the actions of his country. Even in areas where collectivization manifestly appears to be a logical option such as the joint combatting of organized crime and narcotrafficking, Brazil has opted to create a web of bilateral arrangements rather than a unified continental system that might operate through UNASUL frameworks (Muggah and Diniz, 2013). These relational power questions aside, there is a clear sense that the expansion of regional and subregional multilateral frameworks has made an important contribution to the larger foreign policy ambition of shifting how Southern countries conceptualize the structural possibilities of action, giving a sense that Brazil has a strong coalition quietly backing its international initiatives. Within the continent where the US once dominated thinking and was seen as an almost essential interlocutor, the pattern has weakened, with Latin America in general and South America in particular taking a far more direct and active management role in its own regional affairs.

Building a new global multilateralism

The efforts to build alternative regional multilateral structures and quietly push the US out of South America created the foundation for Brazil's push into the global multilateral arena. A proven ability to bring stability to South America and organize regional voices behind Brazilian proposals proved important in the 1990s for the country's entry into global governance talk shops such as the Third Way Summit series set up by advisors to US president Bill Clinton and British prime minister Tony Blair. The proactive role that Brazil took in ending the Ecuador–Peru border war (Herz and Nogueira, 2002; Palmer, 1997; Lampreia, 2009), the lone shooting war on the continent, as well as the quiet stabilization of political affairs in Paraguay provided further weight for the idea of Brazil as a credible international actor (Hirst, 2005/2006: 12–14; Santiso, 2003; Valenzuela, 1997). Weight was added to this by Cardoso's decision to sign the NPT, which provided assurances that while Brazil might be pushing for changes in global governance systems, it was not seeking to tear down the structure or revive any of the more pointed ideas that had circulated in the UN during the 1970s (Cardoso, 2006:

612–617; Lampreia, 1999a: 384–387; Patti, 2010). Equally comforting was the figure of Cardoso himself, a leading international academic who would later win the US Library of Congress's Kluge prize for the study of humanity. His scholarly antecedents and deep network with leading thinkers in the North meant his proposals for global governance reform were taken as the starting point for a relatively sedate conversation about what might be changed and how. More to the point, domestic economic instability in Brazil created a situation where Cardoso's government had limited energy and space to push for substantive changes in multilateral structures beyond the consensual hegemony advancement of his South American project.

Lula's electoral victory in late 2002 brought a significant change to how the global aspect of multilateralism was treated within Brazilian foreign policy. While Cardoso's efforts to have Brazil included as a de facto member of the club of global decision making countries were certainly not abandoned, the approach taken to gaining this position changed. Where the Cardoso years were marked by backroom discussions, Lula's arrival in the Planalto Palace brought a direct and proactive approach to Brazil's use of multilateralism on a global level. Particularly important to this was the appointment of Marco Aurélio Garcia as presidential advisor on foreign affairs and Samuel Pinheiro Guimarães as Itamaraty secretary general. Both figures brought a strong anti-imperialist, staunchly autonomist approach to Brazil's foreign policy that had a strong grounding in structural analyses of global power. Backing these individuals by taking on the sharp end of diplomatic practice, namely the business of international negotiations, was Celso Amorim, who had previously served as foreign minister at the end of the Franco presidency in the 1990s and was also a leading architect of Brazilian ideas of a South American region in the 1980s. As outlined in chapters eight and nine, the result of this personnel shift at the highest levels of foreign policy decision making was a turn to the Global South and the pursuit of intra-Southern regionalism to create a multilateralized base for attempts to magnify Brazil's global voice and thus continue to vouchsafe national autonomy (Almeida, 2003; Cervo 2010; Vigevani and Cepaluni, 2009; Visentini and Silva, 2010).

The extent to which Lula's foreign policy team worked to build strong coalitions to protect the Brazilian position in forums such as the WTO Doha round negotiations is set out in chapter five. In some respects the creation of the G20 trade grouping within the WTO was really more a reflection of coalition shopping after Brazilian negotiators were unable to bring the Australian dominated Cairns coalition to adopt their position (G20 – member trade diplomat, 2007; Veiga, 2005). More significant for the wider argument in this chapter is the background work that allowed formation of the WTO G20, a coalition which grew from efforts to build the South–South grouping known as IBSA (the India, Brazil, South Africa Dialogue Forum). Here the idea was to strengthen direct links between major Southern countries on both a formal and informal level, obviating the need for bilateral or multilateral interactions to pass through Northern dominated institutions. A series of regular meetings were consequently instituted to build links between government bureaucracies, businesses and civil society (Alden and Vieira, 2005; Genésio, 2009). For traditional approaches to international relations the logic behind the grouping proved problematic because there appeared to be an absence of common economic or security considerations. An anchoring point was instead found in a more ideological or conceptual view of the global system, which viewed the existing order as problematic for the developmental aspirations of the member countries (Oliveira, Onuki and Oliveira, 2009). Commonalities in UN voting patterns and approaches to issues in international organizations were isolated by Itamaraty officials as the starting point for the cooperation arrangement, not the trade linkages and security concerns typically associated with the launch of multilateral bodies.

The nature of IBSA highlights the limits to Brazilian engagement with multilateral institutions it may not be able to control. Rather than calling for a permanent secretariat and positioning the grouping as the centre of a new South–South multilateralist policy, IBSA emerges as a loosely organized talk-shop designed to help the countries to get to know each other. Indeed, the multilateral grouping has proven to be spectacularly boring in terms of high profile deliverables, prompting continuous questions about whether it actually matters or has relevance for any of the members. Yet, it is this very vagueness that provides IBSA with its greatest value as a multilateral grouping. It commits the participants to nothing more than talking and seeking new mutual opportunities, incurring almost nothing in terms of substantial costs and obligations for the members. As such it deflects attention away from Northern dominated multilateral bodies and demonstrates that activities can take place independently within the South.

The sense that the South has agency implicit in IBSA activities was amplified by other, softer Brazilian multilateral initiatives such as the CPLP and the series of leader's summits Brazil organized between its South American neighbours and counterparts in Africa, the Middle East and Asia (e.g., Araujo, 2005; Coelho and Saraiva, 2004;). Additional weight to the idea of Brazil as a 'Southern leader' came from the domestic economic and social transformations the country experienced during the Lula presidency (interview with Brazilian diplomats, 2010; van der Westhuizen, 2013). Policy makers from countries such as Angola and Mozambique, for example, point to the poverty reduction successes of Brazil as examples to follow and clear evidence that good ideas can come from the South. As Angolan ambassador Tavares (2014) observed, 'to combat hunger, this is our project for a long time and we can learn much from the Brazilian experience'. The importance of this aspect of Brazil's foreign policy was emphasized by Antonio Patriota (2011a), foreign minister for the first two years of Dilma's presidency, when he noted that an idealistic drive for social development, social justice, poverty eradication, democratic strengthening and sustainable development were central to domestic and international policy. The idea that Brazil was a valuable policy leader, implicit in its reception in the Global South as well as through its foreign policy declarations, was amplified by international organizations such as the IMF and World Bank. Although the conditional cash transfer programme Bolsa Familia has its intellectual traditions in the Mexican programme Progresso (Fenwick, 2015), Brazil succeeded in selling itself to the international community as the chief architect of this sort of social programming and the model to be emulated (Fiszbein et al., 2009). For its part, the IMF has a quiet preference for recruiting Brazilian technical consultants for more than just their facility in Portuguese, focusing equally on the ability of these experts to adjust orthodox policy ideas and processes sensitively to diverse national circumstances (interviews with IMF officials). Lula's rapid expansion and widening of Brazilian development assistance provision followed a similar logic, positioning his country as a non-prescriptive or dictatorial source of advice and collaborative counsel dedicated to poverty alleviation and hunger eradication (Burges, 2014; Inoue and Vaz, 2012; Milani and Carvalho, 2013; Robledo, 2015; Stolte, 2015).

By the mid-2000s expanded engagement across the Global South through soft power avenues, such as South–South Cooperation provision and the hosting of bilateral and multilateral summits, resulted in Brazil's emergence as a de facto 'bridge' between the North and South. Of particular value to both ends of the bridge was the Brazilian diplomatic proclivity for creating consensus over direct imposition, as well as an ability to intrinsically understand the challenges facing industrialized and developing economies. For Brazil the particular value came from being seen as a voice for the Global South, one lacking the sorts of expansionist and economically voracious habits attributed to China's role in regions such as Africa (interviews with Mozambican government officials). For other developing countries Brazil was an attractive interlocutor exactly because it lacked the sort of economic power found in China and thus was forced to take a more measured approach.

Within this context the rise of the BRICS grouping of countries – the emerging market stars of Brazil, Russia, India and China identified by investment bank Goldman Sachs, as well as late addition South Africa – added heft to Brazil's ability to engage the global multilateral arena and quietly push for change. Like IBSA, the BRICS has little formal institutional structure and commits its members to little in terms of concrete action (Stuenkel, 2015). Indeed, a close reading of the various BRICS Summit joint declarations and pre-meeting discussions reveals a notable avoidance of anything that might raise disagreement amongst the members. Given the heterogeneity of the BRICS grouping and the relative reluctance for it to formally solidify as a group – it was only after the start of the Global Financial Crisis that serious moves were made by the four main countries to embrace the externally imposed 'common' identity – it is not surprising that it has focused on high-level global governance reform, not integrationist visions of a pan-Southern future. The strongest actions taken by the BRICS have related to calls for representational change in key global governance institutions such as the IMF and World Bank as well as allied but more technocratically obtuse organizations such as the Financial Stability Forum in the Bank of International Settlements.

In many ways the BRICS grouping highlights the concentration on addressing questions of structural power in Brazilian foreign policy. How Brazil seeks to do this through multilateral mechanisms can be found in the genesis of the BRICS development bank, which tellingly relies on Chinese capital to make it a reality. Rather than trying to overturn the existing international development finance system, emphasis was placed on creating alternatives that allow new ways of financing and pursuing national development, initiatives that would also help to fund the growing number of Brazilian construction companies operating in Africa. Similar emphasis on offering alternate understandings came in the July 2014 BRICS Summit Declaration of Fortaleza announcing the Bank through an instruction by the five leaders that their respective national statistical institutes and social policy ministries cooperate in the creation of joint methodologies to measure indicators of social progress. Indeed, there is virtually nothing within the Declaration of Fortaleza that commits the member countries to maintaining the BRICS grouping or taking meaningful steps to substantively institutionalize it. Rather, the document is more of a joint declaration of common goals and ambitions for the international system, which gain greater weight as issues to be internationally considered thanks to the combined attention of the five leading emerging market countries. The focus is on presenting alternatives to existing patterns of power and practice without actually challenging the underlying ideological basis for world order. There is no challenge to the need for careful statistical analysis to support public policy, but rather a call for further refining processes and adapting them to specific national contexts. Likewise, the move to establish the New Development Bank and the Contingency Reserve Arrangement operate within the existing assumptions about global economic governance, but present venues where the actual decision making on daily questions is not dominated by the North.

International multilateral action

The BRICS also stand as a key example of how Brazil has used its expanded engagement with the Global South to magnify its international voice. A constant refrain in Brazilian speeches and statements was that the relative distribution of global power contained implicit and embedded inequities that threatened sustainable development (for example, survey the documents collected in Guimarães, 2006; Patriota, 2013c). Ideas of rebalancing, restoration of equilibrium and, above all, the sense that countries in the South should and do have agency, particularly on a national and regional level, emerge as themes underpinning quietly rising efforts to build soft multilateral ventures such as something like a South Atlantic security community (Abdenur and Souza Neto, 2014; Abdenur et al., 2014). Above all, the focus on dialogue and consensus has greatly contributed to Brazil being accepted across large areas of the South as an at times representative voice for engaging with the North, although it would be stretching the point considerably to suggest that the countries interacting most with Brazil completely trust it to protect and advance their interests. Rather, Brazil is seen as an international actor that at least faces the same challenges and limitations as other developing countries, and because it is willing to discuss these openly with potential partners, is likely to bring these perspectives to global decision making tables (interviews with Angolan and Mozambican government officials). As the now collapsed G8 Heiligendamm outreach process and the post-Global Financial Crisis G20 meetings demonstrate, the established global powers also demonstrated an at least tacit willingness to turn to Brazil as a representative of the South with the technocratic capability to positively contribute to the management of major issues (interview with WTO official, 2007).

The corollary to Brazil's sort of bridging role is that the established powers also expect Brazil to deliver the South and bring developing countries onboard to support the decisions made at the core global governance decision tables. In a sense the expectation is that Brazil will take on the role of a new generation of middle powers that continue to quietly support the agenda of the traditional core countries (Spanakos and Marques, 2014). For Brazil this expectation is ideal because it also places the country in a place where it can work to reshape the nature of global power structures and thus advance the autonomist agenda that rests at the heart of its multilateral engagement agenda. The challenge for the North comes from how Brazil might understand its role in global affairs, which involves actively rejecting the idea that it is a 'middle power' and instead positioning itself as a soon-to-be great power or intermediate power (Burges, 2013; Soares de Lima and Hirst, 2006). Leaders in the North are consequently often extremely frustrated with Brazil's initiatives because the country subscribes to the idea of a middle power only in as much as it seeks to preserve the existence of a multilateral order; advancing this system is pursued very much in Brazil's distinct, autonomist interests, not the cooptive, Northern centric patterns traditionally associated with middle powers (Jordaan, 2003).

The growing sense of self-confidence that marked Brazilian foreign policy towards the end of the Lula presidency resulted in a very public display of the extent to which the Planalto Palace felt alternate approaches to shared international goals should be pursued. Although Brazil did sign the NPT in 1998, it remains a controversial decision because of the failure of the nuclear powers to fulfill their end of the deal by actively disarming. Beyond the argument about ensuring a nuclear security imbalance, nationalist segments in Brazil complain that a major goal of the treaty is to deny access to nuclear technology even if it is for peaceful use. Much to the consternation of the US, Brazil drew on this logic to justify its attempt to work with Turkey to broker a deal with Iran that would allow Tehran the right to develop enriched-fuel systems in a manner that also satisfied the proliferation concerns of the P5 nuclear powers. The catch was that the three-way talks took place without US oversight and flew in the face of a new drive to stiffen UN-imposed sanctions on Iran. Unsurprisingly, Washington's reaction to the May 2010 triumphal announcement of the deal in Tehran – Lula and his Iranian counterpart president Mahmoud Ahmadinejad paraded before cameras with their arms in the air like World Cup victors – bordered on the apocryphal, with US Secretary of State Hillary Clinton publicly castigating Brazil for an ill-considered venture that threatened global peace and security. For Lula and his foreign policy team the deal was a critical breakthrough for global security that had alluded the established Western powers, demonstrating not only Brazil's ability to deliver concrete global governance goods from its quieter, more consensual approach to international relations (Jesus, 2011; Patti, 2010), but also the ability to pursue security goals in a manner that privileged state autonomy.

A critical concern with the nature of global power structures and national autonomy was embedded within the Brazilian approach to the Iranian nuclear question. On a national level it emphasized that countries should be left free to manage their own internal affairs with international security concerns left as secondary, barring clear and overwhelming evidence of intent to violate the sovereignty of other countries. In the systemic sphere the Brazilian approach appeared focused on limiting the capacity of international bodies to impose sanctions and significantly raising the burden of proof for the imposition of penalties by taking an idealist view that states would keep their word. National development and autonomy issues for Brazil also played a prominent role in the logic behind the effort to broker the deal by focusing on Iran's right to pursue mastery of the full nuclear fuel cycle, something Brazil had itself just completed despite US attempts to slow it down.

Similar preoccupations with domestic self-determination and restrained multilateral enforcement marked Brazil's approach to democracy and human rights in the hemisphere. The difference was that in this policy area the idealist, pro-autonomist undertones of engagement with Iran appeared to be subsumed to broader economic and ideological interests. Although Brazil has never been an advocate of direct intervention to advance democracy by imposing it, the general pattern of post-1986 foreign policy has been to pointedly insist that democratic forms be followed, leaving the details of how this is done to internal negotiations between contending political interests (Daudelin and Burges, 2007). During the Lula and Dilma years this approach appeared to slip, with questions of ideological alignment and economic relations melding with the sustained Brazilian goal of preventing the rise of transnationalized democratic enforcement mechanisms. Active comments from Lula in support of leftist candidates and regimes in the Americas became common and during the Dilma years increasingly morphed into a two-track approach to the advancement of core democratic requisites.

While Brazilian diplomats certainly worked tirelessly behind the scenes to keep neighbouring countries on the democratic path – most notably Bolivia, Ecuador and Paraguay during the 2000s – an overriding factor was ensuring that US-dominated multilateral instruments had little sway in the region. To this end Brazil played a leading role at the 2005 OAS General Assembly by marshalling the members of ALADI around a counter-proposal that sunk the host US's attempts to create an inter-American democratic oversight mechanism. While not explicitly expressed, an extended survey of Brazilian diplomatic discourse from 2003 gives a sense that senior political policy makers in Brasília felt their left-of-centre agenda to be under constant threat. In a foreign policy debate held on the margins of Brazil's 2014 presidential election Marco Aurélio Garcia suggested that the charged political rhetoric of Dilma and opposition candidate Aécio Neves could be traced to the fundamental changes the PT had wrought in Brazil, but which had yet to become deeply institutionalized into the socio-political fabric of the country. Pulling this logic to the global level and its implications for the prevailing structural relationships, Garcia pointed out that part of the disquiet with the PT's foreign policy was that it refused to accept a subordinate role for Brazil, arguing that under his party's rule no Brazilian minister would ever remove their shoes for a US airport security scan as Celso Lafer had done in the US shortly after the 9–11 attacks (Mello, 2014).

Protecting responsibly

The basic principle underlying Garcia's refusal to accept a supine position for Brazil relates back to the overarching foreign policy argument in this book that Brazil is not so much concerned with relational power questions, but rather with how issues of structural power present a constant threat to the core goal of protecting national autonomy. That this prerogative trumps other considerations was highlighted by the Brazilian approach to the UN-sanctioned 2011 interventions in Libya. As Brazilian diplomats point out, the UN issued a limited mandate for intervention in Libya, one which was quickly exceeded when NATO forces began to put soldiers, albeit in limited numbers, on the ground to advise the resistance to Muammar Gaddafi's regime. The clear point made by Patriota (2011b) was that intervention in the internal affairs of another country, as was the case in Libya, remained illegal under international law and was anathema for the principles guiding Brazilian foreign policy. In itself the Responsibility to Protect (R2P) doctrine was not abhorrent to Brazil, a country which had in fact supported its use in Yemen, Burundi and the Central African Republic. More worrying for Brazil's fixation on preserving autonomy was the suggestion from the Libyan case that the traditional core countries in the international system had found a way to turn the principles of the R2P doctrine into a device for further entrenching and perpetuating Northern dominance and privilege (Stuenkel, 2015: chapter seven).

Rather than taking a blunt obstructionist approach to an apparent revivification of the R2P doctrine, Brazilian diplomats at the UN exercised their considerable technocratic expertise to advance the parallel idea that there was also a Responsibility While Protecting. In other words, the intervening force must be accountable for collateral damage caused to civilians during a humanitarian intervention (Kenkel, 2012; Patriota, 2011c). While debate on adoption of Responsibility While Protecting continues, on a more strategic level it had the desired, autonomy-protecting impact of creating a new hurdle that would have to be overcome by future R2P ventures. In part this has proven rhetorically useful for Brazil in its opposition to armed interventions in Syria as well as against the militant Wahabist breakaway attempt to form an Islamic State of Iraq and the Levant.

The issue in all of these Brazilian positions opposing intervention is concern that structural imbalances in the framing of global governance systems neither reflect the purportedly democratic ethos of contemporary global order, nor accurately echo the shifts in global power distribution that should be reducing the relative position of Europe if not also the US. Embedded in this is a sense that the existing multilateral framework is more concerned with maintaining the current configuration of structural power than the developmental principles of human rights and democracy found in Brazil's foreign policy. Dilma's argument to the 2014 UN General Assembly – that 'the use of conflict is incapable of eliminating the underlying causes of conflict' and that 'each military intervention leads not to peace, but to the deterioration of these conflicts' – holds some clear merit if we look to the cases in Iraq and Afghanistan (Rousseff, 2014b). But it also overlooks the reality of the civil war in Syria or the situation in Iraq, leaving the question of how Brazil would address its simultaneous call to not 'allow these barbaric acts to increase, harming our ethical, moral and civilizational values'. As of the writing of this book, a clear answer to this contradiction has yet to emerge from the Brazilian foreign policy establishment, leaving Dilma and Itamaraty open to charges that they callously disregard human rights and are unable to discern the difference between authoritarian and democratic regime along with what this implies for notions of a country's autonomy-based freedom for self-determination (e.g., Florencio, 2011; Magnoli, 2011; OESP, 2010). Instead, the picture that emerges is of a country carefully engaging multilateralism as an avenue for preventing the rise of potentially autonomy-threatening precedents (Patriota, 2013e).

Conclusion

Despite the critical tone in this chapter, the rhetorical importance of multilateralism to Brazilian foreign policy should not be underestimated. After all, multilateral institutions and international regimes provide a mechanism for controlling uncertainty and restraining the arbitrary actions of the powerful. They also provide a useful lever for exerting pressure on how the structures organizing international affairs operate and evolve. The issue is that they hold a decidedly ambiguous position in tactical and strategic diplomatic thinking if Brazil is unable to exert concrete control over the direction the organizations take. This was demonstrated in the starkest terms towards the end of Dilma's first term when Brazil failed to pay its dues to a number of major multilateral organizations. In an act that is itself a strong commentary supporting portions of the hemispheric argument in this chapter, Brazil chose to pay just a single dollar of the USD 8.1 million in dues to the OAS in 2014. Matters were not much better on the global level. Brazil lost its voting rights at the IAEA over a USD 35 million debt to the organization. Within the main UN itself Brazil owed USD 76.8 million for the standard operating costs and USD 87.4 million for peacekeeping activities (Mello, 2015). Only an emergency deposit of USD 15 million allowed José Graziano to stand for reelection at the FAO, a position which was one of the hallmark successes of the internationalization of the PT's domestic social policy achievements (Epoca, 2015). In one sense this is a very rational approach to organizations that Brazil is finding difficult to manipulate. A voice is retained, but the costs deflected until they become avoidable in much the same manner that the country's emerging middle classes have proven able to boost their domestic consumption in recent years. The question for Brazil's larger foreign policy strategy is when will this 'buy now, pay later' approach undercut its credibility and denude its ability to have a voice in these bodies. Evidence from other major powers such as the US suggests that it could take quite some time.

In terms of the larger argument about focusing on structural power over relational power to safeguard national autonomy multilateralism emerges as a central tool. Within South America, and to a certain degree the wider space of Latin America, efforts at building regional and subregional arrangements have succeeded in creating a change in the mindset of other countries that has the effect of reducing US primacy in the Americas. While the US still matters, the sustained work on groupings like Mercosul, UNASUL and CELAC, as well as their issue-specific corollaries in areas like health and defence, has brought a change in focus that now looks inwards for regional solutions, not outwards. For

Brazil this is both a victory and a new challenge. It is a gain in that it contributes to the reshaping of the pattern of structural power that had marginalized Brazil in much the manner discussed by dependentistas. The challenge it brings is a call for greater leadership and cost carrying by Brazil, something which is resisted because this would act as an unwanted restraint on autonomy. Brokering this middle ground between pushing for new multilateral frameworks in the region without imbuing them with significant power stands as one of the primary balancing acts of contemporary Brazilian foreign policy.

Something similar has taken place on an international level, but with less call for Brazil to provide concrete leadership goods. The marrying of persistent calls for a 'democratization' of major international institutions such as the United Nations with efforts to create intra-Southern groupings such as the BRICS, IBSA and the CPLP again has an impact on the structural aspects of global power relations. Dependence on historical colonial centres is quietly eroded through a process of leading by example where Brazil works to find new ways forward with Southern partners and actively includes other Southern countries in its discussion of new ways forward through forums such as the South America-Africa leaders meetings. Again, the resistance is not to the fundamental ideas underpinning existing international institutions, but rather to who gets to interpret these ideas and how. A shift in prioritization is also evident, with sustained pan-Southern development being a serious priority rather than a desired side effect. The sum result is a broadening of the pan-Southern sense that there are alternatives to Northern provided frameworks and policy solutions, a lesson that in the African case also seems to be creeping through with respect to managing relations with China. The overall effect is to open space within existing global institutions for greater consideration of Brazilian interests and, where this appears to falter, create the confidence to try the new paths forward independent of Northern benediction outlined elsewhere in this book. Throughout all these process the focus is redressing what Brazil perceives to be imbalances in structural, not relational power at a regional and global level.

5

Trade policy

The 2003 Cancun WTO ministerial meeting ended with US trade czar Robert Zoellick's thunderous denunciation of Brazil as a wrecker and obstructionist country that had conspired to prevent further progress on global free trade. That Brazil could attract such attention – it usually sits around 21st on world trade activity tables – came as a bit of a surprise to many observers. The anti-globalization forces seized on the opportunity and applauded events in Cancun as a victory of the South over Northern imperialism. While president Lula enjoyed the profile it brought to him as a leader of the South, Brazilian diplomats quietly delivered a different message that may not have resonated so well with the global left: Brazil merely wished to see actual free trade, not a continuation of Northern trade distorting practices such as subsidies, quotas and non-tariff barriers (interview with Brazilian diplomats, 2007). As the WTO Doha round continued, these conflicting views of Brazil's role in international trade negotiations remained the norm, with Brazil simultaneously appearing to be an obstructionist and an orthodox liberal free trader. When viewed in historical context the mere fact that Brazil even had a voice and a role in the WTO talks is anomalous, standing in stark contrast to a long history of protectionist, inward looking trade and economic policies as well as its relatively low rate of participation in international trade. When placed in the context of this book's larger argument the Brazilian stance is not a surprise and represents a clear instance of it challenging the nature and application of structural power in the global system.

In order to unpack the trade side of the Brazilian challenge to existing structural power frameworks this chapter will contextualize Brazil's shift in identity to 'global trader' (Barbosa and Panelli, 1994), exploring what this has meant in terms of trade policy on a regional, South–South and global level. From the early 1980s it became apparent that international trade insertion would play an important role in a country's ability to pursue its own national development and maintain the space it needed to preserve autonomy in the regional and global sphere. Indeed, these became major themes in Brazilian foreign policy from the early 1980s, when explicit attention was given to discerning what options existed for the international sale of Brazilian products and which markets might be opened to sale of the industrial and manufactured goods the country was generating after its period of rapid growth in the 1960s and 1970s. More to the point, as the 1980s progressed it became increasingly clear that autarchy was not going to be an option, and that countries such as Brazil would have to find a manner of inserting themselves into emerging international trade and economic regional arrangements. The question was how this could be done without falling prey to the dependency and peripheralization dynamic long-preoccupying policy makers in Latin America (Bandeira, 2003: chapters twenty to twenty-three; Cason, 2011: chapter three).

At the core of the story is the shift from inward-orientation to export-oriented development that was initiated during the short-lived Fernando de Collor de Mello presidency, which in turn helped drive a deeper internationalization of the Brazilian economy. Over the next twenty years Brazilian government policy worked steadily to encourage national economic sectors to use the domestic and regional market as a springboard for expanded penetration of international markets. The result was an, at times, conflicting pattern of liberalism and protectionism, all wrapped in an approach to trade policy that frequently appeared to subsume it to political priorities. Embedded in this are a series of lags between where Brazilian exporters are going and what the government thinks is taking place. Part of the story was the shifting nature of the Brazilian economy, which first saw some industries protesting that the pace of liberalization was too fast and then later complaining that the government was not doing enough to open new markets and remained excessively dedicated to increasingly politicized regional trade arrangements like the Common Market of the South, Mercosul (Mercosur in Spanish). Viewed more holistically the issue was one of interest intermediation and the ability of competing sectors in the Brazilian economy to get their view before policy makers and reflected in the negotiating stance Itamaraty took to forums such as Mercosul, the FTAA negotiations, and the WTO. Wrapped around this domestic political dynamic were the foreign policy considerations of maintaining relations with neighbours in South America, particularly Argentina, and latterly the efforts of the PT governments to expand Brazilian influence and access throughout the Global South.

Turning to the outside

In many respects the import-substitution industrialization policies followed by Brazil from the 1950s to the 1980s worked. High tariff barriers on imports worked as incentives for international firms to establish local operations and provided Brazilian entrepreneurs with a level of protection as they sought to build their firms (Fleury and Fleury, 2011: chapters six and seven). The result was the formation of a series of national champions in key industries such as mining (Vale), oil and gas (Petrobras), telecoms (Telebrás), and the rise of home-grown companies such as the Odebrecht conglomerate (construction, infrastructure, energy), Embraer (aerospace) and Brazil Foods (meat processing). Embedded within the industrial rise that happened with particular strength in the late 1960s and early 1970s was a production structure that relied on authoritarian governance to keep labour costs down (Cardoso, 1989; Evans, 1979) and the exclusion of external competition to shelter other, globally non-competitive sectors of the Brazilian economy. By the 1980s the result was a financial drain on the national economy with poor quality goods being provided to Brazilian consumers at high prices, and continued tariff protection in sectors such as information technology being driven by political linkages between industry and government (Nelson, 1995).

A brief anecdote related to the author during an interview with a Brazilian civil servant in the early 2000s captures the problems created by the exhaustion of the import-substitution industrialization phase. This official recounted that in the late 1980s and early 1990s every manager worth their salt had close connections with a smuggler who could obtain the equipment necessary to run an office from the black market in Paraguay. The example cited was that of fax machines, which were produced in Brazil, but which seldom worked reliably. Rather than struggling with equipment that did not work, managers would proudly place the (unplugged) Brazilian-made model on public display in the office and quietly make use of a functioning Japanese machine acquired illicitly and hidden away in a drawer.

The costs being incurred by continued protectionist policies presented two problems for the national economy. First, the tariff barriers were creating an additional cost to do doing business by preventing firms from purchasing reliable inputs for their operations at affordable prices. The second was the more obvious impact these elevated costs were having on the national accounts, which were seeing successive waves of financial crisis and roaring inflation. While there had been some halting attempts at economic integration with Argentina on a sectoral basis through the 1986 launch of PICE as part of a mutual confidence building project to support each country's democratic transition process, little happened to create substantively greater economic exchange (Cason, 2011: chapter three; Manzetti, 1993–1994). This changed with the election of Fernando Collor de Mello, a president who wasted little time in engaging his Argentine counterpart Carlos Menem to use a series of presidential summits to restart the discussions and drive through the formation of the trade bloc Mercosur despite cautious foot-dragging from their respective foreign ministries (Cason, 2000: 208; Hage, 2004: chapters three and four).

On an immediate level Mercosul, which also incorporated Paraguay and Uruguay, was important due to structural restraints created by the shape of the global economy. Contemporaneous to Mercosul's negotiation were concerns the world was dividing into a series of competing economic blocs, none of which included Brazil. Moreover, there was an active worry in Brasília and Buenos Aires that some measure of self-help was needed because accession to something like NAFTA would be a difficult path and might be prejudicial to their respective interests. There was also an awareness running through Argentine and Brazilian foreign policy in the late 1980s that the most attractive markets – the US and Europe – were direct competitors in the agro-industrial and industrial goods produced by the two largest South American economies. Regional economic penetration was thus essential, pointing to the idea of some kind of South American Free Trade Area anchored on the Rio de Janeiro-São Paulo-Buenos Aires axis and bridging out to include Chile and the Andean Community (Bandeira, 2003: 465–470). Magnifying these concerns when the FTAA proposal was eventually presented was a sense that Clinton's trade proposal represented little more than a retrenchment of the Monroe Doctrine, capturing the Americas as the exclusive economic sphere – read market – for the US, which did not fit with either Brazilian nor Argentine national development plans (Bandeira, 2003: 494–495).

There was thus an immediate defensive element to Mercosul in the face of structural power imbalances that Brazilian policy leaders saw as permanently impinging their national development prospects. Policy priorities focused on ensuring investments continued to flow to Brazil and markets were preserved for Brazilian firms. Perhaps equally important was the role Mercosul took in Collor's liberalizing reform agenda. Adoption of the bloc's common external tariff of 35% allowed Collor to externalize the need to dismantle some of the industrial policy frameworks that had been established in the boom years of the 1960s and 1970s. Significantly, the common external tariff did not mean the sort of wholesale opening seen in 1980s Chile. Rather, it was positioned as

Table 5.1 Brazil trade with Mercosul (USD millions), 1992–1998

	1992	1993	1994	1995	1996	1997	1998
Exports	4,127.7	5,393.9	5,921.4	6,153.4	7,305.2	9,043.6	8,877.1
Imports	2,208.1	3,576.8	4,593.5	6,858.4	8,270.1	9,647.7	9,448.8

Source: IADB DataIntal

a phased approach that would see Mercosul acting as an 'incubator' to provide Brazilian firms with a period of adaptation for entry into global markets. This transition process was assisted by another aspect of the Mercosul open regionalism model, namely the creation of a larger internal market capable of attracting inward flows of FDI. The presence of an existing industrial infrastructure in Brazil and the reasonably large intra-bloc market meant Brazilian firms were an increasingly attractive site for FDI in the 1990s, which brought not only new flows of capital badly needed to stabilize the country's macroeconomic situation (Cason, 2011), but also the advanced production and management techniques needed to modernize national firms (Amann, 1999; Coutinho et al., 2008).

The direct economic returns from Mercosul to Brazil were substantial. As Table 5.1 highlights, Brazilian exports to the bloc grew quickly until the global financial crisis of 1997, which led to the real's sudden devaluation in early 1999. Over that time period, Brazilian exports to Mercosul went from just over USD 4.1 billion in 1992 to a high of USD 9 billion in 1997. The attractiveness of the Brazilian market as an export destination for the other Mercosul countries similarly surged, becoming particularly attractive as the real became increasingly overvalued after 1996. When put in the larger economic context the importance of Mercosul for Brazilian economic stabilization becomes even clearer. In 1992 the bloc absorbed 11.2% of Brazil's exports, a figure which had risen to 17.4% by 1998. Perhaps more significant was the nature of Brazilian exports to its regional partners; industrial products that employ a larger number of people in manufacturing jobs consistently made up 85–90% of the value of Brazil's exports to Mercosul.

The centrality of the Mercosul and South American market for Brazilian value-added exports had an important impact on the formulation of trade policy in the 1990s. As Figure 5.1 highlights, the manufacturing intensive harmonized system trade code chapters for electrical, machinery and transportation exports comprised between 35 and 45% of Brazilian exports to Mercosul and the rest of South America while representing a much smaller share of sales to North America and the wider global market. The sub-regional and continental markets thus

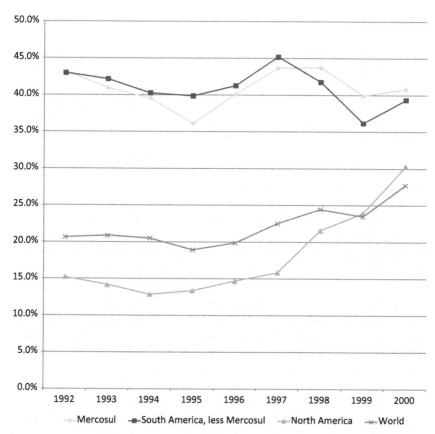

Figure 5.1 Machinery, electrical and transportation as % of exports, 1992–2000

became something important to protect and expand as the Brazilian economy underwent the Collor-initiated transition to greater global insertion, resulting in two important trade policy directions.

First was resistance to the FTAA proposed by the US at the 1994 Miami Summit of the Americas. Brazilian diplomats who worked on the file make no secret of the fact that their government held a pessimistic view of the mooted FTAA, with one publishing a book on how Itamaraty worked to subtly derail Washington's efforts to strike a lightening quick deal (Magalhães, 1999) and another noting that signing the FTAA deal in 1994 would have meant breaking up Mercosul, which was fast becoming a political and economic priority for Brazil (Amorim, 2011a: 502). Their assessment of the proposed deal was that it was too early for Brazil and could result in serious adverse effects for the country's industrial and manufacturing firms. This analysis was also extended to

most of the other countries in Latin America and used to collectivize
Brazil's concerns about the rapid opening sought by the US. The significant point for the larger argument in this book was that the diplomats in
Itamaraty were very aware that Brazil lacked both the economic power
and attractiveness as an alternative market to support a policy of bluntly
opposing the FTAA. The problem they raised was that the FTAA was
being floated extremely quickly by Washington, almost as more of an
easy deliverable for the Miami Summit (Arashiro, 2011: 32–34). Indeed,
suggestions the hosts expected to ink a trade deal in Miami appeared to
catch some of the visiting dignitaries, including president-elect Cardoso,
by surprise (Bandeira, 2003: 496).

Although deeply dubious about the FTAA, Brazil was backed into a
corner and had to engage in the process, which it did by putting forward
the view that any deal would have to be patiently negotiated and carefully
thought through. Moreover, a view was expressed that US ambitions to
use the FTAA to accelerate stalled WTO issues relating to the regulatory
function of states was unacceptable; any possible FTAA would be consistent with the WTO, but not an amplification of what had been agreed
in the world body (Arashiro, 2011: 35–36). Brazil thus built consensus
around a broadly Latin American policy of detailed and inclusive negotiation framed around an understanding that any FTAA agreement would
have to be a 'single undertaking'. This meant a deal would have to be
agreed and implemented in its completed entirety, not piecemeal fashion
as individual elements achieved agreement. Perhaps seeing a structural
shift in domestic political realities throughout the region, former Foreign
Minister Celso Amorim (2011: chapter 19) recalled there was a sense in
Itamaraty that eagerness in Latin America for a deal with the US could
fade as new governments came to power throughout the continent and
other market alternatives developed. The result was a long, drawn out
death for the FTAA, which was effectively interred at the 2005 Buenos
Aires Summit of the Americas when the major protagonists disengaged
from the talks and shifted their attention to bilateral deals and the WTO.

Efforts to delay and derail the FTAA were supported by the second
element of Brazilian trade policy stemming from the pattern in Figure 5.1.
Part of the strategy of derailing the FTAA effectively involved an attempt
to change the structural power realities of regional trade relationships by
positing alternatives to the US. To this end Brazil pushed for an agreement between Mercosul and the Andean Community. In effect Brazil
was suggesting the creation of a South American Free Trade Area, an
idea which had been under discussion within Itamaraty since the mid-
1980s (Amorim, 2003), with some diplomats attributing significant
aspects of its genesis to the thinking of Samuel Pinheiro Guimarães

(interviews, 2007). There was also an awareness in Brasília that a developing economy alternative to the US would be useful not only as an option in place of the FTAA, but also as a balance to potential trade dependence that might come with a hemispheric agreement. By 1995 this had taken more formal shape with the initiation of talks for two bi-regional agreements, one with the Andean Community and the other with the EU. Despite the Cardoso presidency's ambitions and efforts, the realities of intra-Mercosul politics and legal structures rapidly emerged as barriers to these expansionist trade policy ambitions.

One implication of the language in the Mercosul treaty is that members may not individually strike new trade agreements with other countries or regions. While this measure does serve to keep the other bloc members tied to Brazil, it has also consistently blocked Brasília's efforts to expand Mercosul's reach by signing new deals with other parts of the world. In the initial phases of the bloc the provision was particularly important for constraining Argentina, which president Carlos Menem was trying to bring significantly closer to the US by seeking non-Nato ally status and ambitions to join NAFTA. For Brazil the 'all or none' negotiating provisions of the bloc, grounded in late 1980s discussions about collectively maintaining a measure of continental autonomy in the face of US pressure for increased influence, were particularly important because Mercosul had yet to experience its full boom in intra-regional trade. Yet, by the late 1990s the collective negotiating action provisions of the bloc began to be a hindrance as attempts at reaching an agreement with the Andean Community collapsed under Argentine reluctance to introduce a new element of competition for access to the increasingly lucrative Brazilian market; the rapidly rising value of Brazilian imports from Mercosul in the 1990s chiefly reflected the purchase of Argentine goods. Similarly, efforts to strike a bloc-to-bloc deal with the EU were hamstrung by protectionist sentiments in Argentina, some of which were amplified by interest groups within the Brazilian economy. Twenty years after the subject was first breached discussions on a Mercosul–EU deal continued, demonstrating the same tensions between Brazilian and Uruguayan desire for a deal and Argentine reluctance to increase its international economic exposure.

While efforts to build a South American trade bloc were not abandoned, they did undergo a significant shift in approach. The problem was one of non-complimentarity. Mercosul's two big economies – Argentina and Brazil – produced competing, not complimentary products. As Cardoso explains, in the late 1990s there was a tight concentration on trade, which was causing tensions as the different members not only attempted to maximize benefits for their respective competing firms, but also sought to protect themselves from the large currency fluctuations rolling through the bloc after Brazil's 1999 currency devaluation. Drawing on the example of the Ruhr Valley in Europe, Cardoso sought to shift attention away from a strict trade focus to a model more closely aimed at building transnationally integrated production structures by developing international axes of physical infrastructure linking economic centres (Cardoso, 2007). Although attention is often focused on the results in the Merocsul region, which continues to be an important trade locus for Brazil, arguably the most concrete achievements of the physical infrastructure integration strategy agreed at the 2000 Brasília Summit of South American Presidents have been the deepened linkages and expanded cross border trade with Peru and Venezuela with significant impact for the local economies (Gadea, 2012). These successes aside, by the start of the Dilma presidency the expansion of physical infrastructure linking the bloc's different markets had not resulted in the development of significant transnationalized value-chains, with the exception of an illegal cigarette production system (interviews with Brazilian diplomats, 2007). Trade relations within the bloc consequently remained fixed on an attitude of competition amongst similar goods, not the sort of disaggregated collaborative production structures seen in ASEAN, the EU and NAFTA that significantly boosted national insertion into global economic power structures.

The search for something deeper in terms of Brazilian integration with South America became increasingly pressing over the 1998–2003 period. As the figures in Table 5.2 demonstrate, the devaluation of the Brazilian real in early 1999 and then the 2002 Argentine economic crisis had a major negative impact on intra-Mercosul trade. Traditional industrial economic sectors in Brazil expended a lot of effort in 2001 and 2002 lobbying the government to provide additional assistance to not only counteract the negative effects of the Argentine economic crisis, but also to finance the purchase of firms in Argentina facing insolvency. There was also a concomitant surge in protectionism as Argentina began implementing a series of tariff and non-tariff barriers on Brazilian goods as widely variegated as rice, shoes, household appliances and vehicles. Tit-for-tat trade disputes began to mark the bloc, which was unable to

Table 5.2 Brazilian trade with Mercosul (USD millions), 1998–2003

	1998	1999	2000	2001	2002	2003
Exports to	8877.1	6777.8	7732.0	6363.6	3310.7	5671.7
Imports from	9448.8	6743.6	7919.6	7099.1	5667.0	5987.8

manage these ongoing irritants through its dispute settlement procedure because none of the countries appeared willing to accept adverse decisions without either ignoring them or escalating the dispute to the WTO (Gómez-Mera, 2013).

Reconstructing trade policy

Given the importance of the Mercosul market, it would hardly have been surprising if these disruptions had resulted in a notable drop in Brazil's exports. Yet, Brazilian exports continued to grow, increasing from just over USD 55 billion in 2000, to USD 58.2 billion 2001, and USD 60.3 billion in 2002, before taking off to USD 73 billion in 2003 and USD 96.4 billion in 2004.

While attention in the late 1990s and early 2000s was focused on the industrials export potential of Mercosul and how to open US and European markets to manufactured goods, a productivity revolution was quietly taking place in Brazil's agricultural heartland. Reforms in the agro-industrial sector throughout the 1990s brought a surge in productivity and the rise of new powerhouses in the non-industrial sector. Although attention to Brazil as an agro-industrial superpower rose in the mid-2000s as global commodity prices soared, the data in Table 5.3 demonstrates that production levels began their surge in the mid-1990s as the Collor-era economic reforms and the Cardoso-era stabilization of the economy began to take effect. The significant point in the table is that exports of the five selected commodities is measured in weight, not value, and thus controls for variations in price. What becomes clear is that the 1990s were a period in which a major change took place in the productive structure of the agricultural sector and a shift in market focus from the internal to the external, with exports taking off in a serious way while the Argentine economic crisis was hitting Brazil's industrial economy. Particularly notable were the surges in cattle meat exports, growing over 2600% in ten years, and soya beans, which grew just over 680%. Even in areas where Brazil had a long established reputation like sugar, the growth was large, increasing 470% between 1996 and 2006. Brazil was on its way to becoming something close to an agricultural superpower (Barros, 2009), eventually bringing with it a changed relation to global structures of economic power.

By the end of the Cardoso presidency and the start of the Lula presidency the success of the agro-exporting sector was creating a whole new set of domestic pressures on Brazilian trade policy, which diverged significantly from the sorts of trade management issues that had dominated work on Mercosul and relations with the US. Growth in agricultural

Table 5.3 Selected Brazilian agricultural commodity exports by volume (tonnes), 1996–2006

	1996	1997	1998	1999	2000	2001	2002	2003	2004	2005	2006
Meat, cattle	46,652	52,412	80,715	150,554	188,402	367,819	429,831	619,545	923,659	1,083,933	1,221,701
Meat, chicken	558,601	373,771	612,478	770,582	906,753	1,249,288	1,599,923	1,922,042	2,424,520	2,761,966	2,585,713
Meat, pork	52,994	53,138	70,936	73,319	97,941	144,088	229,434	312,120	335,684	389,755	349,530
Soybeans	3,646,934	8,339,590	9,274,752	8,917,210	11,517,260	15,675,543	15,970,003	19,890,467	19,247,690	22,435,072	24,957,975
Sugar, refined	1,288,496	2,527,746	3,575,266	4,273,257	2,158,348	4,083,343	5,724,009	4,560,734	6,198,182	6,568,079	6,063,237

Source: FAO Stat

exports was not a surprise to policy makers, but it did not quite align with the long-standing ambition in national development policy to see Brazil become an industrial and technologically sophisticated powerhouse. Absent from the immediate conscious thinking driving trade policy was the reality of modern agribusiness, which is highly technically advanced, mechanized and dependent on the sorts of innovation long sought by policy makers. More importantly for the trade policy file were the new issues the rise of the agro-industrial sector brought before diplomats negotiating at the WTO or representing exporter interests abroad. The result was that the agro-industrial sector appeared to be having an extremely difficult time accessing policy makers during the second Cardoso presidency, which led to a pointed running argument in the OpEd pages of the major newspapers about Itamaraty's role in trade negotiations and its seeming inability to grapple with the technical intricacies impacting the interests of commodity exporters.

In a reaction that presaged the coming challenges at Itamaraty as foreign policy began to be seen as just another field of public policy, business interests in the agricultural sector were particularly scathing about the failure to advance the trade deals they sought, particularly with respect to combating market-distorting subsidies and quotas in the EU, Japan and the US. The institutional reply from Cardoso's foreign minister Celso Lafer was pointed and highly indicative of the Itamaraty mindset even though he was not himself a career diplomat:

> Major decisions about trade policy are taken within the government by the CAMEX, a committee which includes the Foreign Ministry, the ministries of Development, Finance, Planning and Agriculture and the Chief of Staff's office. Conducting negotiations is the responsibility of the Foreign Ministry, whose tradition and experience in this area date back to the time of the Empire. ... The most recent criticisms that have been raised about the Foreign Ministry's negotiating competence can be likened to a speculative attack by domestic economic and political sectors seeking their own short-term gain at the expense of an asset that belongs to all Brazilians. (Lafer, 2002)

Lafer's comments were forcefully defensive, seeking to establish Itamaraty's capacity to listen while simultaneously reinforcing its rightful place as the outside face of Brazil and final arbiter of negotiating positions. More telling are the clear suggestions that voices criticizing Itamaraty's capacity in trade negotiations are motivated by the advancement of partisan interests and have little regard for the common good of the country; exactly the sort of thing Rio Branco sought to exclude from Brazil's foreign policy process when he took on the minister's job in

1902. An interesting added element is Lafer's description of the departments included in the foreign trade council, CAMEX. Particularly telling
is his reference to the 'Development' ministry, which he headed earlier in
the Cardoso era and which as CAMEX chair bears the full title Ministry
of Development, Industry and Foreign Trade. The implicit denigration
of MDIC's foreign trade expertise was reinforced during interviews in
2001 when senior officials in the Ministry's foreign trade secretariat
expressed their frustration with Itamaraty's resistance to outside technical advice and guidance.

A big part of the issue for critics was the clubiness of Brazil's diplomatic corps, which has a deep sense of its own technocratic and professional superiority embedded into its collective psyche by preparatory
training at the Rio Branco Institute and the general implicit social
contract governing the department within the Brazilian governmental system (Moura, 2007). This was particularly the case during the
Cardoso administration because he drew extensively on diplomats as a
technocratic elite for senior advisor and ministerial positions (Cason and
Power, 2009: 128). Case in point, career diplomat ambassador Sergio
Amaral was MDIC minister from 2001–2002 during the time when the
agro-industrial sector was beginning to push very hard on trade policy.
Although not formally part of the 'old boys' network at Itamaraty
because he was not a career diplomat, Celso Lafer had previously served
as foreign minister in the Collor government and been the Brazilain
ambassador to the WTO and Geneva-based international organizations
from 1995–1998, becoming MDIC minister in 1999 before moving
back to the minister's post at Itamaraty in 2001. At the Planalto Palace
other diplomats drawn from Itamaraty held key presidential advisory
positions. Magnifying Itamaraty's sense that it should be dealing with
these trade-related questions was the 1970s decision to set up the Trade
Promotion Department within the foreign ministry, which was later
moved to MDIC.

For critics of Brazil's trade policy this old boys networked approach
to foreign affairs was a major problem, particularly as it was grounded
in a historical vision that denigrated agricultural exports in favour of
industrial products targeted specifically at the US and Western Europe.
Marcos Jank, an agricultural economist at the University of São Paulo
and the Inter-American Development Bank, as well as founder of the
think tank ICONE, did not mince words: 'Brazil's diplomats have
enormous "know-how" in geopolitical questions, but little experience
in conducting trade negotiations' (quoted in Osse and Cardoso, 2002).
Jank later went on to extol Itamaraty and the quality of its diplomats,
but with a telling technocratic caveat: 'The diplomats do not have

the [technical] conditions to evaluate the impact on a specific export segment of an offer to reduce or raise an import tariff by another country' (Jank, 2003). The crucial point Jank was making was not that diplomats were incapable of conducting negotiations or representing the agricultural sector's trade interests, but rather that there was a new level of technical complexity to the file which appeared beyond Itamaraty's institutional capacity and which consequently placed Brazil at a major structural disadvantage in negotiations impacting national and international economic power.

Complex econometric analyses were needed to understand the impact different subsidy programmes had on global product prices and how this interacted with tariff levels and market access rules. Layered on top of this was the non-tariff barrier component, particularly questions about phytosannitary standards and rules governing the cultivation, harvest, processing and transportation of agricultural commodities and products. Agricultural trade negotiations, essential for Brazilian economic health, was a specialist field being managed by Itamaraty generalists. Adding an additional layer of complication to the issue were the parallel negotiations in the FTAA and WTO, which the US was seeking to use as a venue for advancing different strategic economic agendas. Globally the trade in agricultural commodities became a particularly charged issue as the Doha development round launched with a focus on developing country interests partly to assuage concerns left over from the contentious 1998 Seattle ministerial meeting and as an attempt to try and undercut the discontent with neoliberalism's failures in the 1990s. For Brazil's agro-industrial sector, which was highly organized and carefully examining the details being discussed in the various trade talks underway, the ground was fraught with danger and held a real threat of seeing Brazil and Mercosul marginalized with extremely unfavourable offers in agricultural trade.

The critical inflection point for reconstituting Brazil's trade policy is the commencement of the Lula presidency in 2003, which explicitly recognized the changes not only in the Brazilian economy, but also in the international agricultural trade landscape. Presidential diplomacy certainly continued apace as a force challenging Itamaraty hegemony, but it was also paralleled by the rise of other powerful voices in Brasília. Most notable in this respect were two strong-willed business figures from the agro-industrial sector: Luiz Fernando Furlan left his position as head of the Brazilian food multinational Sadia to head MDIC; and the Ministry of Agriculture was taken over by Roberto Rodrigues, a highly respected agronomist and engineer. These two new ministers proved critical for breaking the Itamaraty deadlock on CAMEX, hammering home the point that the foreign ministry lacked the technical expertise to adequately manage the agricultural issues that had become the country's core trade interest. Significantly, the arrival of Furlan and Rodrigues in the Lula government was paralleled by the formation of ICONE as a non-partisan technical research institute. By May 2003, the work of ICONE had proven its value and Jank and members of his team were included as technical advisors in the Brazilian negotiating teams for the FTAA and WTO (*Gazeta Mercantil*, 2003a).

On a working level, Brazil's diplomats praised ICONE, with Itamaraty Economics Department head ambassador Valdemar Carneiro Leão telling *Gazeta Mercantil* (2003b), 'Icone is a very serious organization and our impression is the best possible.' Despite this praise, the factor to keep in mind is that ICONE, as well as trade economists at peak body groups such as FIESP and CNI, were providing technical analysis of proposals and the econometric modelling to support Brazilian positions, not directly mandating negotiating positions. The primary avenue of influence they wielded came through their technical skill and ability to use economic analyses to nudge the thinking of diplomats in a particular direction. Officials at the Ministry of Agriculture (interviews, 2007) also pointed to the centrality of the informal and responsive nature of government interacation with ICONE, noting that even if the Ministry had the funds to contract the sort of rapid-fire comparative position analysis provided by Jank's grouping, federal contracting laws meant that they would never be able to commission and receive the work in time to use it in negotiating sessions. As one interview subject noted, some of the analysis input by ICONE into Brazil's negotiation preparations was delivered exceedingly quickly and often in the form of an informal spreadsheet that negotiators could immediately use, not the lengthy and often more obtuse materials required to justify tendered research contracts.

The influence ICONE and its private sector counterparts wielded by providing gratis technical analysis was nevertheless tempered by Itamaraty, which retained for itself the strategic thinking and planning role, keeping groupings such as CAMEX as consultative mechanisms that could be subsumed to the foreign ministry's understanding of what was needed for Brazil (interview with Brazilian diplomats, 2007; interview with Casa Civil Advisor 2007). Research interviews conducted with trade officials at the Ministry of Agriculture in 2007 pointed directly to the persistence of frustration with Itamaraty negotiators; Mercosul-country diplomats in Geneva spoke of Brazilian firms approaching them to lobby Itamaraty to alter its negotiating position. Similar complaints came from agro-industrial peak body groups in São Paulo, with some officials expressing severe disdain for Itamaraty and others enormous frustration that the government as a whole was not treating technocratic issues such as phytosanitary monitoring with the requisite seriousness. Indeed, a theme running through one of then Foreign Minister Celso Amorim's memoires on the WTO Doha round is the efforts he had to expend managing Furlan and Rodrigues, going so far to note that 'the principal point was to guarantee Itamaraty's space' (Amorim, 2013: 81).

The voice of the agricultural lobby grew rapidly at the start of the Lula years and then gained strength as commodity exports picked up steam, changing the structure of the Brazilian economy (interview with Casa Civil Advisor, 2007). As Cardoso left office in 2002, the value of primary product exports stood at USD 16.95 billion. By the end of Lula's first year that value had already risen to USD 21.20 billion, pointing to the start of the commodity boom and an eventual 2011 value of basic product exports of USD 122.46 billion (SECEX, 2012). This in turn transformed the composition of Brazil's goods exports between 2002 and 2011. During that time period basic products went from 28.1% of the total to 47.8%; semi-manufactureds from 14.9% to 14.1%; and manufactureds from 54.7% to 36.3% of total value. While production levels and efficiency did improve over this decade, the real story is in the shift in commodity prices. For example, from 2002 to 2012 tonnes exported of all forms of soya rose 161%, but the shipped value went up 435%. Chicken exports went up 230% by volume, but 518% by value. Mineral exports stood out for a 194% increase in volume and a corresponding 940% in value.

The surge in commodity exports, particularly food exports, drove two substantial changes in the range of issues confronting Itamaraty. First was the need for a stronger technocratic capacity on agricultural issues in Brazil's foreign missions, which the Ministry of Agriculture sought to address by having technical officials stationed in foreign missions. Despite the clear need for these specialized officers to protect Brazil's considerable agricultural interests abroad, Itamaraty quietly blocked efforts to establish these posts until compliance was commanded by the Planalto Palace (Faria, 2012: 329–331). This sort of reticence was driving agricultural peak body groups to distraction in 2007 because of the impact it was having on the agro-industrial sector's market access (interview with agro-industrial executives, 2007). A simple totaling of the value of exports to the top four markets for selected commodities highlights the economic scale of the issue. In 2002 the respective values for soya, beef, chicken and pork were USD 6.49 billion, USD 1.83 billion, USD 2.85 billion and USD 1.0 billion. By 2012 these figures had grown, respectively, to USD 18 billion, USD 2.94 billion, USD 3.14 billion, and USD 1.2 billion.

The rise in the value of agricultural exports points to the second set of issues, namely Itamaraty's geopolitical concentration on North America and Western Europe. While there is certainly an element of truth to the proposition that the initial stages of Brazil's foreign policy turn to the South remained very close to the core beliefs of traditional *Petistas* as a soft counter to Lula's continuation of Cardoso-style macro-economic policies (Almeida, 2004), this ideological policy direction was underpinned by some hard economic realities. More than prestige was involved. Lost in the noise of the political debate surrounding the turn towards more Southern linkages in Brazilian foreign policy is the strategic aspect, which was fully in keeping with the standing tradition of autonomy through diversification and the challenge to perceived imbalances in the structural power in the international system (Fonseca, 2004; Vigevani and Cepaluni, 2009). As in the 1980s when energy and agriculture were used to reduce Brazilian dependency on specific bilateral economic relationships (Bandeira, 2003: chapter 20), so too was the case in the early 2000s. The difference was that this time there was a strong focus on varying the destination of Brazil's rising agricultural exports, not distributing the source of its imports.

The story of the impact Chinese economic growth had on commodity prices and thus Brazilian economic stability is well known and set out in more detail later in the book. Less well known are the role countries such as Russia, Saudi Arabia and the wider Global South played in Brazil's rise as an agro-industrial power. In 2002 the only non-European countries for Brazil's soya exports were China (14.6%) and Iran (3.34%). By 2012 this had changed to the point where China absorbed 48.39% of Brazil's soya with Vietnam, Iran, South Korea, Taiwan and Thailand accounting for another 12.9%. Export markets for beef were dominated by Russia (21.08%), Hong Kong (17.84%) and Egypt (11.24%). For chicken the geographic spread was similar. Where in 2002 Germany had ranked fifth (5.10%), Holland seventh (4.30%) and the UK eighth (4.30%), by 2012 only Holland (2.54%) remained on a top ten list dominated by Saudi Arabia (16.80%), Hong Kong/China (14.28%) and Japan (10.23%). In short, the new loci of Brazilian economic interests were moving away from the geopolitical centres that had traditionally preoccupied Itamaraty thinking.

The rise of agro-industrial exports also created a major shift in where Brazilian trade negotiators focused their attention, and opened up significant new space to build linkages with other developing countries dissatisfied with the operational patterns of global structural power. Market access for industrial goods faded as a priority and was replaced by a focus on barriers to agricultural exports. This in turn meant a shift in concentration to issues such as quotas and subsidies as well as the traditional concern with tariff levels. In the FTAA arena it soon became clear that the US and Brazil, by then joint chairs of the negotiations, could not agree on these issues and were increasingly pushing them towards the WTO (Amorim, 2011a: chapter 19). Within the ambit of the WTO Brazil used its collectivization strategy to leverage the technical expertise of groups such as ICONE to build the G20 negotiating coalition (interview with Geneva-based G20 member diplomat, 2007). Initiated by ambassador Luiz Felipe de Seixas Corrêa during his time as Brazilian representative to the WTO, the G20 was brought to full life by Celso Amorim and unveiled at the 2003 Cancun ministerial meeting where it pressed for large reductions in agricultural subsidies as well as significant moves on tariffs, quotas and subsidies in Europe and the US. When negotiations in the Doha round proved faltering, Brazil took to the WTO's dispute resolution panel and used the international structure to push for change. Notable examples amongst the cases brought by Brazil include the 2002 case against the US on cotton, the 2005 procedure against the EU on sugar barriers, a 2006 case against the EU on frozen chicken, a 2007 case against the US on its general agricultural subsidy policy, and a 2008 case against the US over orange juice barriers. As of the writing of this book Brazil had brought forward twenty-six cases itself and entered into proceedings as a third party in a further 84 cases, bringing more actions than all other WTO members save Canada, the EU and the US.

The 2002 cotton case Brazil brought in the WTO against the US stands as an important example of the Brazilian strategy of using trade issues to position itself as the coordinator and voice for other developing countries. In this case Brazil worked with Benin, Burkina Faso, Chad and Mali to bring the procedure forward and, significantly, gain the right to impose retaliatory sanctions in unrelated trade areas like automotive parts or computer software. Similar efforts to represent larger groups as an avenue for strengthening Brazil's voice proved effective in placing Brazilian negotiators at the heart of the WTO Doha negotiating round as part of the 'new quad' of agenda-setting countries. As Amorim (2015b) later noted, 'we worked in a very tough way that changed the pattern of negotiations', which he went on to note brought an emphasis on developing countries 'that had expression within the WTO'. Early in the process Celso Amorim went to considerable effort to bring members of the LDC-dominated G90 negotiating coalition into the Brazilian camp, travelling extensively throughout sub-Saharan Africa and addressing the group's 2004 coordinating meeting in Guyana (Amorim, 2004a; 2013: chapter six). This outwardly collaborative approach continued in

Geneva, where weekly meetings with the other G20 coalition members were held at the Brazilian mission to review negotiating positions and plan responses to new developments (interviews with Geneva-based G20 member diplomats, 2007).

Although the regular briefing and consultations within the G20 did bring a heightened degree of transparency to the WTO negotiation process, as the talks dragged on disquiet began to emerge amongst the negotiating coalition's members. As agricultural commodity prices took off in the mid-2000s it became clear that demand for food was not going to decline and the economic calculation underpinning Brazil's approach to the WTO shifted. By 2007 many Brazilian agricultural commodities had become price-competitive in the EU and US despite producer subsidies in those markets. Moreover, the importance of the traditional Northern markets for Brazilian agribusiness had, as noted above, faded remarkably to be replaced by China and other emerging economies where quotas were not much of an issue. Interviews conducted in 2007 with trade officials from four separate G20 member missions in Geneva all directly questioned Brazilian motives in the WTO negotiating coalition, each pointing to the strong possibility that political ambitions to gain better global political positioning were supplanting economic imperatives in Brazil's management of the group's position within the quad. The perception was that it had become more important for Brazil to make the deal happen and thus garner international prestige not just for the country, but more particularly for president Lula and his foreign minister Celso Amorim (interviews with G20 member trade officials, 2007). While this may have been an instance of creative diplomatic tattle-telling, the reality was that Brazil had recently adopted a far more flexible position to issues such as non-agricultural market access than that discussed in the weekly briefing sessions.

The same element of firmly putting Brazilian interests ahead of the collective became evident as the WTO cotton dispute with the US evolved, which by 2014 saw the Dilma government cutting a final payment deal with Washington in order to put the dispute to rest despite the potential ongoing ramifications for the Cotton-Four countries in Africa (Soto and Hughes, 2014). While lamentable for Brazil's partners at the WTO, none of this was taken as particularly surprising, with one participant in the G20 weekly meetings being quite sanguine in remarking that every country has limits on how far it will stick with a coalition and that at a certain point a parting of the ways should be considered normal. What remained important for the wider diplomatic game in Brazil's WTO trade policy approach was its ability to convene disparate interests and keep discussions alive, skills which helped ambassador Roberto Azevedo win the director generalship of the WTO in 2013 after five years of representing Brazilian interests in Geneva. The ability to consistently convene a group of influential developing countries also proved critical in Brazil's rise as a country of importance in the international system, drawing it into the discussions mapping out how the structures governing the global system would operate.

Politicization of trade policy

The economic stability that came with the surge in global commodity prices and Brazil's success in exporting agricultural products and minerals underpinned an apparent shift in the strategic interplay between trade and foreign policy. A series of summits Brazil organized between South America and Africa (2006, 2009) as well as the Arab world (2005, 2009) kept the same implicit logic of trade expansion found in efforts to move Cardoso's infrastructure integration programme to deeper economic and political cooperation first through the launch of CASA, and then as the South American Union, UNASUL. Where matters shifted was in a move away from the technocratic avenue Cardoso had prioritized through the focus on infrastructure integration towards a more explicit political focus. As Amorim (2013: 126) notes, 'it was clear to us within the Brazilian government that the economic fundamentals were essential for the strength of the political framework'. While this comment focuses on the importance of an economic underpinning, the ultimate objective it highlights is political alignment, coordination and perhaps integration, all with Brazil at the head of the table with an enhanced position to exert some measure of influence on structural power frameworks.

As rising commodity prices removed restrictions on the sorts of trade and foreign policy options the Lula government might consider, an emphasis on rhetorically and to a lesser extent substantively providing concrete support for the strengthening of regional projects grew. Continental groupings like UNASUL and Mercosul in particular took on increasing elements of being a vehicle for consolidating Brazilian leadership and being of less importance as keystones in foreign trade policy (Gómez-Mera, 2013). Indeed, officials from other South American countries complained about market access to Brazil, with Ecuador being a clear example: 'The problems we have with Brazil usually emanates from trade… We have tried to export bananas to Brazil for many years and always there is another reason for them to not import our product. This is also the case for seafood… They're quite protectionist in their trade policy' (Arízaga, 2015). The recurrence of these complaints throughout the region combined with the inability to open new markets and trade deals to kick off a vociferous argument within Brazil about the failures of the PT's trade policy, particularly with respect to a persistent stream of trade distorting policies in Argentina. Proponents of the Lula and Dilma governments' approach pointed to the creation of institutions such as the Mercosul parliament and the Structural Convergence Fund, FOCEM, to deal with the asymmetries embedded in the bloc and strengthen its economic and political substance, something they argue was supported by Venezuela's accession to the bloc and applications for membership by Bolivia and Ecuador (Pereira, 2014). Critics responded that these measures were little more than window dressing and that the bloc had deviated a long way from its original purpose of creating a common internal market for complete free trade amongst its members (R. Barbosa, 2014). Indeed, Venezuelan president Hugo Chávez greeted the beginning of his country's accession to Mercosul with a call to 'decontaminate' the bloc and make it more reflective of his socialist vision of a South American family (Tosta, 2007).

In part, the economic costs of playing politics with Mercosul were fairly low because the bloc had declined in relative importance as a market for Brazilian exports as set out in Table 5.4. As the repeated series of crises rolling through the bloc highlighted – particularly the persistent application of unilateral trade barriers by Argentina, complaints about unresolved structural asymmetries from Paraguay (Lambert, 2016), and desires to sign bilateral deals with extra-bloc countries in Uruguay and latterly Paraguay – the Brazilian response remained largely one of mollification. Both Lula and Dilma effectively resorted to the strategy of 'avoiding mindless opposition' set out in chapter four to bring Argentina back to the negotiating table and delay the need to actually commit concrete resources to addressing the underlying issue. The generally unstated coercive stick at the Brazilian president's disposal was the centrality of their market for Argentine industry, a card which was occasionally played in the form of withdrawing automatic import

Table 5.4 Percentage of total exports to selected regions, 2007–2012

	2007	2008	2009	2010	2011	2012
Mercosul	10.8	11.0	10.3	11.2	10.9	9.5
South America	19.8	19.4	17.6	18.4	17.6	16.7
Europe	29.5	28.0	26.7	25.6	24.4	23.9
USA	15.6	13.9	10.2	9.6	10.1	11.1
China	6.7	8.3	13.2	15.2	17.3	15.9
Africa	5.3	5.1	5.7	4.6	4.8	5.1

Source: IADB Dataweb Intal

Table 5.5 Percentage of exports by value aggregation

	2007	2008	2009	2010	2011	2012
Primary products: agricultral goods, foodstuffs, minerals	43.7	48.2	53.9	56.4	59.1	57.7
Semi-manufactureds: chemicals, rubbers etc	14.6	12.7	13.4	13.0	11.8	11.9
Manufactureds: textiles, metals, machinery, etc	36.3	33.7	27.4	25.7	24.3	25.1

Source: IADB Dataweb Intal

licences for key products when Buenos Aires was proving intractable or complaints from industrialists in Brazil politically difficult.

By 2008 this mollification of Argentina and absorption of the costs of the rolling unilateral trade restrictions being implemented within Mercosur was driving Brazil's industrial exporters to distraction. From 2006 they not only saw their share of global exports declining rapidly, but also witnessed the relative decline of their main Mercosul and South American markets in the larger picture of Brazilian trade policy. The persistent call was for a widening of the country's approach to international trade, most particularly through the signing of new free trade agreements with other potentially significant markets like the US and EU. In response, the government ushered Venezuela into Mercosul after it arranged for Paraguay's political rights in the bloc to be suspended in the wake of the 2012 coup-peachment of president Fernando Lugo. Further advances included announcements from Bolivia and Ecuador that they wished full membership in the bloc. Business, meanwhile, was looking longingly at the potential of the Pacific Alliance that was forming on the West coast of South America and spurning the Brazil-managed Mercosul in favour of options in the Asia-Pacific.

Although trade talks with the EU had been taking place on and off since the mid-1990s, the previous challenges of overcoming European agricultural supports and domestic producer protection policies appeared to be fading towards the end of Lula' presidency, allowing a more forceful restart of the process towards the end of Dilma's first term. The problem for her government was that efforts to negotiate new trade deals, such as the one being discussed with the EU while this book was being written, ran afoul of the requirement that Mercosul do the deal, not Brazil as an individual country. Brazil consequently had to gain the support of Argentina and Venezuela for any putative agreement, which was problematic because there were definite limits to how much pressure the Planalto Palace was willing to put on its reluctant bloc partners, particularly an Argentina that was facing its own severe economic crisis. Further complicating matters was the breakdown in technocratic capacity in Argentina and Venezuela, which made it difficult for these countries to meet deadlines for submitting lists of excluded products for the negotiating sessions with the EU (interviews with Brazilian diplomats, 2010). While the option of simply walking away from Mercosul, or threatening to do so, remained, the political weight that had been given to the bloc on a domestic, regional and international level made this a nuclear option that was perceived to carry unacceptable collateral damage. Power and influence over international trade frameworks ultimately stretched back to the ability to hold the Mercosul market together, making the bloc an essential anchor in the pan-Southern trade policy linkages supporting Brazil's wider foreign policy agenda.

Conclusion

The picture that emerges from this survey of the role of trade policy in Brazil's global insertion is messy. On a domestic level there is a lag between what is actually taking place with Brazilian firms and exporters and the sorts of policies that are being pursued by the government, although this almost inevitably takes place in most countries with sophisticated and diversified economies. In part the challenge is bureaucratic coordination in the form of continuing tension between Itamaraty, which sees itself as the arbiter and manager of all external interventions, and the more technocratic development, trade and agriculture ministries actively involved in seeking to advance Brazil's outward economic insertion. The complication which pervades this relationship is the politicization of trade policy for political ends as seen in the use of Mercosul to advance continental leadership ambitions and the slightly fickle turn that Brazilian leadership of the G20 took as commodity prices soared and the Doha negotiating round stalled.

These complications aside, there is a certain logic to the approach Brazil has taken to trade policy even if it does not always align with demands from the business community. Where Brazil has a competitive advantage despite trade distortions in place, Itamaraty remains quiet. When Brazilian producer competitiveness is being undermined, the response is forceful, including pointed use of the WTO dispute resolution mechanisms to attack core elements of US and EU agricultural policy. The regional level creates a different set of drivers, with heavy emphasis within Mercosur and the wider UNASUL space being placed on access to markets for value-added products. Here the game is slightly trickier for Itamaraty, with diplomats having to walk a delicate line of absorbing bouts of retaliatory trade measures from countries such as Argentina in order to keep open the longer-run market access demanded by Brazilian manufacturers, as well as some sense of political leadership on a continental level. This line of analysis also helps explain otherwise seemingly contradictory initiatives such as bringing the ostensibly anti-liberal trade Venezuela of Hugo Chávez into the trade bloc Mercosur. Finally, the wider South–South dimension enters as a forward-looking strategy to address the growth limits imposed by the small size of South American markets and the relative difficulty of penetrating protected European and North American markets. Proactive trade and investment engagement with Africa and the Arab world emerges in this context as a low-cost bet on a potentially important market in the future, one which Brazil is better equipped culturally to engage than competitors from the North and China.

6

Brazil Inc.

As Brazilians frequently point out, from 1968–1973 their country experienced the sort of economic surge and staggering GDP growth rates we now associate with China. These boom years were not an accident, but the result of focused government policy designed to precipitate rapid industrialization and transformation away from a rural, agrarian economy towards an urbanized, manufacturing economic model. A stable of state industrial champions were placed at the heart of this policy push, all financed and supported by state-run banks and development institutions. Names well known to the international investment community today – Vale, Petrobras, Embrear, CSN, USIMINAS, EMBRATEL, Embraer, and Eletrobras – were founded by civilian and military governments as part of the developmentalist policy track, designed to push Brazil along to the next developmental stage. Frustrated with Brazil's perceived global economic marginalization, the policy vision from government was that these and other firms would not only generate the manufacturing jobs of a modern economy, but also create the strong industrial base that is a prerequisite for any country with pretensions of being a world power. Simply put, the belief was that if a country is to be a serious international player and exercise real influence on global power structures, it must have major international companies.

The problem with the national industrial and development policies of the 1960s and 1970s was that they remained excessively bound to political prerogatives at the expense of economic sustainability. This directly contributed to the debt crisis of the 1980s and saddled the country with an industrial and manufacturing sector that not only was protected from external competition by high tariff walls, but also was seemingly incapable of offering products that worked and were desired by the public, much less in a cost-effective manner. Seeking to rid Brazil of an inefficient corporatist culture that ensured the country had to struggle with a competitive millstone around its neck, Fernando Collor de Mello initiated a process of sweeping liberalization and privatization, which was continued by Fernando Henrique Cardoso (2007), who explained: 'I was in favor of [privatization] for practical reasons because the state did not have enough money to invest, because the managerial capacity of the state bureaucracy prevents a more lively evolution of the company.' When set in the historical context of state-led development and the importance of government owned and supported firms the privatization process of the early 1990s represented a major shift in thinking about how national development could best be achieved. For the Brazilian left this represented a fire sale of the national patrimony and an abandonment of any pretensions of national industrial development. On the right the concern revolved around national security issues and how *Brasil grandeza* would be achieved if the country's industrial base was foreign-owned.

The challenge, as Cardoso (2007) explains it, was 'how can we offer more possibilities for people using either markets or government, using state regulations to force business to open in a certain way'. National development remained the priority, but in a policy direction that would be sustained through the Dilma administration the state moved from the position of prime instigator and director of firm growth to a supporting role, albeit one that waxed and waned depending on the financial strength and ideological proclivities of the government in office. More importantly, there was a sustained awareness in both the PSDB and PT presidencies that autarchy was no longer an option for Brazil. Capital, knowledge and technology needed to be brought in to revitalize the national productive system. Firms also needed to seek international opportunities not only for trade, but also for investment if the Brazilian economy was to follow a path towards the sort of integrated development found in Europe and North America. In this context government and foreign policy had an important role to play not only as financier through institutions such as the BNDES, but also as door opener and match maker for businesses contemplating outward expansion of their activities.

As this chapter will explain, the concerns of both the left and right were misplaced. Through a clever *jeitinho*, privatization divested the Brazilian state of direct ownership, but not control over many important national industrial champions. A complex web of interlinked corporate boards as well as conglomerate-style holdings of privatized company shares by public sector pension funds ensured that the inflow of capital was not matched by a total loss of control. Buttressing this

shift in ownership structures were quiet changes in the operating practices of government financial institutions such as the BNDES to give
the Brazilian government an additional element of control through the
ability to approve or withhold financing in the country's notoriously
tight credit market. An interesting quirk that would come to mark
the country's globally oriented companies was thus introduced to the
Brazilian capitalist model and the historical tradition of the developmentalist government policy. Profit remained the driving motivator for
firms, but with the time horizon for optimal return stretched beyond the
quarterly dictates of Wall Street to a longer-term approach to return on
investment consonant with the developmental policy ambitions of the
Brazilian government.

In an echo of Itamaraty's role in the formulation of economic policy
during the first developmentalist period in the 1940s and 1950s
(Sikkink, 1991: 129–132), the privatization of state-owned enterprises
and the opening of the Brazilian economy had an intimate interplay
with the country's foreign policy. As Dilma's second foreign minister,
Luiz Alberto Figueiredo told the Senate Foreign Affairs and Defense
Committee in February of 2014, 'I will seek to maximize the role of
foreign policy as a tool for national development.' He continued on to
explain exactly why Itamaraty was interested in the internationalization
of the Brazilian economy as part of a pro-development foreign policy:
'Economic diplomacy is absolutely crucial at this stage of national
development, in which, among other challenges, we have to raise our
economy's level of international competitiveness, its level of integration
into international markets to create new employment and income for
Brazilians.' The shift revealed by Figueiredo's testimony and one that
will be traced through this chapter is a move away from the approach
to internationalization under the classical developmentalist policies pre-
dating the military government and still being considered as essential
in the early 1990s (IPRI, 1993: 49). Pre-existing policies focused on
market diversification for exports and imports to avoid vulnerabilities
created by a sole or limited commercial relationship for needed technology, capital goods, and product markets (Hirschman, 1945). The
gradual change that began to emerge clearly at the end of the Cardoso
presidency was to increasingly encourage an expansion of Brazilian FDI
abroad rather than a simple boosting of trade flows. While emerging
markets were clearly on the radar of firms expanding outwards, the Lula
presidency provided a major level of political and financial assistance by
building on regulatory changes initiated in 2000 and 2001.

A clear foreign policy element was thus revealed inside Brazil's neo-
developmentalist model, with actions from Itamaraty, the presidency

and other state agencies like the BNDES working with the country's emerging multinationals to push the economy out into the global sphere, particularly South America and Africa. This is in turn brought expanded influence for Brazilian foreign policy makers throughout the Global South as Brazil became an important source of FDI and economic partnership. Expanded penetration throughout the South also brought an elevated level of economic and political risk for Brazil. The first came through the threat of nationalization and adverse policy decisions by host governments, something particularly evident in Bolivia's 2006 decision to nationalize the natural gas industry. Political risk came not only through the manner in which the Brazilian government might support its capital exporting firms, but also in the conduct of these firms and how it might reflect on the national image factors central to public diplomacy and soft power at the heart of the consensual hegemony approach to contesting the application of global structural power.

The mechanisms through which Brazil Inc. has moved out into the world is complex and variagated, involving not just obvious foreign policy and state financing initiatives, but also quietly integrated cooperation amongst Brazilian firms and trail-blazing by some of the larger former state-owned and private enterprises. To unravel the story this chapter will start with a review of the liberalization of the Brazilian economy in the 1990s before turning to shifts in FDI patterns of the Lula era. These elements then set the stage for an exploration of how foreign policy iniatives have supported the internationalization of the Brazilian economy as a strategy for advancing national development and how the outward expansion of the economy has supported growth of Brazil's influence in South America, Africa and beyond.

Liberalizing and internationalizing

While the bulk of the work on privatization was undertaken during the Cardoso presidency, the economic divestment by the Brazilian state initiated by Collor resulted in a seismic shift in the corporate composition of Brazil and the rise of a series of major enterprises and industrial sectors that began to look not only for wider international opportunities, but also to insulate their balance sheets from domestic financial instability by moving into foreign markets (Fleury and Fleury, 2011: chapter seven). During the period from 1991 to 1998 eighty-six state-owned enterprises were partially or completely privatized, raising a total of USD 54.296 billion (Manzetti, 1999: 169–172). Collor set the scene, but it is the backstory to Cardoso's real plan economic stabilization policies that is particularly important for the larger argument in this chapter. For

Cardoso privatization was not just about quickly raising money to pay down the national debt. A more important element was to modernize the Brazilian economy, bringing much needed new managerial practices and production techniques (Amann, 1999; Bonelli, 1999). This upgrading of the practice of business in Brazil was matched by a vision that encompassed a democratization of ownership in the sense that ordinary citizens now had a stake in the companies either through their own personal share purchases or through the holdings of their pension funds. The point the Vale and Petrobras examples outlined here reinforce is that the large privatized Brazilian multinational corporations and their non-state counterparts are competitive, aggressive companies seeking entry into as many profitable markets and arrangements as possible.

The transformation of equity holdings in Brazil as a result of the privatization process was thus far from a simple off-shoring of corporate ownership. Although constitutional rules initially restricted foreign ownership, loosening of these regulations to allow a complete foreign take over had little real impact. Instead, the equity holdings were taken up by a wide array of Brazilian actors, often with significant international partnership (Manzetti, 1999: 173–179). Further complicating matters was a provision in Brazilian law allowing the collaboration of different entities to create a holding company that then buys equity in another company, which can be yet another holding company. Moreover, these holding companies can encompass a mix of different types of economic actors, sometimes combining pension funds, Brazilian firms and foreign capital within the one holding company. The result is what Sergio Lazzarini (2011) has labelled a 'capitalism of linkages', a pyramidal ownership structure which results in a tight web interconnecting a wide range of actors in the Brazilian economy with seemingly disparate interests, as well as linking them to the state in a manner that gives the government significant input into corporate strategy formulation.

Illustrative of the interconnectedness of the capitalism of linkages is Lazzarini's (2011: 21) mapping of the majority ownership of one of Brazil's most internationalized companies, the mining giant Vale. At the top level two key 'owners' of Vale are identified. One is BNDESPAR, the equity-holding arm of the wholly government-controlled BNDES. The other is a holding company called Valepar, which exists to aggregate together various other holders of Vale stock. At this point the story begins to get complicated. Of the five main equity holders in Valepar only the Japanese firm Mitsui is a standalone shareholder. The other four are holding companies. The government is able to exert some influence over Valepar through its investment via BNDESPAR. Bradesco, one of Brazil's largest banks, is pulled into the mix through the presence of its holding company Bradespar. Another investment firm, Opportunity, has a stake in Valepar through its holding company Eletron. Finally, a series of pension funds control a stake in Valepar through their holding company Litel. Significantly, these pension funds serve major state-controlled enterprises like the oil company Petrobras and the national banks Banco do Brasil and Caixa Econômica. To further complicate matters, holding companies such as Litel, Bradespar and Eletron also have interests in other firms, some of which are themselves holding companies. Just to add an additional layer to the interweaving of public and private economic interests, an important source of project finance for Vale is the BNDES, as well as the state banks that control Eletron, which are in turn run by government appointed executives and board members.

Setting aside the outright theft by government-supporting political parties revealed by the Petrobras corruption scandal that broke during the 2014 presidential election, implicit in the post-Cardoso privatization ownership arrangements is the idea of government influence over business decisions to advance national development policies. Clearly identifying instances where government policy has overruled corporate leadership is difficult to directly identify, although it can be more apparent when the government failed to get its own way (OESP, 2010b). Throughout the Lula era it became clear that state equity holdings and financing were being used to nudge companies in directions consonant with national development policies, the most telling being the use of Petrobras and its control of the sub-salt oil deposits as an engine to drive the petroleum extraction related industries not only by implementing national content requirements for firms exploring the offshore oil and gas fields, but also by pushing Petrobras to prioritize Brazilian suppliers and contractors. While the oil industry proved to be a key site for heavy government pressure on firms to support national development priorities, the overall pattern was one of distinct limitations on government influence dictated by the commercial considerations firms had to honor as publicly listed companies. The result was a degree of tension between policy makers and corporate bosses that reined in some of the worst excesses of political opportunism while still leaving room for use of Brazil Inc. as a foreign policy device.

Perhaps the most direct evidence of the business–government tension can be found in the aftermath of Vale president Roger Agnelli's 2009 decision to lay off workers and cut planned investments when the Global Financial Crisis caused a major drop in company revenues. Lula was incensed and actively sought, unsuccessfully, to pressure Agnelli into reversing the production slowdown. Compounding Lula's ire was Agnelli's decision to have a fleet of Valemax ore-carrying boats built in

China and South Korea rather than Brazil where the costs were higher and the available shipyards too small for the task. It was left to Dilma to exact political retribution after she was inaugurated president in January 2011. Shortly before a March 2011 Vale board of directors meeting Dilma had her finance minister Guido Mantega meet with Brandesco president Lázaro Brandão to discuss Agnelli's future. Brandão appeared amenable to suggestions from Mantega that change was needed at Vale and the next board meeting saw Agnelli removed from his post. The point here is that while Brazilian government attempts to push questionable business decisions can be defied, there can also be consequences. Nevertheless, the public–private mix of shareholdings in firms like Vale means that even those consequences need to contain an element of economic rationality that can be explained to shareholders and that meets the requirements for listing on major international stock exchanges, which is why Agnelli was able to resist two years of efforts to remove him from post and Brandão acquiesced in the context of a new government and a need to revisit Vale's leadership in a post-resources boom era. Perhaps more telling of the personalized nature of Agnelli's removal is that it did not result in a major redirection of Vale corporate policy to mirror the national development plans of the Dilma government.

The commercial logic applied by Agnelli to move production of the Valemax ore carriers offshore and to cut iron production during the Global Financial Crisis was at other times a useful brake on the Planalto Palace's presidential diplomacy. The most notable example of this was deflection of Hugo Chávez's attempts to supplant Brazilian leadership and absorb Petrobras resources as a device for advancing Venezuela's Bolivarian vision for South America. When Chávez first proposed the idea of a 'South American Energy Ring' natural gas pipeline in 2006 to bind the continent together, Lula was enamoured of the idea and thought that Petrobras should embrace it. The reaction from Petrobras president Sergio Gabrielli was dubious, questioning not only if it made economic sense to invest over USD 20 billion in this venture, but also if there were sufficient gas reserves to actually fill the pipeline. For Lula this resistance was at first maddening because Chávez was simply able to command action by Petroleos de Venezuela S.A. (PDVSA), while the public shareholdings of Petrobras meant that similar political commands could be resisted by Gabrielli. This is not to say the political pressure from Lula failed to bring about Petrobras–PDVSA collaboration, but rather that the commercial prerogative of the Brazilian multinational acted as a brake on poor economic policy and pushed attention to more sustainable areas. In this case the result was a Petrobras–PDVSA memorandum on cooperation and the construction of the Abreu e Lima refinery in Pernambuco, a project which remained economically attractive for Petrobras and developmentally useful for Brazil despite repeated failures by PDVSA to meet its financial commitments to the endeavour (Emerson, 2014).

In the pan-Southern context of South America and Africa, Brazilian firms have been seeking a foothold in new countries because these are markets where profits can be made and have often been overlooked by Northern-based firms. This profit motivation is in some senses coincident with and of assistance to the Brazilian foreign policy motivation of seeking expanded influence and power across the Global South, both as an avenue for national development and as a device for staking a clear claim to a seat at global governance decision making tables. As will be discussed below, this effective coincidence of interests did create some risks for Brazil if the multinationals behaved badly in their host countries and opened an avenue for some external influence on Brazilian policy makers. But these costs paled behind the level of impact and influence that were gained by Brazilian policy makers for minimal economic outlay. Invested capital by the government was instead largely political in nature, particularly with respect to supporting Brazilian firms abroad in the same manner many OECD governments do for their international companies, and helping to open new markets for Brazilian FDI. While there was a definite stick held in reserve, the predominant theme that Brazilian foreign policy makers were consequently able to use with varying effectiveness was one of collaborative growth and solidarity, not reconstruction of hierarchy and new relationships of dependency.

Casting the FDI web

The intricate and interweaving pattern of ownership seen in the Vale case is replicated throughout the Brazilian economy. Indeed, just taking Bradespar as a case leads quickly to another group of holding companies that involve partnerships with energy companies, construction engineering firms and holding companies that operate in Brazil and abroad. Crucial to this network is the role of the state as both financier and equity holder. A central challenge in getting Brazilian firms to internationalize was the intertwined questions of risk management and project financing. In the 1990s and 2000s medium- and long-term capital was difficult to come by in Brazil and, when available, costly. Further impeding internationalization ambitions was the difficulty that Brazilian firms had in drawing on global capital markets, particularly for investments in other developing countries. This meant any internationalization plan was largely going to be funded through internal reserves, resulting in a highly risk-averse approach to international expansion.

The critical shift in regulatory frameworks began towards the end of the Carodoso era, focusing on a change in what the BNDES would be allowed to do. Primary capital financing for BNDES operations comes from a payroll tax, which is then used to underwrite Brazilian firms seeking to establish new operations or expand existing plans. One of the consistent conditionalities of BNDES financing is that funds disbursed by the Bank be spent within Brazil, which is part of a recognition that the institution exists explicitly to advance Brazilian social and economic interests, not those of other countries. In April 2001 the expanded view of what it meant to support Brazilian firms and the importance of internationalization formally made its way into the BNDES's regulatory structure with the pursuit of legal changes allowing the Bank to finance Brazilian FDI abroad.

As Bank officials explained, the broadening of lending activities was initially driven by a group of executives from about 200 firms with major interests in the Argentine economy seeking support for further internationalization (BNDES, 2002). Interest was particularly high as the Argentine economy entered into crisis and entrepreneurs in Brazil clamoured for financing to take advantage of fire sale prices for a round of mergers and acquisitions. The official line from Itamaraty drew on this commercial logic with incoming ambassador to Argentina José Botafogo Gonçalves explaining that while Brazil would not provide financial aid, 'Brazil could provide a response. Not in concessions, but with integration of the productive structures of both countries and Mercosul and with the promotion of trade with third markets.' As he explained, the BNDES would be a critical part of making this happen if the bloc's countries could get the appropriate policies and institutional structures in place to make it happen (Marin, 2002). For its part the BNDES had a clear sense that encouraging the internationalization of Brazilian firms was firmly within its mandate because companies able to compete internationally must, perforce, be strong within Brazil and would thus bring benefits back into the country. The challenge that technicians saw in late 2002 was that not many national firms were ready to make the jump to the global market, leaving the Mercosul and Latin American level as a stepping stone (BNDES, 2002). While not an incorrect reading, this analysis aligned with the inherent conservativeness of the BNDES and only loosely forecast the rapid outward movement that would take place as the commodity boom entered into full swing and Brazil's macroeconomic situation stabilized over Lula's first term.

From 2000–2008, 58.2% of Brazilian firms engaged in internationalization used internal financing and 27% obtained loans on international capital markets (Fleury and Fleury, 2011: 185). Until 2005 the BNDES remained largely silent as a source of financing for outward Brazilian FDI despite the work on establishing further export and FDI credit facilities noted above. Significantly, the 2005 decision to open up BNDES financing for outward FDI was matched by major improvements in Brazil's macroeconomic situation, which in turn led to a liberalization in Brazilian private bank attitudes towards the financing of national companies expanding abroad. Perhaps of equal importance was the crystal clear direction from BNDES president Luciano Coutinho (2008) that the rise and spread of Brazilian multinational corporations had a central role to play in national economic expansion and developmental consolidation. The results of these changes in economic circumstances, state-controlled bank lending policy, and clear policy signalling are striking (see Table 6.1). Flows of Brazilian FDI surged, increasing year-on-year 24.9% in 2006, 83.7% in 2007 and 30.3% in 2008. While the Global Financial Crisis in 2008 brought a retraction in the size of outward flows in 2009, new Brazilian FDI did not stop, with nearly USD 26 billion being invested in other countries, rising to just over USD 65 billion in 2012.

Of course, FDI flows can be driven by transient economic phenomenon. For example, there was a big surge in outward flows in 1999 and 2000 as investors sought to protect their funds from the economic uncertainty that came with the floating of the Brazilian real. Indeed, as the economic situation in Brazil stabilized there was a repatriation of capital as demonstrated by the decline in FDI stocks from 2000 to 2001. What matters for the larger story of Brazil's international economic expansion discussed in this chapter are changes in FDI stocks, or the total value of equity assets held abroad. From 2002 Brazilian FDI stocks steadily increased, going from USD 54.9 billion when Lula was inaugurated in 2002 to USD 79.2 billion in 2005. The BNDES financing changes discussed above had a demonstrable influence on the accumulation of Brazilian FDI stocks even if the Bank provided only a tiny portion of the funds at play – reported export support contracts between 2008 and 2012 totalled USD 12 billion (Hochstetler, 2014: 363), which compares to annual disbursements in the USD 80–90 billion range. Brazilian held FDI stocks jumped 43.7% between 2005 and 2006 to hit USD 113.9 billion, and then kept climbing through the Lula years to reach USD 188.6 billion by the end of his second term and USD 232.8 billion halfway through Dilma's first presidential term.

The nature of Brazilian FDI in the post-2006 era also points to a diversification of interests away from a concentration on natural resource extraction and agricultural production to include the processing of these products. With the exception of 2006 when Vale paid CDN 17 billion

Table 6.1 Brazilian outward FDI (USD millions), 1990–2012

	1990	1995	1999	2000	2001	2002	2003	2004
Outward FLOWS	988.8	4405.1	28578.4	32779.2	22457.3	16590.2	10143.5	18145.8
Outward STOCKS	41044.1	44473.6	49664.5	51946.1	49688.5	54422.8	54891.7	69196.2

	2005	2006	2007	2008	2009	2010	2011	2012
Outward FLOWS	15066.2	18822.2	34584.9	45058.1	25948.5	48506.4	66660.1	65271.8
Outward STOCKS	79259.2	113925.1	139885.9	155668.4	164522.8	188637.3	202586.3	232847.9

Year-on-year percentage change in outward FDI

	2001	2002	2003	2004	2005	2006
Outward FLOWS	-31.5	-26.1	-38.9	78.9	-17.0	24.9
Outward STOCKS	-4.3	9.5	0.9	26.1	14.5	43.7

	2007	2008	2009	2010	2011	2012
Outward FLOWS	83.7	30.3	-42.4	86.9	37.4	-2.1
Outward STOCKS	22.8	11.3	5.7	14.7	7.4	14.9

Source: http://unctadstat.unctad.org

to purchase Canadian nickel mining giant Inco in an all cash deal, natural resource extraction and agriculture make up an unexpectedly small proportion of Brazilian outward equity FDI. Services dominate instead, comprising roughly between 50% and 60% of equity FDI in any given year, followed by industrial investments, which range from 34% to 44% of the total annual outflow. Within these subdivisions several specific sectors stand out. In the industry grouping, FDI in basic metallurgy, transportation equipment manufacturing and foodstuffs emerge as important account lines. These in turn align with some of the larger Brazilian multinationals, particularly firms like Gerdau and CSN (steel production), the complex of automotive parts suppliers that feed into the production chains of Marcopolo (buses), Fiat, Ford, GM and Volkswagen operating in Mercosul, and JBS, a meat packing firm which became one of the world's dominant players in the 2000s with a market-making presence not only in Latin America, but also in such diverse countries as Australia and the US.

Other equity exporting areas point to different elements of the Brazil Inc. machine (see Table 6.2). Investment in infrastructure works jumps from USD 36 million in 2007 to USD 310 million in 2008, USD 452 million in 2009, and then oscillates between USD 145 million and USD 335 million from 2010 to 2012. This aligns with the business practice of many of Brazil's *empreiteiras*, the civil construction/engineering firms that have diversified beyond the Brazilian market to establish a presence throughout the world, but particularly in Latin America and Africa. The

Table 6.2 Brazilian outward equity FDI by sector (USD millions), 2006–2012

	2006	2007	2008	2009	2010	2011	2012
Crop, livestock and mineral extraction	15896	280	815.1	519	2417	839.7	1219.3
Industry	3334	5023	7669.1	2666	10304.7	7865.8	5691.1
Services	4775	6342	8825.7	4646	17506.5	14769.8	6807.7
Total	24005	11645	17310	7831	30228.3	23475.4	13718.3

Brazilian outward equity FDI sector as % of total

	2006	2007	2008	2009	2010	2011	2012
Crop, livestock and mineral extraction	66.2	2.4	4.7	6.6	8.0	3.6	8.9
Industry	13.9	43.1	44.3	34.0	34.1	33.5	41.5
Services	19.9	54.5	51.0	59.3	57.9	62.9	49.6

Source: Banco Central do Brasil

largest of these firms is Odebrecht, a company that takes a long view to engagement in a new market. A key corporate strategy for Odebrecht is long-term investment in a host country, which involves not only the creation of locally staffed national subsidiaries in different countries, but also corporate diversification beyond the engineering activities that may have brought the firm to a country into industries as varied as infrastructure systems management, energy production, food production and distribution, and property development and management.

Linking capitalists abroad

The dense networks of Brazilian corporate ownership captured by Lazzarini's 'capitalism of linkages' had an important impact on the internationalization of Brazilian business. While some firms, such as construction company Odebrecht and Andrade Gutierrez, have a long history of foreign operations, particularly in Angola and Cameroon, there was a certain element of 'follow the leader' to the surge in internationalization seen during the Lula years. A combination of complex ownership structures and the difficulties of financing domestic infrastructure and industrial enterprises meant Brazilian firms and their executives have long experience in the formation of consortiums to dissipate risk and pool financial resources.

At the heart of this process are the giant Brazilian energy and resource companies such as Petrobras, Eletrobras and Vale, all of whom have long-established supplier and sub-contracting relationships within Brazil. Moreover, firms such as Eletrobras have a history of entering into joint bids with other national firms, particularly the *empreiteiras*, for the development of expensive and complex projects such as new hydroelectric plants. One particularly strong example of this process can be found in the expansion of Brazilian FDI in Mozambique, which grew from a series of quiet informal exploratory meetings at the start of the Lula years (interview with Mozambican executive, 2015). While a number of Brazilian construction firms, such as Odebrecht and Andrade Gutierrez, have decades of experience in Africa, little attention had been given to developing market share in Mozambique due to a combination of civil war-induced insecurity in the 1990s and a general shortage of state funds for major infrastructure projects in the 2000s. The turning point came in 2004 when Vale was persuaded to bid for and won an international tender to develop the coal deposits around Moatize in the province of Tete (interview with Mozambican executive, 2015; Peres, 2013). To bring the mine into operation Vale was faced with a series of complicated tasks. First was the issue of physically constructing the mine, resulting in a series of contracts for Odebrecht and later Camargo Correa and Andrade Gutierrez. Second was the challenge of ensuring that there was enough energy in place to run the construction and mining machinery, which resulted in collaboration with Eletrobras. The third major hurdle was training the local workforce in order to meet the 90% Mozambican labour quota set by the resource exploitation contract, which prompted ad hoc collaboration with the Brazilian state workplace skills training programme SENAI to establish a technical skills transfer development project to support Vale's investment.

The significant point about Vale's market opening activities for the larger story of Brazil Inc. is that the firms that followed to provide services for the mine's development are now striking out in new directions. In an account that is emblematic of the activities of the *empreiteiras* in Angola, Odebrecht has looked beyond the work building the Moatize mine, collaborating with the government in Maputo to arrange BNDES financing to build a new airport in Nacala, a city in Northern Mozambique. Managers were also drawing on the diversified expertise found in the Odebrecht group conglomerate to explore establishment of a vertical production and distribution system for either cassava or chicken, a project which in turn draws on the Brazilian technical assistance programming to boost agricultural productivity in the country through the ProSAVANA project looking at the viability of transplanting practices from the Cerrado to Mozambique (ProSAVANA, 2015). As a further incentive mirrored by the other *empreiteira* conglomorates, Odebrecht officials frame their negotiations with governments by differentiating their approach from Northern firms, emphasizing that the company also delivers something close to development assistance by training a domestic workforce targeted at a long-term presence, not the short-term importing of labour (interview with Odebrecht executive, 2010; interviews with *empreiteira* executives in Luanda, 2014). A similar account was given by a Luanda-based *empreiteira* executive who noted that 'if you form local professionals then you can stop bringing in expatriot labour, which is expensive' (author interview, 2014). The attractiveness of this approach by Brazilian companies was reinforced by Mozambican foreign minister Baloi (author interview, 2013), who remarked of Vale's investments: 'Brazil is investing heavily in Mozambique. By investing I don't just mean what they are doing in coal, financially investing, but also in terms of capacity building. Human capital. You have a lot of trainees, a lot of students in Brazil.' Although seeming idealistic, there is a hard underlying economic logic to these programmes, with specific mention being made by some executives of local labour being trained as part of a strategy to drop costs low enough to be competitive with Chinese infrastructure companies (author inter-view, Luanda, 2014). Other observers in Maputo note that these 'add ons' helped Vale win slightly more generous contract terms than might otherwise have been expected (author interviews, 2015).

For Brazilian trade officials the activities of companies such as Odebrecht are doubly important. In keeping with the shift encouraging outward FDI flows as a driver for sustained Brazilian domestic develop-ment one government official based in Africa observed that the story is 'now more about investment than trade. Trade was ten years ago' (author interview, 2014). Another noted that Africa was the new frontier of growth and opportunity before observing that governments in the region were pushing hard for inward investment flows (author interview, 2015). For the smaller companies the large firms are critical because they provide a 'sheltered environment' within which they can work and build expertise in new market environments. Once in-country the smaller Brazilian firms are in a position to build their own relationships and diversify their business and investment linkages. Adding to this is the entrepreneurial tilt of some Brazilian executives, who also start up new ventures to take advantage of the opportunities they find. Trade officials and diplomats attempt to support business from their country through introductions and advice about domestic political conditions, chang-ing policy frameworks, and the soundness of potential local partners, which are essential for establishing a lasting presence throughout much of Africa. Brazilian executives were clear that their government was not coordinating the activities of national firms (interview with Brazilian executives, 2010), but in-country observers noted that the monitoring of national development strategies forms a particularly important aspect of Itamaraty work and in the mid-2010s was leading Brazilian officials to encourage their country's multinationals and agro-industry combines to look at investing in African agriculture as national governments raised the prospect of heavily curtailing food imports in a bid to restart stag-nant rural economies. Although the outcomes were uncertain as this book went to press, projects such as Odebrecht's Biocom biofuel initia-tive in Angola, the ProSAVANA research project in Mozambique and an Embrapa experimental farm in Ghana all pointed to possible future expansion of investment and activities in these areas.

As one senior diplomat noted (author interview, 2014), the interna-tionalization of the Brazilian economy has also been very important for Brazil's diplomacy. The example offered was the case of Malawi, which already had three major Brazilian firms with local operations present when a move was made to deepen political relations. Consultations with these firms provided an important intelligence-gathering avenue and helped the incoming ambassador and staff identify with whom they should be meeting as well as assisting with developing the inter-personal relationships critial to building tighter diplomatic linkages. In the Angolan case the senior diplomat noted that Odebrecth has far better intelligence about the country and contacts than the foreign ministry, something which they are continuously seeking to strengthen because of its importance to their ongoing business success. These impressions mirrored accounts given by Brazilian diplomats, APEX officials and corporate executives during field research in Luanda in 2013 when it became clear that there was a habit of informal information sharing. While none of this is unusual diplomatic practice, it does stand to underline a certain degree of symbiosis in the Lula era diplomatic push into Africa.

Without financing, the market development intelligence assistance from the Brazilian government would prove relatively meaningless due to the difficulty of obtaining venture capital at affordable rates from global, African or even private Brazilian sources. The Brazilian financial institution that attracts the most attention is the BNDES because of its enormous annual operations and the impression that it lends vast sums to other developing countries. Reality is somewhat different with export financing for goods and services to South America and Africa measuring under 1% of actual disbursements in a typical year (Hochstetler, 2014). Construction company executives highlight the importance of the BNDES for South American projects, but downplay its role in Africa, something which government officials in Mozambique reiterate with their comments about financing from the Bank not being cheap (interviews with Brazilian executives, 2010; interviews with Mozambique government officials, 2013). Other state-owned financial institutions are also quietly at work, notably the Banco do Brasil, which has an operations office in Angola to coordinate its activities in Africa. What really mattered for the accelerated move into Angola in the mid-2000s was agreements on binational finance guarantees: 'First there were government-to-government relations with Africa after which came the availability of Brazilian lines of credit for Aftrican governments. With this Brazilian firms began to arrive in Africa' (interview with Brazilian construction company executive, Luanda, 2014). Where it proved difficult to implement credit guarantees and asset-backed lines of credit, investment flows proved slower. For this the role of government was important as facilitator of financial risk management. At the time of writing, the Banco do Brasil was running its sixth line of credit tranche for Angola valued at approximately USD 5 billion, with most of the funding directed towards infrastructure projects implemented by the *empreiteiras*. Rather than passing funding through the Angolan government with the attendant risks of corruption, the Banco do Brasil makes direct fund transfers to the Brazilian firms. In a procedure more commonly attributed to China, the national government in Luanda repays its loans by shipping crude oil to Petrobras refineries in Brazil for which the oil company then remits payment to the bank. Similar credit guarantee strategies were not feasible for the smaller contracts undertaken by Brazil's small and medium enterprises (SME) in part because these firms were either unaccustomed to the necessary procedures or lacked a corporate culture comfortable with debt-based expansion (Corrêa, 2014). Efforts were made by the Brazilian government to help through programmes such as the export financing instrument PROEX, which was being targeted at projects of up to USD 200 million, including direct investment in addition to trade. For Angolan officials the perception was that these measures implemented during the Lula presidency did help encourage investment from Brazilian SMEs (Tavares, 2014), although there was some question in Luanda about whether many firms could afford the financial and logistical costs of establishing local operations in the 2000s when opportunities were easily available at home (Corrêa, 2014). Similarly, accounts provided by executives and government officials in Maputo indicated that there had been a limited inward move by Brazilian SMEs despite the desires of the governments in both countries.

This sort of international market penetration by Brazilian firms is not unique to the South. Chances are that if you are having a beer and burger in North America or Western Europe, the meat will have been processed by the Brazilian multinational JBS, the largest food processing firm in the world with operations in 150 countries, and your beer brewed by one of the offshoots of InBev, the world's largest beer producer and owner of Budweiser maker Anheuser-Busch. If you are having this meal in a hub airport waiting for your connection to a smaller centre you will likely be flying out on a regional jet built by the Brazilian aircraft manufacturer Embraer. The cement used to build the airport may have come from a local subsidiary of São Paulo-based Votorantim and the structural steel from a steel company such as Gerdau or CSN. If you have the time to freshen up before getting on your plane, the tiles in the bathroom might might come from the ceramic company Eliane and the cosmetic products you use might be of the Natura brand.

Where the penetration of Northern markets by Brazilian firms differs from similar activities in the South is the supporting role of the government. Service and manufacturing firms have long looked to North America and Western Europe as valuable markets, something which was reflected in the tenor of foreign policy during the Cardoso era. As the case of companies like Odebrecht in Angola and Brazil's wider move into Argentina through Mercosul make clear, there was a clear presence of Brazilian firms throughout Africa and Latin America during the Cardoso years. The point was that it was left quietly understated and received limited support from a government that was struggling to stabilize Brazil's teetering macroeconomic situation (Rocha, 2002). It was during the Lula presidency that an explicit and very public political decision was made that market expansion might also be fruitfully pursued in the South, particularly in neighbouring South America as well as Africa. Government efforts were consequently devoted to encouraging Brazilian FDI in neighbouring countries, particularly by large state influenced firms such as Petrobras. The possibilities of Brazilian FDI were also becoming very apparent to the leaders of other South American nations even before the transition from Cardoso to Lula. Peruvian president Alejandro Toledo wasted little time looking for an expanded Brazilian presence in his country, using a meeting during Lula's inauguration in 2003 as an opportunity to ask for a revitalization of the bilateral economic relationship with a particular focus on investment (Amorim, 2013: 123–127).

For his part Lula was quick to get the internationalization ball rolling, making close to USD 3 billion of BNDES financing available by May 2003. While boosting exports was certainly part of this plan, the impacted industries pointed directly to a rise in Brazilian FDI. A large part of the plan was to help the *empreiteiras* win contracts for infrastructure projects throughout South America (Santos, 2003). Smaller scale, but still highly symbolic acts early in Lula's first term included pardoning USD 52 million of debt owed by Bolivia while simultaneously opening a USD 600 million credit line for the development of Bolivian infrastructure (BBC, 2004), a country that had billions of dollars in Petrobras FDI and was a major energy supplier for Brazil. The significance of these changes was not lost on Brazil's neighbours. For example, a 2005 visit to Ecuador by Brazil's foreign minister prompted an Ecuadorian diplomat to tell the Quito newspaper *El Comercio* that 'Brazil wants to raise its area of influence in the region.' The proposition that Ecuador played an important part in Brazilian ambitions of greater sway on the continent's Pacific coast was emphasized by analysts who highlighted the extent to which Brazilian investment was rising in their country and the potential that the growing relationship had for reducing Us Influence.

The South American FDI figures in Table 6.3 support the idea that Brazil consciously worked to boost its corporate presence throughout the continent, albeit in a manner that reinforced existing strong economic relationships and reflected perceptions of political stability.

Table 6.3 Brazilian FDI flows to South America (USD millions), 2006–2012

	2006	2007	2008	2009	2010	2011	2012
Argentina	1,317	528	620	191	530	1,159	618
Bolivia	3	4	3	12	20.8	5.8	15.3
Chile	41	689	547.3	55	897.6	87.5	1066.3
Colombia	0	0	172.73	18	39	212.7	322.9
Ecuador	4	1	0	0	12.4	2.2	2.5
Peru	27	14	25.5	158	105.3	60	67.4
Uruguay	233	229	482.78	77	184.2	227.8	250.4
Venezuela	0	73	183	1	153	10.1	10.8

Source: Banco Central do Brasil.

Within Mercosur Uruguay consistently received substantial levels of FDI, generally around the USD 225 million mark, but with a spike to USD 483 million in 2008 before falling due to the Global Financial Crisis. The picture in Argentina is more variegated, reflecting not only perceptions of the security of the funds invested in the wake of successive nationalization and appropriation decisions by the Cristina Kirchner government, but also the impact of persistent trade conflicts between the two countries. Indeed, by 2012 concerns over government policy in the mineral and petrochemical sectors were having a negative impact on Petrobras and Vale investment decisions in Argentina that could not be overcome by direct presidential pressure. By 2013 Vale had made one very high profile decision, cancelling its 6 billion Rio Colorado project in Argentina. Flows to Chile, Colombia and Peru find a more conventional grounding in FDI decision making as firms sought to expand into these markets to take advantage not only of the growth prospects brought on by economic and political stability, but also the space for access to new export markets through their respective trade agreements.

Where the immediate economic prospects did not appear as obvious for Brazilian firms, government action helped to prepare the ground for new investments. One avenue that proved remarkably effective during the Lula years was the tying of presidential visits to trade missions. Central to this was the popularity of Lula throughout the Global South and his ability to open doors and smooth regulatory barriers for Brazilian FDI. Classified US diplomatic cables leaked through the Wikileak Cablegate affair make direct mention of the success Brazilian construction firms were having in winning Venezuelan infrastructure contracts (Wikileaks, 2006), a process that was assisted by the practice of Lula and Chavez regularly meeting 'mano-a-mano in Portuñol' to address thorny issues in the bilateral relationship. For Brazilian firms this meant ensuring they were paid for the work completed, something that was not always easy for international enterprises from other countries operating in Venezuela. The value of Lula as interlocutor in market opening and FDI facilitation became clear in 2013 when the newspaper *Folha de São Paulo* broke the story that about half of the former president's international trips since leaving office had been funded by the *empreiteiras*, with an emphasis on travels to Latin American and African countries with substantial infrastructure needs. For their part business and government officials in Africa were clear in a series of separate author interviews during 2012–2014 that Lula had a powerful ability to open doors for Brazilian economic interests and gain access to strategic planners in the continent's emerging markets.

Risk and retaliation

This surge in Brazilian FDI throughout Latin America did not come without significant risks for Brazilian foreign policy as well as leading Brazilian firms. One of the complaints which began to surface from about 2005 was that Brazil was taking on something of an imperial role in the region as its firms bought up local assets, set up production processes, and took leading roles in national economies (Deo, 2012; Flynn, 2007). Speaking in the Mozambican context in late 2012, where Vale suffered major public relations failures over its poor handling of resettlements in Tete, Lula explicitly warned Brazilian companies not to make any 'mega errors' and thus harm the image of Brazil (macua.blogs. com, 2012). For their part Brazilian firms were fully aware that support from Itamaraty would likely only come in extreme circumstances such as the 2006 gas nationalization in Bolivia. One Vale Mozambique noted that he had yet to see the embassy provide the sort of practical backing with business difficulties sometimes seen from countries such as France or the US: 'they are not going to go against the government here for Vale. I think we have never reached a situation of high risk of, say, hardball, where we would need them. I don't think they want to get exposed' (author interview, 2015). Implicit in Lula's warning were the lessons his government learned in the South American context where it not only had to act forcefully to defend Brazilian business interests, but also had to deal with the political repercussions of popular perceptions that Brazilian firms were engaged in malfeasance and callousness. In short, there was a clear awareness on both the part of the government and the Brazilian firms that FDI brought new avenues of influence and pressure that were distanced from direct governmental accountability, but which also carried wider risks that required explicit political backing (interviews with Brazilian executives in Angola and Mozambique, 2013/2014; interview with World Bank officials, 2013).

This tight interconnection between expanded influence, new avenues of economic growth, and widened political risk for the Brazilian foreign policy nexus became exceptionally clear in 2006 when Bolivian president Evo Morales summarily nationalized the country's natural gas industry and used the military to seize Petrobras assets. Reaction in Brazil was furious, particularly given the Lula government's understanding that Morales would negotiate a path to more national control of gas production. Complicating matters for Lula was the timing, coming shortly before the launch of his presidential reelection campaign. When combined with public outrage in Brazil over what many commentators branded a theft of their property and a violation of Brazilian sovereignty, a harsh and aggressive diplomatic reaction might have been expected. Lula's response was instead outwardly measured and focused on negotiation, an approach he could publicly take because the dense network of state-capital linkages in Brazil made other, distanced avenues of pressure possible (interviews with Brazilian diplomats, 2010). Although state-controlled, Petrobras was positioned as something of an independent economic actor and allowed to put enormous pressure on the Bolivian government, which Lula and his team attempted to 'manage' for Morales. Petrobras met initial blockages in contract renegotiations with a consultation of its accounts receivables, which showed Bolivia to be heavily in arrears on its diesel supply account. The message was blunt if unspoken: negotiate in good faith and quickly or risk having the diesel pumps turned off and a consequent paralysis of transportation in Bolivia (EFE, 2006; Lima, 2006). Brazil's government stepped into this context as a restraining force helping Bolivia by attempting to calm Petrobras, a dual role which increased Brasília's influence in La Paz while simultaneously creating space to pressure for a protection on Brazilian economic interests.

Direct pressure on Bolivian transportation networks through threats to cut off diesel supplies were followed up by Petrobras management in October 2006 with the classic multinational corporation strategy of threatening withdrawal from a difficult investment site after large natural gas reserves were discovered off the coast of Brazil. Rumors that Bolivia might seize further assets were met with an observation from Amorim that Petrobras was in a position where it might be able to withdraw entirely from the country, a possibility that had the added credibility of some uncertainty around Lula's cabinet table about what exactly Petrobras executives had planned. Tempers calmed with the resignation later that year of Bolivian Energy Minister Andres Soliz

(Reuters, 2006b), opening a space for a more official governmental response from Brazil. In this vein Brazilian Energy Minister Silas Rondeau bluntly noted that 'If relationships between our countries... do not improve it will not be Brazil's fault but the attitude of the other side' (Bianconi, 2006). These direct public statements were backed with shuttle diplomacy by close Lula political advisors Marco Aurélio Garcia and José Dirceu, resulting in an eventual settlement that former Bolivian president Carlos Mesa (2011: 30) characterized as having changed little of substance other than an important, but still relatively small increase in tax revenue from natural gas exploitation.

Similar direct pressure in support of Brazilian corporate and national developmental interests could be seen in relations with Ecuador in 2008. After failing to resolve an extended dispute with construction firm Odebrecht, Ecuadorian president Rafael Correa announced that his country would not repay the underlying BNDES loan and expelled company officials from the country. The Brazilian foreign minister Celso Amorim was quick to point out that Ecuador must pay its debts, adding 'I don't want to say anything that might sound like a threat. No threat is necessary' (EFE, 2008). This illustrates the extent to which the successful internationalization of Brazilian firms was seen as intrinsic to Brazil's national development model as well as the extent to which government processes had been aligned to support outward FDI. Correa and his advisors were caught by surprise as they had assumed there would be a separation between the affairs of a private Brazilian company and the Brazilian state (EFE, 2008). Rather than easing the pressure, Brazil increased it, pointing out that Ecuador's loan was secured through the ALADI Reciprocal Credit Convention, which allowed member countries to engage in direct currency exchanges to bring risk premiums down from an open-market 12% to 2%. Directly alluding to the BNDES's role as catalytic infrastructure financier, Amorim sought to collectivize continental pressure on Ecuador and the other Bolivarian countries that, following Correa's lead, were talking of auditing their debts: 'The non-payment of loans will have an impact on the granting of new loans for all other countries. This is not a threat. It is a fact' (Chade 2008). By 2012 matters were completely settled, Odebrecht was again working in Ecuador, and a pragmatic approach to bilateral relations had returned. In particular, the importance of Brazil to development in Ecuador became a matter for public comment, with the vice-minister of foreign affairs Arízaga observing in 2015 that 'Brazil has resources, has a development bank and has large companies that know Latin America and that has experience in important strategic projects. So with them we work very well.'

Yet, despite the increased risks to the Brazilian economy that came with expanded international investment patterns and the potential blowback that government actions could have on economic interests and vice versa, the general tenor of foreign policy retained a strong supporting role for the country's companies. Of particular note was the expansion of Brazilian development assistance provision, which the government framed as South–South Technical Cooperation (SSC) to avoid the connotations of colonialism and domination embedded in the language of foreign aid (Robledo, 2015). The clear emphasis on being responsive rather than prescriptive to requests combined with a focus on sharing expertise not resources, to create a sense Brazil was engaged in a partnership for development, which was reinforced by the explicitly consultative approach taken to pan-Southern relations. On a soft power level the impact was palpable with interview subjects from Latin America and Africa consistently expressing an appreciation that the pattern of relations with Brazil was different than with other countries even if there was a clear awareness that the Brazilian government would ultimately place its own priorities first.

The good relations created by the expansion of SSC provision during the Lula years mattered for business, particularly when disputes arose. A case in point was the reaction of Guinean president Alpha Conde to his government's decision to cancel the joint Vale/BSGR concession to develop two iron ore deposits on the grounds of corrupt business practices. While the Israeli firm BSGR was castigated, Conde actively sought the continued presence of the Brazilian company, noting: 'Vale was not involved in the corruption or aware of it and we strongly hope that Vale will participate' (Nebehay, 2014). While Conde's statements about Vale do need to be taken at face value, comments about the general conduct of Brazilian firms operating in other parts of Africa are instructive. Suggestions of direct corruption were avoided, but several interviewees were clear that African partners were essential for a successful investment and that these individuals brought other 'goods' than a direct managerial capacity to advance the business (interviews with Brazilian executives in Africa, 2014). As noted above, assistance in finding the right contacts and building relationships with the right actors in propitious policy contexts was an important service provided by the Brazilian market. When the political landscape shifted the positive relations and public impression of Brazil created by its foreign policy and SSC actions proved equally important in at least keeping doors open even if the situation could not be outright rescued.

Conclusion

The complex interplay of economic and political factors behind governmental support of Brazilian FDI was neatly captured by a Bolivian economist: 'On one hand, companies are eager to win and do not want to lose their investors' money. Then there is the Foreign Ministry, which always takes a hardline institutional response. Finally, there is the presidential diplomacy of Lula and his advisor, who use political and ideological lines to communicate with neighbors' (Charleaux, 2008). Three factors mutually reinforced each other in the internationalization of Brazilian business. First, firms wanted to increase profitability and insulate themselves from shocks that might come if they were entirely dependent on their home market. But, to spread abroad they needed access, financing and political support in the event of disputes. This feeds the second element, which is the Brazilian government's desire to expand and promote national economic development. Significantly, both the centre-right presidencies of Collor and Cardoso, as well as the centre-left presidencies of Lula and Dilma clearly recognized that national economic success requires a strong stable of international corporate champions. Thus, as the macro-economic situation in Brazil solidified, fungible state support for Brazilian outward FDI increased, leading to the post-2005 surge in flows and the rising presence of Brazilian firms in the emerging markets of the Global South. The third factor enters into play at this point, which is the desire in the foreign policy establishment to increase Brazil's international influence without having to engage in politically or economically risky endeavours. Expanded FDI also provided a new avenue of pressure on potential or actual Southern partners, with the prospect of new or expanded investments leveraged through the capitalism of linkages forming attractive bait to retain the interest of leaders in South America and Africa. While the FDI flows coming from Brazil Inc. were certainly not overwhelming, they formed an important strut in the larger foreign policy project allowing Brazil to claim it was making an important contribution to pan-Southern development, which in turn formed a key building block of Brasília's claim it should have direct impact on global affairs at a structural level.

7

Security policy

As former Brazilian ambassador to Washington Rubens Barbosa succinctly put it in 2007, 'Security is not an item on the agenda in South America... The problem here in the region is poverty... Security is an agenda performed by the US' (Barbosa, 2007). When examined through the frame of mainstream international relations theory Brazil sits in a remarkably luxurious security situation. Although there are petty bureaucratic squabbles with the neighbours from time to time, there is no argument about the demarcation of national borders. Rio Branco's success in settling an end to the last disputed frontier in 1904 largely removed the need for Brazilian military planners to worry about a land-based armed invasion. Indeed, the logistical difficulties of engaging in combat along Brazil's Amazonian boundaries have combined with the relatively weak military capacity of most bordering countries to make the risk of war close to zero. Even with respect to Argentina, with whom Brazil had a long-standing strategic contest, distrust was always more a case of rhetorical bluster than concrete action, although it drove significant expenditure by the military on equipment such as Leopard tanks.

The already high level of intra-continental security is magnified by Brazil's geostrategic location in the South Atlantic, far from the main axes of conflict in the North Atlantic and Middle East. Security born of this geographic remove from global hotspots has historically been amplified by the Monroe Doctrine, which Rio Branco embraced as a shield at the start of the twentieth century to keep potentially marauding European powers away from his country's shores (Burns, 1966). External invasion has consequently also been a very remote possibility, further reducing pressures on the traditional security front. Even when it comes to worries about spillover effects of regional security issues Brazil has had relatively little to worry about. While there has been a sparse handful of serious conflicts in South America over the last century, they have either been isolated events that neither party really wanted to pursue – the War of the Chaco between Bolivia and Paraguay (Farcau, 1996) and the Ecuador–Peru border conflict (Herz and Nogueira, 2002) – or internal conflicts such as in Colombia with the FARC and ELN, and in Peru with the Sendero Luminoso. For Brazil the most threatening events were rebel actions in the Andes, but even here the risk was from transnational criminality, not military invasion. With the Ecuador–Peru conflict finally settled in 1998 Brazil consequently has had very little to worry about in terms of regional peace maintenance.

With no real external military threats of its own and an absence of regional conflagrations to bring unwanted international attention and intervention to South America, Brazilian policy planners have been left free to take a more expansive approach to thinking through how security issues might be used to advance national development and foreign policy priorities. As this chapter will explain in the first section, Brazil is the dominant military actor in South America, which in itself brings an added element of security and opens new space for leadership. The next section will look at how this freedom to manoeuver has been worked into national defence and security policy, allowing these ostensibly military fields of public policy to become new vectors for pursuing national development as well as the regional and South–South leadership central to the larger foreign policy priority of reframing the nature and application of structural power. Discussion of security relations with South America, Africa and the US will highlight the persistence of a geopolitical approach to strategic thinking concentrated on maximizing national autonomy and excluding foreign powers from as wide a space as possible around Brazil.

One aspect yet to be thoroughly investigated by scholars is the importance of civilian control of the military. The armed forces answer to civilian ministers who set the policy and give direction to the different branches of the military. More significantly for this book, defence policy is a subset of foreign policy, which in turn requires significant consultation and coordination between the two ministries. While how this operates in practice is still being sorted out, something which is alluded to further in chapter ten on bilateral relations with the US, the extent to which defence policy advanced foreign policy goals and ambitions in South America, the South Atlantic and globally will emerge as a central theme in this chapter. The tight interconnection is itself perhaps one reason why Dilma decided that Celso Amorim would by an appropriate figure to serve as Defence minister for much of her first term.

Defence and security policy in the Brazilian context is about much more than simply defending the national territory. Elements aimed at expanding geopolitical policy influence and advancing national development priorities also stand as central objectives in the policy space. In keeping with the logic of consensual hegemony the quirk in Brazil's approach to regional and South–South security questions has been to pursue and establish a measure of leadership without expending much in the way concrete resources or taking the risk of actively being seen to pursue a preeminent role in coordinated military matters. Ideas and acculturation consequently emerge as particularly important to the Brazilian security project. Although there is meaningful expenditure through training initiatives for other countries, the major avenue of engagement is through the collectivization of Brazil's vision for something vaguely like a security community, perhaps more accurately a 'security identity' not only in South America, but also the South Atlantic, which obviates the need for European or North American intervention. Indeed, with trade relations sometimes strained by competing political priorities in South America or logistical realities in Africa, engagement in the security field quietly emerged during Dilma's presidency as a prime space for linking other countries into the Brazilian vision for global structural reform by feeding a growing sense of regional defence cooperation and independence.

The strategic context

The Brazilian case poses a bit of a challenge for analysts following the structural realist tradition of counting airplanes, ships and troops or measuring other indicators of concrete military capacity (Villa and Weiffen, 2014). In a South American context the proportion of the national economy Brazil devotes to defence spending is commensurate to neighbouring countries at around 1.5% of GDP, which still leaves it lagging significantly behind the 2.2% of Chile, 3.4% of Colombia and 2.7% of Ecuador (Table 7.1). Similar disjunctures are found if we look at the percentage of government expenditure devoted to the military. With a 2014 rate of 3.4% of budgeted spending, down from a high of 5.0% at the end of the Cardoso era, Brazil ranks as one of the most parsimonious regional spenders in proportional terms (Table 7.2). What these numbers obscure is the wide difference in actual nominal spend, which sees Brazil dwarf its neighbouring countries in terms of the total share of defence spending in South America by regularly accounting for at least 52% of the regional total. By comparison Colombia, which has a long-standing serious internal military conflict, sits in second place at 18% (Table 7.3).

While Brazil may dominate in scale and military scope on a sub-regional level, this preeminence is not reflected on the global stage.

Table 7.1 Military expenditure by country as % of GDP, 2000–2014

	2000	2002	2004	2006	2008	2010	2012	2014
Argentina	1.1%	1.1%	1.0%	0.9%	0.8%	0.9%	1.0%	1.0%
Bolivia	2.1%	2.0%	1.9%	1.6%	2.0%	1.7%	1.5%	1.4%
Brazil	1.8%	1.9%	1.5%	1.5%	1.5%	1.6%	1.5%	1.4%
Chile	2.7%	2.5%	2.5%	2.4%	2.5%	2.2%	2.1%	2.0%
Colombia	3.0%	3.4%	3.5%	3.3%	3.7%	3.6%	3.2%	3.4%
Ecuador	1.5%	1.8%	1.9%	2.0%	2.7%	3.1%	2.8%	2.7%
Guyana	1.8%	2.3%	2.8%	2.1%	2.6%	1.4%	1.2%	1.2%
Paraguay	1.4%	1.2%	1.1%	1.1%	1.0%	1.1%	1.3%	1.5%
Peru	1.7%	1.5%	1.3%	1.3%	1.1%	1.3%	1.2%	1.4%
Uruguay	2.5%	2.5%	2.1%	2.1%	2.0%	2.0%	1.8%	1.7%
Venezuela	1.5%	1.2%	1.3%	1.6%	1.4%	0.9%	1.3%	1.1%

Source: SIPRI Military Expenditure Database 2015, http://milexdata.sipri.org

Table 7.2 Military expenditure by country as % of government spending, 2000–2014

	2000	2002	2004	2006	2008	2010	2012	2014
Argentina	4.1%	2.8%	3.0%	2.8%	2.5%	2.4%	2.2%	2.0%
Bolivia	7.1%	6.1%	6.0%	5.3%	5.6%	5.3%	4.1%	3.7%
Brazil	5.0%	4.9%	4.1%	4.0%	3.9%	4.0%	3.7%	3.4%
Chile	11.7%	10.9%	12.1%	12.9%	11.7%	9.1%	8.7%	8.2%
Colombia	11.5%	12.2%	13.1%	11.6%	13.9%	12.4%	11.2%	11.4%
Ecuador	6.3%	8.3%	9.5%	9.6%	7.6%	8.7%	6.7%	6.3%
Guyana	3.7%	4.6%	5.6%	3.5%	5.1%	4.4%	3.8%	3.7%
Paraguay	7.7%	6.0%	6.5%	5.8%	5.9%	5.7%	5.6%	6.5%
Peru	8.3%	7.9%	7.1%	7.3%	5.8%	6.3%	6.1%	6.3%
Uruguay	8.5%	8.4%	7.1%	7.1%	6.8%	6.4%	5.8%	5.0%
Venezuela	5.4%	3.7%	4.0%	4.2%	3.9%	2.7%	3.3%	2.5%

Source: SIPRI Military Expenditure Database 2015, http://milexdata.sipri.org

Despite having the seventh largest economy in the world and ample natural resources, aggregate rankings of military power in 2015 positioned Brazil in 22nd place (globalfirepower, 2015). While not commensurate with Brazil's economic size or productive capabilities, this ranking is nevertheless significantly ahead of the next Latin American country – Mexico in 31st spot – and the closest South American country – Chile in 43rd place, four spots ahead of Argentina in 47th. That Brazil lags behind other emerging market countries such as Turkey and Indonesia is not terribly surprising if we focus on the regional security environment, which is particularly notable for the lack of ongoing conflicts or

Table 7.3 Percentage of South American military expenditure, 2000–2014

	2000	2002	2004	2006	2008	2010	2012	2014
Argentina	5.1	3.9	4.3	4.0	4.6	5.4	6.7	8.5
Bolivia	0.6	0.6	0.7	0.6	0.7	0.5	0.5	0.6
Brazil	58.7	62.7	55.0	52.9	53.0	57.5	54.7	52.0
Chile	7.8	7.2	9.1	9.5	8.8	7.7	7.8	7.7
Colombia	14.2	14.9	17.7	16.3	17.9	16.7	16.0	18.2
Ecuador	1.4	1.6	2.1	2.3	3.2	3.3	3.3	3.4
Guyana	0.0	0.1	0.1	0.0	0.1	0.0	0.0	0.1
Paraguay	0.5	0.4	0.5	0.4	0.4	0.4	0.5	0.6
Peru	3.5	2.9	3.1	3.2	2.7	3.1	3.2	3.7
Uruguay	2.0	1.7	1.5	1.4	1.3	1.3	1.3	1.2
Venezuela	6.1	4.1	6.0	9.2	7.5	3.8	6.0	4.1

Source: SIPRI Military Expenditure Database 2015, http://milexdata.sipri.org

the potential for sudden flashes of hostility. Moreover, the rankings also mask the latent capacity that Brazil has thanks to its highly developed industrial sector, which is particularly strong in fields such as automotive production and aerospace. Indeed, Brazil is an important exporter of light arms, selling over USD 370 million in 2012 alone (Small Arms Survey, 2015: annex 4.1).

A more interesting story about Brazil's latent military capacity is the extent to which extensive re-equipping plans for the military have been used to bolster existing national firms and drive technology transfer from more technically advanced nations. Revitalization of the military's AS365 Panther K2 helicopters resulted in a deal which saw Airbus Helicopter set up a Brazilian subsidiary Helibras in order to not only complete the mechanical work of the upgrade in-country, but also to undertake the various design stages within Brazil. Similar logic underpinned the decision to award Saab a USD 4.5 billion contact to supply a new generation of fighter jets. While Saab likely secured its defeat of Boeing in the decade-long contest for the contract after the US was caught spying on Brazilian government officials (Soto and Winter, 2013), the common element to both bids was the requirement for a high degree of technology transfer and the importance this held for national development plans. Under the terms of the contract Saab will work with Brazilian firm Embraer, the world's third largest passenger aircraft manufacturer, to develop the first supersonic jet built in Brazil. The resultant technology transfer will add capacity to a company that launched the KC-390 medium-sized twin-engine transport aircraft in 2015 and was already producing and exporting the Super Tucano light fighter plane in addition to a successful range of short- and medium-range passenger jets; by June 2015 Embraer had accumulated a USD 23 billion order backlog in its civil aviation unit alone (Jelmayer, 2015). Similar activities were also taking place on the naval front, most notably the agreement to work with France to develop a fleet of up to 21 submarines by 2047, including six possible nuclear-powered boats (Coelho, 2014), which Naval officers highlighted as one of the most technically advanced industrial undertakings that the military could pursue.

The developmental implications of this approach to kitting out the armed forces are obvious, and parallel the approach to national industrial modernization that partly underpinned the privatization of state firms in the 1990s. Lest there be any doubt, successive national defence strategy documents make the connection between security and development crystal clear. The 2005 National Defense Policy begins by quoting a 1990 United Nations meeting in Tashkent where specialists defined security as meaning that a state is free from the danger of military aggression, political pressure or economic coercion such that it can pursue its own development and progress (Ministério da Defesa, 2005). The 2005 document goes on to note in paragraph 6.9 that 'development in defense industries, including mastery of dual use technology, is fundamental for having a secure and predictable supply of defense materials and services'. This linkage is bluntly reinforced in the 2008 National Defense Strategy: 'National defense strategy is inseparable from national development strategy. Each drives the other' (Ministério da Defesa, 2008: 9). By 2012 the theme had almost become embedded as an article of faith in military thinking, becoming more of an assumed fact instead of the subject of extended discursive justification. A bulleted list is used in the 2012 White Paper on National Defense to simply note that developing the national industrial base with a view to ensuring an autonomous supply of critical technology is a central strategic objective for the military (Ministério da Defesa, 2012: 27).

Conceptualizing geostrategic rings

Where the trio of defence strategy documents released during the PT presidencies become particularly interesting is in the direct linkage they make between the national development possibilities of building a military-industrial complex and the realities of Brazil's geostrategic position. For example, the 2008 National Defense Strategy gets straight to the point, stating that firms in the national military-industrial complex will be encouraged to keep costs down by achieving economies of scale through the opening of export markets, with a particular focus on the possibilities of UNASUL (Ministério da Defesa, 2008: 18). Although the economic dimension of this proposition carries obvious benefits for Brazil, the subtler aspect is the strategic dimension. As briefly outlined in the introduction, Brazilian strategic thinking has long been dominated by a geopolitical model that breaks the world into a series of concentric circles. Brazil sits at the centre, surrounded by the circle of South America, the Western Hemisphere and then the global arena. This finds expression in Brazil's National Defense Policy by defining areas of strategic interest as South America, the South Atlantic, Antarctica and some parts of the Caribbean. The geostrategic game for Brazil is to vary the accepted level of 'influence' or 'interference' in each of these circles, with virtually none being accepted in the Brazilian core, and minimal outside influence in the South American field. Symbolically the continued resonance of this mode of thinking is obvious in the 2008 National Defense Strategy: early PDF versions of the document were watermarked with a concentric circle design, and the high-gloss version available online as this book was being written continued to make frequent use of the graphic motif.

Speaking at a 2011 conference in Rio de Janeiro, former defence minister Nelson Jobim tied together the developmental and strategic components of Brazil's defence policy before pointing to how these areas might interact with foreign policy: 'The [National Defense] Strategy states that defence is "the shield of development." That means that defense cannot exist without development and vice-versa... Defense guarantees protection to the development process from any external influences that can prevent or limit our capacity to reach higher standards of civilization' (Jobim, 2011: 2). Reference was again made to regional economies of scale for Brazil's defence industry before attention was turned to mapping out the strategic dimension of the policy: 'There is also room for increasing exchange, strategic dialogues, and common projects of development, among other things. However, Brazil does not intend to encourage the creation of a collective defense organization in the subcontinent based on NATO's format, not least because of a desire to minimize US influence on the continent. There are no reasons for that in our mid- term scenario' (Jobim, 2011: 6). Underpinning Jobim's remarks was a clear desire to create something approximating a regional security community, but with a format that continued to fall short of the full requisites of such an arrangement (Hurrell, 1998).

In part Jobim was pointing towards an approach to regional security aligning neatly with Brazil's autonomist, non-interventionist foreign policy tradition. Indeed, the same tactics found in Brazilian foreign policy marks defence and security engagement, particular the collectivization of action, the building of new organizations and the propagating of new thinking. The focus on engagement following the principles of consensual hegemony to build regional frameworks which might serve as a protective insulation for Brazil's autonomy was explicit: 'This way, we could have a much more intense influence, not only in our South American surroundings, but also in West Africa and in specific points of the world where vital Brazilian interests are at stake' (Jobim, 2011: 6). In effect, Jobim was mapping out a significant diplomatic push under the guise of security engagement to position defence policy as an important contributor to Brazil's wider foreign policy agenda. In this vein Amorim (2015b) recalls that the itinerary for Lula's relatively big visit to Africa in 2005 was partly dictated by a desire to build strategic relationships with countries on the West of the continent like Ghana, Cameroon, Nigeria and Senegal: 'West Africa, after all, is what is facing [the South Atlantic] and you have to do something with these countries.' It is thus perhaps unsurprising that Dilma chose to replace Jobim in August 2011 with Celso Amorim, who as Lula's foreign minister was one of the central architects of Brazil's engagement with South America and Africa.

While there was little in the way of immediate strategic threats to Brazil when Amorim took office at the Defense Ministry, there were real worries about precedents being set that might later make it easier for external actors to impinge upon the national interest. A specific concern was that the Responsibility to Protect (R2P) doctrine was being manipulated by the US and Europe within the UN as a pretext for Western intervention when policy makers in the US and Europe decided it was to their advantage (Cunliffe and Kenkel, 2016; Stuenkel, 2015). In a point echoed by foreign minister Antonio Patriota, Amorim took this up directly in a paper he wrote for a Brazilian journal, pointing out that initiatives such as no-fly zones brought a danger of mission creep, which could see them also used to promulgate regime change, as was the case in Libya (C. Amorim, 2012). When placed within the context of an international system undergoing a transition from unipolarity to multipolarity, the risk to Brazil from this mission creep was seen as being very real (Patriota, 2012; Varadarajan, 2011). As Amorim continued to observe in his paper, there were a range of new security issues that could cause a repeat of the Libyan experience, ranging from the persistence of narcotrafficking, terrorism and maritime security, to growing tensions in West Africa, as seen in Guinea Bissau and Mali. Strategic policy planners in both the Defense and Foreign ministries worried these issues could be used as pretexts for other actors to take an active role in areas considered central to Brazilian security, raising the possibility of conflict with significantly better equipped armed forces such as those of the US.

The answer Amorim (2012: 345) outlined to the potential new range of strategic risks was a clear turn towards collectivization and new organizational development: 'Cooperation with our neighbors is not a free altruistic gesture. It is a way of consolidating peaceful relations and strengthening our influence, always exercised in a respectful manner.' A guiding imperative behind the turn to cooperation as a foundation for mutual security was a deliberate effort to remove the need for great powers to be present in what Brazil judged to be its own zone of influence. For Brazilian defence policy planners this logically meant direct contributions would have to be made to reducing tensions not just in South America, but also in the wider space of the South Atlantic. The view Amorim (2015b) took of countries such as São Tome was that 'these are aircraft carriers in the middle of the Atlantic. There is no way that Brazil cannot be interested.' The security-pursuing goal, as Amorim noted in an article written after his period as foreign minister, was to bring about a benign global multilaterlism: 'Cooperation, integration and peace: It is with these objectives in mind that Brazil desires to contribute, along with its neighbors, to the solidification of a benign multilateralism' (Amorim, 2011b: 372). Within the South American context this meant working to build the South American Defense Council as the premiere location for discussing and coordinating responses to intracontinental security issues (Battaglino, 2012; Teixeira, 2010). Some success in this respect came with the agreement to launch a staff officer training school within the Council, meaning that the region would be able train its most talented officers in South America rather than sending them to the US (Arízaga, 2015). Stepping out to the next concentric circle in the geostrategic model, Brazil turned to African members of the CPLP as well as the West African states with whom diplomatic relations had been strengthened during the Lula years to advance the idea of the South Atlantic as a zone of peace and security (Abdenur et al., 2014).

Building the geostrategic framework

The Lula era idea of creating some version of a South American security community and transforming the Southern Atlantic into a zone of peace and security, known as ZOPACAS (Zona de Paz e Cooperação do Atlântico Sul) to Brazilian policy makers, was not new. As far back as the early 1980s serious strategic attention was being given to the idea of some kind of security pact in the South Atlantic. The apex of ambitious thinking in this direction was talk about a possible South Atlantic Treaty Organization (SATO), which might parallel NATO. In a prescient 1983 analysis Andrew Hurrell noted that while SATO was never a realistic possibility, something reaffirmed by Amorim nearly three decades later, it contained a geopolitical logic irresistible to security thinkers in the region. The pressure to pursue some sort of localized cooperation approach to maintaining security in the area was dramatically heightened by the Falklands/Malvinas War of 1982, which ultimately pushed Brazil in 1986 to propose and win approval of a UN General Assembly resolution creating ZOPACAS. By 1994 the members agreed to a relatively inexpensive, but highly symbolic step to retrench ZOPACAS by jointly declaring the South Atlantic a nuclear weapon-free zone, which for Brazil was a particularly easy move given its adherence to the Treaty of Tlatelolco as well as its bilateral non-proliferation regime with Argentina (Mallea et al., 2015).

The underlying logic behind these initiatives was a sense that the South Atlantic should be demilitarized, which also offered a convenient way of balancing the decidedly limited force projection capabilities of the littoral countries. Added to this was an understanding that there were real and ongoing security issues requiring active engagement in the South Atlantic, most especially the maintenance of open shipping lanes, the provision of search-and-rescue facilities, and the protection of offshore natural resources such as fisheries and oil fields. Cooperation through the auspices of ZOPACAS was put forward as an effective way to provide these security goods, as well as building the mutual confidence necessary to prevent possible future armed conflagrations. As the Cardoso presidency stated, the problem was that Cold War strategic pressures had been removed, leaving the uninstitutionalized and almost informal ZOPACAS as something of an empty shell, member states nearly abandoned. Building on a 1994 meeting of the grouping in Brasília, the members agreed to shift the focus from peace to four key areas: the environment and environmental monitoring; a nuclear-free South Atlantic; increased interpersonal contact; and the bolstering of economic and commercial ties (Pereira, 2013; Venter, 1996).

Despite the diplomatic reinvigoration of the early 1990s, substantial cooperation across the South Atlantic, often referred to as the Blue Amazon by PT-era policy makers, continued to flag in much the same manner as it had in the Amazon basin. Although vastly different geographically, the fundamental concerns military planners had about Brazilian interests and preventing external imposition and military occupation in the South Atlantic were equally present in the approach to the Amazon. In a sense, the Amazon was seen as an enormous strategic vulnerability because it was a region essential to a number of global environmental goods, but also a space over which the Brazilian state had enormous challenges exercising and asserting sovereignty.

Moreover, many of the factors challenging national security interests in the Amazon crossed national borders, whether it be the knock-on effects of environmental damage or criminal enterprises such as illegal forestry, unlicensed mining or narcotrafficking (Azevedo, 1992).

As was the case in the South Atlantic, a central challenge in the Amazon was keeping track of what was going on and then ensuring the state had the capacity to react. Complicating matters was the transnational nature of some of the key security issues in the Amazon basin, particular narcotrafficking, wildcat mining, illegal forestry and abuses of indigenous populations. One central initiative launched during the Cardoso presidency was the Amazon Vigilance System, SIVAM, which deployed a network of remote sensors, satellite surveillance and an improved rapid response facility (Sennes et al., 2006). This improved monitoring system was reinforced by a strengthening of the Calhe Norte programme, which involved a network of military outposts along the Amazonian frontier to establish a concrete state presence and increase the ability to assert sovereignty over the national territory. Although much was also initially hoped of the 1978 Amazon Cooperation Treaty to help coordinate actions to protect the region, by the mid-1990s differences in the actual capacity of the member states to proactively address shared concerns differed widely (Silva, 2013). As the implementation of the SIVAM system in 2002 highlighted, it was Brazil that had the greatest capacity to not only monitor, but also to act to assert a state presence across the forest.

The decision to tender the SIVAM project in 1995 almost sat in a worst-case scenario for Brazil's geopolitical strategists. Just as it was becoming extremely clear that the Amazon Cooperation Treaty would not allow a sub-regional collectivization of the sovereignty-protecting tasks needed to keep external influences out of the forests the US was increasing its proactive narcotics interdiction efforts across the Andes. The massive expansion of US military assistance to Colombia through the 1999 plan Colombia raised particular concern because it brought a direct presence of US military personnel into the Amazonian region, as well as the establishment of significant bases in Ecuador and Colombia. A central concern was thus keeping the US military presence from increasing in the region and out of Brazilian territory, for which SIVAM was seen as being essential (Ballve, 2003). Indeed, SIVAM represented a potentially powerful tool to reduce the reliance of neighbouring countries on US security capacities because the coverage of the surveillance system significantly overlapped Brazil's borders. Nevertheless, by 2004 extended regional sharing of SIVAM data had yet to become common practice, leading Colombian president Alvaro Uribe to make it a theme of an official visit to Brasília, noting, 'In Colombia we have had a bad experience in the Amazon with a portion destroyed for drug production. To protect the forest it is crucial that we have access to important technology like SIVAM' (Maisonnave, 2004). The catch was that Brazil was looking to sell access to SIVAM data, not include it in a more concretized form of joint action through something like the Amazon Cooperation Treaty (Duailibi, 2003).

While the focus on cost recovery did not mean Brazil withheld information when it was most critical, most notably in 2003 when the system was used to help Peru rescue a group of kidnapped pipeline workers, it was not until 2006 that SIVAM was officially extended to include Peru. The agreement broadening the monitoring system's reach reflected the strategic and developmental logic discussed earlier in this chapter. Rather than merely becoming a consumer of SIVAM intelligence, Peru joined as an integrated contributor, which required the erection of several radar stations as well as the purchase of aircraft – equipment that was in part produced in Brazil. On a strategic level the agreement fitted neatly within the emerging Lula government plan to create a 'defence belt' amongst South American countries to allow the internal management of regional issues. By 2009 this approach had begun to achieve more practical application, with a decision to provide Peru free access to the software needed to use SIVAM data for drug interdiction, and progress negotiating similar agreements with Colombia and French Guiana (Sequeira, 2009). Other gaps in the monitoring of Brazil's land frontiers were addressed through the formation of SISFRON (Sistema Integrado de Monitoramento de Fronteira – Integrated Frontier Monitoring System) to provide an integrated platform for securing Brazil's borders and dealing with transnationalized criminality (C. Barbosa, 2014; Landim, 2015).

At the heart of the SIVAM-related and SISFRON-related projects was a desire to know what was going on within Brazil's physical territory and to create space for coordinating responses with neighbouring countries. Turning to the South Atlantic we find a similar logic, marked most notably by the great care the Brazilian Navy took to launch the idea of the 'Blue Amazon' from 2004. A particular emphasis was placed on charting the limits of Brazil's continental shelf – a programme begun in 1989 – in order to have it recognized by the United Nations' Commission on the Limits of the Continental Shelf. While this proved to be a far from straightforward process requiring multiple resubmissions to the UN, it did allow Brazil to develop a serious expertise in underwater surveying that would prove important for inexpensively maintaining strong relations with countries on the West coast of Africa. As Brazilian naval planners noted in 2010, establishing a clear sense of national continental shelf limits, as well as a capacity to monitor the Southern Atlantic, was an important goal, particularly given the presence of small, but strategically located British islets in the area. The complicating factor was that the pertinent partners in Africa for this enterprise lacked the necessary technical and military capacity to substantially engage in the task (Wiesebron, 2013).

On a technical level Brazil responded to the African capacity challenge by providing Namibia with a technical assistance programme that allowed a comprehensive survey of the country's continental shelf for the UN Commission. A similar request was received from Angola, although in this case decision makers in Brazil elected to charge the oil-rich country for the service. In both instances diplomats in Brazil remarked that the initiative was a success and resulted in significant expansion of the offshore claims bringing attendant increased potential sub-surface resources for each country. Building on this positive experience Brazilian policy planners at the start of Dilma's first presidency were looking at expanding the programme to other West African countries with a view to helping them gain knowledge of and control over their littoral regions, an ambition aligning with Brazil's goals of a regionalized approach to providing security in the Southern Atlantic (Wiesebron, 2013: 116). As one Angolan officer noted, such coordination is becoming of increasing interest as the post-civil war stability allows the government to turn its attention to offshore areas. The attraction of Brazil's ZOPACAS approach is the inclusive, discussion-based contrast it presents to the US approach, which is seen to be predicated as a tutelary command model (author interview, 2014).

The practical challenge facing a collectivized approach to managing the South Atlantic is Brazil's lack of viable partners with the capacity to act. Aside from South Africa, with whom Brazil signed a military cooperation agreement in 2003, most West African countries lack the capacity to provide a clear presence in their territorial waters. To help redress this public security and military capacity development, provisions were included in a succession of agreements with African partners: Guinea-Bissau (2006), Namibia (2009), Nigeria (2010), Senegal (2010), Angola (2010), and Equatorial Guinea (2010). Of all of these agreements the most substantive partnership has been with Namibia, a relationship which dates back to a 1994 accord seeing Brazil provide officer training gratis. As the relationship developed, senior diplomats only half-joked that the Namibian Navy operated in Portuguese, pointing to a deepening of the relationship to include establishment of a Brazilian-staffed training school in Namibia, as well as the transfer of reconditioned and brand new naval vessels to the West African country, resulting in Brazil training 1,897 Namibian officers between 2002 and 2013 (Seabra, 2014: 90). Additional joint projects included Brazilian assistance in the formation of a Namibian Marine Corps Battalion (Aguilar, 2013). Brazilian military academies also began to receive candidates from other countries in the region, including Nigeria, Cape Verde, São Tome and Principe, Gabon and Angola.

Through its increasing network of inter-institutional linkages and training programmes Brazil was achieving a certain degree of success in collectivizing its strategic desire to see the South Atlantic managed by regional countries (Seabra, 2014). The particular gain from this process was a further building of mutual confidence, which could help reduce tensions going forward. For Brazil's larger developmental goals the work on surveying continental shelves and assisting with the deepening of national capacities to patrol coastal waters and international shipping lanes meant a reduced need for intervention by major naval powers such as the US or even Britain (Aguilar, 2013). This, in turn, leaves the territorial continental shelf regions free as natural resources, which can be developed as Brazil sees fit, repeating the national security and development logic seen in the Amazon region. Indeed, the encouragement of interoperability and provision of advanced training in the South Atlantic mirrored the sorts of initiatives the Brazilian armed forces had been taking in South America, including the expansion of its jungle warfare school and an increased rhythm of joint exercises along the national borders. In both cases the intent was not to foment the creation of a large collective defence mechanism along the lines of NATO, but rather to build confidence within each region that the constitutive countries have the capacity and joint capability to locally manage defence and security issues without the need for external intervention by Northern powers. While this proposition has yet to become a concrete reality in all areas, when placed in a longer-running historical context, it is clear that both in South America and the South Atlantic there is an expanded willingness and ability to manage issues that previously saw almost immediate requests for international assistance.

Providing security

Implicit in Brazil's ability to coordinate countries in South America and the South Atlantic for regional security management is an assumption that Brazil itself is able to provide these goods. Indeed, the space to be able to pursue this exclusionary strategy is predicated on confidence from world powers such as the US and latterly China that Brazil is in fact a credible security actor, something which was not necessarily taken as a given in the early 1990s. With a distinctly non-bellicose military tradition, the challenge for Brazil's foreign and defence policy planners was to find a way of providing these assurances without contradicting the historical pattern of staunch non-intervention (Kenkel, 2013b). The Cardoso presidency began with the sudden eruption of one such opportunity, namely the resumption of armed hostilities between Ecuador and Peru in 1995. As Cardoso and his foreign minister Luiz Felipe Lampreia have both noted, quickly and peacefully resolving this dispute was an essential task if Brazil was to give any credibility to the idea that South America did not require a tutelary relationship with the US. Although successful in bringing an amicable settlement to the long-simmering war in 1998, this achievement still did not provide the security credentials needed to underwrite Brazil's global ambitions. Further advancement in this direction would wait for the first Lula presidency and a dramatic upswing in Brazil's peacekeeping activities by taking leadership of the MINUSTAH United Nations force in Haiti.

Although packaged by Brazilian policy makers as a relatively benign form of Chapter VI intervention within the UN framework, the reality was that the 2004 peacekeeping action in Haiti bore closer similarities to the more robust Chapter VII pattern of externally imposed intervention sanctioned by the Security Council (Kenkel, 2013b). Although Brazil's leadership of the MOMEP mission in 1995, leading to the 1998 resolution of the Ecuador–Peru border conflict, did involve formal command over US forces engaged in the process, authority was limited to directing personnel and not the physical machinery such as helicopters provided by the US, leaving Washington with a backdoor veto on operations. The difference that came with the MINUSTAH mission in Haiti was that Brazil found itself with much stronger command and planning functions, including the presence of up to 2,200 Brazilian soldiers on the ground. Working directly with a UNSC mandate the Haitian mission consequently provided Brazil with an opportunity to directly demonstrate its ability to not only manage regional security challenges, but also to take the place of the US as coordinator and credible peace keeper should further hotspots arise in the Americas (Sánchez Nieto, 2012).

The decision by the Lula government to take on the MINUSTAH mission in Haiti was not without some substantial controversy (Kenkel, 2013a; Kenkel, 2010). Some critics pointed out that it was a significant change in Brazil's strategic outlook towards the concept of sovereignty (Herz, 2013), which might create a potentially dangerous precedent. Foreign policy decision makers in the Planalto and Itamaraty Palaces put an additional structural power spin on the decision, claiming it offered Brazil an opportunity to prove its bona fides as a security-providing potential permanent UNSC member. More importantly, Haiti offered an opportunity to showcase what Brazilian policy makers felt was a more comprehensive approach to peacekeeping and building. Speaking to a 2004 joint session of the Senate and Chamber of Deputies Commissions on Foreign Relations and Defense, Amorim explained that Brazil was an appropriate actor to take on the MINUSTAH role because it had no stake in the political and economic contests involving Haiti. Amorim continued on to offer a further justification, seeking to distinguish Brazilian intervention from patterns established by the US and European powers: 'we have a conception, which we now truly have a chance to put into practice, that problems of security such as those that undoubtedly exist in Haiti cannot be resolved in isolation from the political situation, nor in isolation from the humanitarian, social or economic situations' (Amorim, 2004b). With this in mind Amorim was clear to the joint Commission that the Lula government wanted a longer-term commitment to MINUSTAH rather than the initially proposed short mission. The priority was to push back on operation of global power structures, questioning the established understanding of how crises are dealt with in order to open space for a more amplified approach to security that prioritized the developmental priorities of a country like Brazil and not just the stability concerns that had driven interventions in the past.

While Brazil's intervention in Haiti has not been an unqualified success (Braga, 2010; Howland, 2006), it has offered a space to articulate a more holistic approach to peacekeeping that seriously takes in questions related to socio-economic development. Indeed, the MINUSTAH mission stands as a watershed moment implicitly positioning peacekeeping operations as a substantive action in Brazil's wider foreign policy engagement repertoire even if a clear overarching strategy was absent (Cavalcante, 2010). The sorts of attitudinal factors set out in chapter nine on Brazil's relations with the Global South would thus seem to position peacekeeping as an ideal avenue for further work with African partners. The reality has been somewhat different with Brazilian decision makers historically reluctant to undertake African operations because of the frequent need to use coercive force as part of the mission (Kenkel, 2013c). Where the Haitian case becomes important for Brazil's broader agenda of becoming a viable global security provider with a focus on South–South questions is in the proof of concept it offered for the holistic approach to conflict resolution and stabilization outlined by Amorim to Congress. The result was an expansion of Brazil's participation in UN missions during the PT presidencies of Lula and Dilma, taking Brazilian forces to the Democratic Republic of Congo (DRC), Cyprus, Lebanon, Sudan, Liberia and Côte d'Ivoire. With the exception of the Haitian and Lebanese cases, in the majority of these examples the number of participating Brazilian troops was small, typically numbering well under ten. Change has instead come in Brazil's comfort with stronger roles requiring the direction of actual coercive force as a sometimes necessary precursor to the sorts of broader approaches launched in Haiti. Indeed, the changes which Brazilian military leaders were able to bring about in Haiti led to the 2013 appointment of General Carlos Alberto dos Santos Cruz, MINUSTAH force commander from January 2007 to April 2009, to lead the MONUSCO mission in the DRC. Direct commands to engage in proactive military strikes to bring peace to Eastern areas of the DRC were an almost immediate part of Cruz's job, which also afforded space for advancing the sort of security sector reform and capacitation projects Brazilian forces had pursued in Haiti (Silva and Martins, 2014). Similar patterns of direct engagement in formerly contentious areas such as democracy promotion in Africa build on this tradition and can be seen in the pattern of work with countries such as Guinea Bissau (Abdenur and Souza Neto, 2013).

Conclusion

Beyond the obvious aims of preventing invasion and vouchsafing national territorial sovereignty, two general imperatives run through the Brazilian approach to defence and security policy. The first is not particularly surprising when placed in the context of overarching Brazilian government policy over at least the last century. Policy planners on a civilian and military level have devoted considerable effort to leveraging necessary expenditures on the armed forces as an avenue for advancing not only the productive capacity of the national economy, but also its technological sophistication. As discussed above, substantial attention has been given to using force modernization programmes as vehicles for acquiring advanced know-how in areas such as aerospace, naval and information technology engineering. Perhaps of equal significance is the effort given to developing the economies of scale allowing the viable export of items such as aircraft, surveillance systems and coastal patrol vessels. These sales throughout the Global South have been bolstered by a vision explicitly viewing interoperability with neighbouring armed forces and the provision of training to other Southern militaries as avenues to encourage the attractiveness of Brazilian military hardware.

The sustained work with armed forces in other South American and South Atlantic littoral countries is also central to the second imperative running through Brazilian security policy. Although notions of a NATO-like alliance structure in either South America or the South Atlantic do not appear to be on the table or hold any real attraction for Brazil's defence policy planners, there is a sense that a hybrid form of a security community is being developed in both spaces. As was detailed in the South Atlantic case, Brazil has worked with African countries surrounding the ocean to not only build their knowledge of what physically exists in the space, particularly in terms of continental shelf limits, but also to improve regional capacity to provide basic security goods such as search-and-rescue, as well as drug and piracy interdiction. An exclusionary imperative is also at play, one which seeks to demonstrate that since there is no need for Northern intervention to 'secure' the seas in the South Atlantic, then navies from countries such as the US, UK and France have no business staging preventative patrols in the region. The same logic is in play with the case of the wider Amazon and the South American region as a whole. If Brazil and its South American partners can prevent the outbreak of hostilities and at least prevent transnational criminality in the area threatening the wider international community then there is no need to even have a discussion about extra-continental intervention. Substantial contributions to peacekeeping operations such as the MINUSTAH force in Haiti directly support this by demonstrating not just contextual, but sustained capacity to engage in security building and provision activities.

It is this last aspect that ultimately is crucial for Brazilian security policy. As long as Brazil is able to maintain adequate levels of security governance in South America and the South Atlantic through a coordinating approach to the region redolent of consensual hegemony models of foreign policy, the US is likely to remain uninterested in getting involved. In other words, while successful implementation of Brazil's security policy does not require US assistance, it does depend on at least tacit acquiescence. The unstated reality is that Brazil lacks the force projection and domestic defence capabilities to keep a determined super power out of the South Atlantic and South America. In terms of the larger argument in this book the structural power game being played by Brazil is one of reconditioning global strategic thinking and international acceptance of what is appropriate in terms of national and regional intervention. Brazilian policy is dedicated to entrenching South America and the South Atlantic first as zones of reliable peace and security and, second, as regions capable of internally managing localized security issues. Successful pursuit of these interlinked strategies has been fed by the mutual confidence and interdependence built by the frequent accompanying joint exercises, advanced training provision and, latterly, sale of increasingly sophisticated military hardware. The awkward question for the ambitious thinkers within the Brazilian foreign policy establishment is how much of this success ultimately rests on the relative global isolation of the two regions in question and the international concentration on a succession of wars in the Middle East and Central Asia.

8

Brazil and Latin America

Latin America more broadly and South America specifically provide the platform on which Brazilian foreign policy architects positioned their main lever for attempting to shift structural power frameworks and the pursuit of their country's particular brand of international insertion. Central to this has been a continental strategic reality particularly propitious for the consensual hegemonic style of leadership sought by Brazil over the last quarter century. While there have been occasional armed contretemps between South American states, the most serious episodes since Brazil's transition to democracy – the 1995 Ecuador–Peru border conflict and the near conflict that would have pitted Colombia against Ecuador and Venezuela in 2008 – have been half-hearted and something the protagonists deeply wished to avoid. More to the point, neither of these incidents presented a threat to Brazil's territorial integrity, and their rapid conclusion, led by Brazil, removed the potential for extra-continental intervention. Strategic threat considerations have consequently been deeply downplayed in regional diplomatic thinking (Schenoni, 2014), creating an enormous amount of space to pursue the sort of patient, ideas-based discussion-centric approaches to foreign policy mapped out in chapter three. The implicit underlying sense of trust and understanding between governments in the region (Merke, 2015) layers on top of this to create a regional environment where Brazil has been able to collectivize its desire to challenge existing regional and global governance frameworks, albeit not without challenges. While this chapter will map out how an unwillingness to provide concrete leadership goods has created resistance to Brazil's leadership, the nature of this resistance paradoxically suggests that key elements of the consensual hegemonic project have been internalized throughout the region resulting in a sustained challenge to prevailing structural power frameworks in the Americas and the wider South. Latin America with a special emphasis on South America thus becomes the central launching pad for the Brazilian foreign policy of challenging not just regional, but also global structural power realities.

It is a point of pride for Brazilian diplomats and a keystone in the country's security framework that the borders with all ten neighbouring nations were peaceably settled at the start of the twentieth century, all but removing the threat of intra-continental war from the list of diplomatic concerns. The resultant space for an engaged continental diplomacy in South America has been amplified since the end of the Cold War by the general absence of US attention to the region (Reid, 2007; Emerson, 2010; Weitzman, 2012), which has allowed Brasília to quietly take on something of a leadership role. This has occurred most particularly through attempts to create a sense of South Americanness, which creates a natural geographical focal point of Brazil. While Brazil's evolving economic relations across South America have underpinned these leadership ambitions, their strength has been limited outside of the Southern Cone, partly because it is only within Mercosul that the Brazilian economic presence really dominates and partly because decision makers in Brasília have been reluctant to commit serious resources to anchoring a continental project. Of course, those with a realpolitik approach would rightly ask why any Brazilian government would expend these resources if it is gaining what it wants from the region on the cheap, which this chapter will argue is a refocusing of South America inwards and away from external Northern power structures in the search for opportunities and solutions to regional challenges.

Despite recent initiatives such as CELAC, the idea that Brazil has strong leadership in Latin America is contestable and was actively contested by Hugo Chávez's Venezuela and a bit less directly by Argentina under the Kirchners. Nevertheless in South America Brazilian leadership is present, but grudgingly accepted as a convenience by others and only weakly asserted and assumed by Brazil. Perhaps the most useful framework for understanding how Latin America fits into Brazilian foreign policy priorities is to draw on the concentric circle model of geopolitics employed by Golbery Couto e Siva in the 1960s. Reinterpreted slightly, the model sees a series of rings extending out from Mercosul to South America then Latin America and finally the Western Hemisphere, with Brazilian influence and sensitivity declining as we travel out from the inner most ring, which effectively only involves Argentina with absorption of the 'buffer' states Paraguay and Uruguay. In strategic terms the overarching policy goal is to exclude external influence from the inner most circles, particularly that of the US, and increase Brazil's influence in the outer circles. The secondary ambition is to shift the structural realities to vouchsafe Brazilian interests and to use the regional context as a platform for strengthening the country's international economic and political insertion, elements which are reflected in more detail throughout the rest of the book.

Brazilian relations with South America have thus often been quietly understated but nevertheless very goal oriented, which explains the careful strategic calculus behind a simultaneously active and detached engagement with the continent. Once a desired goal is secured, further expenditure of resources becomes unnecessary, in some ways leaving regional management questions as the subject of recurring cost-benefit analyses. That Brazil is able to pursue this strategy also indicates that it retains a structural importance to the rest of the region requiring engagement by neighbouring countries. Where matters shift slightly is in the move from the Cardoso era to the Lula/Dilma era. While the structural game during the Cardoso era had a strong focus on the economic element and collective security stabilization to rule out the need for external intervention in the region, the PT presidencies quietly shifted focus to emphasize an agenda of regional *auto-estima* grounded in the thinking behind its domestic social inclusion policies to create a proactive structural shift in the attention of regional countries. The result was a strong sense under Lula and Dilma that Brazil's regional foreign policy had become ideologized, bent on protecting the 'pink tide' in the Americas, or at the very least framed around a leftist reading of regional and world affairs necessitating a new policy approach to prevailing structural realities (Almeida, 2004; Almeida, 2014: chapter nine; Barbosa, 2008; Cervo, 2010). Although this argument certainly has some merit, the story is more complicated, working reflexively to support a regional ambiance backstopping the PT's social inclusion agenda and even making it seem moderate and desirable in the face of the Bolivarian alternative emanating from Hugo Chávez's Venezuela.

South America, not Latin America

Although this chapter is titled Brazil and Latin America, the main story relates to Brazilian relations within South America. The structural realities brought by geography and trade relations create a situation where Brazilian influence in Central America is weak and subject to serious contestation from Mexico, not to mention the larger pressure from the US. Although there was an expansion of Brazilian attention to Central America during the later Lula years and the Dilma presidency, most notably through responses to the 2009 coup in Honduras and an increase in programming by the Brazilian Cooperation Agency along the isthmus, the economic and political limitations on diplomatic action in the region emerge as a clear theme from the early 1990s (Cabral and Weinstock, 2010; Garcia, 2009/2010; IPEA, 2010b; Lampreia, 2009/2010; Legler, 2010; Pino and Leite, 2010). As Lampreia (2009: 203–204) recalls, Mexico's decision to sign the North American Free Trade Agreement created a sea change in intra-Latin American dynamics. Contesting the US for influence in Mexico and Central America was already a virtual impossibility despite challenges through the Contadora Group and its successor the Rio Group. For Brazilian diplomats implementation of NAFTA meant that Mexico had effectively delinked from the wider region, heightening the northward focus of Mexican and Central American policy makers. Nevertheless, efforts were given to maintaining a degree of intra-Latin American coherence. Advice provided by diplomats to decision makers in 1993 was that Brazil not enact the ALADI treaty and erect barriers to Mexico's NAFTA accession because such action would likely sunder the long-standing Latin American Free Trade Agreement, which was still being used to anchor Brazilian continental leadership ambitions (MRE, 1993).

Set in the context of the time, the formation of NAFTA appeared as a serious threat to Brazil's regional and global position. Policy makers worried about the rise of a series of super blocs that might structurally exclude their country on a permanent basis if they were not successful in leveraging the regional space for a greater global profile. Beyond building stronger links with Europe and with parts of the Global South, particularly the Portuguese speaking nations, Itamaraty's 1993 foreign policy review specifically called for 'reinforcing the priority of relations with Latin American neighbors, especially those in South America' (IPRI, 1993: 27). This idea was not new and built directly upon internal Itamaraty thinking in the 1980s about constructing South America as a distinct space, quite possibly in the form of some sort of continental free trade area (Amorim, 2003). Primary focus was subsequently placed on strengthening political, economic and social linkages with security questions such as Narcotrafficking and terrorism being left to an ancillary bracketed clause. In large part this was simply reflective of the work that was already taking place. Brazil's main historical security preoccupation – relations with Argentina – appeared to be a thing of the past, thanks to the rapprochement of the early 1980s at the presidential level (Spektor, 2002), which was bolstered by the launch of sub-regional trade initiatives such as the PICE Accords and the nuclear cooperation agreements (Azambuja, 2009; Baumann, 1987; Manzetti, 1990). As mentioned earlier, traditional security threats on the continent were notable for their absence; new concerns such as drug-related crime remained a question yet to be seriously addressed in a transnational manner outside of US involvement in Colombia and Peru, and certainly were not seen as a major issue for multilateralization in Brazil.

Argentina sits at the centre of the South American concept that came to dominate Brazilian foreign policy thinking for the region in the 1990s. In addition to the long-running historical importance of bilateral relations (Bandeira, 2003), the internal political dynamics also played an important role in keeping Argentina at the heart of Brazilian efforts to build a sub-regional anchor in Mercosul for a wider South American space. For most of the twentieth century Argentina was the sole substantive strategic concern for Brazilian security policy makers, with mutual distrust between the respective militaries extending to a nuclear arms race that looked set to bear fruit in the early 1980s. In part the positive engagement with Argentina that began in the late 1970s when Ernesto Geisel handed the military-led Brazilian presidency on to João Figueiredo was intended to pull the two countries back from a potential nuclear precipice. The debt crisis and transition to democracy provided additional major incentives for bilateral cooperation, creating a framework that, by the 1990s, made it clear that some form of integration with Argentina would be of major importance for magnifying Brazil's ability to resist economic and political pressures coming from the international system. Argentina consequently emerged as an important partner in the early 1990s, not only for the obvious reasons of geography and growing economic interlinkages, but also for the ability it gave Brazil to project a 'collectivized', albeit frequently disputed regional voice on the global stage.

By the late 1980s region building in the Southern Cone emerged as a joint effort by Brazil and Argentina, simultaneously being supported by and supporting of the processes of democratization that were taking place in the two countries, later incorporating Paraguay and Uruguay (Fournier, 1999; Gardini, 2010). On a pragmatic level consonant with the goal of a phased insertion into the emerging globalized international trading system economic liberalization amongst the bloc-member countries also started to create immediate gains for Brazilian firms. As is detailed in Figure 8.1, the mere act of signing the Mercosul-founding Treaty of Asuncion in 1991 precipitated a surge in Argentina's importance as an export destination for Brazilian products, rising from 4.7% in that year to 8.5% in 1992. A further jump came when the bloc began formal operation in 1995, with Argentina going from taking 8.8% of Brazilian exports to 13.3% in 1998. Similar rises in the importance of Brazil to the other bloc countries can be seen over the same time period, with Paraguay increasing from 1.6% in 1991 to 2.5% in 1998, and Uruguay from 1.1% to 1.7%.

The time period of 1991 to 1998 is a bit of an artificial construct because it demonstrates the heyday of Mercosul before a series of economic shocks began to seriously impact the bloc, starting with the 1999 devaluation of the Brazilian real and then the 2002 economic collapse in Argentina. What the data in Table 8.1 highlights is the extent to which the decision to form Mercosul created a surge in trade between the member countries, leaving the relative weight of the other South American markets more or less static. Equally striking is the composition of the exports to the Mercosul countries, which were dominated by Brazil's manufacturing and value-added sector and thus offered wider

Table 8.1 Percentage of total Brazilian exports, 1991–1998

	1991	1992	1993	1994	1995	1996	1997	1998
Argentina	4.7	8.5	9.5	9.5	8.8	11.0	12.9	13.3
Bolivia	0.8	0.9	1.1	1.1	1.1	1.1	1.4	1.3
Chile	2.1	2.6	2.9	2.3	2.6	2.2	2.3	2.0
Colombia	0.5	1.0	1.0	0.9	1.0	0.9	1.0	0.9
Ecuador	0.4	0.4	0.4	0.6	0.5	0.4	0.3	0.4
Paraguay	1.6	1.5	2.5	2.4	2.8	2.8	2.7	2.5
Peru	0.7	0.6	0.7	0.8	0.9	0.6	0.7	0.7
Uruguay	1.1	1.4	2.0	1.7	1.8	1.7	1.7	1.7
Venezuela	1.4	1.2	1.0	0.6	1.0	1.0	1.5	1.4
South America	13.2	18.0	21.1	20.1	20.5	21.7	24.3	24.3
Mercosul	7.3	11.4	13.9	13.7	13.3	15.5	17.2	17.5

Source: World Bank WITS UN Comtrade, 1991–1998

Table 8.2 Manufactureds as % of Brazilian exports, 1991–1998

	1991	1992	1993	1994	1995	1996	1997	1998
Argentina	66.9	76.5	73.2	71.8	67.3	71.9	74.9	75.4
Bolivia	80.2	82.1	80.5	79.4	79.4	79.0	82.2	78.5
Chile	82.4	85.1	87.0	81.5	79.9	79.5	82.0	79.2
Colombia	73.2	82.7	80.9	76.3	77.9	80.2	77.9	75.8
Ecuador	89.7	90.4	91.5	90.6	91.0	89.2	86.1	87.8
Paraguay	70.3	66.0	65.6	64.3	61.2	62.2	61.4	56.7
Peru	87.4	85.6	79.3	84.6	87.5	82.5	85.4	77.6
Uruguay	42.7	51.2	48.5	41.2	45.8	37.9	40.6	40.4
Venezuela	67.2	77.9	70.3	67.2	70.6	71.9	80.6	75.7
World	53.5	55.4	56.5	52.5	50.8	50.4	50.1	50.6

Source: World Bank WITS UN Comtrade, 1991–1998

employment-generating opportunities as well as diversification of the national economy. The next step in the policy formation process came from a comparison of the export potential to South America if a way could be found to broaden membership of Mercosul to something closer to a continental free trade area.

Constructing South America

Although the idea of Latin America is now so commonly accepted that it is assumed to be a natural region, it is an artificial device carefully constructed by France as part of its struggles with the US for territory and influence in the 'New World' (Mignolo, 2009; Smith, 2000). Throughout the 1990s Brazilian diplomats drew on this historical precedent to advance a further sub-division of the Americas to include South America as a valid regional space (FUNAG, 2002a; 2002b). Summarizing the relative strengths and aptitudes of regional economies during a 2000 interview, Cardoso gave some retrospective insight into the thinking that was taking place at the Planalto Palace in the 1990s. He noted that Chile was emerging as a capital exporter and that Brazil was a borrower, investing funds for future industrial development in South America, particularly Brazil. As one of his trade officials noted: 'We are making progress because we reached or are reaching bilateral agreements with virtually every South American country. To Brazil, Mercosur is the tool, but it is not enough. We need a broader integration. With integration I believe the trend will be that of technological and industrial investment concentrating in Brazil' (Spinola, 2000). In effect he was floating a softer version of the sorts of ideas that Darc Costa (2003) would take to the BNDES in the first Lula government and which could be seen in Brazil's South American foreign policy during the 2000s: an inward strengthening of the South American economy around Brazilian economic leadership provided in the form of a large consumption market and source of advanced technical services, all geared as an export platform to the wider continental market.

Other countries in the region, most notably Argentina, were understandably a bit uneasy about the growing Brazilian economic dominance and industrial centrality that were made explicit in Costa's 2003 book. But in terms of the foreign and economic policy project being pursued by Cardoso the important point is his conception of Mercosul as a tool. Rather than seeing the bloc and its expansion as the end point for Brazil's internationalization ambitions, it was instead positioned as the anchor, from which an outward base could be initiated that would see both the spread of Brazilian trade discussed in chapter five and outward

FDI explored in chapter six. Liberalization within the bloc served as an incubator to prepare national firms for the fire of global competition. Articulation and development of transnationalized production processes and value chains involving partnership and collaboration from firms, finance and labour in the various countries of South America was part of a strategy of leveraging a better economic and political insertion for the continent in global affairs, which would naturally position Brazil at the lead due to its sheer economic and geographic size.

Lingering distrust and disquiet in Argentina created significant political barriers for Brazil's outward looking approach to Mercosul. Efforts in the 1990s to expand the bloc to include Bolivia, with a view to an ultimate absorption of the Andean Community, stumbled upon intransigence from Argentina. A similar fate befell efforts to broker a bloc-to-bloc deal with the EU. Perhaps expressing some frustration, German chancellor Helmut Kohl was unequivocal with Cardoso, strongly advising his colleague to take an active leadership role anchoring Mercosul and bringing South America round to a regional formation like Europe (Cardoso, 2006: 617–619). Whether or not Cardoso felt inclined to have Brazil take on the role of economic anchor for a South American region by absorbing the associated costs proved irrelevant after the economy suffered rapid currency devaluation in early 1999, which sent the rest of Mercosul into an economic tailspin and ultimately the Argentine economic collapse of 2001/2002. While the economic crises from 1999 did dramatically illustrate the extent to which the sub-regional economies had become interlinked, the political dynamics also heightened unease and distrust, particularly in Buenos Aires where complaints were loudly voiced about a lack of warning before the 1999 changes in Brazilian economic policy.

Sensing in the late 1990s that political resistance to a deepening of Mercosul and expansion to include South America might become an insurmountable barrier, Cardoso shifted tack to a highly technocratic approach. Rather than addressing the thorny issues of trade and production distribution that had historically derailed South American integration projects, attention was turned to the question of why production chains in the region were all but non-existent, and why meaningful transnational connections so hard to form. From 31 August to 1 September, 2000 the presidents of all South American countries gathered at a summit meeting in Brasília where Cardoso unveiled a plan to integrate the physical infrastructure of the continent along twelve axes of integration. The plan he floated was to build 'corridors' of transportation, energy and communications infrastructure linking the continent's main economic centres. In principle political bickering would be removed from the equation as the countries instead concentrated on providing the foundational support needed by intra- and extra-regional firms to develop new opportunities in South America. The extent to which politics were pushed off the table became clear during discussions about the corridor running along the north of the continent from Colombia to French Guiana, which involved a road crossing several contested frontiers. Similar sidelining of national political posturing was seen in the Andean corridor where the protagonists in the Ecuador–Peru border conflict were strongly enjoined to set aside their past and look together for a more prosperous future.

Two ambitions ran through the infrastructure integration plan that was launched at the 2000 Brasília Summit. The first was to lay down the logistical frameworks that would allow emergence of the sorts of just-in-time production processes and transnationalized value-chains found in Europe, North America and Asia. This was particularly important for Brazilian firms looking to diversify their production systems and for Cardoso's wider ambition of seeing the rise of Brazilian multilatinas with the sort of globally diversified business and investment plans surveyed in chapter six. Indeed, this very process would strengthen Brazil's leadership in the region through what might best be described as a new application of dependency theory that would see economically essential linkages driving support for Brazilian positions in international forums by creating an implicit harmonization of interests around the agenda set in Brasília. This directly points to the second ambition, which was to solidify Brazil's de facto role as regional leader and international interlocutor, a position that was already being softly seen in Cardoso's inclusion in groupings such as the 'Third Wave' leaders' summits and Brazil's central voice in the FTAA negotiations (Arashiro, 2011; Feinberg, 1997).

Rough regional roads

Although the logic underlying Cardoso's approach to continental integration was grounded in an attempt to bring about the economic gains for Brazil and the region, the interesting aspect for what was to come with the Lula presidency was the initiative's strong element of social capacitation and inclusion by placing an emphasis on the consensus creation, discussion, and national and intra-continental self-determination strategies mapped out in chapter two. Beyond the political capital required to convene the Brasília Summit, the actual costs to Brazil for leading this integration vision were remarkably low because the expense of building the infrastructure would fall to the individual countries. In some ways the benefits to Brazil even outstripped those of neighbouring countries as Brazilian construction firms bid for the contracts, often with highly competitive financing from state institutions like the BNDES or international financial agencies such as the Inter-American Development Bank. In terms of the structural power argument in this book, the biggest gain came on a political level where the project contributed to keeping the attention of neighbouring states on intra-continental issues managed by regional actors, not seeking interventions from North America or Europe. The infrastructure networks were planned and agreed within the region, giving the participating countries a clear and self-interested sense of ownership of the integration project that had been missing in visions focused on the politically sensitive questions of trade and industrial production distribution.

Whether or not the turn to infrastructure integration, a policy continued by the Lula and Dilma presidencies, was an effective idea remains a question of debate. Figures 8.1 and 8.2 highlight the limited nature of the trade gains from using infrastructure integration as a device to increase Brazil's importance to regional countries. The largest spike found within Mercosul involves associate-member Bolivia and can be almost entirely attributed to the natural gas pipeline opened and operational before the 2000 Brasília Summit. Despite improvements in transnational

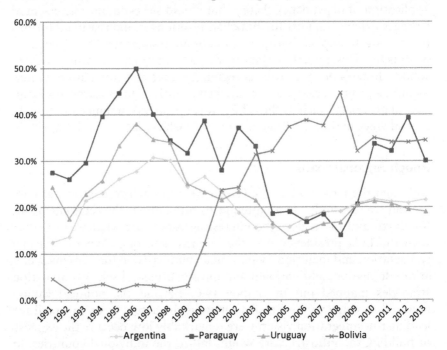

Figure 8.1 Mercosul country exports to Brazil as % of total exports, 1991–2013

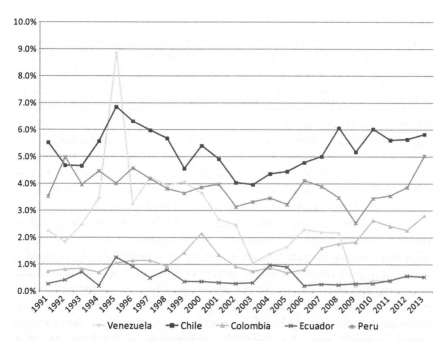

Figure 8.2 Exports to Brazil as % of total exports, non-Mercosul countries, 1991–2013

transportation linkages, in both the Uruguayan and the economically more significant Argentine case, the general trend in the 2000s was down from the peaks of the 1990s despite investment in improved road linkages. These disappointing results reflect the continued absence of sub-regional value chains of any meaningful scale, particularly in such key areas as the automotive industry. While the situation appears far more dynamic than with the non-Mercosul countries covered in Table 10.2, Brazil's importance as a trading partner nevertheless remains minimal, peaking at just under 6% with Chile. Nevertheless, the non-Mercosul case does provide evidence that building logistics networks has been providing some results, even if they were localized to the frontier regions in Colombia and Peru where deliberate effort has been given to strengthening trade across the Amazonian frontiers (Gadea, 2012).

Mindful of the importance of further binding the continent to Brazil, one of the early foreign economic policy decisions of the Lula government was to make up to USD 3 billion in financing available to neighbouring countries to encourage the importation of Brazilian goods and services (Santos, 2003). Symbolic, if only moderately substantive acts were added such as forgiving USD 52 million in Bolivian debt, which appears rather less altruistic if we note that this opened the way for a new USD 600 million line of credit that allowed the government in La Paz to contract Brazilian construction firms for a series of infrastructure projects (BBC, 2004). Lula also continued Cardoso's attempts at building something like a South American Free Trade Area, using sidebar meetings at the 2004 Rio Group meeting to broker a deal between Mercosul and the Andean Community. While the bloc-to-bloc arrangement was a half-hearted affair and lacked participation from Chile, it did create the impetus needed to further advance the South American agenda. When continental leaders met in Peru at a December 2004 summit they signed the Cusco Declaration, which served as a letter of intent to form CASA, which later transformed into UNASUL, launched at the 2008 Third Summit of Heads of State of South America held in Brasília.

During events leading to the formation of UNASUL intimations of an overt Brazilian desire for leadership were noticeable by their absence. This approach was part historical legacy of a tradition of disavowing leadership, part reflection of the power realities of a still-weak national economy, and part reaction to the rise Hugo Chávez's oil-fueled competing leadership project. Lula's meetings with his presidential colleagues consequently focused on building quiet links orienting attention towards Brazil. Expenditure on South–South Cooperation for development began to quietly increase as an avenue for underpinning Brazilian soft power and regional solidarity (Burges, 2014; Cabral and Weinstock, 2010; IPEA, 2010b). Efforts were made to liberate financing through state financial institutions, such as the BNDES, Banco do Brasil and Caixa Econômico, in order to facilitate expanded Brazilian FDI throughout South America. The Ministry of Development, Industry and Foreign Trade quietly started an import-substitution programme that encouraged Brazilian firms to seek cost and quality competitive alternate suppliers in the region instead of Europe or North America (Oxford Analytica, 2005b).

Bolivarian challenge

During the 2000s Brazil faced active opposition to its South American leadership attempts. As oil prices rose and Hugo Chávez consolidated his hold on power after the 2002 coup attempt against him, Venezuela began to actively advance a competing regional project built on the socialist principles ascribed to Simon Bolivar's legacy. Chávez launched programmes such as Petrocaribe to entice allegiance from Caribbean and Central American countries with highly subsidized oil. In South America the Bolivarian project was advanced through the vocally anti-neoliberal bloc ALBA, which attracted membership from Bolivia and Ecuador, as well as curious glances from a Paraguay contemplating an opportunity to play Brasília off against Caracas. Heft was added to Chávez's revisionist ambitions by his decision to pull Venezuela out of the Andean Community and to greet the invitation to join Mercosul with a ringing condemnation of what he saw as its neoliberal ethos (Espin, 2006; Otta, 2007). What most inflamed Lula's foreign policy team and Brazilian sentiment in general was the revelation that Bolivia's 1 May 2006 nationalization of Petrobras assets was not only morally encouraged by Chávez, but actively supported with commitments of financial and logistical support (OESP, 2006).

By mid-2006 it was thus becoming increasingly apparent that Chávez's actions had the potential to undo the complex mix of regional and global connections that Lula's team was fashioning to bind South American to Brazil. In response, the foreign policy makers in the Planalto and Itamaraty palaces turned again to the techniques outlined in chapter three and the traditions implicit in a consensual hegemony approach to foreign relations. Although the Brazilian government was deeply angered by Chávez's role in the Bolivian nationalization process, and disenchanted with the disjuncture it highlighted in the two countries' approaches to Southern solidarity, diplomats kept quiet and publicly took a consoling attitude; private comments and discourse at multilateral meetings was another matter. As one official noted, the first thing that Brazil and a number of other countries tried to do at inter-American meetings was marginalize the Venezuelan representative. On a procedural level a mid-career diplomat was reassigned and tasked with the sole responsibility of tracking Chávez and coordinating a control strategy (interview with Brazilian diplomats, 2007). After an extended frost in bilateral relations in 2007, which saw no contact between Chávez and Lula for nearly seven months (Valente and Mascarenhas, 2015), renewed political backing was given to the Venezuelan management question. A series of tri-annual meetings between the two presidents was instituted to hash out thorny issues 'mano-a-mano em portuñol', which Brazilian diplomats pointed out were a near necessity because of the extent to which decision making in Venezuela had been concentrated in Chávez's office (author interviews, 2010).

Three Venezuelan policy proposals emerged as particularly important to Brazil's desire to derail Chávez's regional ambitions: Chávez's plans for a Bank of the South; a Venezuelan nuclear industry; and a gas pipeline ring around South America. While none of these major projects was particularly liked in Brasília, none was explicitly opposed. Instead, a strategy of co-option and diversion was employed, explicitly including Venezuela in projects and initiatives in order to contain and manage Chávez (interview with Brazilian diplomats, 2007). The Bank of the South was prevented from becoming a Bolivarian slush fund by the Brazilian proposition that it support approved infrastructure plans and follow the model of Brazil's highly successful National Bank for Economic and Social Development (BNDES). Nuclear proliferation in Venezuela was neatly diverted by the Brazilian suggestion that rather than reinventing the wheel Caracas join its soon-to-be Mercosul partners in the Argentina–Brazil nuclear cooperation arrangement. The South American gas pipeline ring project and other attempts by Chávez to deploy Venezuela's state oil company as a political device across the continent were sidelined by a series of partnerships with Petrobras (Emerson, 2014), which insisted that any venture be driven by an economic calculus, not a political one. On a wider regional level, the most notable change in response to Chávez's challenge was a modification in Brazilian discourse to drop an explicit language of leadership. Attention was instead turned to elaborating UNASUL as an important coordinating body for pragmatic work toward regional integration.

Leading quietly

Despite the subtle speeches, careful actions and strategic positioning by Lula and his foreign policy team it was becoming abundantly clear to other South American countries that Brazil was pursuing a project of regional leadership. As early as 2005 Ecuadorian officials were quietly noting Brazil's desire to take on the preeminent role in the region and suggesting that their country might play an important role in these plans (*El Comercio*, 2005). Others began to float the idea that Brazil was acting in an imperialist manner and that it might be wise to start playing Brasília off against Caracas (Flynn, 2007; Sant'anna, 2009; Trevisan, 2005). Evo Morales in Bolivia went further, using the army to publicly take Petrobras's assets during the May Day 2006 nationalization of the natural gas industry. While Morales's decision was driven by domestic considerations explained to Lula in early 2006 during a reportedly clandestine meeting by Bolivian vice president Álvaro Marcelo García, the impression in Brasília was that the process would be negotiated, not a sudden, televised seizure that seemed to find encouragement from Chávez (interview with Brazilian diplomats, 2007). In a similar, although significantly lower value incident in 2009 discussed in chapter six, Ecuadorian president Rafael Correa refused to honor a BNDES loan to Odebrecht for what he labelled faulty work on the San Francisco hydroelectric project.

The reaction from Brazil to these incidents illustrates the extent to which specific national interest questions were privileged, but not at the expense of derailing the wider South American strategic project and maintaining the fictitious plausible deniability of Brazilian leadership. Initial blockages in gas contract negotiations resulted in Petrobras threatening to withhold diesel fuel shipments due to outstanding accounts receivables, which would have paralysed Bolivia's transportation system (EFE, 2006; Lima, 2006). Complete withdrawal was raised as a possibility when Bolivian energy Minister Andres Soliz suggested further nationalizations, with his subsequent resignation perhaps reflecting Bolivian economic dependence on the Brazilian owned pipeline and gas market (Reuters, 2006a; 2006b). Corporate pressure from Brazil's state oil company and diplomats was matched with shuttle diplomacy by Lula advisors Marco Aurélio Garcia and José Dirceu. By 2007 the tone had changed, with Morales noting that hearing Lula speak was 'a great school' (Neto, 2007).

The political and social inclusion element embedded within the infrastructure integration approach would be particularly important as the Lula presidency took over the South American project and carried it forward in a more politicized direction. The centrality of South America to the wider structural agenda in Brazil's foreign policy agenda was neatly captured by foreign minister Luiz Alberto Figueiredo in a 2014 interview: 'The entire neighborhood has to have peace, concord, security, harmony between neighbors, energy and communication. In the end, you work together as a neighborhood or your house, in isolation, does not work.' Figueiredo's main point was that integration – or at least the political pressure of pursuing integration – is essential and not optional for Brazil and, as the trade numbers above suggest, that Brazilian development depends on regional and not just national advancement (A. Barbosa et al., 2014). As Marco Aurélio Garcia recalls, the economic approach to regionalism was looking rocky in the early days of the first PT presidency under Lula when successive integration projects stalled in the face of competing trade blocs and different conceptions of how trade relations with the wider world should be managed. Like Cardoso, the vision taken by Lula's team was the physical integration referenced by Figueiredo, focusing on the sorts of energy and logistical patterns found in Asia rather than a formation of a large free trade bloc. More particularly, Garcia notes that the idea was to 'open another perspective on integration. One of Lula's personal successes was his ability to put the idea of integration above the ideological differences of the region.' The major divergences between three disparate groups such as Chile/Colombia, Brazil and the ALBA bloc were sidelined with recognition that 'integration which includes a diversity of political views is of fundamental importance', which in turn opened the space for more inward-oriented collective focusing on creating regional mechanisms to manage continental challenges (Oualalou, 2014).

In a 2011 article Garcia provided more insight into how the South American concept fitted into Brazil's wider multilateralist agenda and foreign policy, forming the foundation for his country's pursuit of the more democratic international order flagged in the 1993 Itamaraty policy review (Garcia, 2011; IPRI, 1993). On a continental level the focus was widening, with the strengthening of existing institutions such as Mercosul, the articulation and political solidification of new bodies such as UNASUL, and the launching of related offshoots such as the South American Defence Council. Tellingly, the manner in which Garcia sets out the case for Brazil's South American policy points to an underlying attitude towards the region that sees it almost as something subservient and oriented around Brazil, leaving his country as a near-natural conduit for South American inputs into global multilateral organizations. The critical response from Lampreia (2011), who launched the South American infrastructure initiatives as Cardoso's foreign minister, is that the gains coming from these processes appear to have been rather one-sided, causing many in the region to question whether it is worth acceding to Brazilian leadership (Malamud, 2011).

Bolivian economist Gonzalo Chávez offers an explanation of why Brazil experienced such conflicted reactions from countries like Bolivia, Ecuador and Paraguay: 'On one hand, companies are eager to win and do not want to lose their investors' money. Then there is the Foreign Ministry, which always takes a hard-line institutional response. Finally, there is the presidential diplomacy of Lula and his advisors, who use political and ideological lines to communicate with neighbours' (Charleaux, 2008). Scholars from neighbouring countries point to Lula's personal charm and credibility as central to keeping bilateral relations positive despite growing charges of imperialism created by corporate conduct and diplomatic statements (Mesa Gisbert, 2011: 40; Sant'Anna, 2009). Although Brazil responded with a steady stream of statements that it wanted to absorb more regional value-added exports and was working to provide development assistance and expanded infrastructure financing, the achievements consistently fell short of expectations, keeping questions about Brazilian imperialism alive (Deo, 2012; Flynn, 2007).

The idea that the Mercosul benefits flow mostly to Brazil is not new and is consistently reiterated by diplomats from Argentina, Paraguay and Uruguay. A large part of the problem is that while Brazil has pushed the regionalist agenda and encouraged neighbouring countries to look to it for leadership this has not been accompanied by a corresponding willingness to create substantive governance institutions as discussed in chapter four on multilateralism. This is most marked within Mercosul where both the dispute resolution mechanism and the bloc parliament lack any real enforcement powers, which in the case of trade disputes often means issues go to the WTO if they cannot be settled at the presidential level (Gómez-Mera, 2013; Malamud and Dri, 2013; Pretti, 1999). The same situation was seen at the meetings founding UNASUL, where the relatively straightforward approximation of Mercosul and the Andean Community advocated by Brazil contrasted with the Venezuela's ALBA-bloc call for a strongly institutionalized vision capable of advancing the Bolivarian 'revolution' (Amorim, 2013: 136). Unwilling to absorb the economic, political and sovereignty-sacrificing costs of anchoring a sub-regional or regional bloc along the European terms that Kohl pressed upon Cardoso in the 1990s, Lula and Dilma took a softer approach predicated on shifts in attention and changes in thinking. As Amorim explained to a trainee diplomat asking about the logic behind Lula's Latin American and Caribbean project, 'we are trying to build CELAC precisely to bring these other countries into our environment' (Amorim, 2011a: 406). Influence and reorientation of attention, not outright compulsion is the theme, using the prominent space Brazil occupies in the thinking of others as a device to exert pressure without seeming to impose.

The wider point of interest to the argument in this book is that the regional entities advanced by Cardoso, Lula and Dilma worked to turn attention away from traditional centres of structural power such as the US and EU. Clearly, there was some aspiration that this intra-continental shift in focus would look towards Brazil, placing Brasília in a central coordinating position through a series of relatively low cost instruments for collectivizing its policy decisions. Mercosul and UNASUL reaction to the Paraguayan Senate's exceptionally cynical June 2012 political impeachment of president Fernando Lugo stands as a case in point. Paraguay had its political rights suspended from both organizations despite what appeared to be the strenuous objects of Uruguayan president José Mujica, who protested at the Mercosul Summit by sitting in the back row and placing his foreign minister at the side of Dilma and Argentina's Christina Kirchner. At issue was the *jeito* Brazil and Argentina extracted from Paraguay's political upheavals and their manipulation of Mercosul to collectivize their desires. In this case it involved using the crisis as an excuse to remove the last barrier to Venezuela's full Mercosul membership, namely the Paraguayan Senate's refusal to approve the bloc's enlargement.

Changed terrain

In some respects the Brazilian push to redirect attention without providing the corresponding leadership goods or rewards did contribute to a sense there might be a need to balance Brazil's growing regional power (Flemes and Wehner, 2013; Flemes and Wehner, 2015; Schenoni, 2014). One of the recurrent weaknesses in critical analyses of Brazil's South American leadership project and the sorts of regional institutions to which it has acquiesced is the persistence of an almost maximalist interpretation, making the ability to control and easily direct others the natural endpoint. Here the ambiguity in the Brazilian approach to regional leadership captured in the concept of consensual hegemony becomes critical for understanding how the larger structural power agenda has been advanced through the South American policy space.

From at least the beginning of the Cardoso presidency a key imperative of Brazilian foreign policy has been to lead the region. Where nuance comes into play is with what is meant by 'lead', which Itamaraty secretary general Osmar Chohfi (2002) explained in the following manner: 'When we say that we don't want to be the leader, we don't want to impose … The idea is to strengthen our own positions and to have a better possibility of negotiating something that is favorable for everybody, but good for us too.' Structural realities dictate that the continental context is essential not only for preserving Brazilian autonomy, but also vouchsafing security in areas ranging from traditional security and economics through to energy supplies and environmental management. An ability to retain some measure of influence in discussions relating to all continental themes, as well as a capacity to dampen outside voices, thus becomes an important part of Brazil's foreign policy agenda, which in turn impacts Brazil's ability to assert its interests on the global stage, themes articulated in the 1993 review of the country's coming international challenges (IPRI, 1993: 52–58).

Where Cardoso set the stage and created the frame, the sustained continental political engagement by Lula and its quieter continuation by Dilma have succeeded in revising South American orientations to the point where Brazil becomes a central frame of reference, sometimes to the exclusion of the US. Brazil has played a critical role in calming almost every democratic disruption throughout the region since 1998, taking an important bilateral role in, for example, Paraguay (1998, 1999) and Peru (2000), and via multilateral frameworks based in the continent for episodes in Venezuela (2002, 2013), Ecuador (2005, 2010) and Bolivia (2005, 2008). The strength of this shift in South American countries looking towards their continent for regional solutions to crises is highlighted by two conflicts involving Ecuador. The 1998 resolution of the Ecuador–Peru border war was conceived and brokered by Brazil, but required official benediction from a White House press conference to make it stick. Conversely, the possibility of a war pitting Colombia against Ecuador and Venezuela in 2008 after Bogota had its air force bomb a FARC rebel base just over the border in Ecuadorian territory was avoided through a rapid meeting of the Rio Group and calm restored to relations through UNASUL.

Even when Brazil fades from central stage, the frameworks it helped establish such as UNASUL remain. More importantly, the sorts of ideas pursued through groupings like UNASUL by other regional countries point to a certain degree of internalization of the structural reform agenda to push attention away from the North. By 2015 the possibilities of CELAC and UNASUL had become apparent to foreign policy makers in other countries. In one example Ecuador has been working to build consensus around a new regional financial coordination mechanism that would allow the retraction of reserve holdings from Northern financial centres to be held in South America (Arízaga, 2015). In part this idea plays on a further development and activation of the Bank of the South first floated by Venezuela and grudgingly accepted by Brazil with significant governance qualifications in 2009. But it also points to a more profound reform of the international financial system, seeking to deepen the ALADI Reciprocal Credits Convention to expand trade-related direct currency swaps and reduce use of the US dollar as a medium of intra-regional commerce.

The element highlighted by Ecuador's regional financial engineering ambitions is that other South American actors are now actively pushing to change the application of structural power in the region in a self-interested manner, which is also consistent with Brazilian foreign policy ambitions. Pushing the point a bit we can even begin to argue that the Pacific Alliance is an indicator of Brazil's success in incultating the structural power reform agenda throughout South America via its consensual hegemony strategy. In this case the four leading liberal Latin American economies – Chile, Colombia, Peru and Mexico – have combined to form a new type of regional grouping to cooperatively explore international engagement. While the Pacific Alliance does look West and thus away from Brazil, it explicitly involves collaboration amongst its members to find an improved economic insertion that is not reliant upon the US as a savior market. A certain sense of synchronicity between the Pacific Alliance and the Brazilian vision also appears to be in place, as evidenced by the initiation of inter-bloc talks as this book was being written (Opera Mundi, 2014).

Conclusion

The argument in this chapter has been that Latin America and specifically South America are essential foundation stones for Brazil's larger
foreign policy agenda of pushing structural reform at a global level.
Existing arguments point to the same political management and trade
relationships outlined in this chapter to suggest that it is the continental
level that furnishes the economic stability and international credibility
necessary to have a global voice. The element added particularly towards
the end of the discussion here is one of identity and ideational transformation which sees Brazil's sense of a need for change in the configuration of structural power spreading amongst its neighbours. This takes on
two elements. First is acquiescence to Brazilian plans and cooperation
(or at least studied silence) as the resultant policies are developed and
implemented. A more interesting second element is also emerging and
causing the very resistance of Brazilian leadership, which prompts critical scholars to question whether the continent will continue to follow
Brazil. In keeping with the logic inherent to consensual hegemony the
argument developed towards the end of this chapter is that other countries in the region have internalized the structural resistance element
of Brazil's overarching foreign policy agenda and are autonomously
advancing it. While this does not automatically mean that the policies
advocated by other South American countries will necessarily be seen as
entirely positive by Brazilian policy makers – we might well look at the
early days of the Pacific Alliance here – the underlying reality is that they
are consistent with the idea of looking 'inward' and seeking routes for
national and regional development that do not rely on the US or the EU.
The extent to which China may supplant the US and Europe in Latin
American dependency is still an unanswered question with important
implications for the ultimate success of the sort of reform agenda being
quietly pushed by Brazil.

   All of these changes are critical for Brazil's ability to project itself onto
the international stage and positively position its hemispheric economic
and political interests. Even if Brazil is not the chief protagonist, the
turn towards South American solutions and alternatives for national
and intra-continental challenges almost automatically ensures that
Brazil will have at least a consultative role. The proliferating presidential
meetings linked with the exclusive South American and Latin American
groupings might be disappointing in terms of high profile deliverables
and further progress towards a 'European' integration, but they do serve
an important soft power imperative. Each meeting provides an opportunity for formal and informal consultation with Brazil and with the

other South American and Latin American countries, which this chapter has suggested creates an important shift in orientation away from the traditional power centres of North America and Europe inwards to the continent and often Brasília. For officials at Itamaraty this is critical because the preparation for these meetings and the resultant frameworks increases interaction between the region and Brazilian officials, further subtly entrenching Brazil as a preferred partner. This in turn allows Brazil to position itself as an aggregator of continental thinking (even if its neighbours do not always accept it in this role) and leverage this into a seat at major international decision making tables. Payoffs for business are similarly important, particularly for the Brazilian multilatinas which have spread into the Americas as both investors and traders. As Figueiredo noted in his summary of long-standing Brazilian diplomatic strategy, Brazil's neighbourhood is the foundation for its inward and outward success.

9

Brazil and the Global South

Brazil has traditionally had a somewhat ambiguous view of its position in the Global South. Brazilian diplomatic discourse has episodically adopted a 'country of the South' rhetoric, but outside the flag of convenience role the idea of Brazil as a 'Southern' or developing country has never sat particularly well with the traditional national elite. Instead, the guiding logic within the Brazilian foreign policy establishment has historically been that the country's natural affinity is with Western Europe and North America, not the Spanish-speaking republics of Latin America and certainly not the countries of sub-Saharan Africa. Underpinning this aspirational tilt to Brazil's international identity was a general lack of engagement with the Global South. Trade and cultural links driven by the elite were firmly focused on the North, leading to the challenge identified by then foreign minister and future president Fernando Henrique Cardoso in 1992: the world had just undergone a major systemic change with the fall of the Berlin Wall and the end of the Cold War, which in turn necessitated a major revision of how Brazil understood the regional and global system as well as what implications these held for the sorts of policies Brazil might pursue. To address these challenges Cardoso commissioned a sweeping consultation exercise to review not only the guiding principles of Brazilian foreign policy, but also the strategic approach that Itamaraty would take to continue vouchsafing the country's sovereignty in a new and uncertain global context. The result was a 351-page report, *Reflexões Sobre a Política Externa Brasileira*, which summarized and synthesized a series of public and internal seminars to provide a set of guiding principles and understandings for Brazilian foreign policy in the post-Cold War era (IPRI, 1993).

Twenty-two years later the *Reflexões* report remains important because it laid the intellectual groundwork for the story in this chapter – Brazil's turn to seeing inclusion in the South as an opportunity, not a pejorative label. Lula's sweeping embrace of Latin America, Africa and the Middle East drew on Brazilian identity self-conceptions that the country truly is a mix of the many races and peoples who immigrated by choice or force to Brazil, which are in turn grounded in the Cardoso era ideas of the South as an area of partnership that could be leveraged for greater international advantage. While glossed over in the *Reflexões* report, a central conceptual principle here is the inversion of Fanonian ideas of identity set out by Jerry Dávila (2010), which sees Brazil using its mixed racial heritage as proof that it is a true citizen of the world at home in any country, not a disjointed nation seeking to reconcile conflicting notions of self. This self-professed cultural affinity with the South sat in the background in the 1990s, but was on constant display during the Lula years and was leveraged through a succession of summits with leaders from Africa, the Middle East and Asia to form a key arm of a multi-pronged strategy to advancing Brazil's ambitions of affecting substantial structural change in the prevailing pattern of global governance (interview with Brazilian diplomats, 2010).

On a political level, efforts to coordinate and express the 'Southern' view have become an effective lever in the structural power game, vaulting Brazil to a seat at key global governance decision making tables. Economically, a turn to the South is offering a double benefit, as discussed in chapters five and six. China's rapacious desire for commodities, set out in chapter eleven, has driven the surge in raw material prices that forms the basis for Brazil's new wealth, but also created new economic dependence challenges that became apparent with the Chinese economic slowdown. Parallel rises in income in the Americas and Africa have created an increased demand for FDI and large infrastructure projects, which are major export sectors of the Brazilian economy. Programmes of enhanced political consultation and more active South–South technical cooperation for development have consequently emerged from Brasília to support the country's economic penetration of the South and bolster a sense of political leadership that is in turn needed for pushing changes in understandings of what is possible in the international system. The prestige and positive presence that these programmes bring are needed because Brazil faces competition across the South, most notably from two of its main Southern partners – China and India – as well as from more traditional rivals in the North.

As this chapter will explain, the Brazilian engagement with the South is a multi-faceted game that often requires simultaneous cooperation and competition. The South offers potentially lucrative opportunities, but it also brings costs. For Itamaraty a central challenge is how to manage these tensions, which has led diplomats to return to Brazil's pattern of weak institutionalization of multilateral forums and the diversion of tension and conflict to exhaustive discussion at the negotiating table. This chapter will focus on the key questions driving Brazil's engagement with the South. Attention will first be turned to the dependency analysis underpinning the Southern agenda. In the next section institutional frameworks and the rise of development cooperation provision policy will be taken up as strategies that Brazil is using in an attempt to manage engagement with the South. Finally, attention will be turned to highlighting the inherent contradictions that come from the competing ambitions and lack of homogeneity across the South to suggest there is little new in the foreign policy track launched by Lula other than a geographic diversification of Brazil's foreign relations, which Dilma has quietly maintained.

Reflecting on Brazil's place and potential in the world

The Baron of Rio Branco José Maria de Silva Paranhos, Junior, founded Brazil's modern foreign policy in the early twentieth century around an approximation with the US in order to use the Monroe Doctrine as a defensive shield against potentially predatory European powers thinking of annexing parts of his country (Burns, 1966; Smith, 1991). In the early 1990s a similar sort of structural concern was at play, only this time it focused on deflecting US interventionist attention away from Brazil. The *Reflexões* report (pp. 52–53) makes clear mention of the US interventions in Panama, Haiti and Peru before turning to highlight the extent to which issues such as human rights, narcotrafficking and the environment were increasingly being seen in Washington as appropriate grounds for violation of a country's sovereignty. While the concern was not so much with the threat of direct US intervention, serious questions were raised about how these external pressures would limit Brazil's domestic policy autonomy and ability to influence continental agendas. More specifically, questions were raised about the potential costs of opposing US punitive initiatives proxied through the OAS and designed to discipline perceived transgressors in these areas.

For Brazil the question was thus one of what does a country with very limited power resources – at best a 'middle power' (IPRI, 1993: 62) – do to protect itself in the emerging international system, particularly when it does not necessarily agree with the course of action being advocated by a hegemonic power or the constraints inherent in extant patterns of structural power. In simple terms, the ideal order advanced in the report was one that assured the prevalence of international rules and law over the naked application of force (IPRI, 1993: 56). Yet this in itself presented a central challenge to Brazil because the framework of international norms, rules and regulations that might constrain naked use of force and direct inter-state relations was itself in flux to cope with new issues arising from changes in global political order and technological innovations. Moreover, the forums in which these discussions were taking place were not viewed as being particularly 'democratic', reflecting more de facto power capabilities over principles of equal member participation. A central problem for a developing country like Brazil with limited hard power resources was thus how to maintain and exert a voice in the management and evolution of the international system (IPRI, 1993: 56–58), yet avoid the risk of being tied down by existing or new multilateral instruments that might restrict national policy autonomy (Daudelin and Burges, 2011; Vigevani and Cepaluni, 2009).

Two critical understandings about how to gain a voice in the international system emerged from the *Reflexões* discussions (IPRI, 1993: 59–61). First, the report concluded 'those who want to influence the debate on rules must demonstrate a national capacity to construct good rules', which translated into policy terms as having a strong domestic record on human rights, honouring democratic principles and guaranteeing economic liberty – broadly the key objectives of the Cardoso presidency. The symbolic or ideational power that went with tackling these internal issues – part of the foreign policy identity dialectic developed by Lafer (2001a) – twinned neatly with the second understanding. Traditional instruments of power such as ideology, military force and economic strength had lost much of the immediate impetus they held during the Cold War. The emerging norm of sustained discussions for framing laws and agreements consistent with a consensual hegemony (Burges, 2008), rather than balder forms of coercion, opened an interesting space where the diplomatic skill and patient negotiating tactics set out in chapter three created potential opportunities for Brazil. As the report noted, success through this new approach required a measure of economic strength as well as credibility and prestige. Advancing individual projects required a clear sense of what Brazil would pursue, as well as the ability to create flexible alliances and coalitions tailored to particular issue sets. Ideas, in other words, had a new or renewed power in international politics.

The next question was with which partners Brazil could effectively leverage these ideas to shift global governance frameworks: 'The major foreign policy effort will thus be to place the country in diplomatic situations that allow it to find emerging niches of opportunity for the exercise of an 'active role' in the construction or application of new rules, dedicating itself in parallel to the construction of new realities of conduct' (IPRI, 1993: 61). Actually pursuing this sort of engaged, innovative policy required overcoming a relative position in the international system that saw Brazil varying between being a demandeur and demandee depending on the actors being engaged. More specifically, the report's compilers summarized the discussion as saying: 'it seems clear that, as a middle power, we find ourselves in various situations in the international system that range from hegemony to dependence' (IPRI, 1993: 62). For the universalist foreign policy strategy adopted by Brazil this presented specific problems: 'one of the perennial problems for our foreign policy is the dissonance between a universal presence and restricted instruments of influence' (IPRI, 1993: 130). The answer which began to emerge during the Cardoso presidency and crystalized during the Lula years was to draw on Brazil's status a nascent middle income country to push a new vision of South–South relations and parlay this into a form of 'bridge' between the North and South.

Building a regional anchor

The idea that emerged from the *Reflexões* exercise was to turn to the South as a point of leverage for gaining access to and influence in global governance forums. A focus on the immediate regional neighbourhood was the first step in rebuilding Brazil's credibility as a serious country and as an international actor. Stabilization of the economy provided the crucial first domestic step, which was further bolstered by the deepening of a series of important structural reforms in the Brazilian economy, not least of which was the initiation of a strategic privatization process (Manzetti, 1999). The next step was to take some measure of charge of the regional context to ensure stability within the Southern Cone and the wider space of South America as a sign that Brazil belonged at major decision making tables. In his Portuguese-language memoires Cardoso (2006b: 607–612) spends some time discussing the shifts in Brazil's energy import patterns that he encouraged first as foreign minister and then as president. Overturning the until then dominant strategic concerns that Argentina was a threat, Cardoso pushed Petrobras into shifting its purchases to acquire more oil from its Southern neighbour as well as another supplier to the North, Venezuela. Raising oil imports from these countries from virtually zero to status as important suppliers was paralleled by work with Bolivia to develop that country's natural gas fields and build a pipeline to the São Paulo industrial heartland (Holanda, 2001) and the development of Angola as another important production site for Petrobras.

These efforts to bind neighbouring countries more closely to Brazil through economic ties were mirrored in the political arena, where attention was quietly devoted to consolidating a sense of Brazilian leadership. As Cardoso noted in an interview with the author in 2007, 'our strategy is to reinforce our position here, to never put aside our global perspective'. The challenge which he went on to describe was how to go about this without actively proclaiming leadership and thus opening Brazil to blocking tactics by other countries. To this end, attention was given to quietly resolving regional crises and acting as a sober voice of counsel, and more particularly pursuing both of these roles free of the imperial baggage and looming sense of hegemonism carried by the US. This was the model on display when armed hostilities broke out again between Ecuador and Peru shortly after Cardoso was sworn in as president. Brazil took charge of the four guarantor nations and engaged in an extended process of quietly forceful mediation between the two countries, ultimately leading to a resolution of the fifty-year dispute in 1998 by convincing Ecuador to accept the status quo and give up dreams of pushing Peru out of the headwaters of the Cenapa River (Cardoso, 2006: 637–640; Herz and Nogueira, 2002; Lampreia, 2009: 148–164).

Perhaps the central area where Cardoso most established Brazilian credibility as a regional leader was that of democracy promotion. Brazil repeatedly offered support to Paraguay as it worked its way through a reluctant democratic transition. Fears of a coup in 1996 caused Paraguayan president Juan Carlos Wasmosy to make a clandestine flight at night to Brasília for a secret meeting with Cardoso where assurances that Brazil would press for the maintenance of institutionality were given (Cardoso, 2015: 545–547). In a similar vein, Cardoso persuaded Raul Cubas Grau to resign from the Paraguayan presidency in 1999 when it appeared that the country was set to implode in the aftermath of vice president Luis Maria Argaña's assassination (Cardoso, 2006: 634–636; Valenzuela, 1997). Similar succor and support was given to Ecuador when Jamil Mahuad was toppled from the presidency in 1999. The 2000 attempted coup against Venezuelan president Hugo Chávez drew a swift response with Brazil organizing a Rio Group call for a return to constitutionality in that country. Likewise, electoral disputes surrounding the 2002 Peruvian presidential ballot returning Alberto Fujimori to office were summarily dismissed by Brazil with a call for the people of Peru to be allowed to deal with their own political processes through the appropriate domestic institutions.

Indeed, the precedents that the Cardoso era set went a long way to positioning Brazil as a reliable interlocutor in times of regional crisis during the Lula years, resulting in Ecuador again turning to Brazil when

Lucio Gutiérrez was overthrown as president in 2005. Bolivia also turned to Brazil in 2005 after Carlos Messa was forced into resignation by mass protests. In 2008 Brazil was at the centre coordinating regional efforts to calm tensions after Colombia violated Ecuadorean sovereignty to bomb a FARC base. By the time Dilma came to power this element of constructive pro-democracy conflict resolution had spread to relations outside the Americas, resulting in Brazil playing an important role in Guinea-Bissau (Abdenur and Souza Neto, 2013) and easing tensions in Mozambique during 2013 when there were fears that the Renamo and Frelimo political movements might reignite the country's civil war. The regional challenge was that towards the end of the Lula years an increasing level of ideology appeared to creep into Brazil's treatment of neighbouring countries, with Lula not shying away from expressing his preference for particular candidates, generally of the left. This tendency grew stronger during the Dilma presidency and was manifest in the very quiet response to the growing political tensions in Venezuela that saw the leftist Chávez and Maduro presidencies flirt with the limits of democratic acceptability and the severity with which Brazil reacted to the hyper-accelerated June 2012 impeachment of Paraguay president Fernando Lugo, suspending Paraguay's political rights in Mercosul.

The characteristic that came to dominate Brazil's regional relations under Cardoso and create the frame for its insertion into the Global South under Lula and Dilma was an ideas-based soft power, focusing on a gentle touch and the sort of engagement-based tactics mapped out in chapter three. As the democratic protection examples in the previous paragraph demonstrate, an added dimension was an explicit respect of the principle of national self-determination, something Cardoso claims set his country apart from the US and which senior diplomats continue to argue gives them expanded access and credibility with the vast majority of the UN's membership (Cardoso, 2006a: 222). Amplifying this sense of constructive leadership were the efforts Brazil was giving to building the South American region in a literal sense through the 2000 Brasília Summit of South American presidents, which advanced a comprehensive physical infrastructure integration programme. The presidential diplomacy of Cardoso bolstered these processes, particularly his skill dealing with Carlos Menem in Argentina, the intellectual respect he commanded from Chávez, and the personal friendships he had developed with the Chilean political elite during his period of exile in Santiago during the Brazilian military government. Wrapped around these elements was the impact of the discussion-based consensual approach to decision making on the regional level. While Brazil may have quietly talked neighbouring countries into submission to its view, the notable characteristics were a lack of the sorts of coercive tactics used by Northern powers to compel support, and Itamaraty's willingness to flex on non-core elements to maintain collective consent. Despite grumbles from countries like Paraguay and Uruguay over the inevitability of their adoption of Brazil's stance on many global issues, there was grudging recognition that working with Brazil did at least offer them a chance of getting their views and concerns onto the global decision making table. Similar views were expressed by Mozambican officials about their engagement with Brazil during the Lula and Dilma years, highlighting how sustained dialogue with Brazil provided an important intelligence source for understanding what was going on in the inner corridors of global governance institutions.

Outside of South America, Brazil began to be viewed as a critical interlocutor and leader with the continent. At the ninth Iberoamerican Summit in Havana, Spanish Prime Minister Aznar sought a private meeting with Cardoso for a frank discussion about Spain–Latin America relations (Cardoso, 2007). German chancellor Kohl repeatedly sought to push Brazil's presence in South America by encouraging Cardoso to take on the role of 'anchor' to a deepened Mercosul which might move to something similar to the EU (Cardoso, 2006: 617–619). Relations with the US also remained strong, if understated, and often resulted in Cardoso taking on a quiet management role at regional summits to constrain voices such as that of Venezuela's Chávez or helping to resolve extra-regional tensions like the 2001 collision between a US spy plane and a Chinese military aircraft (Dianni and Braga, 2001). Perhaps the ultimate accolade handed to the direction Cardoso was taking Brazil came in the form of inclusion in the 'Third Way' leaders club, which brought together US president Bill Clinton, UK Prime Minister Tony Blair, Italian Prime Minister Romano Prodi and German chancellor Helmut Kohl to discuss new forms of governance and public policy management for the twenty-first century. In a similar vein Cardoso teamed with his Portuguese counterpart Mário Soares to launch a new institutional framework that exploited linguistic and cultural links across the Global South by forming the CPLP (Cardoso and Soares, 1998).

Broadening the Southern reach

Drawing on the findings of the *Reflexões* report, a clear theme through Cardoso's public statements was that Brazil had to engage with both its neighbourhood and the wider South if it was to achieve the national development and autonomy it sought. During the Cardoso presidency overtly engaging in this process was difficult in part because of the fiscal challenges that marked the 1990s and then the rolling economic instability between the real's devaluation in 1999 and the collapse of the Argentine economy in 2002. While these uncertainties remained in place during the first years of the Lula presidency, the policy context had changed with the arrival of a more Southerly oriented group of foreign policy makers in the form of presidential advisor Marco Aurélio Garcia and newly appointed Itamaraty number two Samuel Pinheiro Guimarães. The major shift brought by the new regime was a changed view of the potential the South offered for Brazil. Rather than seeing a strong position within the South as a way of making Brazil credible to the North, the Lula team further developed the logic to turn intra-Southern positioning into a lever for challenging existing structural power realities. Intrinsic in this was an expanded engagement across the South, which drove a renewed interest, in addition to the standing work with Latin America addressed in chapter eight.

At the time, Lula's turn to the South was seen as an ideologization of Brazilian foreign policy, placing notions of global leftist solidarity within the PT ahead of the established common sense of Itamaraty's European and US orientation. Viewed retrospectively, the turn to the South for which Lula's foreign policy was strongly criticized emerges as more than a simple ideological sop to keep his party base happy while the Cardoso-era liberal economic policies were continued, although this element did come into play. As one Geneva-based G20 diplomat mused in 2007, Brazil was assuming a sort of 'spiritual leader' role, working to resolve intra-Southern conflicts while staying above the fray (author interview). Certainly, there was an element of prestige-seeking necessary for gaining global position (Stolte, 2015). But, there were also pragmatic and concrete reasons for engaging the wider South that matched up with a search for the new investment and trade opportunities discussed in chapters five and six. As Lula pointed out at the 2006 Africa-South America Summit in Nigeria, Brazil's ambitions to change global patterns of structural power were the main preoccupation: 'If we want a different globalization, one that is more equitable and marked by solidarity, we need strategic partnerships that bring together developing countries' (Nossa, 2006). Business actors were far more direct, noting not only that Africa was set to rise, but also that the trick was to get into a new market early, which in turn opened space to help shape a country's regulatory climate and political standards in a manner sympathetic to the Brazilian business interests (interviews with Brazilian executives, 2010). As one construction company executive in Africa noted, 'it was the Lula government which encouraged the move by Brazilian firms to other continents, principally Africa' (author interview, 2014). Another executive was more direct, opining that 'Itamaraty was not prepared for this. They like to go the UN and say okay "free the Palestinians", but not on a business oriented perspective. That is not what we have had' (author interview, 2015).

The reality was that Brazil already had an important presence throughout the Global South, including in Africa where the changes introduced by the Lula government were particularly striking. On a government-to-government level Brazil was already providing scholarship programmes to educate Africans at national universities in a tradition that dated back to the 1960s, but which accelerated rapidly during the Lula years, including the 2011 establishment of Unilab, the Universidade da Integração Internacional da Lusofonia Afro-Brasileira (Milani, 2015). Military engagement, while understated, was active to the point where the Namibian Navy is equally comfortable operating in Portuguese as English, thanks to long-standing officer training and exchange programmes with Brazil (interview with senior Brazilian government official). On the economic front major Brazilian companies had well-established operations in Africa, as discussed in chapter six. Most notable in this respect were the activities of the *empreiteiras*. Trade between the two continents also has a long tradition, although never in the sort of high volumes that elicit much political excitement. Nevertheless, links with Africa have been important as an alternate source for oil supplies and as a market for some Brazilian manufacturing and agribusiness enterprises discussed in chapter five. More significant has been the flow of FDI from Brazilian firms into Africa. Overarching these elements was a sort of comparative advantage for Brazilian entrepreneurs that tracks back to the cultural melting-pot nature of Brazilian society, which has combined with the country's historical traditions to create a business class that intrinsically understands how formal rules interact with equally dominant informal norms in a manner that is not necessarily redolent of corruption, but also dissonant from the strict legality found in the North.

The economic underpinning of Brazil's engagement with Africa and the wider South reaches back to the logic in the *Reflexões* report, that Brazil needs to look beyond the North for opportunity. At the core of the *auto-estima* – self-belief – vision for Brazil and the wider South advanced by Lula was a sense that developing countries were missing out on opportunities within their own markets and between each other. To this end Lula started off his presidency with a call to reshape international trading relations into a new global economic geography that would build intra-Southern logistical routes to facilitate South–South exchange (Lula da Silva, 2004). In this vein a particularly telling development was the 2003 launch of the India-Brazil-South Africa Dialogue Forum (IBSA), which was created to foster inter-government, inter-society and inter-business cooperation to maximize pan-Southern synergies. While spectacularly uninteresting in terms of headline grabbing surges in trade flows or the announcement of high profile deliverables with a clear potential to transform the global system, IBSA has nevertheless quietly worked to bolster enhanced trilateral coordination in technical areas and introduce the three countries to each other and their respective neighbourhoods. The parallels are with the spread of Brazilian multinationals discussed in chapter six, with the expansion of non-Northern intermediated coordination quietly helping to advance an alternate agenda in global governance forum such as the WTO, G20 and UN, as well as providing an umbrella for a slow but steady growth in business and civil society linkages.

As was set out in the introduction to this book, Brazil lacks the hard power resources necessary to move quickly into a position of prominence across the Global South. Again, the emphasis was on the quiet tactics mapped out in chapter three, with Lula expanding upon the process of quiet dialogue and engagement seen during the Cardoso years. While sitting as president, Lula visited 21 African countries during 12 separate trips and received in Brazil visits from 47 African leaders representing 27 nations. His foreign minister Celso Amorim was even busier, undertaking 67 official visits to 34 different countries on the continent, often involving travel conditions that he described as 'uncomfortable' (Amorim, 2013: chapter 7). Attention during the Dilma years dropped off on an official level, but she nevertheless did travel to South Africa, Mozambique and Angola in 2011, as well as attending the 50th anniversary celebrations of the African Union in 2013, where she announced the cancellation or restructuring of USD 900 million in debt owed by twelve African countries. The sentiment was that under Dilma Africa had faded from the presidential agenda. As one Mozambican official revealingly noted, Dilma had visited once and was aware of the continent, which was all that was necessary in a context where engagement had moved more from the political to the working level. More significantly, there remained a sense on the working level that the lines of communication with Brazil remained open and that projects planned during the Lula years were continuing (Gubo, 2015).

In the private sector, lines of government influence on Brazilian firms in Africa appeared to have retracted. As one oil executive in Luanda noted, while Petrobras was never a major producer in Angola, its presence by 2014 was becoming almost irrelevant with daily production of only about 4,000 barrels per day. More telling was Petrobras's absence from the 2011 auction for blocs in the Kwanza offshore field (author interview, 2014). Although this likely represented business considerations trumping political imperatives – sub-salt investments in Brazil were creating a considerable financial strain and the geology of Angola is complicated – the decision stands in contrast with operations in South America which see Petrobras working to ensure it maintains a substantive presence in neighbouring countries (interviews with Brazilian diplomats, 2010). Similar changes were ocurring in Mozambique by 2015 where Vale was actively exploring options for lowering its exposure by acquiring a substantial equity partner for its Moatize and Nacala corridor operations. Private sector activities in Angola's oil and gas sector demonstrated a similar hedging with Odebrecht managing its 15% share of a deep water drilling bloc from its petroleum headquarters in Houston despite the estimated USD 5 billion cost of the operation (interview with oil executive in Luanda, 2014).

Nevertheless, the sense from the wider Brazilian business and diplomatic community towards the end of Dilma's first presidential term was less optimistic about their country's engagement with African partners. During the Lula years bilateral presidential visits were paralleled by a series of summits that Brazil organized to bring South American leaders together with their counterparts from sub-Saharan Africa and the Arabic-speaking world. Although the concrete deliverables from these events were often underwhelming – indeed, Argentine president Nestor Kirchner stormed out of the 2005 South America-Arab Summit in impatience as a ploy to rein in Brazilian ambitions – the often overlooked point is that they did create direct face-to-face contact unintermediated by Northern powers or geography, opening the space for a major reshaping in how policy ideas were thought through and coordinated across the South. Underpinning these visits was an enormous amount of bureaucratic effort to coordinate activities and agree on the declarations and joint statements announced during the meeting of dignitaries, which deepened desk-level linkages between governments. This in turn prompted a rapid expansion in diplomatic representation, with Itamaraty increasing the number of embassies in Africa from 17 in 2002 to 37 in 2012.

On a practical level the expanded engagement with Africa paid major dividends in the UN. As one senior Brazilian diplomat noted, where he previously had to rely on the parsed institutional reporting or private intelligence services such as Stratfor or *The Economist*, Brazil's network of embassies and even multinational corporations allowed diplomats to gather their own intelligence and conduct analyses consonant with the needs of their foreign policy. This was highlighted as being particularly important for Brazil's more active foreign policy and efforts to coordinate critical, but positive engagement with the institutions of global structural power. Although countries such as Argentina, Colombia and Mexico are seeking to open more missions, Brazil remains the only Latin American country with direct and widespread penetration into Africa, which is particularly important for engagement in conflict zones such as Sudan and the Democratic Republic of Congo. As the senior diplomat pointed out, the unvarnished reporting available from his diplomatic missions in or near these conflict zones is becoming increasingly important as Brazil becomes something of a fixture in a whole range of international peace and security forums. From the Brazilian point of view the critical point is that the information they operate with has not been filtered to meet with the interpretations suggested as reasonable by a Northern analytical lens. This is turn builds Brazilian credibility throughout the South as a credible interlocutor and framer of alternatives even if it does at times also result in a position and interpretation that seems strange to established powers.

Although the engagement with Africa remained significant through the transition from Lula to Dilma, there was a distinct shift in the importance of Africa in diplomatic thinking at the highest levels. As the Mozambican official cited above noted, engagement continued, most notably through regular conferences and seminars that brought Brazilian and African officials together to discuss technical questions of mutual interest. But without the sustained political pressure of the Lula years, bureaucratic attention in Itamaraty appeared to drift and offer quiet resistance. While some ranking diplomats remarked that there was a new breed of diplomat at Itamaraty who saw Africa as the land of opportunity, not a penance to be served before joining the Elizabeth Arden circuit in London, Rome and Paris (interview with Brazilian diplomats, 2014), this view appears to be more applicable to an entrepreneurial minority who took a wider view of their future career prospects to encompass possibilities outside government service. Indeed, the overt signals from Dilma were not helping encourage career focus on Africa, with one former ambassador to the continent complaining in a 2014 interview that the lack of presidential engagement was undermining their hard work at not only opening markets and investment opportunities for Brazilian firms, but also at building the government-to-government linkages critical for sustaining support of Brazil's international initiatives, itself a critical activity to redress perceived global structural power imbalances.

One of the factors afflicting the diplomatic engagement with Africa has been a shortage of staff in the region; as of late 2012 Brazil was short about 40 diplomats and 45 assistants in its African missions. While anecdotal, a common theme in field research during the 2010s was the shortage of accredited diplomats in the region, including the presence of empty offices in many of the missions visited. Matters were further complicated by massive cuts which Dilma brought to Itamaraty, dropping funding by the end of her first term to less than half of what it was when Lula left office. This had a telling impact on relations with Africa by radically contracting the resources available to meet the rapidly rising demand for South–South technical cooperation from Brazil; available funds fell from USD 20.2 million in 2010 to USD 9.7 million in 2012 (Rossi, 2013). Perhaps more disturbing for the general practice of diplomacy was that the budget cuts left Itamaraty unable to finance the physical infrastructure of their new missions in Africa. Meeting basic operating costs such as internet, water and electricity effectively devolved to a personal responsibility of Brazilian diplomats as funds failed to materialize in embassy bank accounts (Mello and Fleck, 2015). Problems with payments to the diplomatic support staff posted in the embassies further exacerbated issues and created additional challenges keeping the missions running.

The pattern under Lula, as described by one ranking diplomat, was to pursue high-level political engagement to back specific processes. To this end a strategic bilateral partnership was formed with South Africa and similar plans were being discussed with Angola in 2010. Strategic dialogue processes were also part of relations with Algeria, Egypt and Nigeria, with plans to add Kenya. Similar engagement efforts came to fruition in early 2015 with agreement on bilateral investment treaties with Angola and Mozambique. In these and similar processes the focus was on the sort of policy consultation on both bilateral and multilateral issues that underpinned Brazilian work within the WTO and marked intra-Latin American relations. On a practical level engaging in these processes gave many of Brazil's partner countries an opportunity to have direct input into core discussions in global governance forum such as the WTO and the G20, institutions in which the North was increasingly looking to Brazil as a bridge with the South.

Patterns of penetration

To help propel the engagement process during the Lula years attention was also returned to some initiatives from the Cardoso era, particularly the CPLP, which one Mozambican official described as being particularly useful because it increased the political weight of the smaller countries by allowing them to regularly consult and link with Brazil and Portugal (author interview, 2013). This idea of expanded influence through coordination was publicly highlighted by Mozambican president Armando Emilio Guebuza (2013) when he noted that one of the greatest advantages of the CPLP is that its members are also members of the subregional groupings where they are geographically located, i.e., South America, East Africa, West Africa, ASEAN and the EU, which allows for greater coordination possibilities and the potential for leverage. Conversations with executives in Angola and Mozambique reinforced this theme, although with a greater focus on the personality of Lula than the innate characteristics of Brazil. As one individual put it, the personal charisma of Lula had an enormous impact on the ability of Brazilian firms to gain access to these new markets. Diplomats at Itamaraty recognized this with some going so far as to quietly acknowledge that Itamaraty was generally trailing behind Lula and the Planalto Palace (interviews with Brazilian diplomats, 2010). The Vale investment in Mozambique in particular was highlighted as a case where the attention of the Brazilian president and the emphasis on a corporate strategy that promised developmental outcomes, as well as a cash inflow, resulted in the mining company winning the contract despite not having perhaps the most generous bid on the table. Money mattered, but inclusion in a larger project and the sense of solidarity in dealing with perennial challenges of poverty from Brazil appeared to give Vale that critical extra competitive edge.

It is this sustained engagement on substantive matters with African colleagues that is perhaps the greatest shift under Lula that supported a deepening of engagement. One observer in Luanda put forward the suggestion that the PT engagement with Africa was really a continuation of the foreign policy trajectory started by Cardoso, but with the added twist of Lula's personal attention to the continent (interviews with Brazilian diplomats). Looking back on his time as foreign minister, Amorim (2015b) noted that 'Africa was in our minds all along... Our policy did not really change during the Cardoso government. I was ambassador in the UN and the WTO, and we always tried to coordinate with the Africans.' What Amorim did see was a shift from Cardoso to Lula with respect to Africa:

> The Cardoso government did not really pick up as much as it could because his vision was more that Brazil should look for better integration with the Western world. Not because of any prejudice, but because of the economic convictions that were there... With the Lula government it was exactly the contrary. It was very clear for Lula that we had to strengthen our relations with the other countries of the South, big countries, but also the African countries. (Amorim, 2015b)

In practical terms this helped propel wider interest from Brazilian business and government, something bolstered by Lula's practice of taking a large private and public sector delegation with him on official visits, although it took some effort to get participation for the first couple of trips.

The optics of the post-2003 Brazilian policy changes to Africa prompted Viana da Silva Magalhães, the second deputy speaker of the Mozambican National Assembly to note that Lula brought important changes in attitude and approach to engagement (author interview). The extent of this shift in mentality was set out by a Brazilian executive who recalled a meeting in Sierra Leone where that country's president commented that the Brazilian delegation looked more European than the European delegation (author interview, 2010). The executive went on to explain that in many respects the senior officials at Itamaraty have tended to look and think like Europeans, which means they try to play international politics by European rules and norms. The big change that Lula brought was a clear decision that Brazil was neither interested nor disinterested in that game, but would instead play its own game and work to best position Brazilian interests and priorities, which in this context meant taking attitude of equals to interactions with African counterparts. Brazilian corporations gave at least some substance to this rhetoric through their practice of hiring as many locally based staff as possible, although at times this approach was not perhaps as evident at senior executive and board levels as national governments might have wished (interviews with government officials in Angola and Mozambique, 2014/2015).

One important element of the shift that Lula's government brought to general patterns of engagement with the Global South was the expansion of Brazil's provision of technical cooperation. Brazilian officials are very careful to be clear that they do not provide 'foreign aid' or 'official development assistance', phrasing which they see as carrying connotations of the sort of hierarchical relationship they are deliberately trying to avoid through the various political engagement processes. The language is instead one of cooperation and collaboration, emphasizing the transfer of Brazilian knowledge and expertise as well as opening the possibility that the Brazilian experts might learn from the operation, too. These activities are coordinated by the ABC (Agência Brasileira de Cooperação) and do not involve the direct transfer of funds, but rather the lending of technical experts to help set up projects and share expertise.

Data on Brazilian technical cooperation programming is not updated in the same way as for a OECD-DAC-member development agency because there are not the same reporting and oversight pressures. Indeed, since Dilma came to power the budget for ABC has been slashed, resulting in a dramatic decline in the number of projects that can be undertaken, although the ABC internet presence paradoxically increased during the same period. For officials at Itamaraty this is particularly difficult because their counterparts in Africa frequently request assistance with specific projects where Brazil does have the necessary expertise. The state of engagement by Brazil under Dilma thus declined from the height of the Lula years, but still encompassed technical cooperation agreements with Botswana, Sudan, Burkina-Faso, Benin, Gambia, Equatorial Guinea, Zambia, Tanzania, the AU, Rwanda, Swaziland, Sierra Leone and, as of 2009, agreements under negotiation with Ethiopia, Mali Comoros, Burundi, Liberia and Chad. This does not include major projects such as experimental farms, national public health system development, and anti-retroviral factories that were being pursued in countries such as Ghana, Senegal, Angola, Namibia and Mozambique. In an overview publication from 2009, ABC reported 115 cooperation actions in Africa as of 2008 in fields ranging from education, agriculture, livestock, health, environment, public administration, energy, urban development and professional training. Significantly, 74% of the resources directed towards Africa were spent in the CPLP countries.

In many respects the motivations underlying the Brazilian approach to development assistance provision do not differ greatly from those found amongst traditional donors. The same power and prestige ambitions found in the North are equally present in the higher level motivations in Brazil, although mixed with a far more pressing engagement with the reality of poverty and an awareness that South–South linkages will be critical for national development (Burges, 2014; Robledo, 2015; Stolte, 2015). Where matters are significantly different is in the extent to which the provision of technical assistance for development is linked to larger national industrial strategies in Brazil. Where countries such as Australia and Canada are explicit that their development assistance programming should support their international firms – largely in the resource extraction sector – by helping to create the governance and human capital conditions necessary to support FDI by their nationals, Brazilian programming lacks this sort of joined-up thinking, focusing more on building influence and presence across the globe (interviews with Brazilian diplomats, 2010). Questions to Brazilian executives in Africa about linkages to ABC programming were often met with confused looks and one or two instances of questions back at the author, wondering if there might be possibilities for the firm to advance its training activities through this modality.

Similar surprise could be found in Brazil, where one of the biggest complaints in Brasília about ABC's activities is this very lack of over-arching strategy. As Amorim (2015b) recalled, 'It was not planned, but it was not haphazard. We had an awareness that we needed more resources and, of course, the demand – the demand is huge.' He con-tinued on to note that South–South Technical Cooperation provision was not purely responsive, 'that's an oversimplification. It was reactive, but we went there and said "we are here. If you ask us we will see what we can do."' In keeping with these observations, projects are selected on a reactive basis in response to requests from the partner country. While some initiatives such as the ProSAVANA agricultural research programme in Mozambique clearly have the potential to open space for Brazilian firms in the future, this sort of medium- to long-term plan-ning is not driving project development at the outset. The end effect is to leave more of the altruistic veneer of being genuinely interested in helping through a sense of solidarity than is found in the case of many traditional donors. It also undercuts any sense that the projects have a coercive element of requiring compliance from the recipient for continuation, something which is further bolstered by their relatively restrained size and the avoidance of the sort of direct budgetary support programmes that can raise concerns about aid dependency (Easterly, 2006; Moyo, 2009).

The Brazilian provision of technical assistance carries with it two factors that are particularly important for engagement with Africa. First, and shared with the other BRICS countries, is that assistance from Brazil is not linked to specific conditionalities and is responsive to recipient requests. This has important implications for in-country management and the empowerment of the receiving government in a manner that may well be more consistent with the Paris Declaration principles of aid effectiveness than OECD-DAC-member approaches. The second is specific to the CPLP countries. When asked about differences between Chinese and Brazilian technical assistance, Mozambican foreign min-ister Baloi (author interview, 2013) replied that there are 'slight dif-ferences, virtually none significant. All of them attach a very high importance to training and education. Simply when it comes to Brazil it is easier because there is no language barrier. That is a very big plus.' The ease of transferability of Brazilian programming carries through into the corporate sector where enterprises such as Vale and Odebrecht ocassionaly turn to capacity building programmes from their home countries to help with their own training and CSR activities, but not through the auspices of ABC and more often by sending their employees to Brazil for specific educational courses. The training programmes of the Brazilian companies are highly significant in their own right, with a single programme from Vale seeing over three hundred Mozambican maintenance workers in Brazil and over two hundred truck drivers with four of the five simulators owned by the company being brought to Tete (author interview, 2015).

Implicit in the expanded provision of technical cooperation is an attempt to increase influence that aligns with ideas of soft power. Brazilian assistance is definitely not large enough to create issues of aid dependence, but it does have a very direct impact on key public policy areas. More significantly, it has the effect of building relationships on a person-to-person level that access directly into the Brazilian government and position Brazil as a responsive, not directive partner. Additional elements of the development assistance agenda, particularly the provision of university scholarships – including Lula's setting up of Unilab in Fortaleza – creates lasting linkages back to Brazil as the individuals passing through the programme pursue their careers in much the same manner as the US Fulbright scheme and the British Chevening Scholarship programme. Government-to-government linkages are futher developed by the inclusion of foreigners in Brazilian state agency training programmes. In terms of foreign policy the most notable example of this is the provision of 'scholarship' spots at the Rio Branco training institute to counterparts from other Southern nations as well as the regular convening of intensive short courses on diplomatic practice. While none of these programmes are sufficient to vouchsafe Brazilian influence and win contracts for Brazil's firms, they do help open the door and create a positive image for the country.

Reaping the rewards?

On one level the engagement strategy with the Global South has been a huge success for Brazil. In the mid-2000s the members of the G8 turned to Brazil as one of the key countries to engage through the Heiligendamm outreach process with a view to using Brazil as a bridge to bring the wider Global South inline with Northern economic and security planning priorities. Although Brazil quickly rejected its assigned role as a junior adjunct to the G8 members, in other forums such as the WTO the patient work with Southern partners bore fruit and resulted in a leading role in the Doha round negotiations as a member of the 'new quad' drafting the main discussion texts. Similar rewards were found towards the end of Lula's presidency and at the beginning of Dilma's when Brazil was successful in mobilizing support to have ambassador Roberto Carvalho de Azevêdo elected as director general of the WTO in 2013 and Lula's minister for food security José Graziano elected as director general of the Food and Agriculture Organization in 2011.

While both of these are high profile positions, it is telling that neither sit at the core of Northern political, economic or security interests. Brazilian attempts to have ambassador Luiz Felipe de Seixas Corrêa elected as WTO director general in 2005, during the height of US and European hopes that the Doha round would be completed, failed utterly in the face of competition from EU trade commissioner Pascal Lamy and perceptions that the bid was an act of retribution against Uruguayan Carlos Pérez del Castillo for advancing the US/EU text at the 2003 Cancun ministerial meeting (interview with Brazilian diplomats, 2007; WTO official, 2007). Despite brave words from the WTO under Azevedo's tenure, the sense is that trade liberalization efforts have somehow moved past the WTO to various regional and bilateral agreements, particularly efforts to forge a Trans-Pacific Partnership and a Trans-Atlantic Trade and Investment Partnership. José Maurício Bustani's removal as director general of the Organization for the Prohibition of Chemical Weapons provides an even clearer example of the limitations to Brazilian leadership in international organizations. Despite being unanimously reelected for a second term a year early in 2000, the US engaged in an aggressive lobbying campaign to have him removed from his post in 2002 when it emerged he was working to bring Iraq into the organization and thus gain access to detailed records on Saddam Hussein's chemical weapons holdings which might have made US invasion plans more problematic.

A common characteristic of Brazilian efforts to engage the Global South under Cardoso, Lula and Dilma has been the focus on ideas and rhetoric over the allocation of serious resources. Although the amount of direct development assistance and trade diversion provided by Brazil does matter and did increase as the country's fiscal situation improved during the Lula years, the actual fungible resources flowing out to Southern partners remained quite small, particularly when compared to the size of flows and trade absorption from China, the EU and US. The problem, as one scholar has noted in the South American context, was that Brazil was becoming a 'leader without followers' (Malamud, 2011). Growing economic disatisfaction with Brazil despite the ideological affinities that came with the 'pink tide' in the Americas created a conflicted regional context. The centrality of the Brazilian economy to Argentina, Bolivia, Paraguay, Uruguay and Venezuela meant that these countries had limited recourse and were in effect captives bound to limit their political resistance lest such action prove excessively costly. Other continental countries led by Chile, Colombia and Peru retained some political affinity with

Brazil due to a geographically and developmentally induced alignment of interests, but by the Dilma years were increasingly forging out to create a separate destiny, most notably through the formation of the Pacific Alliance bloc with Mexico and latterly Costa Rica.

In part the issue was that under Dilma the seductive veneer of Brazil's Southern engagement strategy, embodied first in the urbane persona of Cardoso and then the raw charismatic power of Lula, began to crack under the pressure of the Brazil-first technocratic policy decision style that she brought to Brasília. Part of this contradiction became clear in July 2013 when plans were announced for a new Africa strategy. On the positive side the project included renegotiating over USD 900 million of African country debt, with a significant portion of it being erased. This was balanced by proposed organizational changes that would move the ABC from the foreign ministry to the MDIC and include it in a special secretariat that would focus on increasing exports and FDI to Africa. Although the idea of increasing trade and investment flows is consistent with dominant visions of the importance of sustainable economic interaction over aid, there remains a distinctly mercantilistic hue to the proposal which aligns it with the much critiqued approaches of China and the North, not the altruistic rhetoric of Lula's Southern solidarity.

The extent to which this is not a surprise to government officials in Africa is reflected in their comments that despite the gentler rhythm of interactions with the Brazilian government and firms, the same commercial prerogatives found elsewhere nevertheless remain firmly to the fore. A particularly pointed example of the limits this brings to Brazil's ability to retain the sort of preferential treatment historically achieved by the British, French and US came in April 2014 when Guinea Bissau stripped Vale of its rights to exploit the Simandou and the Zogota iron ore deposits in response to a government panel's finding that the concession was won through corrupt means. Instead, the reaction was in keeping with positive popular views of Brazil measured against hard business decisions with a soft nod towards protecting the bilateral relationship. Engagement through the CPLP and extensive technical assistance for development and work to support Guinea's democratic transition was apparently translated into an invitation from Conde for Vale to seek a continued engagement with resource extraction development in his country (Abdenur and Neto, 2013; Nebehay, 2014). In what looks a lot like a mirroring of the Brazilian approach to separating friendship and business, blame was wholly attributed to Vale's partner in the project, Guernsey-based BSG Resources, and the opportunity taken by Guinea to improve the concession terms negotiated under the authoritarian regime in 2008 despite the nearly USD 1 billion reportedly invested in the project by Vale.

Conclusion

There is one marginal point that should not be excluded from consideration of why Brazil pushed so forcefully into the Global South and Africa under Lula, particularly in the Brazilian foreign policy context of presidential diplomacy and leadership being key for new departures. As his presidency progressed Lula enjoyed something akin to rock star status, not only amongst the global Left, but also throughout the South. He enjoyed this status on a personal level and clearly sought to use it to not only advance Brazil's position internationally, but also to establish a legacy for himself. Indeed, one of the tales of distress told by Brazilian diplomats connected to the foreign aid file in 2010 was that the Brazil-funded anti-retroviral factory in Mozambique would not be ready in time for Lula to open it before the end of his second term in office. While a battle with cancer slowed Lula down after he left office, during his final years as president it did appear that he was angling for some kind of major international office with some at one point mooting the idea of UN secretary general. What is clear is that Dilma brought a major shift in tone to Brazilian foreign policy that demonstrated considerably less personal interest in foreign affairs (Casarões, 2014), which in terms of African engagement translated into a notification to Brazilian businesses that their government was now going to follow, not break the trail (Peres, 2013).

It is in this respect that the central weakness in Brazil's engagement with the Global South emerges. As set out in the introduction, the power resources available to Brazil to pursue expansive foreign policy ventures are limited and Brazil's natural position of centrality in the world questionable. Clearly there were returns for both Brazil and its Southern partners from the diversification of relations throughout the Cardoso and especially the Lula years. But, as was alluded to in chapters five and six, much of this engagement would have occurred without major direction and assistance from the government. The presence of an eager and active charismatic president in the form of Lula gave a sense of depth and substance to the largely ideas-based ambitions of Brazilian foreign policy in the Global South, and while ideas do matter and are essential for the construction of new realities, ultimately hard resources are needed to create lasting structures. This is where Brazil falls down, both in terms of its ability to commit the sort of massive financial resources seen in Northern and Chinese engagement with the South, and

in terms of the construction of concrete and functional alternate institutional structures, which Brazil recognizes as an authority, something
that in turn would effectively require a diminution of sovereignty that
Itamaraty is simply unwilling to accept.

10

Brazil and the United States

A major theme running through this book is the sense of tension between Brazil and the US that periodically arises across a range of policy areas. Indeed, much of Brazilian foreign policy can be read as an explicit attempt to assert autonomy from the US, reflecting the reality that in no other area is the distinction between relational power and structural power so important for gaining analytical insight as the case of Brazil–US bilateral relations. Although this line of argumentation overlooks the enormous degree of pragmatic cooperation between the two countries, it does have roots in the wider attempts to contest structural power that inevitably require negotiation with American interests. More often than not the interests of each country run in close parallel, and cooperation is far more prevalent than most observers recognize; the overarching tenor of the relationship is one of misunderstanding and at times an almost willful ignorance of the motivations and ambitions of the other actor. As this chapter will argue, a significant factor in what some (Hirst, 2005) have called the 'long road of unmet expectations' between Brazil and the US is the perception in significant portions of the Brazilian foreign policy community that the US is generally playing a relational power game designed to structurally marginalize the South American country. Conversely, policy makers and analysts in Washington often fail to grasp the extent to which Brazil is playing a revisionary, not revolutionary structural power game, set in a context where something more than zero-sum approach is often assumed an option in Brasília. The result is misunderstanding and stunted communication that actively retards what is sometimes a mutually desired collaboration.

The fundamental problem marking the Brazil–US bilateral relationship is a clash between the political perceptions of both sides and the accompanying expectations of what the other side should do. In this context history matters, with Brazil pointing to repeated US failures to provide promised assistance such as development aid after World War Two or substantive economic growth support throughout the Cold War period. For its part the US points to repeated Brazilian refusals to assist with what Washington saw as major geopolitical priorities such as the Korean War, the Vietnam War and, most recently, the two wars in Iraq and Afghanistan. All of this is played out in public with Brazilian politicians finding rhetorical attacks on the US to be a convenient method of bolstering domestic political support. Within the halls of government the picture is more complicated. Where the US stumbles, blockages often stem from simple ignorance about the policy priorities and logic in Brazil; along the Esplanada in Brasília there are strong bureaucratic factions, especially within Itamaraty, that view any collaboration with the US as a dangerous dance with the devil. But cooperation and collaboration remain the rule, with those disputes that do arise often little more than passing contretemps in a generally pragmatic bilateral relationship. An important part of the story thus becomes not only the disjuncture between public utterances and working-level collaboration, but also the inter- and intra-departmental disputes in Brasília about where the US fits into the larger picture of Brazilian public and foreign policy.

An unspoken, but abiding reality in Brazil–US relations is the inherently unequal nature of the relationship (interviews with Brazilian diplomats, 2007; 2010; 2014). From time to time Brazil is a useful partner for the US and can greatly smooth policy initiatives in the Americas and beyond – something that will be discussed below – but the US ultimately does not need Brazil. Conversely, Brazil does need the US. Whether it be as a market or as a source of benediction of national economic policies or political stability, acquiescence and support from Washington is repeatedly sought by governments of all ideological stripes, although generally quietly and through diplomatic channels. This creates a fundamental identity crisis for staunchly nationalist segments of Brazil's foreign policy elites who dream of their country being an autonomous world power fully free to act independently of pressures from Washington. Unable to redress the relative power imbalance and persistent elements of dependence, significant portions of Brazilian foreign policy become about structural power games designed to minimize potential US influence, which is the story through much of the rest of this book. This preoccupation on the part of important segments of Brazil's foreign policy and political elite introduces irritants not only into the bilateral relationship, but also into inter-departmental governmental relationships in Brasília. Matters are only complicated by the failure of official Washington to understand Brazil and plan its policy approaches accordingly.

In order to provide a sense of how relations with the US fit into Brazil's global insertion, this chapter will begin with a rapid historical survey concentrating on the Baron of Rio Branco's 1902 decision to shift his country's diplomatic focus away from Europe and to the US. The importance he foresaw the US having for Brazil will be surveyed in the following section by looking at trade and investment flows in the post-Cold War era, setting the economic ground for the contradictions examined in the subsequent sections. Tensions of structural versus relative power will be unpacked by looking at the extent to which Brazil actively cooperates with the US and the corresponding 'nationalist' backlash that runs as a consistent background theme. The narrative that emerges across the PT governments of Lula and Dilma is consequently one of a certain tetchiness from Brazil, which is aggravated by serious US missteps, and frustration from US foreign policy makers that their Brazilian diplomats take a different view of the world even when interests are seemingly aligned. Ultimately, there is little in the way of 'right' or 'wrong' in how the bilateral relationship is viewed by either side, but rather a sustained lack of mutual understanding.

Turning to the North

Drawing on his time as a diplomat posted to the UK, Germany and the US at the end of the nineteenth century, José Maria da Silva Paranhos Junior, the Baron of Rio Branco, presciently forecast a major shift in global power from Europe to North America at the start of the twentieth century. Under Rio Branco's leadership as foreign minister, the Monroe Doctrine was clearly and openly embraced as Brazil's official view of international power relationships, positioning it as a shield that could be used to protect Brazil's long and vulnerable coastline from resource-hungry European capitals. Setting the tone for contemporary Brazil–US relations, obeisance to Washington was not what Rio Branco had in mind when he deployed the Monroe Doctrine as a defensive device. He instead envisioned a practical division of responsibilities in the hemisphere. The US would vouchsafe territorial integrity in the hemisphere and Brazil would use its already considerable negotiating capabilities to manage the situation in South America. In effect, Rio Branco was explicitly recognizing Brazil's weakness in terms of relative power, and seeking to build a hemispheric structure that could be used to manage pressures from Europe, allay fears from the US, and consolidate a leading position for his country in South America (Burns, 1966).

While there was certainly logic to Rio Branco's plan, by the 1920s some of the flaws in terms of mutual interest in this strategic relationship were becoming evident. The decade was marked by a period of US indifference towards Brazil, with Brazilian support in international and regional policies being assumed as a given by officials in the White House and State Department without a need to engage in substantial degrees of reciprocity (Crandall, 2011; Smith, 1991). In the years after World War One Washington seemingly only took note of Brazil when US interests such as warship construction contracts were at stake or a Latin American pathbreaker was needed for a US-backed international treaty. By 1930 the Brazilian government had become fed up with this treatment and pointedly refused to sign the Franco-American treaty that would explicitly outlaw war in the Americas (Smith, 2010: chapter four). Nevertheless, the turn to the US was not abandoned. In the 1930s president Getúlio Vargas reversed the Washington Luís presidency trend of rising tension between Brazil and the US, advancing a 'good neighbours' foreign policy approach that sought to use close links with Washington as a platform to facilitate expanded industrialization and accelerated modernization in Brazil (Smith, 1991). The central problem identified by Vargas was that Brazil required massive levels of investment and technology. While taxing the land-owning elite and existing industrialists in Brazil was one option for mobilizing the necessary capital, Vargas recognized that this was a dangerous strategy in a country still sorting out regional rivalries and social cleavages. Simply borrowing the money in international capital markets was also out of the question because lending to states such as Brazil had stopped as a result of the financial pressures of the Great Depression. Direct help from Washington seemed the only alternative, but in a continuation of a long-standing pattern the White House did not appear to be listening.

With the outbreak of World War Two US policy makers returned their attention to Brazil, using the North coast of the country as an important staging point for the Southern Atlantic convoy route. Although officially neutral for most of the war, Brazil was drawn into hostilities in August 1942 after 36 of its ships were sunk by Axis powers, and eventually took part in the Italian campaign towards the end of the conflict. Part of Vargas's logic for helping the Allies was an expectation of concrete assistance with national development, ideally through something similar to the Marshall plan in Europe. These hopes were disappointed and proved to be defining lessons that would guide foreign policy and domestic development policy for the next forty years. On the foreign policy front the chief lesson was that irrespective of the desires of Itamaraty or the military, the US was at best an ambivalent partner.

A major break in Brazilian foreign policy came with the inauguration of the fiercely nationalist president Jânio Quadros in 1961. Although

Quadros was soon pushed out of office after making the spectacular political blunder of tendering his resignation as a tactic in a dispute with Congress, his vice-president João Goulart continued the *política externa independente* (independent foreign policy). The basic principles of this new approach were mapped out for the English-speaking world in an article Quadros (1961) published in the journal *Foreign Affairs*. Beyond the near-obligatory statements about promoting peace and disarmament, Brazil's new foreign policy concentrated on using the UN to balance the role of the US and its perceived proxy the Organization of American States in the Americas (Burns, 1966). Under the *política externa independente* Brazil effectively attempted to disengage from the Cold War. While relations with the non-aligned movement were kept at the level of 'observer status', diplomatic relations were restarted with Cuba and the USSR partly as a political statement, but also to open the door to the transfer of technology and potential increases in trade. For US policy makers, as well as the military in Brazil, this foreign policy shift was alarming because it paralleled domestic political changes that raised concerns the country was undergoing a process of Cubanization. On 1 April 1964 Goulart was ousted by a coup and the *política externa independente* reversed.

The first military president (1964–1967), Marshall Humberto de Alencar Castelo Branco, initiated a period of flux in the strategic orientation towards the US, pulling Brazil back into close alignment with the US. Serious effort was devoted to supporting US efforts at pan-American engagement and the isolation of potential communist threats, including severing relations with Cuba and aiding the US with an OAS-bannered invasion of the Dominican Republic in 1965. In an approach that continues to have repercussions for bilateral relations to this day, the anti-communist stance also included internal threats, resulting in a national security doctrine that pursued a systematic campaign of repression. Under this doctrine, which would remain in place until 1985, future presidents received special attention: Fernando Henrique Cardoso was forced into exile, Dilma Roussef was detained and tortured, and Lula was imprisoned for his union leader activities. Countless others on the left also suffered, including many key Lula policy figures such as José Dirceu and Marco Aurélio Garcia.

Significantly, the adoption of this strict national security doctrine and the short-lived foreign policy realignment with the US did not result in a complete reversal of key aspects of the policy track launched by Goulart. The developmentalist prerogative he had continued from Vargas and Kubitschek remained firmly in place, focusing on the industrialization of Brazil and the creation of advanced productive frameworks. This in turn would eventually push Brazil back to a foreign policy of autonomy and independence in order to acquire the necessary capital and technology, yet again raising questions about the reliability of the US as a strategic partner well disposed to Brazilian development. Castelo Branco's successor as military president Artur da Costa e Silva consequently redirected his country's foreign policy to something approximating the *política externa independente*. In a pattern that has parallels with the PT foreign policy of the 2000s, Brazil moved to a foreign policy of 'resposible pragmatism', becoming a Third World country pushing for structural changes in global economic governance and actively campaigning to head the Group of 77. Regional coordination efforts focused on creating horizontal frameworks and using the Ibero-American heritage to sideline the OAS and US as a regional arbiter. The foreign policy and economic tensions this created with the US were echoed in the security sector where Brazil not only refused to sign the non-proliferation treaty, but also insisted on developing a national nuclear capacity in partnership with whomever was interested in helping.

Brazil's American economic anchor

The subsequent military presidencies moderated the independent tone somewhat to accept concrete bilateral engagement as appropriate in some policy areas. In particular there was recognition during the debt crises of the 1980s that the relationship with the US was key to safeguarding Brazil's economic security even if direct assistance in the form of economic or technology transfers was unlikely. The problem for Brazilian policy makers was that the sort of orthodox stabilization plans proposed by the IMF and backed by the US Treasury proved ineffective. Strong suggestions from Washington that Brazil and the rest of the Americas pursue the sort of unilateral economic opening and liberalization seen in Chile were also rebuffed as not being entirely helpful for a country such as Brazil, which was then suffering through serious inflation crises due to a highly indexed economic model that automatically injected inflationary shocks into the system (Fishlow, 2011: chapter three; Bandeira, 2004: 50–55; Roett, 2010: chapter five).

From a US perspective, events leading up to the launch of the real plan in 1993 did little to build confidence in Brazil's ability to formulate and successfully implement independently created heterodox economic stabilization plans. It was thus not entirely surprising that requests for US support with debt refinancing and a new IMF stabilization agreement to support the plan in September 1993 were greeted with skepticism. Officials such as Lawrence Summers, then serving as Undersecretary for

International Affairs of the United States Department of the Treasury, took an almost tutelary tone to Cardoso's economic team, effectively lecturing the Brazilians on the need to announce and pursue sweeping privatizations as a sign of seriousness if they wanted US support for an IMF support programme. Although Cardoso ultimately succeeded in bringing Brazil's soaring inflation under control without direct US backing, the interaction left a nasty aftertaste and a strong sense that policy makers in Washington lacked any meaningful understanding of the very different set of economic challenges facing reformers in Brazil (Prado, 2005: 152–160). This same sense of disquiet and misunderstanding was repeated in 1998 when, in the wake of the 1997 Asian Financial Crisis, officials at the US Treasury and the IMF called for sweeping changes to macroeconomic policy inconsistent with the reality in Brazil, prompting Cardoso (2006b: 397) to write in his diaries: 'Everyone is a pessimist. They do not know the situation in Brazil and want a fiscal adjustment of enormous proportions that is absolutely not feasible.' Doubt within the IMF remained rife and pressure from the US Treasury to follow a more orthodox path, including raising interest rates and devaluation of the real, grew, creating yet again a very difficult negotiating environment for Brazilian economic officials (Cardoso 2006b: 403–407). From Brazil's point of view the important change was that US support was forthcoming and the IMF did back the Brazilian approach to the economic crisis, even if reluctantly.

Two things stand out about the US role in supporting Brazil during the 1998 economic crisis and 1999 devaluation of the real. Where Brazilian macroeconomists had largely been dismissed by Treasury officials in 1993, the real plan's subsequent success stabilizing the national economy without active US help built the credibility needed to at least open the avenue for serious discussion about policy options. Building on this was the second factor, which was the strong personal relationship and mutual confidence that had developed between Clinton and Cardoso. As some of Cardoso's aides commented, summit meetings required tactful management because the two leaders were quite happy to forgo sleep and spend the entire night in earnest conversation. The pay-off in policy terms for Brazil was substantial, particularly during the 1998 economic crisis. Summarizing the importance of his relationship with the US president, Cardoso (2007) recalls: 'Because of Clinton the IMF accepted our views and gave us an enormous amount of money to counter-attack the speculation crisis.' While this did not stop a whispering campaign on Wall Street suggesting Brazil's position was weaker than IMF actions would suggest, it bought Cardoso time to plan the way forward during a moment of very turbulent markets. Perhaps more significantly, the relationship also helped to remove one source of pressure on Cardoso during the sudden devaluation of the real in February of 1999.

The 1998 lessons about the centrality of US support and good interpersonal relations between the US and Brazilian presidents were not lost on foreign and economic policy makers in Brazil. International markets reacted to the apparent certainty of a Lula victory in the 2002 presidential election by again putting pressure on the real, forcing its value down to 3.99 to the US dollar and placing the future of the Brazilian economy on a knife edge. Cognizant that major statements of international support would be required to prevent collapse, Cardoso quietly engaged in a proactive diplomatic programme designed to make markets comfortable with Lula and to convince White House policy makers that the PT leader was credible and responsible. Efforts began by assisting senior PT advisors with trips to Washington and New York to meet with officials at the Treasury and IMF as well as major financial institutions on Wall Street, helping create the confidence needed to secure a USD 30 billion IMF standby agreement shortly before first round voting. More intriguing were the 18 days in November after Lula secured victory in the run off ballot. A delicate diplomatic dance was coordinated between Lula's transition team, the Planalto Palace, the Itamaraty Palace, the Brazilian embassy in Washington, and the US embassy in Brasília to secure a meeting between the president-elect and US president George Bush. On a working level the goal was to reassure officials in Washington that the Lula government did not represent a radical departure as seen in Venezuela. At a leader's level the ambition was to establish Lula as a serious figure in the eyes of Bush. Success was achieved on both fronts with the added bonus of a surprising level of natural chemistry between the two presidents that forged a collegial friendship transcending their substantial ideological differences (Spektor, 2014). While the value of this personal connection would eventually fade as the US and Brazil grappled with contending approaches to various policy issues, it did provide an initial anchor of credibility that helped the Lula administration through its first two years in office and on to the commodity boomfuelled path of economic growth and social development (Barbosa, 2011: chapter 7).

Difficult dependency

One way of reading the US influence on the decade-long process of stabilizing the Brazilian economy is to cast the White House in the sort of veto-wielding role attributed to core actors in dependency models of international political economy. While Brazil's growing ability to pursue

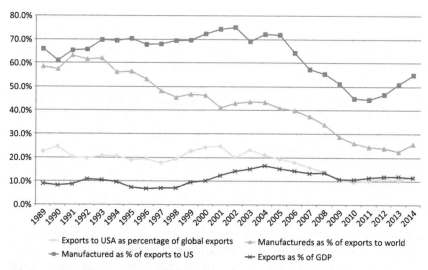

80.0%
70.0%
60.0%
50.0%
40.0%
30.0%
20.0%
10.0%
0.0%
1989 1990 1991 1992 1993 1994 1995 1996 1997 1998 1999 2000 2001 2002 2003 2004 2005 2006 2007 2008 2009 2010 2011 2012 2013 2014

Exports to USA as percentage of global exports   Manufactureds as % of exports to world
Manufactured as % of exports to US   Exports as % of GDP

Figure 10.1 Brazilian exports to the US and the world, 1989–2014

endogenously created macroeconomic policy solutions points to cracks in this argument, what is abundantly clear is that the US continued to be the central economic partner. Indeed, even after accounting for Brazil's relatively low export to GDP ratio, and the rise of China as an export market, the importance of the US economy for Brazil is unmistakable.

Figure 10.1 tells the story of exports in the Brazilian economy in general and where the US fits into this picture. The bottom line on the chart tracks the export of goods and services as a percentage of GDP. Brazil stands apart from other major international economies in that exports account for a surprisingly small proportion of the economy, sitting around 10% of GDP in the early 1990s. From that point the picture changed and exports dropped to as low as 6.7% in 1996 before rebounding to the 14–16% range during the commodity boom of the 2000s. Throughout this period the US remained the preeminent export destination, absorbing 19–24% of foreign goods and services sales in the 15 years to 2004. More significant than the volume of exports absorbed by the US is the type of products sold to that market. Up until about 2004 the sort of manufactured exports underpinning the developmental-ist aims of Brazilian economic and foreign policy accounted for roughly 20–25% of the country's global exports. Within this context the US market becomes extremely important with manufactureds growing from a 61% share in 1990 to a high of 75.1% in 2002. The steady decline in the share of manufactureds in Brazilian exports to the US from 2003 until 2010 tracks roughly against the appreciation of the real, which was driven up in value by the global commodities boom. As the collapse in commodity prices after the Global Financial Crisis and economic mismanagement worked to drive down the value of the real, the proportion manufactures in the export basket rebounded, recovering from a low of 44.5% in 2010 to 55% in 2014.

A second important element of the US export market for the Brazilian economy is revealed by the opposite tracks followed in Figure 10.1 by the share of manufactureds in the exports to the US and the proportion of Brazilian exports going to that market. Until the rapid appreciation of the real began in the mid-2000s the US value-added market was growing for Brazilian producers. The argument here is that the US market remained an extremely important one for Brazilian firms despite the 'turn to the South' that took place during the Lula and Dilma presidencies. One of the critiques fiercely levelled against the Lula governments from 2005 on was that an ideologization of foreign policy was resulting in serious losses in the US market (Almeida, 2014; C. Barbosa, 2014; Barbosa, 2011: chapter seven; Milani and Almeida, 2011). When viewed from the perspective of Figure 10.1 this critique holds water and even accelerated during the first Dilma presidency. Indeed, Figure 10.2 clearly highlights that the percentage of exports going to the US fell precipitously during the Lula and Dilma years, seeing China take over top spot as the main Brazilian trading partner.

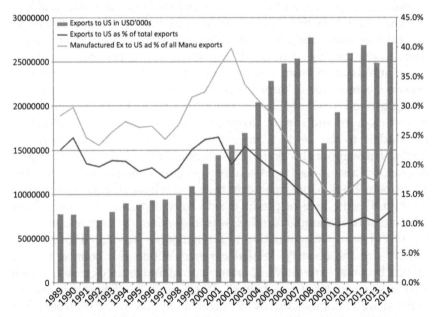

Figure 10.2 Brazilian exports to the US in nominal and % of total, 1989–2014

While technically correct, this widely circulated critique missed two important points. First, the decline in the US share of national exports tracks almost exactly with the surges in both commodity prices and exports by volume discussed in chapter 5. In other words, the boost in market share held by other countries such as China reflects not only the increased export of agricultural and mineral commodities, but also a major multiplier factor caused by the massive increases in the prices of these products in the mid-2000s. The second factor is that despite the decline in proportional terms as a market, the nominal value of goods and services exported to the US soared, doubling over the eight years from 2000 to 2008. Moreover, throughout this surge in the nominal value of total exports, manufactureds accounted for over 68% of the trade from 1993 to 2005, before tapering down to a low of 45% in 2010 as the twin effects of global recession and an overvalued real bit into the competitiveness of Brazilian firms. As the real began to weaken from 2012 both the nominal value and the proportion of manufactureds exported to the US began to recover, reaching, respectively USD 27.14 billion and 55% by 2014. During the height of the Argentine economic crisis the US share of total Brazilian manufactured exports climbed to a high of 39.8%, before tapering rapidly with the rising value of the real, rebounding again from a low of 14.2% in 2010 back to 23.2% in 2014 as the currency depreciated. The US market share of total Brazilian manufactured exports followed a similar trajectory, only one more tightly linked to currency valuation as demonstrated by the rapid increase from 2010 as the value of the real declined. On a strictly trade level the answer to critics of the PT government is thus while the Chinese market was providing an unexpected windfall for the mineral and agricultural sectors, the US market remained a critical destination for high value-added exports. But as will be unpacked later in this chapter, there was a decided shift in tone amongst key foreign policy elites that made enhanced Brazilian government interaction with the US difficult.

The importance of the US for the Brazilian economy is amplified if we turn to the FDI story since the turn of the century. Table 10.1 sets out some of the main sources of inward FDI flows to Brazil from the end of the Cardoso presidency to the mid-point of Dilma's first term in office, highlighting the centrality of the US as a source of capital. At first blush the Netherlands and the Caribbean appear to be major investors, but the story is more complicated. Much of the money flowing in from the Caribbean is actually Brazilian capital moving in and out from offshore tax havens, a reality highlighted by the outward stocks catalogued in Table 10.2. The case of the Netherlands is more nuanced. Dutch laws provide special tax treatment to income earned from FDI, making the

Table 10.1 FDI inflows (USD millions) and % of total FDI stocks held in Brazil, 2001–2012

	2001	2002	2003	2004	2005	2006	2007	2008	2009	2010	2011	2012
World total	18,765	17,118	9,320	18,570	15,045	15,373	26,074	30,064	19,906	48,506	66,660	65,272
USA	20.8%	14.4%	18.5%	18.6%	24.4%	14.3%	10.9%	7.3%	6.4%	11.0%	8.4%	20.7%
	3,902	2,459	1,720	3,455	3,673	2,192	2,851	2,207	1,277	5,348	5,572	13,509
Caribbean	15.3%	11.5%	16.5%	8.7%	8.9%	8.5%	9.5%	9.0%	3.0%	8.9%	2.4%	2.1%
	2,880	1,971	1,539	1,614	1,339	1,311	2,479	2,717	598	4,340	1,578	1,357
Netherlands	9.9%	18.9%	14.2%	39.9%	6.0%	19.1%	26.2%	10.4%	19.1%	5.6%	26.9%	18.4%
	1,852	3,238	1,326	7,405	900	2,939	6,840	3,136	3,803	2,736	17,908	12,003
Spain	14.6%	3.0%	-1.9%	4.7%	-1.3%	3.6%	6.6%	8.6%	15.1%	0.6%	14.7%	3.2%
	2,741	510	-174	878	-188.316	547	1,732	2,594	3,016	313	9,779	2,073
China	0.1%	0.1%	0.2%	0.0%	0.1%	0.0%	0.1%	0.1%	0.4%	1.0%	0.6%	0.5%
	28	10	16	4	7.56	7	24	38	83	480	432	325

Source: UNCTAD FDI/TNC database, based on data from Banco Central do Brasil

Table 10.2 Brazilian FDI stocks abroad (USD millions) and % of total FDI stocks held abroad, 2001–2012

	2001	2002	2003	2004	2005	2006	2007	2008	2009	2010	2011	2012
World total	49,689	54,423	54,892	69,196	79,259	1,14,175	1,40,036	1,55,942	164 523	1,88,637	2,02,586	2,66,252
USA	3.10%	3.90%	4.20%	4.10%	5.50%	3.70%	4.60%	6.80%	6.90%	7.50%	6.80%	8.50%
	1,535	2,110	2,293	2,816	4,338	4,228	6,479	10,640	11,363	14,067	13,816	22,635
Tax havens*	67.70%	70.20%	70.40%	65.60%	58.70%	53.30%	49.70%	50.90%	45.80%	41.80%	34.80%	36.80%
	33,626	38,223	38,641	45,401	46,527	60,878	69,628	79,436	75,367	78,891	70,409	97,867
Netherlands	1.20%	0.70%	1.40%	1.70%	3.70%	2.90%	1.60%	1.60%	2.30%	5.90%	10.40%	11.00%
	580	374	742	1,178	2,951	3,358	2,184	2,466	3,768	11,073	21,066	29,372

*Caribbean Islands, Luxembourg, Isle of Man, Jersey, Switzerland
Source: elaborated from UNCTAD FDI/TNC database, based on data from Banco Central do Brasil

Netherlands a favoured corporate base for large multinational firms and suggesting that these capital flows are not necessarily indicative of decision making by that country's domestic firms. Although Spain began to rival and in some years surpass the US as an FDI source from 2008 on, much of that activity was concentrated in the financial sector and the result of expanding retail and commercial banking activities by Spanish banks. With Chinese investment flows being largely insignificant, the US emerges as the largest single consistent source of capital inflows into Brazil. By 2013 the Central Bank of Brazil ranked the US as the second largest source of FDI stocks, attributing 15% of the total for a value of USD 87.5 billion, well ahead of Spain's USD 65.8 billion, but significantly behind the strategically routed investment from the Netherlands at USD 163.4 billion (BCdoB, Censo de Capitais Estrangeiros – resultados 2010–2013).

If we turn our attention to where Brazilian firms are engaging in FDI as part of their outward expansion we find a similar pattern as that seen with the inward flows. Again, the US stands as a significant destination, rising from 3.1% in 2001 to 8.5% in 2012. Tax havens and the Netherlands again assume importance for much the same reasons highlighted in the discussion about inward FDI flows. The argument that the US was waning in importance for Brazil during the PT governments loses even more heft if we turn our attention to the increases in FDI stocks held in that market compared to the developing markets critics charge were prioritized. Over the twelve years covered by the table the value of Brazilian FDI stocks held in the US grew almost fifteen fold whereas stocks in developing economies grew just two and a half times (UNCTAD, 2014). In all likelihood these official figures understate the true extent of flows and stocks because there was no bilateral investment treaty between the two countries, a situation which had not changed as of the writing of this book. While Brazil had signed sixteen bilateral investment agreements of the sort firms seek to ensure their assets are not summarily seized, none of these instruments were in force and the US was not a party to any of them.

Pragmatism v ideology

While perhaps not as tight and deep as some in Brazil and the US would like, on an economic level the links between the two countries nevertheless were and remain strong, surpassing the depth and complexity seen throughout most of the twentieth century. Indeed, where Brazil was nearly begging for assistance with the establishment of steelworks in the 1930s and 1940s, by the 1990s Brazilian firm Embraer was exporting hundreds of commuter jets to various American airlines and just fifteen years later investment companies such as Jorge Paulo Lemann's 3G Capital were approaching a dominant position in the beer and fast food market in the US. This sort of qualitative shift in relations was also seen on the political front, with linkages moving past the idea of exploratory discussions about where Brazil and the US might work together during the 1970s (Spektor, 2009) to take on a more proactive and at times informal nature in the 1990s and 2000s. As Cardoso's foreign minister Luiz Felipe Lampreia (1999a: 111) explains it, '[Brazil and the US] have an identity of shared values – democracy, respect for human rights, a belief in the liberty of man, a conviction in the superiority of market economics – that make us natural partners.' Indeed, prestigious US institutions such as the Council on Foreign Relations built on this theme and during the Lula and Dilma years were unequivocal that Brazil was a critical partner, a position repeated inside official Washington in the Clinton, Bush and Obama presidencies (Barbosa, 2011; Bodman et al., 2014; Farnsworth, 2015; Spektor, 2014). The result was a rising pace of cooperation and mutual support, but also a certain carelessness in relationship management that spoke to ideologization and naiveté on the Brazilian side and benign neglect and carelessness from the US.

The precedents for close collaboration in issues of mutual concern were steadily built throughout the 1990s and 2000s. To pick but a few examples, the first would be the reaction to the 1996 attempted coup in Paraguay by General Lino Oviedo. Besieged president Juan Carlos Wasmosy was on the cusp of resigning when parallel efforts from Brazil and the US persuaded him to hold fast and Oviedo to back down. While not necessarily explicitly coordinated, actions from Brasília and Washington bolstered each other without getting bogged down in advancing a claim for credit or influence in Asunción (Cardoso, 2006: 634–635; 2015: 552–554; Dias, 2015; Valenzuela, 1997). This pattern was continued over the next six tumultuous years of democratic consolidation in Paraguay and mirrored the sort of collaboration seen in the settling of the Ecuador–Peru border conflict where Brazil led the negotiations and commanded US troops in the peacekeeping force (Herz and Nogueira, 2002). While there was little secret to this collaboration, quieter and subtler initiatives were also underway. One telling example occurred in April 2001 when a US and Chinese military aircraft collided off the coast of China. Although matters were amicably settled, at the time it appeared as if there would be serious difficulties obtaining the release of the US Air Force personnel who had managed an emergency landing in China. Looking to the Latin American tour by president Jiang Zemin, the Bush White House put out soft feelers to see if Cardoso might work as an intermediary to resolve the crisis when he hosted his Chinese counterpart (Cardoso, 2006: 652). Indeed, 2001 was a bit of a busy year for back channel cooperation between Brazil and the US, with Bush also asking Cardoso if he might help reign in Chávez at the Quebec City Summit of the Americas (Cardoso, 2006: 623).

Despite this symphony of shared interests and core values there were real differences in how policies should be pursued (Castro Neves and Spektor, 2011). As detailed earlier in this book, the FTAA negotiations process represents one example where the basic idea might have been shared, but views on how it should be pursued diverged markedly. For Brazil this presented a challenge because it underlined the enormous differences in relative and structural power of the two countries. The telling point made by former Brazilian ambassador to Washington Rubens Barbosa (2011: 182) is that disagreement with the US in trade talks was viewed as an obstructionist unwillingness to negotiate, which is more or less the charge that USTR Robert Zoellick (2003) levelled at Brazil after the 2003 Cancun WTO ministerial meeting concluded without closing the Doha development round talks. Unease with Brazilian failure to follow the US lead continued to grow during the Bush presidency, beginning with Brazil's unwillingness to celebrate the toppling of Hugo Chávez in 2002 and continuing on through both the Cardoso and Lula presidencies' unwillingness to sign on to the War on Terror as well as the conflicts in Afghanistan and Iraq. Indeed, Brazil was a bit of a persistent problematic voice on these issues, consistently asking if armed intervention was the correct way forward. While this stance did not bolster bilateral relations, neither did it excessively damage them. In part this was because there was sufficient mutual understanding that Brazil could engage in honest, open and civil disagreements with the US, something made more palatable in Washington by the relatively muted Brazilian influence in global affairs at the time.

Although the Lula presidency began with a certain degree of euphoria after the successful November 2002 meeting with Bush, consistently building on the positive start proved difficult. As some Washington observers noted, relations between the two countries were amiable, but also marked by considerable discord (Hakim, 2015: 278). The impression given by Lula's first ambassador in Washington was that while there was real progress on the bilateral file, most notably through very warm presidential summits and the launching of strategic policy consultation processes, there was resistance within nationalist sectors of the Brazilian government to deeper and wider ranging cooperation. Framed in the theoretical terms underpinning this book, Lula's advisors were pursuing a clear structural foreign policy deliberately seeking to build alternatives to US influence in the region and the world, something which Brazil was able to pursue more forcefully as the commodity boom gained serious momentum in the mid-2000s and Washington's attention was taken up with simultaneous wars in Iraq and Afghanistan (Barbosa, 2011: chapter seven). Suggestions that Lula's government was being less than serious about deepening the bilateral relationship and pursuing its possibilities were given a significant boost when Barbosa's successor in Washington, Roberto Abdenur, retired from the post and gave an eye opening interview to news magazine *Veja* criticizing Lula's South–South foreign policy focus and worrying about how the Brazil–US relationship would fare in what he saw as an increasingly ideologized context (O. Cabral, 2007).

Abdenur's interview set off a firestorm in the establishment newspapers and prompted an invitation from the Senate Foreign Relations and National Defense Committee to further explain his comments. The arguments he put before the Commission are telling for the larger story in this book and point to the deeply embedded desire for global structural change in the Brazilian foreign policy community as well as the sense in nationalist sectors that the US was the prime barrier to Brazil's global advancement. For Abdenur a central challenge within the Lula government was the tendency of some powerful voices in Brasília to believe that 'Brazil is a peripheral country and that there is a centre, which is dominated by the US with an imperialist posture' (CRE, 2007: 366). Drawing on his experience in Washington, as well as Germany, Austria and China, Abdenur suggested this was an overly pessimistic view of Brazil's global presence and potential and that 'Brazil should stop defining itself in relation to the US on the global stage... We should confront the US where we have conflicts and strong contradictory interests. We should dialogue when there is space for convergence, agree when these convergences are found' (CRE, 2007: 367). Framed differently, he was calling for a pragmatic approach where the US should not constantly be seen as a threat to Brazil, but rather as a partner in the international system with whom much can be done and with whom there will sometimes be honest differences.

In effect Abdenur was calling for a maturation of Brazilian identity as part of its global structural reform agenda, allowing the country to take an independent voice and role in regional and global affairs, one that would actively and enthusiastically cooperate with the US where this made sense. On a practical level this is precisely what was happening across most of the Esplanada and even within Itamaraty (Pinheiro and Milani, 2012). The factor that led to the provocative *Veja* story and Abdenur's frustration was the obstructionist approach to the bilateral relationship by empowered nationalist factions at Itamaraty. Reporting from US diplomats in the second half of the decade is unequivocal on this point. Referring to a series of conversations with Lula's foreign policy advisor and career diplomat Marcel Biato, US ambassador Clifford Sobel reported that many of the innovative proposals, such as a Brazil–US energy cooperation agreement, were being driven by the Planalto Palace, not the Itamaraty Palace (Wikileaks, 2009a). The sense that nationalist sectors in Itamaraty were deliberately blocking a deepening of bilateral relations was bluntly emphasized by the US Charge D'Affaires shortly after Antonio Patriota moved from the embassy in Washington to take over as Itamaraty secretary general, characterizing him as a 'definite improvement over his predecessor, the anti-American and obstructionist Samuel Pinheiro Guimaraes'(Wikileaks, 2009b).

Reflecting on his time as ambassador to the United States, Antonio Patriota (2013d: 46) began his period as foreign minister with an interview to *Veja* where he noted: 'In the last government there was a very good, natural connection [with the US]. There might have been specific difficulties here and there, but nothing that contaminated the overarching relationship.' Nevertheless, the US embassy had a sense that specific segments within Itamaraty were a central barrier to enhanced bilateral relations is a strong and consistent theme in the State Department cables from Brasília released by Wikileaks. In a scene setter for Brazilian defence minister Nelson Jobim's 2008 visit to Washington Sobel wrote:

> While relations between the U.S. and Brazil are generally friendly, often the USG encounters major difficulties in gaining the cooperation of senior policymakers on issues of significant interest to the US. The difficulty is most apparent in the Ministry for External Affairs (MRE) which maintains an anti-American slant and has tried to block improved DoD–MOD relations. In planning for Jobim's visit, the MRE actively campaigned to limit Jobim's time in Washing to one largely ceremonial day with little substance. (Wikileaks, 2008a)

Despite the resistance from Itamaraty, the Ministry of Defense had been pushing for more cooperation with the US on a range of security issues both in the Americas and beyond. Indeed, a 2010 interview with a US government official posted to Brasília about a recently signed defence cooperation agreement elicited strong expressions of relief that Brazil had finally come to the table. The diplomat continued on to explain that the US had for years been seeking to build on the positive joint forces cooperation experience settling the Ecuador–Peru border conflict in the 1990s and the more recent Brazilian-led UN peacekeeping activities in

Haiti. From the US perspective there was little problem leaving regional security management to Brazil. The issue instead was getting cooperation and coordination frameworks in place, as well as getting the right people in the Brazilian government to sign off on the cooperation and actively take on the task.

Echoing the concerns raised by Abdenur before the Senate Commission, one scene setter prepared by the US embassy in Brasília actually contained the subheading 'Relations with the United States: Can Brazil Overcome Its Inferiority Complex' (Wikileaks, 2009c). There was, in part, a strategic aspect to the obstreperous attitude at Itamaraty, with Defense Minister Nelson Jobim almost suggesting to Sobel a need to play a *frenemy*-like game lest Brazil lose its ability to influence countries such as Venezuela, who would not react well to an overly friendly Brazil–US bilateral relationship (Wikileaks, 2008b). Indeed, desk-level diplomats at Itamaraty in the mid-2000s were clear that there was a great deal of quiet communication with Washington about potentially troublesome regional actors such as Venezuela and how possible threats to stability in the Americas might be deflected (interviews with Brazilian diplomats, 2007). Such strategizing aside, during much of the Lula presidency in US eyes there remained 'an influential segment within both senior policy circles and Itamaraty that actively seeks to avoid and minimize ties to the United States' (Wikileaks, 2008c). The impact in practical terms was enormous because most of the international affairs secretariats in the various government ministries along the Esplanada were headed and staffed by career diplomats on secondment. While there are numerous examples of how the combination of the anti-US attitude from Itamaraty filtered into other government ministries, one of the most banal comes from a cable about a NASA-run school education programme blocked by the International Affairs secretariat of the Ministry of Education over concerns that data collected by Brazilian high school students would not be sufficiently protected because the US had yet to ratify the Convention on Biological Diversity (Wikileaks, 2007).

Bad assumptions

Difficulties aside, there was a clear sense in the US embassy in Brasília that many opportunities for collaboration existed and that the mission's work should be dedicated to highlighting areas where national interests aligned and cooperation and collaboration would prove fruitful (Wikileaks, 2008d). Indeed, the larger relationship was following this track through the establishment of a strategic dialogue mechanism in 2011 to at least create a framework for building relations (Muxagato,

2015). The problem was that the message appeared not to circulate widely and Washington was not necessarily listening to its posts in Brazil, lending credence to nationalist elements in Brasília arguing the US was not a reliable partner. In keeping with the central argument in this chapter a key challenge was the prevalence of poor assumptions about the motivations and behaviour of both countries. For their part policy makers in Washington seemingly expected Brazil to simply understand what it was doing and not see any potential nefarious content in new policy actions. American diplomats in Brasília were consequently kept busy fighting small brushfires as nationalistic segments in the Brazilian foreign policy community reacted to new US initiatives. A prime example of this was the 24 April 2008 announcement that the US was reactivating the Fourth Fleet in the Western Hemisphere. Even though the announcement was made shortly after the confirmation of massive offshore oil and gas reserves on Brazil's continental shelf it appears there was little serious effort given to an ongoing process of briefing in key Brazilian actors. The result was a strained reaction in Brazil with more paranoid voices pointing to US plans to seize the country's newfound oil reserves (Arraes, 2008; S. Dávila, 2008; Pecequilo, 2015).

Although the matter was quickly settled in discussions between Amorim and Sobel, the US diplomatic cable detailing the affair is blunt:

> Amorim stressed that this was a politically sensitive issue, and based on friendly and open relations, he was surprised that he had received no communication on this issue from the State Department. When asked about the Fourth Fleet during Mercosul, President Lula turned to Amorim to ask him for guidance, who was forced to reply that he only knew what had appeared in the press. The Ambassador noted that Admiral Stavridis had briefed Admiral Moura Neto and the Brazilian military on the Fourth Fleet, but acknowledged that we had failed to brief the Foreign Ministry. Amorim ended by noting that he would tell President Lula that he had talked to Ambassador Sobel and that Secretary Rice would be sending comprehensive material on the Fourth Fleet. He stressed that more detailed information and a call from Secretary Rice on this matter would be welcome, adding that he was prepared to reach out to her on the issue. (Wikileaks, 2008e)

The space for poor assumptions and misunderstanding stems from the very strengths isolated by this micro case, namely that such a potential issue can so quickly and easily be addressed and remedied. In a sense the problem lies in the very openness and friendliness of the relations identified by Amorim. For policy makers in Washingon there appear to be striking parallels to relations with Canada, where it is safe to assume officials in Ottawa will either have tracked and analysed the situation to avoid misunderstanding or the correct messaging will seep through via the dense network of formal and informal working-level connections between the two bureaucracies. This latter assumption is problematic in the Brazilian case because of the often-terse relations between Itamaraty and other internationally oriented ministries, something which was constantly reiterated to Washington in cables sent from the American embassy in Brasília between 2006 and 2010.

Nowhere was the failure of these assumptions more evident than in Brazil's work with Turkey to negotiate a deal with Iran to end concerns it was enriching uranium to weapons grade as part of a bomb development programme. As Amorim (2015: 28) recounts, at the 2009 L'Aquila G8 outreach process Obama asked Lula if Brazil would be willing to try and bring Tehran to the negotiating table. Although Brazilian diplomats were dubious about the rationality of this proposition, Lula accepted it and tasked Amorim with bringing it about. Viewing the process retrospectively, Amorim (2011: p 287, note 3) quietly acknowledges signs were present throughout the latter stages of 2009 that key decision makers such as Hillary Clinton had become fundamentally uninterested in seeing Brazil succeed, instead investing great energies in lining up support in the UNSC for a new round of sanctions in the belief the talks would fail. Even an April 2010 letter from Obama reaffirming support for Brazil's work was accompanied by quiet signals that this impossible task should not be seriously pursued. Amorim nevertheless kept on course and to the surprise of nearly everyone succeeded in brokering the agreement signed by Lula, Turkish Prime Minister Recep Tayyip Erdogan, and Iranian president Mahmoud Ahmadinejad on 17 May 2010 (Amorim, 2011a: chapter 12; Jesus, 2011; Lampreia, 2014).

Although the P5+1 deal negotiated in 2015 would have many similarities to the agreement brokered by Brazil and Turkey, US reaction to the 2010 diplomatic settlement was not positive; Hillary Clinton was reportedly furious that Brazil had 'naively' charged ahead with a deal it would not be able to monitor or enforce. The result was a series of terse diplomatic exchanges between Brasília and Washington that are less important for their specific content than the larger insight the affair gives to the bad assumption plaguing the bilateral relationship. Throughout the process Brazil took the US at face value, accepting that a request to seek a diplomatic resolution would result in support for a final deal irrespective of what other processes were underway in Washington and the larger political ambitions of individual actors involved in the affair. For their part, US policy makers appeared to assume that Brazil would be unable to broker a deal, overlooking the increasingly influential role the country was taking up across the Global South. The impact on Amorim (2015) is palpable in his ninety-two page account of the affair. Disdain for Obama made clear through references to the US president's 'paternalistic' tone towards Lula (Amorim, 2015a: 28, 37) is paralleled by persistent disquiet with the attitude and deportment of senior State Department officials who appeared to believe that Brazil would fail at this impossible task.

Significantly, there is little suggestion in Amorim's text of an awareness that any potentially workable deal would have to be quietly 'pre-approved' by the US to be successful. While not stated so directly, in an aftermath State Department press conference Senior Official Number Two notes:

> Well, if they had come to us, I guess, and said look, we have the makings of a deal, we'd like you to react to this draft agreement, we could have reacted to that. But they didn't do that. They went to Tehran and they announced the deal. We didn't know what was in the deal before they made it public, so we didn't have an opportunity to comment on its deficiencies ahead of time. (State Department, 2010)

A theme throughout the press conference is whether or not the US 'tasked' Brazil with finding a negotiated solution, something the US denied and Brazil claimed. What is clear is that there were very different underlying assumptions about the nature and direction of the negotiations, with both sides assuming that their actions and intent were clear to the other. For Brazil, the implications of the process were obvious: the Tehran nuclear deal was a clear attempt by Brazil to demonstrate that it is a major world power capable of delivering the sort of global security goods necessary to have a permanent seat on the UN Security Council. Embedded in this attitude was an attempt to reshape relative power relations and their impact on the larger structural question through sheer effort of will by simply acting as if the terrain had shifted and legal restraints would govern international affairs. Lost in this approach was a clear appreciation of the realities of international power and the extent to which the US will ultimately do as it pleases.

The overarching reality that the US has enormous freedom of space to manoeuver in the global system and retains the right to grant or withdraw the ability of other countries to engage in global governance activities was pointedly reinforced in 2013. Edward Snowden's release through the Wikileaks platform of details on US foreign communications monitoring activities, which included the tracking of emails and telecommunications by senior Brazilian government and corporate officials, starkly set out the differences in relative power capabilities and attitudes to good neigbhourliness. Condemnation from Brazil was swift and forceful, resulting in the 'postponement' of an official visit by Dilma to Washington and, some would argue, the cancellation of the USD 6 billion fighter jet contract that likely was not going to the US anyway (Hakim, 2014; Vucetic and Duarte, 2015). While Brazil was not alone in receiving this treatment from the US, the reaction in Brasília was more forceful, with efforts being turned to creating alternate telecommunication routings for internet signals to and from Brazil. Perhaps more importantly, efforts were also being given to developing more secure email and cell phone systems for the Brazilian government, possibly responding to the habit that some ranking figures had for using applications such as gmail and whatsapp for their work communication (Spektor, 2013).

Again, two central assumptions underpinning the relationship become clear through the NSA affair. First is the assumption that Brazil is a reliable US ally, an opinion not shared throughout Washington, largely due to a misunderstanding of Brazilian foreign policy ambitions fed by publicly voiced tetchiness in Brasília. One former US ambassador went so far as to note that for the US such monitoring was a simple decision because 'from Washington's perspective, the Brazilian government is not exactly friendly' (Montaner, 2013). Put less provocatively, most diplomats and senior government officials around the world generally expect periodic surveillance attempts from friendly, much less hostile countries. Many senior figures in the Brazilian foreign policy establishment were consequently unsurprised that these activities had been taking place. Nevertheless, the revelations were a clear shock to Dilma, with the emotive impact perhaps being best captured by one of Brazil's senior diplomats, ambassador Paulo Cordeiro Andrade de Pinto: 'A country like Brazil makes a huge effort to develop. And when you see something like those slides [detailing communications monitoring] – you feel slightly vulnerable' (Nolen and Freeze, 2013). The end result was a period of official toxicity in the bilateral relationship driven by the impossibility of Dilma finding a way past the affront during the run up to the 2014 presidential election. As some of the more pragmatic observers noted, delaying the 2013 official visit to Washington until 2015 was probably more of a relief than headache for most bureaucrats given that the affair was going to be largely symbolic and light on concrete substance (Hakim, 2014). Either way, once the public relations fallout of the 2014 election had passed, the visit was rescheduled and attention returned to pragmatically continuing to build the bilateral relationship.

Conclusion

The relationship with the US touches upon two major flashpoints in Brazilian foreign policy. First, and the theme in this book, is the ambition to reform regional and international power structures to afford Brazil a larger voice in global governance frameworks with a view to protecting national autonomy. Although this element has sat largely as a background theme throughout this chapter, it is a constant thread running throughout the book. In many respects an important part of the story in the other chapters has been how Brazil has sought to counterbalance US influence or shift structures and understandings to dilute US pressure and influence. This points to the second and central point to the current chapter, which is the extent to which nationalist elements within the Brazilian foreign policy community struggle with their country's relationship with the US. Despite efforts to increase autonomy and freedom to pursue national development, the US continues to exercise incredible influence over Brazil's economic and political prospects, much as it does with most other countries. Ironically, the more Brazil has been able to establish a measure of independence, the closer the two countries have become on a practical level (Muxagato, 2015), pointing to an often unexplored pragmatic and sweeping pattern of cooperation across a plethora of policy areas. In many respects this is precisely what ambassador Cordeiro was highlighting in the previous paragraph: despite over a decade of enormous domestic social and economic gains, paralleled by growing regional and international influence, Brazil's arrival on the global stage is not yet an irreversible fact.

Brazil remains very much a junior partner to the US, much to the chagrin of nationalist foreign policy elites in Brasília. The identity argument presented by ambassador Abdenur to the Brazilian Senate consequently assumes central importance to deciphering what is transpiring in the bilateral relationship, pointing to a tendency by some on the Brazilian side to overplay its hand or to not take a pragmatic enough analytical frame to how Washington will react to specific foreign policy initiatives – the attempt to negotiate a nuclear deal with Iran being a particularly glaring example. This results in conflict and superb soundbites, ensuring that this aspect of the relationship receives a lot of attention. Of course, the corollary to this is that decision makers in Washington do not devote a great deal of thought to what is going on Brazil and why particular policy patterns may be advanced from Brasília. The result, as is argued in this chapter, is an extremely close bilateral relationship on a non-governmental level, paralleled by significant interest convergences often missed or misinterpreted by senior political actors using poorly informed or ideological assumptions to guide the political relations. For Brazil the uncomfortable bottom line is that the US remains at least the dominant actor, not just in global affairs, but regional and bilateral relations. The point not entirely noticed by the nationalist elements of the foreign policy community, but embraced by many, is that this relative power relationship often does not matter and that pragmatic cooperation and coordination can significantly advance the structural agenda in Brazilian foreign policy.

11

Brazil and China

Since the turn of the century, perhaps no country has proven as important or confusing to Brazilian foreign policy makers as China. It is both the key to Brazil's rise and the bane to its ambitions of becoming a truly global power with real influence over structural power frameworks. While Brazil's foreign policy establishment initially hoped that China's rise would be a major boost for the country's economic development, and that Beijing would join it in a Southern alliance pushing for the global governance changes sought by Brasília, events during the PT presidencies of Lula and Dilma have demonstrated that such expectations were overly optimistic. China has vaulted from relative obscurity in Brazil's panoply of bilateral relationships to be one of the central partnerships that must be carefully managed by both Itamaraty and the presidency.

It is in the word 'partnership' that Brazilian confusion about China arises. The foreign policy logic driven by the Lula administration was predicated on ideas of Southern solidarity and cooperation based on a sense of a bifurcated global order broadly split into the North and the South. Within this framework China clearly appears to be part of the South due to its own challenges with development, poverty, and scientific and technological modernization. Yet the reality has proven to be considerably more complicated, seeing relations with China vary from partner to rival to competitor to antagonist depending on issue area being discussed and the temporal period under consideration. Adding to the confusion is the economic impact of China's rise, which has simultaneously helped to pull Brazil from the edge of a financial abyss and subjected large swathes of the country's industrial sector to massive competitive shocks in regional and domestic markets.

The larger argument in this chapter is that Brazil has consistently sought to leverage its links with China, particularly by strengthening the BRICs frameworks, to advance a South–South foreign policy and trade agenda. For its part China has kept an open ear, but a closed wallet, strategically deciding to go along with Brazil only when it advances its own narrowly defined interests. More significantly, China has proven adept at separating different aspects of the bilateral relationship so that matters may appear extremely positive on the scientific collaboration front even though substantive economic tensions are continuing to grow. This has presented a quandary for Brazil and highlights the structural limitations of Brazilian power and influence in the global and regional system. Notions of a deep strategic alliance and partnership with China have floundered, yet an ability to get a hearing in Beijing has remained an important strut of Brazil's rising influence at world decision making tables. Matters are further complicated on Brazil's regional and domestic front. The rise of China has simultaneously helped and harmed Brazil. Insatiable Chinese demand for raw materials and food commodities has powered Brazil's latest economic miracle, but at the price of accepting large inflows of Chinese manufactured goods that are decimating often coddled Brazilian industry. More worrying for Brazil's regional ambitions is the growing proclivity of other Latin American countries to look towards China for cheap imports, a deep market for their own products, as well as investments.

This chapter will draw out Brazilian confusion regarding China by focusing on the economic and political factors at play. Attention is first turned to the basis for the relationship, which grew out of good intentions and optimistic readings of the global system. As will be discussed, this 'Southern solidarity' approach has offered some results in the science and technology spheres, but nevertheless coloured Brazilian perceptions of what can be done with China. The following section maps out how China's surging economic growth contributed to the economic foundations of Brazil's rise to an important position on the global stage. But there is another side to this story, which sees Chinese demand for raw materials being paired with the rise of new sources of competition that have impacted Brazilian industry in the domestic and regional markets. Simultaneous gain and loss are also present in the following section, which examines Brazilian efforts to mobilize Chinese support for global governance reform projects. Despite the tentative solidification of groupings such as the BRICS, Brazilian efforts to leverage relations with China to advance major international reforms have proven problematic, pointing to the thinness of the underlying assumptions of solidarity that appeared to guide the Lula administration's approach to Beijing.

Southern solidarity?

From the 1970s through to the 1990s the assumption in Brazil, as in most of the rest of the world, was that the key partner country in the Asia-Pacific would be Japan, not China. Early efforts to build stronger trade links with China stemming from the reopening of bilateral relations in 1974 stumbled upon the unavoidable reality that China had little to offer for sale other than a small sampling of artisanal goods (Altemani, 2006). The pattern over the next two decades was largely one of quiet cooperation, which was fed by a parallel agenda of encouraging changes within the UN and the global governance system to remove systemic barriers to development (Vizentini, 2003b). During the 1980s specific attention was given to increasing scientific cooperation in order to reduce dependence on Western sources and circumvent technology transfer controls imposed by the US. Some twenty bilateral agreements were signed in the 1980s, with the most significant and arguably successful being the China-Brazil Earth Resource Satellite agreement of 1988 (Becard, 2011: 33–34), which has subsequently led to a series of joint satellites and remains a highlight of presidential speeches commenting on bilateral scientific cooperation.

Similarities in the size of GDP and a reading of UN voting behaviour that saw much agreement between the two countries provided an optimistic platform for making grandiose bilateral relations statements during the Sarney and Collor presidencies (Cabral, 2003; Pereira and Neves, 2011). This contributed to the 1993 signing of a strategic partnership agreement. Significantly, the account given of the bilateral relations in the 1990s by Cardoso (2006b: 651–652) emphasizes that it was Chinese leaders who sought to build and deepen the relationship, which he retrospectively attributed to awareness in Beijing that access to a reliable source of raw materials and agricultural products would be required to feed sustained economic growth. The trade aspect and the potential for a useful partnership were of sufficient interest to Brazil during the 1990s to incite some caution in management of the bilateral relationship, prompting Cardoso (2015: 347) to muse in his diaries during a December 1995 visit to Beijing that China would have 'a major influence, potentially decisive, in the coming century and that Brazil needed this relationship'. Bilateral relations were subsequently managed very carefully. For example, a 1999 visit by the Dalai Lama to Brazil was treated with kid gloves and explicitly explained to the Chinese as a meeting between Cardoso and an important religious leader, not a deposed Tibetan head of state.

Cardoso's (2015: 820–821) accounts of a late 1996 meeting with Chinese prime minister Li Peng point to a growing sense that the countries shared an interest in developing a multipolar global order and that China had major interest in Brazilian mineral and agricultural production. The brief account of bilateral relations offered by Lampreia follows this track, highlighting that an official visit by Cardoso to China in 1995 set the stage for what would be a commercially oriented relationship. Tellingly, Lampreia (2009: 294) is clear that the Chinese premier Zhu Rongji frequently made references to the 'strategic partnership', but that details of what this meant were scarce, signifying that while the phrase was not simply empty rhetoric it lacked sufficient urgency to compel concrete and quick action to deepen it. For Brazil this slow approach during the 1990s was likely a blessing as Cardoso sought to maintain economic stability through the 1999 devaluation of the real and then keep the economy afloat through the collapse of main trading partner Argentina in 2001 and 2002. As Cardoso noted after his meetings with Li Peng: 'The Chinese are seeing Brazil as a disant ally and therefore one that is not a problem.'

The situation for the Lula presidency from 2003 was different. As was explained in chapter nine, Lula brought a new foreign policy optic to Brasília explicitly focusing on opportunities across the Global South in addition to existing relationships in the North. Of particular interest to his foreign policy team was the potential of China as a key development partner. Relations with China were set in the context of the 'auto-estima' he was bringing to Brazilian foreign policy. Specifically, China simultaneously represented an option for expanded partnerships and an example of how a Southern country might follow its own path and bring about rapid national development (Lula, 2003). The strong sense within the Lula presidency that there were many avenues of opportunity to explore in the bilateral relationship was given deeper expression during Lula's May 2004 visit to Beijing when it was agreed to form the Comissão Sino-Brasileira de Alto Nível de Concertação e Cooperação (COSBAN). Ambitions were sweeping in scope and looked for cooperation in areas such as international politics, economics, trade, science and technology, and culture and education. The joint declaration of the first COSBAN meeting in 2006 gives a strong sense that the areas which carried the strongest resonance were the joint China-Brazil Earth Resource Satellite programme and the establishment of phytosanitary rules to govern the import of Brazilian agricultural products into China (Itamaraty, 2006). While not quite bluntly stated amidst the flurry of principled statements of solidarity and cooperation, the bilateral relationship was clearly emerging as one driven by economic considerations. But there were two strutural problems to deepening the relationship. First was the geographic, which Patriota (2013f: 275) identified in 2011 as a key problem, particularly for people-to-people linkages. The second issue was more pressing for management of the relationship, which was a lack in Brazil of the requisite expertise to deal with China. As Patriota (2013e: 100) noted, seventeen months into Dilma's first presidency, 'We have a knowledge deficit about China in Brazil. At Itamaraty we are encouraging a growing number of diplomats to learn Mandarin.'

Brazil's China effect

As suggested above, the idea of China as an important trade partner developed very quickly in the early stages of the Lula presidency, particularly as the agricultural and mining lobby gained a strong voice at the cabinet table in the form of MDIC minister Fernando Furlan and agriculture minister Roberto Rodrigues. In 1986 Brazil imported just USD 410.7 million of goods from China, and sold it only USD 411.7 million. While these values rose throughout the 1990s, exports and imports each plateaued around the billion-dollar mark. The transformation in the trading relationship coincided with the start of the Lula presidency when the Chinese economy took off and developed a near insatiable appetite for the primary products so easily produced by Brazil. When Lula took office, exports to China stood at USD 4.5 billion and imports at USD 2.4 billion, numbers which exploded to, respectively, USD 30.7 billion and USD 25.5 billion by the end of his presidency, before climbing even higher to USD 46 billion in exports and USD 37 billion in imports by the third year of Dilma's first term in office (see Table 11.1).

The overriding characteristic of this surging bilateral trade was the extent to which it was dominated by the Brazilian sale of minerals, which in itself stood at close to the total value of Brazil's imports from China. When combined with the important increases in exports of agricultural commodities as well as manufactureds and fuels, the effect of rising bilateral trade with China was to bring a new measure of economic stability to Brazil that effectively financed Lula's expansive pan-Southern foreign policy. By driving the price of energy, agricultural goods and minerals to unprecedented heights, China overturned much of the mainstream economic logic to arguments that resource dependency would inherently limit growth prospects. It also literally ripped apart the 'structuralist' thinking at the heart of the Brazilian version of economic orthodoxy and left in tatters the idea that the region could only progress if it banded together to form a unified regional bloc to facilitate the growth of continental production systems. For Brazil, with its immense reserves of minerals, possibly massive extractable oil and gas assets, as well as the largest unused reservoir of arable land on the

Table 11.1 Brazilian bilateral trade with China (USD 000s), 2003–2013

	2003	2004	2005	2006	2007	2008	2009	2010	2011	2012	2013
Exports											
Agricultural	4,533,363	5,441,746	6,834,997	8,402,369	10,748,814	16,403,039	20,190,831	30,752,356	44,314,595	41,227,540	46,026,153
Minerals	360,179	680,115	565,267	331,134	699,075	1,318,792	986,050	2,014,417	3,024,462	3,267,023	3,050,877
Fuels & chemicals	2,559,627	3,273,548	4,209,819	5,860,572	7,382,423	11,444,417	14,913,816	22,301,707	33,276,606	29,411,433	35,652,658
	127,616	358,720	751,921	1,095,417	1,081,959	1,888,369	1,845,840	4,390,336	5,413,673	5,425,336	4,444,593
Manufactures	1,485,054	1,126,553	1,305,276	1,110,580	1,530,756	1,744,194	2,436,298	2,045,887	2,573,360	2,936,867	2,841,126
Others	887	2,810	2,713	4,666	54,601	7,266	8,828	9	26,494	186,881	36,900
Imports											
Agricultural	2,147,795	3,710,470	5,354,507	7,989,295	12,617,739	20,040,014	15,911,143	25,535,684	32,788,424	34,248,497	37,302,150
Minerals	22,298	25,781	57,517	74,228	87,524	242,014	187,143	412,915	545,414	599,190	765,037
Fuels & chemicals	17,156	15,282	27,158	39,968	65,209	121,684	86,190	107,592	167,973	169,870	206,198
	618,222	815,029	776,775	935,322	1,655,539	3,012,907	1,842,267	2,508,696	3,835,749	3,667,669	4,461,071
Manufactures	1,490,045	2,854,375	4,493,016	6,939,507	8,553,780	16,662,636	13,794,747	22,505,089	28,237,564	29,804,519	31,866,816
Others	75	3	42	271	2,255,687	773	797	1,393	1,724	7,249	3,029
Trade balance	2,385,568	1,731,276	1,480,490	413,074	−1,868,925	−3,636,975	4,279,688	5,216,672	11,526,171	6,979,043	8,724,003

Source: COMTRADE via World Bank World Integrated Trade Solutions (WITS)

planet, the new pattern of trade looked a lot like a guaranteed minimum income on which to build for decades to come.

Positive impacts from China's economic rise extended significantly beyond Brazil's improved balance of payments situation, which allowed foreign currency reserves to top USD 366.6 billion by May 2015. Brazil's manufacturing sector is large and diversified and includes the world's third largest aircraft manufacturer Embraer, as well as the fourth largest auto sector, with a production equivalent to about 60% of US output. For Brazilian manufacturing companies, the availability of cheap components from China meant lower production prices and thus higher competitiveness for their products, both domestically and internationally. Brazil's economy, like those of essentially every country in the world, benefited from the lower prices imparted to global value chains by the low price of the Chinese links in the chain. These gains were passed on to Brazilians in the form of lower prices for products ranging from consumer goods, to electronics, to textiles, shoes and myriad other items contained in the USD 28–31 billion of manufactured imports from China over the initial years of Dilma's presidency. More to the point, the economic stability brought by rising resource royalties and taxes allowed a dramatic widening and deepening of Brazilian social programming, particularly hallmark initiatives like the conditional cash transfer programme Bolsa Familia (Fenwick, 2015), which provided an additional boost to national consumption that in turn provided strong domestic reinforcement to resources-boom incited growth. Resultant success with poverty alleviation and economic stabilization also provided an additional element to Brazil's international influence and credibility by allowing the Lula and Dilma presidencies to present the country's developmental triumphs as an additional reason for having a leading role in the Global South (van der Westhuizen, 2013; White, 2010).

The benefits of the commodity boom were felt across South America, which in turn pushed a rise in the consumption of the sort of manufactured and machinery goods that have long made up a majority of Brazil's regional exports. In 2003 Brazilian exports of manufactureds and machinery to South America stood at just under USD 7 billion. Despite a blip in 2009 due to the Global Financial Crisis, this number had increased to USD 27.9 billion by 2011, before taking a fall in 2012 to USD 23.7 billion. Yet the implications for Brazilian industry were contradictory. As Figure 11.1 demonstrates, while the nominal value of Brazil's manufactured and machinery exports to South America may have been growing, its market share was actually decreasing. More troubling for Brazilian industry was that it was losing market share to China in sectors where it had traditionally been strong. The trend since 2005

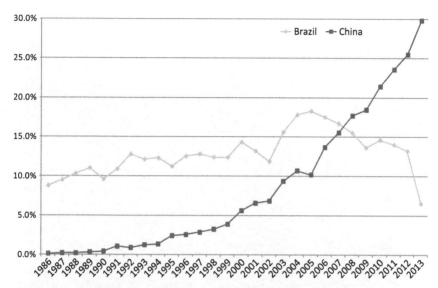

Figure 11.1 Brazilian and Chinese share of South American manufactured imports, 1995–2013

is thus one of declining relative importance of Brazilian value-added exports to the previously strong South American export market. More worrying for the longer-term outlook of Brazil's industrial complex was that market share losses in lower-technology products associated with Chinese exports were not replaced by higher value-added or technologically sophisticated Brazilian products (Jenkins, 2014).

The contradictions in the pattern of market penetration for manufactureds in South America provide a window into the nature of the evolving Sino-Brazilian relationship. A quick glance suggests a level of symbiosis as sketched out above. Yet the deeper reality was that the nature of the trade relationship was skewed in terms of what is being exchanged, as illustrated through figures 11.2 and 11.3. Although global commodity prices did soar in the 2000s, this did not appreciably feed the evolution of further value-added exports to China or an increase in the technological sophistication of Brazil's wider export offerings. Industrial sectors in Brazil could also take little comfort from the positive trade balance with China seen in Table 11.1. The vast preponderance of Chinese exports to Brazil were in the manufacturing sector and sales to China in this area were rapidly declining in relative importance. More significantly, these Chinese products bought by Brazil were not 'import-substituting' for goods from Northern markets as Lula periodically suggested should happen with his call for a new South–South economic geography. Rather,

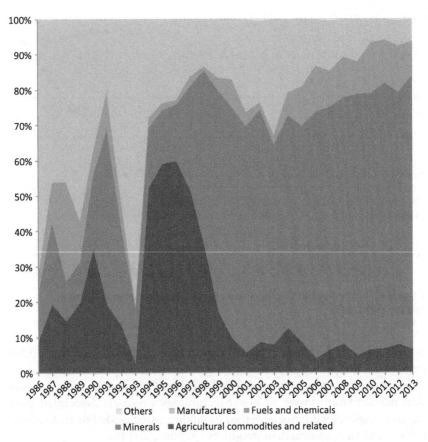

Figure 11.2 Brazilian exports to China, 1995–2013

the Chinese products were entering into direct competition with domestic Brazilian firms and forcing into insolvency those firms unable to adapt to a rapidly changing domestic market context (Jenkins, 2012).

Business is business

From as early as 2004 Brazilian policy makers were aware of the tensions that were being created by the growing economic relationship with China. Part of the motivation for Lula's May 2004 official visit to China was to combine the idea of South–South solidarity, which he had being expounding, with the rapidly increasing bilateral trade to deepen and strengthen the strategic partnership and use it to boost his country's diversified economic growth rate. For their part the Chinese seemed to be on message, but driven by a different prerogative, contrasting a

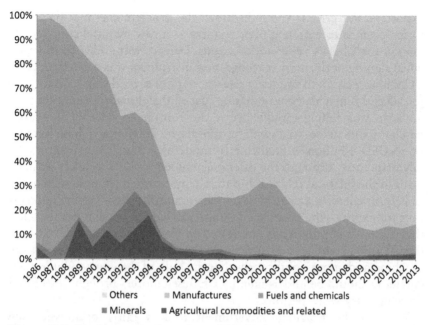

Figure 11.3 Brazilian imports from China, 1986–2013

hard-nosed business first approach to the Brazilian president's more expansive rhetoric, which appeared to miss key indicators of where Brazil might exert leverage. Perhaps the most striking example came in the preparations for the two summits in 2004. In one preparatory meeting MDIC Minister Luiz Fernando Furlan reported that the Chinese negotiator asked 28 separate times for formal recognition as a market economy within the WTO framework, which would make it more difficult for Brazil to bring anti-dumping actions against China (Oxford Analytica, 2004). Brazilian industrialists counselled against the move, worrying that it would lead to precisely the sort of bilateral trade situation illustrated in Figure 11.3. The point continued to be pushed, and Chinese president Hu Jintao won agreement from Lula at their meeting in Beijing.

The reaction in Brazil to Lula's market recognition decision was skeptical. While China did demonstrate some clear and substantive reciprocity, it was not in keeping with the changes that would come in the economic relationship. The two key elements granted by Hu were a declaration of Brazil as an official tourist destination by the Chinese government, which it was suggested would see approximately 100,000 new tourists each year with a collective vacation spend of USD 250–300 million. More substantive was the signing of a series of health agreements that opened the Chinese market up to Brazilian beef, pork and chicken exporters. For critical voices in Brazil the problem was that these 'victories' seemed to entrench their country as a raw material supplier and market for China's value-added goods. Density was added to this view when signing of the market recognition instrument was accompanied by a Chinese decision to suddenly reject receipt of several ship loads of soya for alleged fungicide contamination just as the global spot-market price for soya was falling rapidly below the contracted price of the cargo. Similar issues were seen with proposals in 2004 that China provide up to USD 4 billion in financing to modernize Brazilian transportation infrastructure. Although the offer was lauded by Lula as a key achievement in the bilateral relationship that demonstrated Chinese willingness to help Brazil with a critical developmental difficulty – getting goods to port for export – the proposal ultimately collapsed when it became clear that China was only really interested in financing transportation links that would deliver ore and agricultural commodities to the coast for sale to China and, more significantly, that the bulk of the work to build these corridors should be undertaken by Chinese laborers brought into Brazil on temporary work permits.

Whereas the Brazilian government took a fairly optimistic view towards relations with China and assumed that mutual cooperation and advancement was the overriding driver, the imperatives dictating decisions in major Brazilian firms were considerably different. The case of mining company Vale stands out in particular because it became a central actor in the bilateral relationship through its supply of iron ore. Rather than relying on global spot market prices, Chinese steel mills negotiated annual contracts for ore and coking coal with Vale. While the Brazilian miner periodically made noises during the mid-2000s about abandoning contracts for the spot market due to rapidly rising global prices, pre-arranged pricing remained the practice, with annual increases of 40–70% being well within the norm. The commercial bonanza this presented for Vale had one drawback: the distance and logistical cost of getting Brazilian ore to market. To resolve this issue Vale decided to build a series of 400,000 tonne Valemax ore carriers, which were 10% larger than existing ships and promised transportation cost savings of 20–25%. Although Vale commissioned the Chinese shipbuilder Jiangsu Rongsheng Heavy Industries to build twelve of the vessels in 2008, lingering rancour over the Brazilian company's success in pushing up ore prices in the 2000s seemed to influence regulatory decisions, which declared the main ports unready to safely receive the ships, forcing Vale to set up a regional distribution hub in Malaysia.

Similar contrasts could be found in the area of national industrial policy and the recruitment of FDI. Both Beijing and Brasília pursued clear policies of putting in place market restrictions and regulations to discourage the importation of high value-added products and their substitution with local production, particularly in information technology and aerospace products. The difference that emerged was the extent to which each was willing to allow market-driven investment factors to run in the place of strategic national decisions to deliberately form national champions in place of inward FDI flows. For Chinese firms Brazil emerged as an opportunity where firms could invest to capture large shares of a relatively empty market, as was the case with computer manufacturer Lenovo's substantial move into Brazil throughout the 2000s (Barbosa, Tepassê and Biancalana, 2014). A parallel market-seeking investment behaviour was demonstrated by Brazilian regional aircraft manufacturer Embraer, which was seeking to gain a significant portion of the Chinese regional passenger aircraft market (Goldstein, 2006). While Brazil allowed Lenovo to pursue its productive investments and even encouraged matters through government procurement contracts, Embraer's attempts to develop a manufacturing capacity in China fell afoul of state development ambitions to see the country effectively emerge as an aerospace competitor. By 2012 China had wrapped up its manufacturing partnership with Embraer and withheld a production licence that would have seen the Brazilian firm producing 100-seater regional jets in the country's north. Embraer was forced to be content with permission to produce executive jets locally, with the knowledge that global competition for its main business line was likely coming from a state-backed competitor (Murphy, 2012). No similar reaction to China's presence in the information technology sector was seen in Brazil. Indeed, quite the reverse took place with Brasília working hard to attract further investment from consumer electronics manufacturers Huwaie and Foxconn as well as China's growing automotive sector.

The distinction these examples illustrate between economic and national interest decisions, and separate initiatives for cooperation and political dialogue between China and Brazil, did not appear to be immediately clear in Lula's perception of the relationship and its implications for his country's impact on global governance. For Lula (2009) the key point appeared to be that both China and Brazil had grown significantly, prompting his observation that, 'today it is practically impossible for the traditional rich countries to hold a meeting to make a decision about something in the world without taking into account the existence of China, without taking into account the existence of Brazil, without taking into account the existence of the other countries who comprise the emerging nations.' While this statement was largely true, it lacked an important level of subtlety that took into account how Brazil's relationship with China impacted the sort of influence Lula felt he was enjoying on the world stage. Lula's rhetoric was instead full of positivity, telling journalists in Beijing that Brazil and China could become equals as major economies, improving the lives of the people and gaining a greater say in global governance decisions that might bring greater equilibrium to international relations.

Interests before solidarity

For their part officials in Beijing said little to directly contradict Lula's hopeful musings, relying instead on more subtle patterns of signalling and dissension. On some issues the disappointment of Brazilian dreams was quite direct. In the same press conference where he expounded the potential of the strategic partnership Lula (2009) attempted to spin away failure to obtain Chinese support for Brazil's full membership in the UNSC, opining that China's concerns were not with Brazil, but with one of its partners pushing for reform, Japan. In other areas China seemed to support Brazilian efforts, as was seen in quiet cooperation by Beijing within the G20 WTO coalition through much of the active period of attempts to negotiate the Doha development round. Although the pattern that emerged was one of studied non-confrontation, this does not imply there was a sustained and natural consonance of interests. Nor should it necessarily be taken for granted that there was an implicit equality in the bilateral relationship. Rather, the binding element was one of desiring to see changes in global governance structures and hierarchies. What exactly this would mean in practice was less clear, with Brazilian leaders seemingly assuming more shared space than might actually have existed.

At the heart of the matter was the demonstrated separation in Chinese thinking between the utility of pan-Southern solidarity as an instrument for global governance change and the interest-impacting costs of proactively engaging in a forceful pursuit of change, most notably by underwriting the costs. Signs of this first began to appear in the G20 WTO negotiating coalition in the mid-2000s. Although China was a member of the coalition, it tended to take a quiet role in the grouping, allowing Brazil and India to do most of the work of framing positions and organizing support. Of particular interest to China was the technical skill of Brazil's negotiators and their ability to meld the sometimes competing positions of the coalition's members into a common stance that could be taken to the 'Quad' meetings with the US and EU. The sense of tacit acquiescence and support that appeared to characterize the first four years of Chinese participation in the coalition began to erode by 2007 when rapidly rising agricultural prices helped drive a softening of Brazil's approach towards the US and EU. Steady support for Brazil slipped as China began to align more closely with India and the G33 group of developing countries on questions relating to the support of subsistence agriculture support. More significantly, China diverged from the Brazilian position on market access questions to do with services and manufactured products, reflecting the sort of strategic industrial policy decisions found in the aerospace industry discussed above (interviews with Chinese diplomats, 2007).

The Chinese approach to Brazilian leadership of the WTO G20 negotiating coalition was to accept it when interests aligned, but to quietly disagree when positions diverged. At issue was the idea that Brazil could not represent China within the WTO, not only because there had been no formal selection process, but also because there were too many policy questions that placed the respective national interests in conflict. This is not to suggest that there was dissatisfaction with Brazil's pursuit of its own national interests within the WTO, but rather that China expected that there would be differences, that Brazil had a right to advance its own agenda, and that this implied notions of alliance would be transitory and issue-specific. While this is not a particularly surprising approach and one likely applicable to most states, the critical point for unpacking the disjuncture in Sino-Brazilian relations is the Chinese assumption of differences despite an overarching rhetoric of solidarity and a clearly shared ambition of seeing shifts in the patterns of structural power bounding the international system.

A clear awareness of the limited possibilities of cooperation and combination was more apparent within the realm of the United Nations Framework Convention on Climate Change. Brazil and China, along with India and South Africa, found they held a shared defensive position with respect to the US and Europe over issues relating to mandatory restrictions on carbon emissions, as well as the question of who should underwrite the costs of climate protection. The result was the apparent creation of a new coalition at the 2009 Copenhagen conference, the BASIC group of countries (Brazil, South Africa, India and China). Yet, the unity of the grouping proved more symbolic than substantive. Over the coming years the members consistently deferred to the larger collective of the G77 as pressure for specific positions became stronger and threatened to highlight divisions amongst the four members of the grouping and their other Southern partners. Even though China and Brazil were both engaged in substantial domestic environmental protection investments, by 2010 it was clear there was disagreement over what kind, if any, form of international legal codification of the responsibilities of emerging-market countries should be permitted (Hochstetler, 2012; Hochstetler and Milkoreit, 2013; Hochstetler and Viola, 2012).

The pattern in the BASIC coalition of Brazil and China running in parallel, but not necessarily consonant directions repeated the trends within the BRICS grouping of countries. Although the BRICS captured a great deal of international attention, it began life within the Brazilian view as something transitory and of questionable longevity (interview with Brazilian diplomats, 2010). Unlike IBSA, it was seen to have little glue to hold it together other than being a forum for the member countries to discuss international issues of mutual concern without the presence of European or American interlocutors. Full onset of the Global Financial Crisis in 2008 appeared to change the calculus as it became apparent that the BRICS group of emerging market countries would be critical for maintaining global economic stability (Stuenkel, 2015). Brazil and China duly combined to press for changes to voting quotas and governance structures in the Bretton Woods Institutions, efforts which were accepted by the US and Europe, but which as of writing had yet to be implemented. A more forward reaching attempt to shift global economic governance came from Brazil, with the idea that the BRICS countries might provide balance of payments support to floundering members of the Euro (Leahy, 2011). Implicit in the idea of a BRICS rescue fund was an apparent assumption that China would provide the major part of the capital, something which Beijing quietly decided against, leaving Dilma on her own to publicly muse about the possibilities of Brazilian financial aid for former colonial master, Portugal.

The BRICS coalition highlights some of the limitations to the bilateral relationship. While the grouping appears to be gathering strength as China turns it to suit its needs and Russia finds it a more welcoming forum than Western-dominated groupings (Stuenkel, 2015), the institutional structures remain vague, and major advances such as the formation of a BRICS Development Bank have proven more contingent on Chinese approval than active engagement from Brazil or the other members. Indeed, at the 2014 BRICS Summit in Fortaleza, Brazil typified the different emphasis given to the grouping. Where Dilma and her diplomatic corps saw the summit as a crucial initiative for Brazilian diplomacy and her re-election campaign, the political importance of the meeting was somewhat lower for Beijing. At China's quiet insistence the timing of the summit was changed to allow president Xi Jinping, an avid soccer fan, to attend the World Cup Final. The fact that the summit date was moved, and then that Xi Jinping did not accept Dilma's invitation for all of the BRICS leaders to watch the game in Rio as a meeting precursor, raises questions about the depth of China's attachment to the BRICS as a central construct in their foreign policy framework. For China the economic possibilities that come through acquiescence to the BRICS far outweigh the political utility of the group. The bolstering of sustained bilateral engagement that comes through the grouping likely helped drive decisions such as a USD 30 billion currency swap agreement in 2013 to reduce transaction costs in bilateral trade (Biller and Galvao, 2013). More telling for what was becoming an increasingly structurally imbalanced economic relationship was the 2010 agreement that helped anchor Brazil's aggressive plans to retain control of its vast sub-salt deep-water oil fields by having Petrobras at the centre of their development through an investment plan of over USD 200 billion. In addition to joint exploration agreements with Chinese state oil firms Petrobras entered into a loan agreement redolent of China's resource extraction practices in Africa, guaranteeing a USD 10 billion loan with a commitment to supply 200,000 barrels of oil per day over a ten year period (Trevisan, 2010).

Neo-dependency?

A theme in this chapter is one of structural differences in both relative power and importance given to the bilateral relationship. This was neatly, albeit obliquely summarized by China's ambassador to Brazil, Li Jinzhang during a keynote speech to the 2012 Brazil-China Business Council meeting in São Paulo. Cultural context and hierarchy were discretely set out with Jinzhang speaking in Mandarin, not the Portuguese that we might expect from an ambassador to an important global player such as Brazil. Neither did he choose the common language of international business, English. The talk was given in a wider environment of increased calls within Brazil for higher protection against the Chinese imports discussed above. Cautioning against such moves, Jinzhang told the story of a small Chinese village that, like Brazil, was a predominantly agrarian community, which through hard work and innovation transformed itself into an industrial powerhouse. Although gently delivered, the lesson for the gathered Brazilian business leaders was very simple: China is not going to slow the pace of exports and it is up to you to innovate and compete. More chillingly for Brazil's leading agro-industrial business sector, Jinzhang also noted that a central policy goal of the new administration in Beijing was food security with an ultimate aim of self-sufficiency.

As Dilma's first presidential term drew to a close Brazil was finding itself faced with an awkward transition threatening to generate a new type of dependency relationship, this time with China. The Chinese ambassador's story cited above came during a period of intense public debate in Brazil about the threat posed by China to national industry, something which Dilma herself brought up directly with the leadership in Beijing in 2011 and which was raised again during the 2012 COSBAN meeting. As Patriota noted, 'China excepted these complaints as valid'. He then continued on with what can be read as an attempt to grapple with an increasingly unequal power relationship: 'still, overcoming this concentration of [Brazilian] exports in a few products is not an easy question' (Patriota, 2013e: 98–99). Although post-dating the temporal period covered in this book, the May 2015 visit of Chinese premiere Li Keqiang to Brasília provides a great deal of insight into how the bilateral relationship had moved from being one of near equals to one where China held the sort of clear, but unstated preeminence attributed to Brazil's South American relations in chapter eight. The tradition of renewing standing cooperation through COSBAN was continued through the holding of the Commission's fourth high-level meeting (MRE, 2015). Of more interest to the media were the economic announcements from the two leaders. In what appeared to be a direct addressing of Brazil's ongoing infrastructure revitalization investment woes, Keqiang committed the Industrial and Commercial Bank of China to investing USD 50 billion with Caixa Econômica to set up an infrastructure development fund, which could include a trans-Andean rail link to a Pacific Ocean port. A separate USD 7 billion agreement was also announced between Brazil and China to provide another tranche for exploration and development financing for Petrobras, which was facing difficulties underwriting the continued exploitation of offshore oil and gas fields due to global hydrocarbon price drops and the corruption scandal surrounding the state oil company (Brics Post, 2015a). The sorts of Brazilian deindustrialization concerns highlighted above were later addressed through an agreement to set up a joint USD 20 billion fund to support collaborative projects to increase industrial productivity in Brazil and China (Brics Post, 2015b).

While politely avoided as an overt subject, the tenor surrounding this new wave of bilateral cooperation was very much one of a strong economy helping the weaker. Viewed with a critical eye, the sum of the initiatives appeared aimed at quietly binding Brazil to China, albeit with a mesh of silk threads, not chains. The series of 2015 announcements added project financing to the market access dependency of major Brazilian firms such as Vale and Petrobras. Other Brazilian national champions were given partial victories, such as the announcement of a USD 1.3 billion jet purchase from Embraer, although this did not extend to redressing the in-country manufacturing blockages discussed above.

The agro-industrial sector was also rewarded with a decision to lift a standing ban on Brazilian beef imports following a mad cow disease scare in 2012. More general items, such as enhanced market access to China, were included but with provisos specifying that this was for competitive products, suggesting it was not intended to be a general support of the Brazilian economy. A common factor in all of these decisions was that they were the exclusive preserve of China to either grant or withhold, and quite possibly could be revoked. Brazil had little to no leverage short of the self-immolating option of banning all agricultural and mineral exports to China pending improvements in the commercial relationship. In terms of relational power, which China has notably shied away from using in the Sino-Brazilian bilateral context, Brazil was clearly subordinate. More telling for the larger foreign policy analysis elaborated in this book, the suggestion was clearly that Brazil's structural power was becoming contingent on sustained positive relationships with China to provide the economic underpinnings for Brazilian international engagement and, on an operational level, at least a measure of implied acquiescence – or at least non-opposition – from Beijing.

Conclusion

While there has been a certain degree of mutual dependence in the bilateral relationship, the account here strongly suggests it is skewed in China's favour. A predominant challenge in Sino-Brazilian relations has been that foreign policy makers in Brasília placed themselves in a position where they started with assumptions of shared interests and solidarity while their counterparts in Beijing remained focused on national interests without allowing questions of solidarity to overly impinge upon decision making. Indeed, many aspects of the bilateral relations story paint a picture of China using the tactics outlined in chapter three to manage Brazil, allowing counterparts in Brasília to float ideas or test the waters for proposals that Beijing may find interesting, but does not necessarily want to answer for.

The result is almost a contradiction for the argument presented in this book. China's rise has clearly been a critical factor in allowing Brazil to pursue a foreign policy agenda focused on reforming structural power frameworks in the global system. Indeed, in many places the two countries agree that there needs to be change and even agree on many of the broad outlines of the sought change. But the devil rests in the details, as we can see through the evolution of the BRICS grouping. For Brazil this may prove problematic in the future as policy makers realize that the space for autonomous foreign policy development and implementation they thought they had was in fact contingent upon at least tacit Chinese agreement or benign disinterest. Conceptually, this continues to place Brasília in the sort of system-supporting middle power role (Jordaan, 2003) and raises questions about how China will continue to impact Brazil's international insertion (Spanakos and Marques, 2014). The problem for Brazilian foreign policy makers is that they do not self-identify as middle powers and have consistently shown a reluctance to act as an archetypical middle power in their relations with the US (Burges, 2014). While this chapter has mapped out an increasing position of weakness in power politics terms in Brazil's bilateral relationship to China, there is little to suggest that this will translate into the sort of consistently overt support for Chinese foreign policy that we would expect of a reoriented middle power. The result is a continued challenge for Brazil's ambition of being a great power and a need to continue its more measured, consensually hegemonic approach to advancing change in the nature of structural power in world order.

12

Conclusions and future possibilities

The argument made in this book is relatively simple in nature, but one that is counter-intuitive to first inclinations when analysing a country's foreign policy. Simply put, the point I have sought to make is that Brazilian foreign policy is primarily concerned with questions of structural power, not relative power. Brazil is not seeking power over other states or regional dominance simply to enforce its own will. Instead, the focus is on influencing a deeper and more profound type of power, an effort which seeks to embed Brazilian interests in the very fabric of the regional and international system. For at least a quarter of a century Brazilian foreign policy has focused on questions of structural power, on shifting the rules and norms of the regional and global system to create the space necessary to advance the country's developmental prerogatives and to prevent precedents from arising that might later impinge on national policy autonomy. In this context power takes on a subtler character, revolving more around the ability to pull others into a particular way of thinking such that they appropriate Brazilian ideas and views as their own. This in turn creates limitations on the range of imaginable policy options open to other states such that they intrinsically reflect Brazil's priorities. Rather than wielding power through imposition or coercion, the attempt is to reorient the policies and actions of other states through engagement and discussion.

Clearly Brazilian foreign policy is not bereft of conflict and competition with other international actors, which occasionally manifests in quiet attempts from Brasília to exert some external pressure, particularly on neighbouring countries. Foreign policy in practice is not, after all, a realm of absolute theoretical purity and binary simplicity. The difference that comes with the Brazilian focus on structural power considerations over relative power preoccupations is one of tone and conduct. Disagreements are seen as transitory issues that will ultimately be resolved and might well create the space for new and productive innovation. As was discussed in the chapter on Latin America this certainly proved to be the case in disputes with Bolivia and Ecuador. Indeed, the quieter approach to managing Bolivia's 2006 nationalization of Petrobras gas assets continues to draw condemnation from critical observers of Brazil's foreign policy, including former ranking diplomats who in the past practiced such measured strategies themselves (Barbosa, 2016). While Brazil certainly could have strangled the Bolivian economy in response to the nationalization process – indeed, Petrobras all but threatened this by reviewing its accounts receivables for diesel shipments – the softer process resulted in a settlement with relatively minor economic impact on Brazilian interests and a largely symbolic victory for Bolivia's political leadership (Mesa, 2011). The longer-term pay-off for Brazil was keeping Bolivia onboard its South American initiatives and retaining close access to decision makers in La Paz. In the Ecuadorian case of threats to not repay BNDES loans, the benefits of this measured approach was particularly apparent as the Correa government moved during the Dilma administration to autonomously advance some of the economic coordination and integrationist initiatives necessary for a reshaping of elements of the hemispheric political economy (Arízaga, 2015).

The challenge that has confronted Northern capitals is that the emphasis on structural power does hold the potential to create misunderstandings if a more comprehensive analysis is not undertaken. This is particularly the case in Brazil's engagement with multilateralism. It is in this area where the core interest divergence with the North is also most apparent and the importance of the structural over the relational game clearest. Although not often repeated so baldly, the fundamental critique Brazil brings to its engagement with multilateral structures is that the norms driving the system and the rules used to enforce them are designed to privilege the North and limit the policy autonomy needed throughout the South to advance national developmental priorities. On a global level this approach has served Brazil well, particularly within international economic institutions such as the WTO where the G20 trade negotiation coalition was developed to push the agricultural market access and infant-industry protective measures critical to many of the world's poorer economies. At first blush this can seem like a deliberate attempt to exclude Northern countries to advance a relative power game. But, as was suggested in the wider discussion of South America and Africa in this book, the imperative driving Brazil is more about creating additional space for innovation, which in turn leads to

greater development opportunities. At a fundamental level elements of
the revisionist structural game being advanced by Brazil thus take on
system-supporting characteristics that further entrench the norms of
market economics, democratic political processes and security provision
in a way that could almost be likened to a traditional middle power but
for the Brazilian tendency to not privilege the interests of core Northern
countries (Jordaan, 2003). Although deliberately marginalized in many
of the initiatives led by Brazil, there is nevertheless real value for countries like the US in Brazil's South–South multilateralist efforts because
they further distribute the work of maintaining a rules-based global
system amongst a new group of states who previously had serious cause
to question its utility for their own national development. Again, success
in this venture is not absolute and Brazil has certainly not been vaulted
to an unquestioned position of leadership. But, taking the security
field as an example, it is clear that programmes such as the CDS and
ZOPACAS are driving an attitudinal shift across the Global South that
reframes existing structures in a manner supportive of the Brazilian goal
of vouchsafing national policy autonomy.

The focus on structural power over relative power also allows a
broader understanding of how a generalized national agenda might
be advanced through non-state instruments. Central to Brazil's foreign
policy since at least the early 1990s has been the expansion of South–
South linkages to create new, alternative pathways to development, security and political consolidation. Where the Cardoso presidency focused
mostly on South America, the Lula and Dilma governments pushed this
vision out to actively include Africa and the wider Global South. While
political engagement and security coordination were important elements
throughout these three presidencies, perhaps of equal note was the role
played by state-directed and private economic actors. The idea, which
was neatly captured by Lula with his call for a new international economic geography, was not a tearing down of the global system as hard-
line *dependentistas* might advocate, but a subtler approach more along
the lines of the Cardoso and Faletto (1979) argument that new spaces
for capital accumulation and exchange can be created in the periphery.
Encouraging new patterns of trade and investment flows certainly played
an important role and one which government policy could assist in an
important way. But, as the chapters on Brazil Inc. and relations with the
Global South and China suggest, private economic actors engaging in
long-term FDI and trade relationships have also played a very significant
autonomous role in making other countries believe that it is possible to
redirect at least elements of the structure of the international economic
system. This is not to argue that the Brazilian state directed these private

actors, although it did provide encouragement. Rather it is to suggest that there is something larger in the Brazilian project that has roots in more than just the country's foreign policy establishment, which suggests the patterns set out in this book will continue irrespective of who is occupying the presidency.

Another aspect of the focus on structural over relational power questions is that it emphasizes the long-term continuity in Brazilian foreign policy and the ability to maintain policy tracks when economic or political oxygen is in short supply. In this respect two aspects of this book stand out. First is the extent to which events in the 1990s were important for setting the stage for the Lula government's rapid push out into global and not just South American affairs. As recounted in several chapters, but emphasized in the discussion of bilateral relations with the US, the 1990s were not a period of economic strength for Brazil. Nevertheless, this period marked a real move to push the structural agenda, to create new alternatives, and to retrench foreign policy as a device for advancing national development ambitions. Lula was able to expansively build on this foundation thanks largely to his charisma; although the commodity boom brought a period of fiscal stability to Brazil and thus more resources for foreign policy, the resources provided to Itamaraty have never been enormous in scale. Arguably what mattered most was the sixteen years of active presidential engagement from 1995 to 2010 and the parallel outward push of autonomous business actors such as the resource companies and empreiteiras.

Interestingly, the centrality of an internationally active president for the 'boom' years in Brazilian foreign policy also points to the second important part of the narrative in this book with respect to the political oxygen and economic resources given to Itamaraty. There is a broad consensus amongst scholars, analysts and even diplomats that foreign policy was not a priority for Dilma during her first term as president, something which changed little during her second; as this book entered the production process Dilma was awaiting her impeachment trial and José Serra had been appointed foreign minister by interim-president Michel Temer with an apparent agenda to make foreign policy a significant driver in plans to restart the Brazilian economy. The sorts of sweeping innovations seen during the Cardoso and Lula years were largely absent under Dilma's stewardship. In part this is not unreasonable. As Celso Amorim (2015b) notes, under Dilma Brazil became more introspective, responding to the demands of hosting a succession of major international events such as the Rio+20 environment summit in 2012, the 2013 Papal visit, the 2014 FIFA World Cup, and the 2016 Olympic Games. The result was serious pressure on Itamaraty, a relatively small ministry that played an important role in organizing aspects of all of these events. If we add to these events the need to consolidate the foreign policy expansion of the Lula years and the serious economic crisis that was well and truly beginning to set in by 2013, it becomes reasonable to expect less attention from Dilma to foreign policy in the face of serious domestic challenges. Indeed, one of the most notable policy acts Dilma took on the foreign policy front was a sustained process of cutting the Itamaraty budget to the point where simply keeping the lights on in some embassies became a serious challenge. That the diplomats at Itamaraty managed to keep Brazil seriously engaged with the world to the extent that it was in this context was no small achievement.

One suggestion prevalent in the literature is that Brazilian foreign policy collapsed during the Dilma years. If we take this book as the basis for a comparison Lula is mentioned almost three times as much as Dilma. Even Cardoso, whose presidency forms more of a foundation for the contemporary account in these pages is mentioned twice as often as Dilma. On a ministerial level, virtually no mention is made of Dilma's three foreign ministers Antonio Patriota, Luiz Alberto Figueiredo and Mauro Vieira, whereas there are copious references to Lula's sole appointee to that post, Celso Amorim, and regular references to Cardoso's two ministers, Luiz Felipe Lampreia and Celso Lafer. This is not to suggest that Dilma's ministers were unimportant, but rather that there was a distinct shift in the profile of foreign policy during her presidency, not a collapse. What is different is the absence of the at-times hyper activity of the previous two presidencies. The Dilma presidency does hold an important place in the analytical narrative of this book, particularly with respect to the chapters on trade, Brazil Inc., security policy and bilateral relations with the US and China. Throughout these chapters the structural power agenda attributed to Brazilian foreign policy continued in various forms, albeit with reduced ability to provide incentives, something particularly apparent in discussions of relations with African countries. This foreign policy strategy could continue despite a shortage of political and economic oxygen in part because of a historical disinterest in the Brazilian polity for foreign affairs – something particularly evident in congressional engagement with foreign affairs – which has to an important extent carved this public policy area off as something only of interest to the professionals at Itamaraty. Likewise, the general pattern of pursuing a structural power agenda seeking to open further space for Brazil in regional and global systems was able to continue, albeit at a reduced pace, despite economic and political crises marking the Dilma presidency.

Indeed, the expertise and professionalism at Itamaraty proved crucial during the Dilma years for keeping the foreign policy project in motion despite presidential disinterest. More revealing is why this was been possible, which points back to the centrality of how Brazilian diplomacy works to build support behind its agenda through long-term processes of discussion, engagement and inclusion. This is manifest not just in the extended political dialogues to build a South American sense of regionness, but also in the manner in which the armed forces have worked to create a distributed sense of responsibility for security across the continent and the South Atlantic. Although not government directed, similar processes are seen on the trade and especially the investment front, where Brazilian firms differentiate themselves with the long-term commitment to investing and thus assisting the development of other emerging economies (Freitas and White, 2015).

Future possibilities

The unanswered question in Brazilian foreign policy is how long Itamaraty can keep the foreign policy project moving forward without fresh injections of economic and political capital. As this book was entering the production process in May 2016 the scene was particularly grim, although much hope was being held out for the Serra ministry and his stated commitment to winning the hard budgetary fights on the Esplanada and using a trade focus to make foreign policy relavent to other ministries and the Brazilian public (Serra, 2016). The economic and political crises of 2015–2016 significantly depressed the value of the Brazilian real. For Itamaraty this created a severe budgetary challenge as many of its expenses are denominated in US dollars. Matters were further complicated for Itamaraty when it became clear that virtually no new moneys would be forthcoming and that there would in fact be a further BRL 40 million budget cut (Fleck, 2015). Throughout 2015 stories began to emerge that some embassies were having problems meeting basic operating costs such as internet, electricity and water bills (Mello and Fleck, 2015). Other diplomats quietly spoke of cancelled events or important invitations declined because the funds were not available to send a representative. Perhaps the highly publicized low point came in mid-August 2015 when it emerged that the Brazilian government had not paid over one hundred thousand dollars in car rental bills incurred during Dilma's official visit to the US earlier in the year (Bilenky and Ezabella, 2015). The reputational damage of unpaid dues to various international organizations set out at the end of chapter four continued throughout 2015, creating challenges for Brazilian representatives in the UN. By early 2016 the sense of financial distress and shrinking capacity to act at Itamaraty filtered out into the public consciousness through an article in *GQ Brasil*, which led with the stark hook: 'Contrary to the splendour of past decades, Itamaraty is confronting its worst crisis with budget cuts, late payments, and even a shortage of toilet paper in embassies' (Bancillon, 2016).

Matters were not helped by a widespread perception that Dilma was actively hostile to the foreign ministry. Anecdotes abound and can quickly be turned up with a cursory search on the internet, most of which align with the impression given in some interviews for this book that briefing the president and advancing foreign policy priorities to the Planalto Palace became a somewhat fraught task for career diplomats during the Dilma era. While there is a strong temptation to launch a searing critique blaming Dilma for the collapse of Brazilian foreign policy during her tenure, a somewhat measured approach is more revealing. As one senior diplomat mused, it is far from certain that the Brazilian people are ready for the country's arrival on the global scene, and the popular consciousness has not adjusted to a new reality that sees Brazil being invited as a key participant in many global decision making forums. Given the serious domestic challenges facing Brazil during the Dilma years, public and political attention was understandably focused on practical solutions to immediate local problems, something the president herself repeatedly emphasized in addresses to her trainee diplomats. Less clear was whether or not politicians saw value in the long-game traditionally played by diplomats and that would require Brazil to play the role of good global citizen as an avenue for opening future opportunities.

The irony afflicting Itamaraty during the Dilma presidency was that many of the international trade and investment gains made by Brazilian firms had been greatly advanced by slow and patient work in foreign policy that often appears abstract and disconnected from daily public policy pressures. Relations with South America and Africa were substantially advanced by diplomatic activity, as was the relationship with key partners such as the US and China. In other words, at a time when resources were being cut for foreign policy activity the gains were starting to arrive. This was reinforced as this conclusion was being written. Two stories appeared in the press within days. First, Dilma highlighted the importance of the international context during a meeting with Ecuadorian president Rafael Correa at the CELAC Summit, noting: 'We are very aware that Brazil cannot resume its capacity for growth, that Brazil cannot reestablish the conditions for sustainable growth in this international context without growth in the other Latin American countries, without the other Latin American countries themselves also having the conditions to recover' (Fonseca, 2016). Reaction in the region was remarkably swift with Venezuelan foreign minister Delcy Rodríguez seemingly leaping on Dilma's remarks during a meeting with Mauro Vieira to request government help in getting Brazilian firms to invest in Venezuela and help kick start its flagging economy (Folhapress, 2016). Although not recognized through budgetary decisions, the importance of foreign policy to Brazilian developmental ambitions appeared clear to Dilma. Moreover, the potential Brazil brought as a partner was also apparent to neighbouring countries. What appeared to be missing was an understanding of the indirect nature of the pay-offs from the consistent and engaged foreign policy that marked the Cardoso and Lula presidencies.

Another theme that emerges from reporting in 2015 is the consistency with which diplomats have continued to formulate and implement Brazil's foreign policy despite a reduction in the political and economic capital provided by the presidency. In the eyes of many, foreign policy reverted to the longer-run norm of being something that could largely be ignored and left to Itamaraty. That said, foreign policy was drawn directly into the political fray in May 2015 when the appointment of Guilherme Patriota as ambassador to the OAS was voted down in the Senate 38 to 37 (Guerreiro, 2016). Rather than being a sudden substantive engagement with the policy area and a congressional assertion of leadership, it quickly emerged that Patriota was being used as a pawn in a power struggle with the president. More interesting and substantive events going on in the background were seemingly passed over by congress, including negotiation of a series of bilateral investment treaties with countries such as Angola and Mozambique (Nasser and Sato, 2015). Indeed, interviews in Africa in 2015 made it clear that there was still a Brazilian presence, just one that was greatly restricted in terms of government funded activity and formal interest, but still marked by high levels of good will and bolstered by the activities of the new panoply of internationally oriented actors in Brazil that emerged during the Lula years.

While it is too early to say anything definitive about what impact the Dilma presidency will have on the long-term trajectory of Brazilian foreign policy, some initial propositions are nevertheless possible. The main point, and the anchor for this conclusion, is that the emphasis on structural, not relative power questions will continue to guide foreign policy strategizing. Indeed this was reflected in the ten policy priorities set out by Serra (2016) in his foreign minister investiture speech, which restated the importance of actively engaging the international system and building many of the bilateral and regional relationships discussed in this book. Related to this is the clear emphasis on retaining policy autonomy to advance national development priorities. Beyond these macro level propositions that represent decades-old principles the major area of challenge and change is likely to be in the institutional form and governmental insertion of Itamaraty itself, an area which the subtext of this book suggests might need some serious rethinking. In his speech welcoming the newest class of diplomatic recruits to the Rio Branco Institute Mauro Vieira (2016) dwelled on a line attributed to former foreign minister Azeredo Silveira in 1975: 'The best tradition of Itamaraty is its ability to reinvent itself.' He continued on to explain how diplomats would have to work hard to open new markets and opportunities for Brazil, to ensure that their country had a positive and fruitful insertion into the regional and international system.

More telling in Vieira's (2016) introductory address was an extended passage dealing with changes to the public policy making process for international questions and how Itamaraty should respond:

> The public policy formation process in Brazil has changed greatly in recent years. Our foreign policy is that of a democratic country, where increasing interactions with internal and external actors are making the policy formulation process more complicated. This enriches and gives greater legitimacy to Brazil's positions. Our duty is to ensure an open and transparent Itamaraty, one which reinforces the belief in Brazilian society that the country has a highly qualified and professional foreign ministry serving as a bulwark in defense of Brazil's most fundamental interests....
>
> In order to remain in tune with the aspirations of Brazilian society and have the means necessary to formulate and execute Brazil's foreign policy we must ensure the fluidity of our contacts with other parts of the Executive Branch and the National Congress, with other units of the federation, and with non-governmental organizations... In short, we increasingly have to look not only outside, but also inside the country.

Unspoken in this speech was a sense that the major failure of Brazilian foreign policy during the Dilma years was the internal battle to maintain the prestige and position Itamaraty held during the Cardoso and Lula presidencies. Equally important is the near-direct instruction to diplomats that they practice their art internally to not only mobilize domestic support, but also to tap into established and emerging partners within Brazil who can advance the country's international agenda. In short, Vieira was calling for the sort of more holistic approach to foreign policy making and international insertion at the bedrock of this book, one which at times sees non-diplomatic actors as potentially critical players in the game.

Vieira's speech also points directly to the area where we are perhaps most likely to see innovation in Brazilian foreign policy in the coming years, namely in the policy formulation process at a tactical level and a substantial innovation in how Itamaraty interacts with its growing range of domestic stakeholders. While there is no shortage of critical literature analysing tactical and transactional aspects of Brazilian foreign policy, the larger strategic questions have a surprising degree of, although not all encompassing, consensus. Where there is significant dissent and disquiet is in how Itamaraty interacts with other internationally engaged governmental bodies as well as the wider polity and its mix of business and civil society interests. In a sense what critical voices are calling for, and what Vieira appeared to be tacitly acknowledging in his speech, is that Itamaraty needs to undergo a process of 'reinvention' to bring it fully into the democratic age for defensive and offensive reasons. Defensive because wider engagement, if executed properly, will build support for the institution and generate greater awareness of the centrality of the international context for many pressing domestic issues. Offensive in the sense that there is much untapped expertise and capacity in Brazil which might be used to further advance the country's foreign policy, something most acutely seen during the WTO Doha round negotiations.

When viewed from the outside the institutional changes that appear to be brewing at Itamaraty will likely bring subtle changes in style, but not much in substance. As this book has demonstrated, the long-term pattern in Brazilian foreign policy is to play the structural game. The chief motivator will continue to be national development, shifting the norms and rules in the regional and global system so that policy autonomy can be preserved to advance this goal, creating new space for advancing norms such as liberal democracy and variants of market economics. For external partners this is perhaps the central point to keep in mind when Brazilian counterparts seem obstructionist or willfully difficult. For international relations scholars it points to an equally important reminder, namely that there are other ways of conceptualizing global and regional order predicated on priorities that are different, but not necessarily antagonistic to the current order. Moreover, Brazil will continue to be a player that needs to be accounted for in analyses of regional and global affairs. The Cardoso and Lula presidencies brought Brazil out into the world, a process which continued during the Dilma presidency despite a reduction in the resources available for international engagement. Given that Brazil's current global profile is in many ways simply an extension of a long-term trajectory, the variation going forward is likely to be how expansive Brazil is in its global role, not whether it will continue.

References

Abdenur, Adrian Erthal and Danilo Marcondes de Souza Neto (2013), 'South–South Cooperation and Democracy in Africa: Brazil's Role in Guinea-Bissau', *Africa Review* 5 (2): 104–117.

Abdenur, Adriana Erthal and Danilo Marcondes de Souza Neto (2014), 'Region-Building by Rising Powers: The South Atlantic and Indian Ocean Rims Compared', *Journal of the Indian Ocean Region* 10 (1): 1–17.

Abdenur, Adriana Erthal, Maiara Folly, Kayo Moura, Sergio A. S. Jordão and Pedro Maia (2014), 'The BRICS and the South Atlantic: Emerging Arena for South–South Cooperation', *South African Journal of International Affairs* 21 (3): 303–319.

African Business (2012), 'The Brazilians Are Coming: Top Brazilian Companies In Africa', *African Business* (10 December): Factiva Doc.

Aguilar, Sérgio Luiz Cruz (2013), 'The South Atlantic: Brazil–Africa Relations in the Field of Security and Defense', *Austral: Bzilian Journal of Strategy and International Relations* 2 (4): 47–68.

Alden, Chris and Amnon Aran (2012), *Foreign Policy Analysis: New Approaches* (Abingdon: Routledge).

Alden, Chris and Marco Antonio Vieira (2005), 'The New Diplomacy of the South: South Africa, Brazil, India and Trilateralism', *Third World Quarterly* 26 (7): 1077–1095.

Allison, Graham T. (1969), 'Conceptual Models and the Cuban Missile Crisis', *American Political Science Review* 63 (3): 689–718.

Almeida, Paulo Roberto de (2001), 'Dez Regras Modernas de Diplomacia', *Revista Espaço Acadêmico* 1 (4) (September).

Almeida, Paulo Roberto de (2003), 'A Política Internacional do Partido dos Trabalhadores: Da Fundação à Diplomacia do Governo Lula', *Revista Sociológica Política* 20: 87–102.

Almeida, Paulo Roberto de (2004), 'Uma Política Externa Engajada: A Diplomacia do Governo Lula', *Revista Brasileira de Política Internacional* 47 (1): 162–184.

Almeida, Paulo Roberto de (2012), *Relações Interancionais e Política Externa do Brasil: A Diplomacia Brasileira no Contexto da Globalização* (Rio de Janeiro: LTC).

Almeida, Paulo Roberto de (2014), *Nunca Antes na Diplomacia... A Política Externa Brasileira em Tempos não Convencionais* (Curitiba: Appris).

Altemani de Oliveira, Henrique (2006), 'China–Brasil: Perspectivas de Cooperación Sur–Sur', *Nuevo Sociedad* No. 203 (May/June).

Amann, Edumnd (1999), 'Technological Self-Reliance in Brazil: Achievements and Prospects: Some Evidence from the Non-Serial Capital Goods Sector', *Oxford Development Studies* 27 (3): 329–357.

Amorim, Celso (2003), *Celso Amorim (Depoimento, 1997)* (Rio de Janeiro: CPDOC).

Amorim, Celso (2004a), 'Statement by Minister Celso Amorim at the G-90 meeting', Georgetown, Guyana (3 June), www.mre.gov.br.

Amorim, Celso (2004b), 'Audiência do Ministro das Relações Exteriores, Embaixador Celso Amorim, em Sessão Conjunta das Comissões de Relações Exteriores e Defesa Nacional do Senado Federal e da Câmara dos Deputados', Brasília (12 February).

Amorim, Celso (2011a), *Conversas com Jovem Diplomatas* (São Paulo: Benvirá).

Amorim, Celso (2011b), 'Uma Visão Brasileira do Panorama Estratégico Global', *Contexto Internacional* 33 (2): 265–275.

Amorim, Celso (2012), 'Defesa Nacional e Pensamento Estratégico Brasileiro, *Revista Política Hoje,* 21 (2): 330–349.

Amorim, Celso (2013), *Breves Narativas Diplomaticas* (São Paulo: Benvirá).

Amorim, Celso (2015a), *Teerã, Ramalá e Doha: Memórias da Política Externa Ativa e Altiva* (Rio de Janeiro: Benvirá).

Amorim, Celso (2015b), Author interview, Rio de Janeiro (4 September).

Amorim, Neto (2012), *De Dutra a Lula: A Condução e os Determinantes da Política Externa Brasileira* (Rio de Janeiro: Elsevier).

Antonioli, Silvia (2014), 'Rio Tinto Sues Vale, Steinmetz, BSGR Over Guinea Iron Deposit Rights', *Reuters* (30 April).

APANEWS (2011), 'Brazilian Coal Mining Firm to Invest US$9bn in Mozambique', *APANEWS* (19 March).

APANEWS (2012), 'Brazilian Construction Group Expects $1bn Post Turnover in Mozambique in 2020', *APANEWS* (20 November).

Arashiro, Zuleika (2011), *Negotiating the Free Trade Area of the Americas* (Basingstoke: Palgrave Macmillan).

Araujo, Heloísa Vilhena de (2005), *Diálogo América do Sul – Países Árabes* (Brasília: FUNAG).

Arízaga, Leonardo (2015), Viceministro de Relaciones Exteriores e Integración Política Ministerio de Relaciones Exteriores y Movilidad Humana, Republica del Ecuador. Author interview, Canberra, Australia (13 May).

Armijo, Leslie Elliott and Saori N. Katada, eds (2014), *The Financial Statecraft of Emerging Powers: Shield and Sword in Asia and Latin America* (Basingstoke: Palgrave Macmillan).

Arraes, Virgílio (2008), 'Estados Unidos: Um Possível Significado para a Quarta Frota', *Meridiano 47* No. 97 (August): 25–27.

Arrighi, Giovanni (1993), 'The Three Hegemonies of Historical Capitalism', in Stephen Gill, ed., *Gramsci, Historical Materialism, and International Relations* (Cambridge: Cambridge University Press).

Aurujo, José Tavares de (2009/2010), 'Infraestrutura e Integração Regional: O Papel de IIRSA', *Política Externa* 18 (3): 33–48.

Azambuja, Marcos C. de (2009), 'A Brazilian Perspective on Nuclear Disarmament', in Barry M. Blechman, ed., *Brazil, Japan, and Turkey* (New York: The Henry Stimson Center).

Azevedo, Paulo C. de (1992), 'Security of the Brazilian Amazon Area', Study Project, Army War College Carlisle Barracks.

Ballve, Marcelo (2003), 'Brazil's New Eye on the Amazon', *NACLA Report on the Americas* 36 (6): 32–38.

Ban, Cornel (2013), 'Brazil's Liberal Neo-Developmentalism: New Paradigm or Edited Orthodoxy?' *Review of International Political Economy* 20 (2): 298–331.

Bancillon, Deco (2016), 'Após Décadas de Glamour, Diplomacia Brasileira Acumula Dívidas', *GQ Brasil* (January).

Bandeira, Luiz Alberto Moniz (2003), *Brasil, Argentina e Estados Unidos: Conflito e Integração na América do Sul (Da Tríplice Aliança ao Mercosul, 1870–2003)* (Rio de Janeiro: Editora Revan).

Barbosa, Alexandre de Freitas, Ângela Cristina Tepassê and Marina Neves Biancalana (2014), 'Las Relaciones Económicas entre Brasil y China a Partir del Desempeño de las Empresas State Grid y Lenovo', in Enrique Dussel Peters, ed., *La Inversión Extranjera Directa de China en América Latina: 10 Estudios de Caso* (Mexico: Unión de Universidades de América Latina y el Caribe).

Barbosa, Andrezza, Bruno Quadros e Quadros, Laura Delamonica and Lucianara Andrade Fonseca (2014), 'Entrevista com o Ministro de Estado das Relações Exteriores Embaixador Luiz Alberto Figueiredo Machado', *JUCA: Diplomacia e Humanidades* 7 (34): 33–36.

Barbosa, Cristiano Guimarães (2014), 'O Sistema Integrado de Monitoramento de Fronteiras: Uma Ferramenta de Cooperação Regional', *Anais do I Congresso Brasileiro de Geografia Política e Gestão do Território* (Porto Alegre: Editora Letra1).

Barbosa, Rubens (2007), Author interview, São Paulo (28 March).

Barbosa, Rubens (2008), 'A Política Externa do Brasil para a América do Sul e o Ingresso da Venezuela no Mercosul', *Interesse Nacional* (April/June): 11–21.

Barbosa, Rubens (2011), *O Dissenso de Washington* (Rio de Janeiro: Agir).

Barbosa, Rubens (2014), 'Mercosul: Retórica e Realidade', *Política Externa* 22 (4) (April/May/June).

Barbosa, Rubens (2015), 'FHC e Lula, Políticas Externas Divergentes', OpEd, *Folha de São Paulo* (29 November).

Barbosa, Rubens (2016), 'A Nova Agenda Exeterna para o Brasil em um Mundo em Transformação', *Interesse Nacional* 8 (32) (Jan–March).

Barbosa, Rubens Antônio and Luís Panelli César (1994), 'O Brasil Como "Global Trader"', in Gélson Fonseca Júnior and Sérgio Henrique Nabuco de Castro, eds, *Temas de Política Externa Brasileira II, vol. I* (São Paulo: Paz e Terra).

Barros, G. S. A. C. (2009), 'Brazil: The Challenges in Becoming an Agricultural Superpower', in Lael Brainard and Leonardo Martinez-Diaz, *Brazil as an Economic Superpower?* (Washington, DC: Brookings Institution Press).

Battaglino, Jorge (2012), 'Defence in a Post-Hegemonic Regional Agenda: The Case of the South American Defence Council', in Riggirozzi, Pía and Diana Tussie, eds, *The Rise of Post-Hegemonic Regionalism: The Case of Latin America* (London: Springer).

Baumann, Renato (1987), 'A Integração Econômica entre Brasil, Argentina e Uruguai: Que Tipo de Integração se Pretende', in Renato Baumann and Juan Carlos Lerda, eds, *Barsil-Argentina-Uruguai: A Integração em Debate* (Brasília: Editora Universidade de Brasília).

BBC (2004), 'Brazil's Lula Pardons Debt, Pledges Support for Bolivia', *BBC Monitoring Americas* (9 July).

Becard, Danielly Silva Ramos (2011), 'O Que Esperar das Relações Brasil-China?' *Revista Sociologica Política* 19 (Sup.) (November): 31–44.

Belém Lopes, Dawisson (2013a), *Política Externa e Democracia no Brasil* (São Paulo: Editora UNESP).

Belém Lopes, Dawisson (2013b), 'Titubeios e Tergiversações: Epitáfio para a Era Patriota', *Revista Insight Inteligência* (July/Aug/Sept): 72–81.

Belém Lopes, Dawisson (2013c), 'Quem precisa do Itamaraty?' *Observatorio da Imprensa*, 17 (782) (26 Feb): www.observatoriodaimprensa.com.br/news/view/_ed735_quem_precisa_do_itamaraty.

Belém Lopes, Dawisson (2015), *Política Externa na Nova República: Os Primeiros 30 Anos* (Belo Horizonte, Brazil: Editora UFMG).

Belém Lopes, Dawisson and Carlos Aurélio Pimenta de Faria (2014), 'Eleições Presidenciais e Política Externa Brasileira', *Estudos Internacionais* 2 (2) (July–December): 139–148.

Berger, Peter L. and Thomas Luckman (1966), *The Social Construction of Reality: A Treatise in the Sociology of Knowledge* (New York: Doubleday).

Bianconi, Cesar (2006), 'Bolivia Freezes Plan to Take Petrobras Assets', *Reuters* (14 September).

Bilenky, Thais and Fernanda Ezabella (2015), 'Viagem de Dilma aos EUA dá Calote de US$1000 mil em Aluguel de Limusines', *Folha de São Paulo* (17 August).

Biller, David and Arnaldo Galvao (2013), 'China, Brazil Sign $30 Billion Swap Accord to Bolster BRICS', *Bloomberg* (27 March).

BNDES (2002), Author interview with BNDES Technicians, Rio de Janeiro (11 October).

Bodman, Samuel W., Julia E. Sweig and James D. Wolfensohn (2014), *Global Brazil and US–Brazil Relations*, Independent Task Force Report No. 66. Council on Foreign Relations.

Bonelli, Regis (1999), 'A Note on Foreign Direct Investment and Industrial Competitiveness in Brazil', *Oxford Development Studies* 27 (3): 305–327.

Boulos, Guilerme (2014), 'Eles Venceram Outra Vez', *Folha de São Paulo* (2 October).

Bourne, Richard (2008), *Lula of Brazil: The Story so Far* (Berkeley, CA: University of California Press).

Braga, Carlos Chagas Vianna (2010), 'MINUSTAH and the Security Environment in Haiti: Brazil and South American Cooperation in The field', *International Peacekeeping* 17 (5): 711–722.

Brainard, Lael and Leonardo Martinez-Diaz (2009), *Brazil as an Economic Superpower?* (Washington, DC: Brookings Institution Press).

Brics Post (2015a), 'Brazil, China Ink Multibillion Dollar Trade Deals', thebricspost.com (19 May): http://thebricspost.com/brazil-china-ink-multibillion-dollar-trade-deals [accessed 3 July 2015].

Brics Post (2015b), 'Brazil, China to Set Up New $20bn Fund to Boost Production', thebricspost.com (28 June): http://thebricspost.com/brazil-china-to-set-up-new-20bn-fund-to-boost-production/ [accessed 3 July 2015].

Burges, Sean W. (2007), 'Building a Global Southern Coalition: The Competing Approaches of Brazil's Lula and Venezuela's Chavez', *Third World Quarterly* 28 (7) (October): 1343–1358.

Burges, Sean W. (2008), 'Consensual Hegemony: Theorizing the Practice of Brazilian Foreign Policy', *International Relations* 22 (1) (March): 65–84.

Burges, Sean W. (2009), *Brazilian Foreign Policy After the Cold War* (Gainnesville, FL: University of Florida Press).

Burges, Sean W. (2012), 'Strategies and Tactics for Global Change: Democratic Brazil in Comparative Perspective', *Global Society* 26 (3) (July): 351–368.

Burges, Sean W. (2013), 'Mistaking Brazil as a Middle Power', *Journal of Iberian and Latin American Research* 19 (2): 286–302.

Burges, Sean W. (2014), 'Brazil's International Development Cooperation: Old and New Motivations', *Development Policy Review* 32 (3): 355–374.

Burns, Bradford E. (1966), *The Unwritten Alliance: Rio Branco and Brazilian–American Relations* (New York: Columbia University Press).

Cabral, L. and J. Weinstock (2010), *Brazilian Technical Co-operation for Development: Drivers, Mechanics and Future Prospects* (London: Overseas Development Institute).

Cabral, Otávio (2007), 'Nem na Ditadura', *Veja* (2 May).

Cabral, Severino (2003), 'Brasil e China – Aliança E Cooperação para o Novo Milênio', in Samuel Pinheiro Guimarães, ed., *Brasil e China: Multipolaridade* (Brasília: FUNAG).

Candeas, Alessandro (2012), 'Educação e Política Externa: Por Uma Parceria Diplomacia-Universidade', in Leticia Pinheiro and Carlos R. S. Milani, eds, *Política Externa Brasileira: As Prácticas da Política e a Política das Prácticas* (Rio de Janeiro: Editora FGV).

Cardoso, Fernando Henrique (1989), 'Associated-Dependent Development and Democratic Theory', in Alfred Stepan, ed., *Democratizing Brazil: Origins, Policies and Future* (New Haven, CT: Yale University Press).

Cardoso, Fernando Henrique (1996), 'Impacto da Globalização nos Países em Desenvolvimento: Riscos e Oportunidades', Converência no Colégio de Mexico, Cidade do Mexico (20 February).

Cardoso, Fernando Henrique (1999), 'Discurso por Ocasião de Abartura da IX Conferência Ibero-Americana', Havana, Cuba (15–16 November).

Cardoso, Fernando Henrique (2000), 'Brazil and a new South America', *Valor Econômico* (30 August).

Cardoso, Fernando Henrique (2001), 'A Política Externa do Brasil no Início de um Novo Século: Uma Mensagem do Presidente da República', *Revista Brasileira de Política Internacionais* 44 (1): 5–12.

Cardoso, Fernando Henrique (2002), 'Towards a Democratic Global Governance – a Brazilian Perspective', The Cyrill Foster Lecture, Oxford, England (13 November).

Cardoso, Fernando Henrique (2006), *A Arte da Política: A História que Vivi* (Rio de Janeiro: Editora Civilização Brasileira).

Cardoso, Fernando Henrique (2007), Author interview (São Paulo, 30 August).

Cardoso, Fernando Henrique (2015), *Diários da Presidência, 1995–1996* (São Paulo: Companhia das Letras).

Cardoso, Fernando Henrique and Enzo Faletto (1979), *Dependency and Development in Latin Ameirca*, trans. by Marjory Mattingy Urquidi (Berkeley, CA: University of California Press).

Cardoso, Fernando Henrique with Mauricio A. Font (2001), *Charting a New Course: The Politics of Globalization and Social Transformation* (Lanham, MD: Rowman & Littlefield).

Cardoso, Fernando Henrique and Mário Soares (1998), *O Mundo em Português: Um Diálogo* (São Paulo: Paz e Terra).

Cardoso, Fernando Henrique with Brian Winter (2006), *The Accidental President of Brazil: A Memoir* (New York: Public Affairs).

Carnegie Endowment for International Peace (2010), 'The New Geopolitics: Emerging Powers and the Challenges of a Multipolar World', transcript of a foreign policy public forum by Celso Amorim, Thomas Friedman and David Rothkof (30 November).

Casarões, Guilherme (2014), 'Itamaraty's Mission', *The Cairo Review of InternationalAffairs* (17 February): www.aucegypt.edu/GAPP/CairoReview/Pages/articleDetails.aspx?aid=522.

Cason, Jeffrey W. (2000), 'Democracy Looks South: Mercosul and the Politics of Brazilian Trade Strategy', in Peter R. Kingstone and Timothy J. Power, eds, *Democratic Brazil: Actors, Institutions and Processes* (Pittsburgh: University of Pittsburgh Press).

Cason, Jeffrey W. (2011), *The Political Economy of Integration: The Experience of Mercosur* (Abingdon: Routledge).

Cason, Jeffrey W. and Timothy J. Power (2009), 'Presidentialization, Pluralization and the Rollback of Itamaraty: Explaining Change in Brazilian Foreign Policy Making in the Cardoso-Lula Era', *International Political Science Review* 30 (2): 117–140.

Castro Neves, João Augusto de, and Matias Spektor (2011), 'Obama and Brazil', in Abraham F. Lowenthal, Theodore J. Piccone, Laurence Whitehead and Ted Piccone, eds, *Shifting the Balance: Obama and the Americas* (Washington, DC: Brookings Institution Press).

Cavalcante, Fernando (2010), 'Rendering Peacekeeping Instrumental? The Brazilian Approach to United Nations Peacekeeping During the Lula da Silva Years (2003–2010)', *Revista Brasileira de Política Internacional* 53 (2): 142–159.

Cervo, Amado Luiz (2010), 'Brazil's Rise on the International Scene: Brazil and the World', *Revista Brasileira de Política Internacional* 53: 7–32.

Chade, Jamil (2008), 'Brasil Pode Suspender Crédito a Vizinhos', *O Estado de São Paulo* (3 December).

Charleaux, João Paulo (2008), '"Imperialismo" Brasileiro Perocupa Região', *O Estado de São Paulo* (23 October).

Cheibub, Zairo Borges (1984), 'Diplomacia, Diplomatas e Política Externa: Aspectos do Processo de Institucionalização do Itamaraty', Master's Thesis, Instituto Universítario de Pesquisas do Rio de Janeiro (June).

Cheibub, Zairo Borges (1989), 'A Carreira Diplomática no Brasil: O Processo de Burucratização do Itamarati', *Revista de Administração Pública* 23 (2): 97–128.

Chohfi, Osmar (2002), Author interview with Osmar V. Chohfi, Secretary-General, Brazilian Ministry of Foreign Affairs, Brasília (8 October).

Coelho, Janet Tappin (2014), 'Brazil Navy Submarines Nuclear France', *IHS Jane's Navy International* (16 December).

Coelho, Pedro Motta Pinto and José Flávio Sombra Saraiva (2004), *Brazil-Africa Forum on Politics, Cooperation and Trade* (Brasília: IBRI).

Cohen, Jillian Clare and Kristina M. Lybecker (2005), 'AIDS Policy and Pharmaceutical Patents: Brazil's Strategy to Safeguard Public Health', *The World Economy* 28 (2): 211–230.

Colombia Reports (2008-03-05). 'Bolivia Calls Unasur Meeting on Colombia-Ecuador Crisis', http://colombiareports.com/colombia-news/news/277-bolivia-calls-unasur-meeting-on-colombia-ecuador-crisis.html [accessed 8 September 2010].

Corrêa, Cleber (2014), Author interview with Cleber Corrêa, President of the Associação de Empresários e Executivos Brasileiros em Angola, Luanda (23 September).

Costa, Darc (2003), *Estratégia Nacional: A Cooperação Sul-Americana Como Caminho para a Inserção Internacional do Brasil* (Rio de Janeiro: Aristeu Souza).

Coutinho, Luciano, Célio Hiratuka and Rodrigo Sabatini (2008), 'O Investimento Direto no Exterior Como Alavanca Dinamizadora da Economia Brasileira', in Otavio de Barros and Fabio Giambiagi, eds, *Brasil Globalizado* (Rio de Janeiro: Elsevier).

Couto e Silva, Golbery de (1967), *Geopolítica do Brasil* (Rio de Janeiro: José Olympia).

Cox, Robert W. (1987), *Production Power and World Order: Social Forces in the Making of Modern History* (New York: Columbia University Press).

Crandall, Britta H. (2011), *Hemispheric Giants: The Misunderstood History of US–Brazilian Relations* (Lanham, MD: Rowman & Littlefield Publishers).

CRE – Senado Federal Comissão de Relações Exteriores e Defesa Nacional (2007), 4a Reunião Extraordinária da Comissão de Relações Exteriores e Defesa Nacional, da 1a Sessão Legislativa Ordinária da 53a Legislatura (27 Feb).

Cunliffe, Philip and Kai Kenkel (2016), *Brazil as a Rising Power: Intervention Norms and the Contestation of Global Order* (London: Routledge).

Danese, Sérgio (1999), *Diplomacia Presidencial: História e Crítica* (Rio de Janeiro: Topbooks).

Daudelin, Jean (2005), 'Bubbling up, Trickling Down, Seeping Out: The Transformation of Canadian Foreign Policy', in Fen Osler Hampson, Norman Hillmer and David Carment, eds, *Canada Among Nations* (Montreal: McGill-Queen's University Press): 103–122.

Daudelin, Jean and Sean W. Burges (2007), 'Brazil: How Realists Defend Democracy', in Thomas Legler, Sharon F. Lean, and Dexter S. Boniface, eds, *Promoting Democracy in the Americas* (Baltimore: Johns Hopkins University Press).

Daudelin, Jean and Sean W. Burges (2011), 'Moving in, Carving out, Proliferating: The Many Faces of Brazil's Multilateralism Since 1989', *Pensamiento Próprio* 16 (33) (Jan-June): 35–64.

Dávila, Jerry (2010), *Hotel Trópico: Brazil and the Challenge of African Decolonization, 1950–1980* (Durham, NC: Duke University Press).

Dávila, Sérgio (2008), 'Sob Polêmica, EUA Reativam sua Quarta Frota', *Folha de São Paulo* (13 July).

Deininger, Klaus and Derek Byerlee with Jonathan Lindsay, Andrew Norton, Harris Selod and Mercedes Stickler (2011), *Rising Global Interest in Farmland. Can it Yeald Sustainable and Equitable Benefits?* (Washington, DC: The World Bank): http://siteresources.worldbank.org/INTARD/Resources/ESW_Sept7_final_final.pdf.

Deitos, Marc Antoni (2012), *Processo Decisório em Política Externa no Brasil: A Participação do Empresariado Nacional* (Porto Alegre: Editora UniRitter).

Deo, Anderson (2012), 'Apontamentos Sobre o Imperialism Brasileiro nos Governos Lula e FHC', *Novos Rumos, Marília* 49 (1) (Jan–June): 127–138.

Dianni, Cláudia and Isabel Braga (2001), 'Bush Pede Ajuda a FHC para Superar Impasse com a China', *O Estado de São Paulo* (11 April).

Dias, Marcio de Oliveira (2015), 'Quando o Brasil Ajudou a Impedir o Golpe de Oviedo', OpEd, *O Globo* (29 November).

Dinardo, Ana Carolina (2012), 'Itamaraty Oferece 30 vagas', *Correio Braziliense* (4 January).

Duailibi, Julia (2003), 'Brasil Quer Vender Dados do Sivam ao Peru', *Folha de São Pauo* (24 August).

Easterly, William (2006), *The White Man's Burden* (New York: Penguin).

EFE (2006), 'Bolívia Estuda Punir Petrobrás por Falta de Diesel no País', *O Estado de São Paulo* (6 June).

EFE (2008), 'Brazil Warns Ecuador of Possible Trade Cutoff', *EFE News Service* (15 October).

El Comercio (2005), 'Ecuador es Clave en el Projecto de Brasil', *El Comercio* [Quito] (18 August).

Emerson, R. Guy (2010), 'Radical Neglect? The "War on Terror" and Latin America', *Latin American Politics and Society* 52 (1) (Spring): 33–62.

Emerson, R. Guy (2014), 'Strong Presidentialism and the Limits of Foreign Policy Success: Explaining Cooperation between Brazil and Venezuela'. *International Studies Perspectives*: DOI: 10.1111/insp. 12071.

Epoca (2015), 'Brasileiro é Candidato Único em Nova Eleição da FAO', *Epoca Negocios* (2 February).

Espach, Ralph (2015), 'The Risks of Pragmatism: Brazil's Relations with the United States and the International Security Order', in Oliver Stuenkel and Matthew M. Taylor, eds, *Brazil on the Global Stage: Power, Ideas, and the Liberal International Order* (New York: Palgrave Macmillan).

Espin, Patricia Rondon (2006), 'Chávez Abandons Andean Trade Bloc', *Miami Herald* (24 April).

Evans, Peter (1979), *Dependent Development: The Alliance of Multinational, State and Local Capital in Brazil* (Princeton: Princeton University Press).

Farcau, Bruce W. (1996), *The Chaco War: Bolivia and Paraguay, 1932–1935* (Westport, CG: Praeger).

Faria, Carlos Aurélio Pimenta de (2008), 'Opinião Pública e Política Externa: Insulamento, Politização e Reforma na Produção da Política Exterior do Brasil', *Revista Brasileira de Política Internacional* 51 (2): 80–97.

Faria, Carlos Aurélio Pimenta de (2012), 'O Itamaraty e a Política Externa Brasileira: Do Insulamento à Busca de Coordenação dos Atores Governmentais e de Cooperação com os Agentes Societários', *Contexto Internacional* 5 (25): 20–43.

Faria, Carlos Aurélio Pimenta de, Joanna Laura Nogueira and Dawisson Belém Lopes (2012), 'Coordenação Intragovernmental para a Implementação da Política Externa Brasileira: O Caso do Fórum IBAS', *Revista Dados*.

Farnsworth, Erich (2015), 'America Must Take Brazil Seriously', *National Interest* 15.

Feinberg, Richard E. (1997), *Summitry in the Americas: A Progress Report* (Washington, DC: Peterson Institute).

Fenwick, Tracy Beck (2015), Avoiding Governors: Federalism, Democracy, and Poverty Alleviation in Brazil and Argentina (Notre Dame, IN: University of Notre Dame Press).

Fishlow, Albert (2011), *Starting Over: Brazil since 1985* (Washington, DC: Brookings Institution Press).

Fiszbein, Ariel, Norbert Schady, Francisco H. G. Ferreira, Margaret Grosh, Niall Keleher, Pedro Olinto and Emmanuel Skoufias (2009), *Conditional Cash Transfers: Reducing Present and Future Poverty* (Washington, DC: World Bank).

Fleck, Isabel (2015), 'Contra Crise, Itamaraty Faz Plano de Cortes', *Folha de São Paulo* (8 August).

Flemes, Daniel and Leslie Wehner (2013), Reacciones Estratégicas en Sudamérica ante el Ascenso de Brasil, *Foreign Affairs Latinoamérica* 13 (4): 107–114.

Flemes, D. and Wehner, L. (2015), 'Drivers of Strategic Contestation in South America', *International Politics* (special issue).

Fleury, Afonso and Maria Tereza Leme Fleury (2011), *Brazilian Multinationals: Competences for Internationalization* (Cambridge: Cambridge University Press).

Florencio, Sérgio Abreu e Lima (2011), 'A Ponta do Iceberg', OpEd, *O Estado de São Paulo* (23 May).

Flynn, Matthew (2007), 'Between Subimperialism and Globalization: A Case Study in the Internationalization of Brazilian Capital', *Latin American Perspectives* 34 (9) (November): 9–27.

Folhapress (2016), 'Chanceler Pede Ajuda ao Brasil para Reerguer Economia na Venezuela', *Gazeta do Povo* (29 January).

Fonseca Jr., Gelson (2002) 'O Brasil no Conselho de Segurança da ONU: 1998–1999', *Brasília: Ipri/Funag*.

Fonseca Jr., Gelson (2004), *A Legitimidade e Outras Questões Internacionais: Poder e Ética entre as Nações* (São Paulo: Paz e Terra).

Fonseca, Pedro (2016), 'Dilma diz que Situação Internacional é Adversa e Brasil Precisa da América Latina para Crescer', *Epoca Negócios* (27 January).

Forjaz, Maria Cecília Spina (2011), 'O Congresso e a Política Externa (1999–2006)', in José Álvaro Moisés, ed., *O Papel do Congresso Nacional no Presidencialismo de Coalização* (Rio de Janeiro: Konrad-Adenauer-Stiftung).

Fournier, Dominique (1999), 'The Alfonsin Administration and the Promotion of Democratic Values in the Southern Cone and the Andes', *Journal of Latin American Studies* 31 (1): 39–74.

Freitas, Amy and Lyal White (2015), 'Brazilian Firms in Africa: What Makes them Different?' in Ifedapo Adeleye, Kevin Ibeh, Abel Kinoti and Lyal White, eds, *The Changing Dynamics of International Business in Africa* (New York: Palgrave Macmillan).

Freitas, Marcus V. (2010), 'Honduras and the Emergence of a New Latin America', *Latin American Policy* 1 (1): 157–161.

FUNAG (2002a), *Seminário: Rio Branco, a América do Sul e a Modernização do Brasil* (Brasília: FUNAG/IPRI).

FUNAG (2002b), *Anais do Seminário: América do Sul, Quito, 15 e 16 de Julho, 2002* (Brasília: FUNAG/IPRI, FLACSO Quito).

FUNAG (2007), *Cronologia da Política Externa do Governo Lula, 2003–2006* (Brasília: FUNAG).

Gadea, Rosario Santa, ed. (2012), *Integración Física Sudamericana: Diez Años Después* (Lima: Universidad del Pacífico; BID-INTAL; CEPEI).

Garcia, Marco Aurélio (2009/2010), 'O que está em Jogo em Honduras', *Política Externa* 18 (3) (Dec/Jan/Feb): 123–130.

Garcia, Marco Aurélio (2011), 'Respostas da Política Externa Brasileira às Incertezas do Mundo Atual', *Interesse Nacional* 4 (13) (April–June).

Gardini, Gian Luca (2010), *The Origins of Mercosur: Democracy and Regionalization in South America* (New York: Palgrave Macmillan).

Gardini, Gian Luca (2016), 'Brazil: What Rise of What Power?' *Bulletin of Latin American Research* 35 (1): 5–19.

Gazeta Mercantil (2003a), 'Negociadores Brasileiros Terão Apoio Privado', *Gazeta Mercantil* (5 May).

Gazeta Mercantil (2003b), 'Itamaraty Elogia Criação de Instituto', *Gazeta Mercantil* (7 May).

Genésio, João (2009), *O Fórum de Diálogo Índia, Brasil e África do Sul (IBAS): Análise e Perspectivas* (Brasília: Funag).

Globalfirepower (2015), 'Countries Ranked by Military Strength', globalfirepower. com (1 April): www.globalfirepower.com/countries-listing.asp [accessed 14 July 2015].

Goldstein, Andrea (2006), 'The Political Economy of Industrial Policy in China: The Case of Aircraft Manufacturing', *Journal of Chinese Economic and Business Studies* (4) 3: 259–273.

Gómez-Mera, Laura (2013), *Power and Regionalism in Latin America: The Politics of MERCOSUR* (Notre Dame, IN: University of Notre Dame Press).

Gonçalves, José Botafogo (2013), 'Vamos renegociar o Mercosul?' *Política Externa* 22 (2) (Oct/Nov/Dec): 42–49.

Gramsci, Antonio (1957), 'The Modern Prince', in Antonio Gramsci, *The Modern Prince & Other Writings* trans. Louis Marks (New York: International Publishers).

Gubo, Rogério Samo (2015), Author interview with Rogério Samo Gubo, President, Câmara do Comércio *Moçambique e Brasil*, Maputo (14 January).

Guebuza, Armando Emilio (2013), 'Speech by H. E. Armando Emilio Guebuza to the Australian Institute of International Affairs', Canberra, Australia (14 March).

Guerreiro, Gabriela (2016), 'Em Derrota de Dilma, Senado Rejeita Embaixador Indicado para OEA', *Folha de São Paulo* (19 May).

Guimarães, Samuel Pinheiro (2006), *Desafios Brasileiros na Era dos Gigantes* (Rio de Janeiro: Contraponto).

Hage, José Alexandre A. (2004), *As Relações Diplomáticas Entre Argentina e Brasil no Mercosul: Princípios de Hegemonia, Dependência e Interesse Nacional no Tratado de Assunção* (Curitiba: Editora Juruá).

Hakim, Peter (2014), 'The Future of US–Brazil Relations: Confrontation, Cooperation or Detachment?' *International Affairs* 90 (5): 1161–1180.

Hakim, Peter (2015), 'The Strange Case of the Missing Relationship: Brazil and the US', in Jeffrey D. Needell, ed., *Emergent Brazil: Key Perspectives on a New Global Power* (Gainesville, FL: University Press of Florida).

Haslam, Paul Alexander and Edison Rodrigues Barreto (2009), 'Worlds Apart: Canadian and Brazilian Multilateralism in Comparative Perspective', *Canadian Foreign Policy* 15 (1) (Spring): 1–20.

Herz, Monica (2013), 'Assumptions on Interventions and Security in South America', in Kai Michael Kenkel (2013), *South America and Peace Operations: Coming of Age* (Abingdon: Routledge).

Herz, Monica and João Pontes Nogueira (2002), *Ecuador vs. Peru: Peacemaking Amid Rivalry* (Boulder, CO: Lynne Rienner).

Hirschman, Albert O. (1945), *National Power and the Structure of Foreign Trade* (Berkeley, CA: University of California Press).

Hirst, Mônica (2005), *The United States and Brazil: A Long Road of Unmet Expectations* (New York: Routledge).

Hirst, Moníca (2005/2006), 'As Relações Brasil–Paraguai: Baixos Incentivos no Latu e Strictu Sensu', *Política Externa* 14 (3): 11–22.

Hirst, Monica and Maria Regina Soares de Lima (2001), 'Contexto Internacional: Democracia e Política Externa', *Política Externa* 11 (2) (Sept/Oct/Nov): 78–98.

Hochstetler, Kathryn Ann (2012), 'The G-77, BASIC, and Global Climate Governance: A New Era in Multilateral Environmental Negotiations', *Revista Brasileira de Política Internacional* 55 (special issue): 53–69.

Hochstetler, Kathryn (2014), 'The Brazilian National Development Bank Goes International: Innovations and Limitations of BNDES' Internationalization', *Global Policy* 5 (3) (September): 360–365.

Hochstetler, Kathryn and Manjana Milkoreit (2013), 'Emerging Powers in the Climate Negotiations: Shifting Identity Conceptions', *Political Research Quarterly* 20 (10): 1–12.

Hochstetler, Kathryn and Eduardo Viola (2012), 'Brazil and the Politics of Climate Change: Beyond the Global Commons', *Environmental Politics* 21 (5): 753–771.

Holanda, Franciso Mauro Brasil de (2001), *O gás no Mercosul: Uma Perspectiva Brasileira* (Brasília: FUNAG).

Hopewell, Kristen (2013), 'New Protagonists in Global Economic Governance: Brazilian Agribusiness at the WTO', *New Political Economy* 18 (4): 603–623.

Howland, Todd (2006), 'Peacekeeping and Conformity with Human Rights Law: How MINUSTAH Falls Short in Haiti', *International Peacekeeping* 13 (4): 462–476.

Hudson, Valerie M. (2007), *Foreign Policy Analysis: Classic and Contemporary Theory* (New York: Rowman & Littlefield).

Hunter, Wendy (2010), *The Transformation of the Workers' Party in Brazil, 1989–2009* (New York: Cambridge University Press).

Hurrell, Andrew (1983), 'The Politics of South Atlantic Security: A Survey of Proposals for a South Atlantic Treaty Organization', *International Affairs* 59 (2): 179–193.

Hurrell, Andrew (1998), 'Security in Latin America', *International Affairs* 74 (3): 529–546.

Hurrell, Andrew (2010), 'Cardoso e o mundo', in Maria Angela D'Incao e Hermínio Martins, eds, *Democracia, Crise e Reforma: Estudos Sobre a era Fernando Henrique Cardoso* (São Paulo: Paz e Terra).

Hurrell, Andrew (2013), *The Quest for Autonomy: The Evolution of Brazil's Role in the International System, 1964–1985* (Brasília: FUNAG).

Hurrell, Andrew and Amrita Narlikar (2008), 'A New Politics of Confrontation? Brazil and India in Multilateral Trade Negotiations', in *Global Society* 20 (4); 415–433.

Inoue, Cristina Yumie Aoki and Alcides Costa Vaz (2012), 'Brazil as "Southern Donor": Beyond Hierarchy and National Interests in Development Cooperation?' *Cambridge Review of International Affairs* 25 (4): 507–534.

IPEA (2010a), 'Dimensão, Evolução e Projeção da Pobreza por Região e por Estado no Brasil', *Comunicados do IPEA* No. 58 (13 July).

IPEA (2010b), *Cooperação Brasileira para o Desenvolvimento Internacional: 2005–2009* (Brasília: Instituto de Pesquisa Econômica Aplicada, Agência Brasileira de Cooperação).

IPRI – Instituto de Pesquisa de Relações Internacionais (1993), *Reflexões Sobre a Política Externa Brasileira* (Brasília: Ministério das Relações Exteriores, Subsecretaria-Geral de Planejamento Político e Econômico, Fundação Alexandre de Gusmão, Instituto de Pesquisas de Relações Internacionais).

Itamaraty (2006), 'Ata Final da Primeira Sessão da Comissão Sino-Brasileira de Alto Nível de Concertação e Cooperação', *Nota No. 204* (24 March).

Jank, Marcos (2003), 'Suporte para Negociações Externas', Op-Ed, *Gazeta Mercantil* (6 May).

Jatkar, Archana and Laura McFarlene (2013), 'Brazil in the WTO Dispute Settlement Understanding: A Perspective', *CUTS Briefing Paper* No. 1.

Jawara Fatoumata and Aileen Kwa (2004), *Behind the Scenes at the WTO: The Real World of International Trade Negotiations* (London: Zed Books).

Jelmayer, Rogerio (2015), 'Brazil's Embraer Delivers 60 Planes in Second Quarter', *Wall Street Journal* (15 July).

Jenkins, Rhys (2012), 'China and Brazil: Economic Impacts of a Growing Relationship', *Journal of Current Chinese Affairs* 41 (1): 21–47.

Jenkins, Rhys (2014), 'Chinese Competition and Brazilian Exports of Manufactures', *Oxford Development Studies*, DOI: 10.1080/13600818.20 14.881989.

Jesus, Diego Santos Vieira de (2011), 'Building Trust and Flexibility: A Brazilian View of the Fuel Swap with Iran', *The Washington Quarterly* 34 (2): 61–75.

Jobim, Nelson (2011), 'Brazil and the World – Opportunities, Ambitions and Choices', transcript of speech delivered to CEBRI – Centro Brasileiro de Relações Internacionais (7 April).

Jordaan, Eduard (2003), 'The Concept of a Middle Power in International Relations: Distinguishing Between Emerging and Traditional Middle Powers', *Politikon* 30 (2) (November): 165–181.

Kenkel, Kai Michael (2010), 'South America's Emerging Power: Brazil as Peacekeeper', *International Peacekeeping* 17 (5): 644–661.

Kenkel, Kai Michael (2012), 'Brazil and R2P: Does Taking Responsibility Mean Using Force?', *Global Responsibility to Protect* 4: 5–32.

Kenkel, Kai Michael, ed. (2013a), *South America and Peace Operations: Coming of Age* (Abingdon: Routledge).

Kenkel, Kai Michael (2013b), 'Out of South America to the Globe: Brazil's Growing Stake in Peace Operations', in Kai Michael Kenkel, ed. (2013), *South America and Peace Operations: Coming of Age* (Abingdon: Routledge).

Kenkel, Kai Michael (2013c), 'Brazil's Peacekeeping and Peacebuilding Policies in Africa', *Journal of International Peacekeeping* 17 (3–4): 272–292.

Kindleberger, Charles P. (1973), *The World in Depression, 1929–1939* (Harmondsworth: Penguin Books).

Kleiman, Alberto with Gustavo de Lima Cezario (2012), 'Um Olhar Brasileiro Sobre a Ação Internacional dos Governos Subnacionais', in Leticia Pinheiro and Carlos R. S. Milani, eds (2012), *Política Externa Brasileira: As Prácticas da Política e a Política das Prácticas* (Rio de Janeiro: Editora FGV).

Lafer, Celso (2000), 'Brazilian International Identity and Foreign Policy: Past, Present, and Future', *Dædalus* 129 (2) (Spring 2000): 207–238.

Lafer, Celso (2001a), *A Identidade Internacional do Brasil e a Política Externa Brasileira* (São Paulo: Editora Perspectiva).

Lafer, Celso (2001b), 'ALCA: Futuro', Discurso do Senhor Ministro de Relações Exteriores, Embaixador Celso Lafer, ao Seminário 'O continente Americano e o future das inegrações regionais', São Paulo, Memorial da América Latin (4 April).

Lafer, Celso (2002), 'Suspeitas, Interesses e as Negociações da ALCA', *Folha de São Paulo* (30 June).

Lafer, Celso (2013a), 'Descaminhos no Mercosul', *Política Externa* 21 (3) (Jan/Feb/Mar): 19–28.

Lafer, Celso (2013b), 'O Brasil na America do Sul', speech at the Instituto Fernando Henrique Cardoso, São Paulo (18 April): http://politicaexterna.com.br/140/brasil-america-sul/ [accessed 23 October 2014].

Lambert, Peter (2016), 'The Myth of the Good Neighbour: Paraguay's Uneasy Relationship with Brazil', *Bulletin of Latin American Research* 35 (1): 34–48.

Lampreia, Luiz Felipe (1996), 'A Política Exterior Brasileira e as Relacões Brasil–Bolívia no Context da Integração Sul-Americana', La Paz, Bolivia (23 February), reproduced in Lampreia 1999.

Lampreia, Luiz Felipe (1999a), *Diplomacia Brasileira: Palavras, Contextos e Razões* (Rio de Janeiro: Lacerda Editores).

Lampreia, Luiz Felipe (1999b), 'Speech at the Opening of the General Debate of the 54th Session of the United Nations General Assembly', New York (20 September).

Lampreia, Luiz Felipe (2009), *O Brasil e os Ventos do Mundo: Memórias de Cinco Décadas na Cena Internacional* (Rio de Janeiro: Editora Objetiva).

Lampreia, Luiz Felipe (2009/2010), 'Brasil Comete Erro de Avaliação em Honduras', *Política Externa*, 18 (3) (Dec/Jan/Feb): 117–122.

Lampreia, Luiz Felipe (2010), *Luiz Felipe Lampreia – Depoimento, 2008* (Rio de Janeiro: FGV-CPDOC).

Lampreia, Luiz Felipe (2011), 'Agenda para a Política Externa do Governo Dilma', *Interesse Nacional* 4 (13) (April–June).

Lampreia, Luiz Felipe (2014), *Aposta em Teerã: O Acordo Nuclear entre Brasil, Turquia e Irã* (Rio de Janeiro: Editora Objetiva).

Landim, Hiarlley Gonçalves Cruz (2015), 'SISFRON: Ferramenta de Ampliação da Diplomacia Militar Brasileira e Fortalicimento do CDS', *Revista Política Hoje* 1 (24): 137–147.

Lazzarini, Sérgio G (2011), *Capitalismo de Laços: Os donos do Brasil e suas conexões* (Rio de Janeiro: Elsevier).

Leahy, Joe (2011), '"Brics" to Debate Possible Eurozone Aid', *Financial Times* (13 September).

Legler, Thomas (2010), 'Learning the Hard Way: Defending Democracy in Honduras', *International Journal* 65 (3): 601–618.

Legler, Thomas (2013), 'Post-Hegemonic Regionalism and Sovereignty in Latin America: Optimists, Skeptics, and an Emerging Research Agenda', *Contexto Internacional* 35 (2): 325–352.

Lessa, Mônica Leitie, Miriam Gomes Saraiva and Dhiego de Moura Mapa (2012), 'Entre o Palácio Itamaraty e o Palácio Capanema: Perspectivas e Desafios de uma Diplomacia Cultural no Governo Lula', in Leticia Pinheiro and Carlos R. S. Milani, eds (2012), *Política Externa Brasileira: As Prácticas da Política e a Política das Prácticas* (Rio de Janeiro: Editora FGV).

Lima, Kelly (2006), 'Bolívia Ficou sem Diesel por Atraso de Pagamento', *O Estado de São Paulo* (1 June).

Lima, Laura (2015), *Worlding Brazil: Intellectuals, Identity and Security* (New York: Routledge).

Lima, Sérgio Eduardo Moreira (2014), 'Diplomacia e Academia: O IPRI como Instrumento de Política Externa', *Política Externa* 22 (3) (Jan/Feb/March).

Lins da Silva, Carlos Eduardo (2002), 'Política e Comércio Exterior', in Bolívar Lamounier and Rubens Figueiredo, eds, *A Era FHC: Um Balanço* (São Paulo: Cultura Editores Associados).

Lula da Silva, Luiz Inácio (2003), 'Discurso do Senhor Presidente da República, Luiz Inácio Lula da Silva, na Solenidade de Abertura do Seminário Brasil-China-BNDES', Rio de Janeiro (30 April).

Lula da Silva, Luiz Inácio (2004), 'Discurso no Encontro com Lideranças Empresarias Indianas', New Dehli, India, 27 January.

Lula da Silva, Luiz Inácio (2009), Entrevista Coletiva Condeida pelo Presidente da República, Luiz Inácio Lula da Silva, a Jornais Chineses, Pequim, China (20 May).

macau.blogs.com (2012), 'Lula Avisa Empresas Brasileiras para não Cometerem "Megaerros" em Moçambique' (19 November): http://macua.blogs.com/moambique_para_todos/2012/11/lula-avisa-empresas-brasileiras-para-n%C3%A3o-cometerem-megaerros-em-mo%C3%A7ambique.html [accessed 20 November 2012].

Magalhães, Fernando Simas (1999), *Cúpula das Américas de 1994: Papel Negociador do Brasil, em Busca de Uma Agenda Hemisférica* (Brasília: IRBr/FUNAG/Centro de Estudos Estratégicos).

Magnoli, Demétrio (2011), 'Atenção, Dilma, ele Assina em Teu Nome', OpEd, *O Estado de São Paulo* (18 August).

Maia, João M. E. and Matthew M. Taylor (2015), 'The Brazilian Liberal Tradition and the Global Liberal Order', in Oliver Stuenkel and Matthew M. Taylor, eds, *Brazil on the Global Stage: Power, Ideas, and the Liberal International Order* (New York: Palgrave Macmillan).

Maisonnave Fabiano (2004), 'Coca Ameaça Amazônia, afirma Uribe', *Folha de São Paulo* (23 June).

Malamud, Andrés (2005), 'Presidential Diplomacy and the Institutional Underpinnings of Mercosur: An Empirical Examination', *Latin American Research Review* 40 (1): 138–164.

Malamud, Andrés (2011), 'A Leader Without Followers? The Growing Divergence Between the Regional and Global Performance of Brazilian Foreign Policy', *Latin American Politics and Society* 53 (3): 1–24.

Malamud, Andrés and Clarissa Dri (2013), 'Spillover Effects and Supranational Parliaments: The Case of Mercosur', *Journal of Iberian and Latin American Research* 19 (2): 224–238.

Mallea, Rodrigo, Matias Spektor and Nicholas J. Wheeler, eds (2015), *The Origins of Nuclear Cooperation: A Critical Oral History Between Brazil and Argentina* (Washington, DC / Rio de Janeiro: Woodrow Wilson International Center for Scholars / Fundação Getúlio Vargas).

Manzetti, Luigi (1990), 'Argentine–Brazilian Economic Integration: An Early Appraisal', *Latin American Research Review* 25 (3): 109–140.

Manzetti, Luigi (1993–1994), 'The Political Economy of Mercosur', *Journal of Interamerican Studies and World Affairs* 35 (4) (Winter): 101–141.

Manzetti, Luigi (1999), *Privatization South American Style* (Oxford: Oxford University Press).

Marin, Denise Chrispim (2002), 'Brasil não Dará Ajuda Financeira, diz Botafogo', *O Estado de São Paulo* (11 January).

Marin, Denise Chrispim (2004), 'Mudanças Beneficiam "engajados" no Itamaraty', *O Estado de São Paulo* (3 March): A10.

Marin, Denise Chrispim (2005), 'Para Recuperar Poder, Amorim Muda Itamaraty', *O Estado de São Paulo* (12 June).

Martins Filho, João R. and Daniel Zirker (2000), 'Nationalism, National Security, and Amazonia: Military Perceptions and Attitudes in Contemporary Brazil', *Armed Forces & Society* 27 (1): 105–129.

Matta, Roberto da (1984), *O Que Faz o Brasil, Brasil?* (Rio de Janeiro: Editora Rocco).

Mello, Mariana (2014), 'Estereótipos Marcam Debate Eleitoral Sobre Política Externa', *Carta Capital* (18 October).

Mello, Patrícia Campos (2015), 'Brasil dá Calote de US$ 8.1 Milhões na OEA', *Folha de São Paulo* (10 March).

Mello, Patrícia Campos and Isabel Fleck (2015), 'Faltam Luz e Água em Embaixadas Brasileiras, Dizem Diplomatas', *Folha de São Paulo* (21 January).

Merke, Federico (2015), 'Neither Balance nor Bandwagon: South American International Society Meets Brazil's Rising Power', *International Politics* 52 (2): 178–192.

Mesa Gisbert, Carlos D. (2011), 'Bolívia e Brasil: Os Meandros do Cominho', *Política Externa* 20 (2) (Sept/Oct/Nov): 23–42.

Mignolo, Walter D. (2009), *The Idea of Latin America* (New York: John Wiley & Sons).

Milani, Carlos and Cristina Almeida (2011), 'Les Rapports Bresil-Etats-Unis: Quelle Complementarite?' *AFRI: Annuaire Français de Relation Internationales* Vol. 22.

Milani, Carlos R. S. and Tassia C. O. Carvalho (2013), 'Cooperação Sul-Sul e Política Externa: Brasil e China no Continente Africano', *Estudos Interancionais* 1 (1): 11–35.

Milani, Carlos R. S. (2015), 'International Development Cooperation in the Education Sector: The Role of Brazil', UNESCO Paper Contract Number 4500229657, Education for All Global Monitoring Report 2015, ED/EF A/MRT/2015/PI/46.

Ministério da Defesa (2005), *Política de Defesa Nacional* (Brasília: Presidência da República).

Ministério da Defesa (2008), *Estratégia Nacional de Defesa: Paz e Segurança para o Brasil* (Brasília: Ministério da Defesa).

Ministério da Defesa (2012), *Livro Branco de Defesa Nacional* (Brasília: Ministério da Defesa).

Mintz, Alex and Karl DeRouen Jr. (2010), *Understanding Foreign Policy Decision Making* (New York: Cambridge University Press).

Montaner, Carlos Alberto (2013), 'Why We Spy on Brazil', *Miami Herald* (25 September).

Montero, Alfred P (2014), *Brazil: Reversal of Fortune* (Malden, MA: Polity Books).

Morgenthau, Hans J. (1967), *Politics Among Nations: The Struggle for Power and Peace* (New York: Alfred A. Knopf).

Moura, Cristina Patriota de (2007), *O Instituto Rio Branco e a Diplomacia Brasileira: Um Estudo de Carreira e Socialização* (Rio de Janeiro: Editora FGV).

Mourão, Gonçalo Mello (2013), 'Seria a Política Externa Brasileira um Problema para o Itamaraty', *Política Externa* 22 (2) (Oct/Nov/Dec).

Moyo, Dambisa (2009), *Dead Aid: Why Aid is Not Working and How There is a Better Way for Africa* (New York: Farrar, Straus and Giroux).

MRE – Ministério de Relações Exteriores (1992), 'Ostensivo: Memorandum para o Sr. Subsecretário Geral de Assuntos Econômicos: Organismos Econômicos. Cargos Diretivos. Quadro Geral. Interesses Brasileiros', 039/DPC(DOE) (1 September).

MRE (1993), 'SGIE Memorandum para o Sr Secrtário-Geral, ALADI/GT ad hoc. Revisão do TM-80. Futuro da ALADI', SGIE/035 (15 February).

MRE (2015), 'Ata da Quarta Reunião da Comissão Sino-Brasileira de Alto Nível de Concertação e Cooperação (COSBAN)', Nota 247 (26 June): www.itamaraty.gov.br/index.php?option=com_content&view=article&id=10340:ata-da-quarta-reuniao-da-comissao-sino-brasileira-de-alto-nivel-de-concerta-cao-e-cooperacao-cosban&catid=42&lang=pt-BR&Itemid=280 [accessed 3 July 2015].

Muggah, R. and Diniz, G. (2013), 'Securing the Border: Brazil's "South America First" Approach to Transnational Organized Crime', Igarapé Institute Strategic Paper No. 5.

Murphy, Tom (2012), 'Brazil Embraer CEO: Focus in China Will Be Executive Jets', *Dow Jones News Service* (21 November).

Muxagato, Bruno (2015), 'Brésil-États-Unis: De L'alignement à L'autonomie', *Outre-Terre* No 42: 131–152.

Narlikar, Amrita and Diana Tussie (2004), 'The G20 at the Cancun Ministerial: Developing Countries and Their Evolving Coalitions in the WTO', *The World Economy* 27 (7): 947–966.

Narlikar, Amrita and Rorden Wilkinson (2004), 'Collapse at the WTO: A Cancun Post-Mortem', *Third World Quarterly* 25 (3): 447–460.

Nasser, Rabih and Nathalie Sato (2015), 'O Novo Modelo Brasileiro de Acordos de Investimento', OpEd, *Valôr Econômico* (12 May).

Neack, Laura (2008), *The New Foreign Policy: Power Seeking in a Globalized Era*, 2nd edn (Lanham, MD: Rowman & Littlefield).

Nebehay, Stephanie (2014), 'Guinea President – Vale Did No Wrong, Can Bid to Reclaim Mining Permits', *Reuters* (30 April).

Nelson, Roy C. (1995), *Industrialization and Political Affinity: Industrial Policy in Brazil* (London: Routledge).

Neto, J. C. (2007), 'Evo Morales diz que Bolívia precisa de Petrobras', *Valor Econômico* (18 December).

Nolen, Stephanie and Colin Freeze (2013), 'Spying Not a Shock to Former Brazilian Diplomat', *Globe and Mail* (18 October).

Nossa, Leonencio (2006), 'Cúpula Fracassa e Lula Pede "Outra Globalização"', *O Estado de São Paulo* (12 January).

Ocampo, José Antonio and Juan Martin (2003), *Globalization and Development: A Latin American and Caribbean Perspective* (Palo Alto, CA/Washington, DC: Stanford University Press/The World Bank).

Odell, John S. (2000), *Negotiating the World Economy* (Ithaca, NY: Cornell University Press).

O'Donnell, Guillermo (1999), 'And Why Should I Give a Shit? Notes on Sociability and Politics in Arentina and Brazil', in Guillermo O'Donnell, *Counterpoints* (Notre Dame, IN: University of Notre Dame Press).

OESP – fvO *Estado de São Paulo* (2002), 'Sobre Política Agricola', *O Estado de São Paulo* (31 March).

OESP (2003), 'Brasileiro é Acusado de Gravar Reunião', *O Estado de São Paulo* (23 July).

OESP (2004), 'A Tentativa de Aparelhamento do Itamaraty', Editorial, *O Estado de São Paulo* (6 March): A3.

OESP (2006), 'Bolívia e Venezuela Viram Sócias', *O Estado de São Paulo* (11 December).

OESP (2010), 'Cúmplice da Barbárie', Editorial, *O Estado de São Paulo* (24 November).

OESP (2010b), 'Lula quer Mandar na Vale', Editorial, *O Estado de São Paulo* (21 October).

Oliveira, Amâncio Jorge Nunes de, Janina Onuki and Emmanuel de Oliveira (2009), 'Coalizões Sul–Sul e Multilateralismo: Países Intermediaries e o Caso

IBAS', in Maria Regina Soares de Lima and Monica Hirst, eds, *Brasil, Índia e África do Sul: Desafios e Opportunidades para Novos Parceiras* (São Paulo: Paz e Terra).

Oliveira, Henrique Altemani de (2005), *Política Externa Brasileira* (São Paulo: Saraiva).

Opera Mundi (2014), 'Mercosul e Aliança do Pacífico Fazem Primeira Reunião Bilateral e Buscam Objetivos Comuns', *Opera Mundi* (2 November).

Oppenheimer, Andrés (2007), *Saving the Americas: The Dangerous Decline of Latin America and What the U.S. Must Do* (Mexico: Random House Mondadori).

Osse, José Sergio and Cíntia Cardoso (2002), 'Agropecuária Perde US$ 7.8 Bi por Ano', *Folha de São Paulo* (19 August).

Otta, Lu Aiko (2007), '"Se Não o Quiser Ficar, Não Fica", Diz Lula Sobre Chávez no Mercosul', *O Estado de São Paulo* (5 July).

Oualalou, Lamia (2014), 'Marco Aurélio Garcia, Assessor de Dilma: "Para nós, América do Sul é um Grande Ativo"', *Opera Mundi* (18 October).

Oxford Analytica (2004), 'BRAZIL/ARGENTINA: China Exerts Economic Muscle', *Oxford Analytica Daily Brief Series* (19 November).

Oxford Analytica (2005a), 'BRAZIL: Leadership Ambitions Face Economic Obstacles', *Oxford Analytica Daily Brief Series* (25 October).

Oxford Analytica (2005b), 'Limited Traction for Landlocked Group', *Oxford Analytica Daily Brief Series* (23 August).

Palmer, David Scott (1997), 'Peru–Ecuador Border Conflict: Missed Opportunities, Misplaced Nationalism, and Multilateral Peacekeeping', *Journal of Interamerican Studies and World Affairs* 39 (3): 109–148.

Patriota, Antoino de Aguiar (2011a), 'Brasil, Interlocutor Incontornável nos Grandes Debates da Agenda Internacional', Discurso Proferido por Ocasião das Comemorações do Dia do Diplomata, Brasília (20 April).

Patriota, Antonio de Aguiar (2011b), 'Tempos de Mudaças no Mundo Árabe', *Política Externa* 201 (1) (June–Aug).

Patriota, Antonio de Aguiar (2011c), 'Conselho de Segurança das Nações Unidas – Debate Aberto Sobre Proteção de Civis em Conflito Armado', Media Release No. 436, New York (9 November).

Patriota, Antonio (2012), 'Entre a Responsibilidade Coletiva e a Segurança Coletiva', Discurso Proferido por Ocasião de Debate Sobre Responsibilidade ao Proteger na ONU, Nova York (21 February).

Patriota, Antonio Aguiar de (2013a), 'Diplomacia e Democratização', *Política Externa* 22 (2) (Oct/Nov/Dec): 9–16.

Patriota, Antonio de Aguiar (2013b), 'Um País Sul-American Convicto, Um Ator Global', in Antonio de Aguiar Patriota (2013c), *Política Externa Brasileira: Discursos, Artigos e Entrevistas, 2011–2012* (Brasília: FUNAG).

Patriota, Antonio de Aguiar (2013c), *Política Externa Brasileira: Discursos, Artigos e Entrevistas, 2011–2012* (Brasília: FUNAG).

Patriota, Antonio de Aguiar (2013d), 'Desafios Novos, Objetivos e Valores Perenes', in Antonio de Aguiar Patriota, *Política Externa Brasileira: Discursos, Artigos e Entrevistas, 2011–2012* (Brasília: FUNAG).

Patriota, Antonio de Aguiar (2013e), 'Uma Âncora Regional e Outra, Global', in Antonio de Aguiar Patriota, *Política Externa Brasileira: Discursos, Artigos e Entrevistas, 2011–2012* (Brasília: FUNAG).

Patriota, Antonio de Aguiar (2013f), 'China: Para Além da Complementaridade', in Antonio de Aguiar Patriota, *Política Externa Brasileira: Discursos, Artigos e Entrevistas, 2011–2012* (Brasília: FUNAG).

Patti, Carlo (2010), 'Brazil and the Nuclear Issue in the Years of the Luiz Inácio Lula de Silva Government', *Revista Brasileira de Política Internacional* 53 (2): 178–197.

Pecequilo, Cristina Soreanu (2015), 'The Brazil–United States Bilateral Relations in the Dilma Rousseff Administration, 2011–2014', *Austral: Brazilian Journal of Strategy and International Relations* 3 (6): 11–36.

Pereira, Analúcia Danilevicz (2013), 'The South Atlantic, Southern Africa and South America: Cooperation and Development', *Austral: Brazilian Journal of Strategy and International Relations* 2 (4): 31–46.

Pereira, Carlos and João Augusto de Castro Neves (2011), 'Brazil and China: South–South Partnership or North–South Competition?' Foreign Policy at Brookings Policy Paper No. 26 (March).

Pereira, Ruy (2014), 'O Valor do Mercosul', *Política Externa* 22 (3) (Jan/Feb/March).

Peres, Miguel (2013), Odebrecht Managing Director, Mozambique. Author interview, Maputo (27 February).

Pinheiro, Leticia (2007), 'How Much Foreign Policy Teaching can be Foreign Policy Making?' Paper presented to the 4th Annual APSA Conference on Teaching and Learning in Political Science, Charlotte, North Carolina (9–11 February).

Pinheiro, Leticia and Carlos R. S. Milani, eds (2012), *Política Externa Brasileira: As Prácticas da Política e a Política das Prácticas* (Rio de Janeiro: Editora FGV).

Pino, B. A. and I. C. Leite (2010), 'La Cooperación Sur–Sur de Brasil: Instrumento de Política Exterior y/o Manifestación de Solidaridad Internacional?' *Mural Internacional* 1 (1) (Jan–June): 20–32.

Prado, Maria Clara R. M. do (2005), *A Real História do Real: Uma Radiografia da Moeda que Mudou o Brasil* (Rio de Janeiro: Record).

Pretti, Fúlvio (1999), *Mercosul: A Instituição e o Sistema de Solução de Controvérias* (Blumenau: Editora da FURB).

ProSAVANA (2015), Author interview, Maputo, Mozambique (20 January).

Putnam, Robert D (1988), 'Diplomacy and Domestic Politics: The Logic of Two-Level Games', *International Organization* 42 (3) (Summer): 427–460.

Raile, Eric D., Carlos Pereira and Timothy J. Power (2010), 'The Executive Toolbox: Building Legislative Support in a Multiparty Presidential Regime', *Political Research Quarterly* 20 (10): 1–12.

Reid, Michael (2007), *Forgotten Continent: The Battle for Latin America's Soul* (New Haven, CT: Yale University Press).

Reid, Michael (2014), *Brazil: The Troubled Rise of a Global Power* (New Haven, CT: Yale University Press).

Reuters (2006a), 'Brazil says Petrobras Exit from Bolivia an Option', *Reuters* (15 September).

Reuters (2006b), 'Bolivia Energy Minister Quits after Brazil Row', *Swiss Info* (16 September).

Ricupero, Rubens (2000), *Rio Branco: O Brasil no Mundo* (Rio de Janeiro: Contraponto Editora).

Ricupero, Rubens (2013), 'A Maior Mudança da Política Externa', *Política Externa* 21 (3) (Jan/Feb/March): 95–100.

Riggirozzi, Pía (2014), 'Regionalism Through Social Policy: Collective Action and Health Diplomacy in South America', *Economy and Society* 43 (3): 432–454.

Riggirozzi, Pía and Diana Tussie, eds (2012), *The Rise of Post-Hegemonic Regionalism: The Case of Latin America* (London: Springer).

Robledo, Carmen (2015), 'New Donors, Same Old Practices? South–South Cooperation of Latin American Emerging Donors', *Bandung: Journal of the Global South* 2 (1): 1–16.

Rocha, Angela de and Carl H. Christensen (2002), 'Como as Empresas Brasileiras Exportam: Revisão dos Estudos Sobre Exportação (1978–1990)', in Angela da Rocha, ed., *A Intenacionalização das Empresas Brasileiras: Estudos de Gestão Internacional* (Rio de Janeiro: Editora Mauad).

Rocha, Geisa Maria (2002), 'Neo-Dependency in Brazil', *New Left Review* 16 (July/Aug): 5–33.

Roett, Riordan (2010), *The New Brazil* (Washington: Brookings Institution Press).

Rohter, Larry (2010), *Brazil on the Rise: The Story of a Country Transformed* (New York: Palgrave Macmillan).

Rojas Aravena, Francisco (2010), 'The Community of Latin American and Caribbean States: A Viable Option to Consolidate Latinamerican Multilateralism?' in Thomas Legler and Lesley Martina Burns, eds (2010), *Latin American Multilateralism: New Directions* (Ottawa: Canadian Foundation for the Americas): 18–23.

Rossi, Amanda (2013), 'Governo Dilma Implementa "Agenda África" para Ampliar Relações', *O Estado de São Paulo* (29 October).

Rousseff, Dilma (2014a), 'Entravista com Dilma Rousseff', *Política Externa* (web) (19 September): http://politicaexterna.com.br/2549/resposta-da-presidente-dilma-rousseff/ [accessed 15 December 2014].

Rousseff, Dilma (2014b), 'Statement at the Opening of the General Debate of the 69th Session of the United Nations General Assembly', United Nations, New York (24 September).

Salomón, Mónica (2012), 'A Dimensão Subnacional da Política Externa Brasileira: Determinantes, Conteúdos e Perspectivas', in Leticia Pinheiro and Carlos R. S. Milani, eds, *Política Externa Brasileira: As Prácticas da Política e a Política das Prácticas* (Rio de Janeiro: Editora FGV).

Sánchez, Alex (2008), 'The South American Defense Council, UNASUR, the Latin American Military and the Region's Political Process' (Washington DC: COHA). www.coha.org/the-south-american-defense-council-unasur-the

-latin-american-military-and-the-region%E2%80%99s-political-process/ [accessed 2 December 2009].

Sánchez Nieto, W. Alejandro (2012), 'Brazil's Grand Design for Combining Global South Solidarity and National Interests: A Discussion of Peacekeeping Operations in Haiti and Timor', *Globalizations* 9 (1): 161–178.

Sant'Anna, Lourival (2009), 'Nacionalismo de Esquerda Regional Explora "Imperialismo" do Brasil', *O Estado de São Paulo* (17 May).

Santiso, Carlos (2003), 'The Gordian Knot of Brazilian Foreign Policy: Promoting Democracy While Respecting Sovereignty', *Cambridge Review of International Affairs* 16 (2): 343–358.

Santos, Chico (2003), 'BNDES Distribui Crédito a Países Vizinhos', *Folha de São Paulo* (7 May).

Schenoni, Luiz Leandro (2014), 'Unveiling the South American Balance', *Estudos Internacionais* (2) 2: 215–232.

Scolese, Eduardo and Leonencio Nossa (2006), *Viagens com o Presidente: Dois Repórteres no Encalço de Lula do Planalto ao Exterior* (Rio de Janeiro: Editora Record).

Seabra, Pedro (2014), 'A Harder Edge: Reframing Brazil's Power Relation with Africa', *Revista Brasileira de Política Internacional* 57 (1): 77–97.

SECEX (2012), 'Exportção Brasileira por Fator Agregado – 1964 a 2011', Ministério do Desenvolvimento, Indústria a Comércio Exterior, Secretaria de Comércio Exterior, www.desenvolvimento.gov.br/sitio/interna/interna.php?area=5&menu=1113&refr=608 [accessed 15 February 2013].

Senado (2005), 'Ata da Quarta Reunião Ordinária da Terceira Sessão Legislativa Ordinária da Quinquagésima Segunda Legislatura da Comissão de Relações Exteriores e Defesa Nacional, Realizada do Dia Trinta e um de Março de Dois Mil e Cinco', *Diário do Senado Federal – Suplemento* (30 July): 250–265.

Sennes, Ricardo, Janina Onuki and Amancio Jorge de Oliveira (2006), 'The Brazilian Foreign Policy and Hemispheric Security', *Revista de Fuerzas Armadas e Sociedad* Vol. 1 No. SE.

Sequeira, Claudio Dantas (2009), 'Peru Integrará Seus Radares aos do Sivam', *Folha de São Paulo* (22 March).

Serra, José (2016), 'Leia o Primeiro Discurso de Serra como mInistro das Relações Exteriores', *Folha de São Paulo (online)* (18 May): www1.folha.uol.com.br/mundo/2016/05/1772567-leia-o-primeiro-discurso-de-serra-como-ministro-das-relacoes-exteriores.shtml [accessed 20 May 2016].

Sikkink, Kathryn (1991), *Ideas and Institutions: Developmentalism in Brazil and Argentina* (Ithaca, NY: Cornell University Press).

Silva, Igor Castellano da and José Miguel Quedi Martins (2014), 'National Army and State-Building in Africa: The Brazilian Approach in the Case of the Democratic Republic of Congo', *Austral: Brazilian Journal of Strategy and International Relations* 3 (5): 137–180.

Silva, Rodolfo Ilário da (2013), 'O Multilateralismo Amazônico, entre Êxitos Geopolíticose Entraves Executivos: Trajetória do Processo de Cooperação de 1978 a 2012', *Brazilian Journal of International Relations* 2 (3): 534–559.

Small Arms Survey (2015), *Small Arms Survey 2015: Weapons and the World* (Geneva, Small Arms Survey): www.smallarmssurvey.org/de/publications/by-type/yearbook/small-arms-survey-2015.html [accessed 14 July 2015]

Smith, Joseph (1991), *Unequal Giants: Diplomatic Relations Between the United States and Brazil* (Pittsburgh: University of Pittsburgh Press).

Smith, Joseph (2010), *Brazil and the United States: Convergence and Divergence* (Athens, GA: University of Georgia Press).

Smith, Peter H. (2000), *Talons of the Eagle: Dynamics of U.S.–Latin American Relations* (Oxford: Oxford University Press).

Soares de Lima, Maria Regina and Monica Hirst (2006), 'Brazil as an Intermediate State and Regional Power: Action, Choice and Responsibilities', *International Affairs* 82 (1): 21–40.

Sotero, Paulo (2003), 'Senador dos EUA: Brasil levou Cancún ao fracasso', *O Estado de São Paulo* (18 September).

Sotero, Paulo (2004), 'Brasil vai Testar Novo Modelo de Investimento', *O Estado de São Paulo* (26 April).

Sotero, Paulo (2011–2012), 'Uma Reflexão Sobre a Frustrada Iniciativa Brasil-Turquia para Superar o Impasse Nuclear entre o Irã e a Comunidade Internacional', *Política Externa* 20 (3) (Dec/Jan/Feb): 75–80.

Soto, Alonso and Krista Hughes (2014), 'U.S. to pay $300 Million to End Brazil Cotton Trade Dispute – Officials', *Reuters* (9 September).

Soto, Alonso and Brian Winter (2013), 'Saab Wins Brazil Jet Deal After NSA Spying Sours Boeing Bid', *Reuters* (18 December).

Souza, Amaury de (2009), *A Agenda Internacional do Brasil: A Política Externa Brasileira de FHC a Lula* (Rio de Janeiro: Elsevier).

Souza, André de Mello de (2012), 'Saúde Pública, Patentes e Atores não Estatais: A Política Externa do Brasil ante a Epidemia de Aids', in Leticia Pinheiro and Carlos R. S. Milani, eds (2012), *Política Externa Brasileira: As Prácticas da Política e a Política das Prácticas* (Rio de Janeiro: Editora FGV).

Spanakos, Anthony Peter and Joseph Marques (2014), 'The Chinese Contribution to Brazil's Rise as a Middle Power', in Bruce Gilley and Andrew O'Neil, eds, *Middle Powers and the Rise of China* (Washington, DC: Georgetown University Press).

Spektor, Matias (2002), 'O Brasil e Argentina entre a Cordialidade Oficial e o Projecto de Integração', *Revista Brasileira de Política Internacional* 45 (1): 117–145.

Spektor, Matias (2009), *Kissinger e o Brasil* (Rio de Janeiro: Editora Zahar).

Spektor, Matias (2013), 'Cancelada', Column, *Folha de São Paulo* (18 September).

Spektor, Matias (2014), *18 Dias: Quando Lula e FHC se Uniram para Conquistar o Apoio de Bush* (Rio de Janeiro: Editora Objetiva).

Spinola, Noenio (2000), 'Cardoso Interviewed on Development', *O Estado de São Paulo* (30 January): FBIS-LAT-2000-0202.

State Department (2010), 'Background Briefing on Nuclear Nonproliferation Efforts with Regard to Iran and the Brazil/Turkey Agreement', special briefing by senior administration officials via conference call, Washington,

DC (28 May): www.state.gov/r/pa/prs/ps/2010/05/142375.htm [accessed 22 November 2015].

Stolte, Christina (2015), *Brazil's Africa Strategy: Role Conception and the Drive for International Status* (New York: Palgrave Macmillan).

Strange, Susan (1994), *States and Markets*, 2nd edn (London: Pinter).

Stuenkel, Oliver (2015), *The BRICS and the Future of Global Order* (Lanham, MD: Lexington Books).

Stuenkel, Oliver and Matthew M. Taylor, eds (2015), *Brazil on the Global Stage: Power, Ideas, and the Liberal International Order* (New York: Palgrave Macmillan).

Tavares, Rodrigo (2013), 'Foreign Policy Goes Local: How Globalization Made São Paulo into a Diplomatic Power – *Foreign Policy Goes Local*', *Foreign Affairs* (Web): www.foreignaffairs.com/articles/140091/rodrigo-tavares/foreign-policy-goes-local [accessed 14 December 2014].

Tavares da Silva Neto, Agostinho (2014), Author interview with Agostinho Tavares da Silva Neto, ambassador of the Republic of Angola to Canada, Ottawa (29 July).

Teivaninen, Teivo (2002), *Enter Economism, Exit Politics: Experts, Economic Policy and the Damage to Democracy* (New York: Zed Books).

Teixeira, Augusto Wagner Menezes (2010), 'Segurança Sul-Americana e a Centralidade do Conselho de Defesa Sul-Americano para a Ordem Regional', *Meridiano 47* n. 117 (April): 15–17.

TELAM (2010), 'Kirchner: "We Latin Americans Have Proved We Can Solve Our Own Problems"'. http://english.telam.com.ar/ index.php?option=com_content&view=article&id=9909:kirchner-we-latin-americans-have-proved-we-can-solve-our-own- problems&catid=42:politics (8 November) [accessed 8 December 2010].

Tosta, Wilson (2007), 'Chávez quer Reforma no Mercosul e diz que vai "Descontaminar" o Bloco', *O Estado de São Paulo* (19 January).

Tourinho, Marcos (2015), 'For Liberalism without Hegemony: Brazil and the Rule of Non-Intervention', in Oliver Stuenkel and Matthew M. Taylor, eds (2015), *Brazil on the Global Stage: Power, Ideas, and the Liberal International Order* (New York: Palgrave Macmillan).

Trevisan, Cláudia (2005), '"Império Brasileiro" Emerge na Bolívia', *Folha de São Paulo* (22 May).

Trevisan, Cláudia (2010), 'Petrobrás Negocia US$ 10 bi com a China', *O Estado de São Paulo* (27 May).

UNCTAD (2014) UNCTAD FDI/TNC Database: http://unctad.org/Sections/dite_fdistat/docs/webdiaeia2014d3_BRA.pdf [accessed 25 November 2015].

Valente, Rubens and Gabriel Mascarenhas (2015), 'Lula e Chávez Ficaram 7 Meses sem se Falar, Revela Telegrama', *Folha de São Paulo* (17 June).

Valenzuela, Arturo (1997), 'Paraguay: The Coup That Didn't Happen', *Journal of Democracy* 8 (1): 43–55.

van der Westhuizen, Janis (2013), 'Class Compromise as Middle Power Activism? Comparing Brazil and South Africa', *Government and Opposition* 48: 80–100.

Varadarajan, Siddarth (2011), 'Let's Not Make the Situation in Libya Worse: Antonio Patriota', *The Hindu* (11 March).

Veiga, Pedro Motta (2005), 'Brazil and the G20 Group of Developing Countries', in Peter Gallagher, Patrick Low and Andrew L. Stoler, eds, *Managing the Challenges of WTO Participation – 45 Case Studies* (Cambridge: Cambridge University Press).

Venter, Denis (1996), 'South Africa, Brazil and South Atlantic Security: Towards a Zone of Peace and Co-Operation in the South Atlantic', in Samuel Pinheiro Guimarães, ed., South Africa and Brazil: Risks and Opportunities in the Turmoil of Globalization (Brasília: IPRI).

Vieira, Mauro (2016), 'Aula Inaugural do Ministro Mauro Vieira no Instituto Rio Branco – Brasília, 18 de Janeiro de 2016', Speech (18 January): www. itamaraty.gov.br/index.php?option=com_content&view=article&id=12898 &catid=42&Itemid=280&lang=pt-BR [accessed 4 February 2016].

Vieira de Jesus, Diego Santos (2009–2010), 'Mídia e Política Externa: Democratização ou Instrumentalização? A Política Externa Brasileira Segundo a Folha de São Paulo (1998–2002)', *Política Externa* 18 (3) (Dec/ Jan/Feb): 189–204.

Vigevani, Tullo and Gabriel Cepaluni (2009), *Brazilian Foreign Policy in Changing Times: The Quest for Autonomy from Sarney to Lula* (Lanham, MD: Lexington Books).

Villa, Rafael A. Duarte and Brigitte Weiffen (2014), 'South American Re-armament: From Balancing to Symbolizing Power', *Contemporary Security Policy* 35 (1): 138–162.

Visentini, Paulo G. Fagundes and André Reis da Silva (2010), 'Brazil and the Economic, Political and Environmental Multilateralism: The Lula Years (2003–2010)', in Denis Rolland and Antônio Carlos Lessa, eds, *Relations Internationales du Brésil: Les Chemins de la Puissance* (Parisk: L'Hamarttan).

Vizentini, Paulo Fagundes (2003a), *Relações Internacionais do Brasil: De Vargas a Lula* (São Paulo: Editora Fundação Perseu Abramo).

Vizentini, Paulo G. Fagundes (2003b), 'As Nações Unidas na visão Brasileira e Chinesa: Políticas Externas Comparadas (1945–2000)', Samuel Pinheiro Guimarães, ed., *Brasil e China: Multipolaridade* (Brasília: IPRI, FUNAG): 215–246.

Vucetic, Srdjan and Érico Duarte (2015), 'New Fighter Aircraft Acquisitions in Brazil and India: Why Not Buy American?' *Politics & Policy* 43 (3): 401–415.

Weitzman, Hal (2012), *Latin Lessons: How South America Stopped Listening to the United States and Started Prospering* (Hoboken, NJ: John Wiley & Sons).

Wendt, Alexander (1992), 'Anarchy is What States Make of it: The Social Construction of Power Politics', *International Organization* 46 (2) (Spring): 391–425.

Wiesebron, Marianne L (2013), 'Blue Amazon: Thinking the Defense of Brazilian Maritime Territory', *Austral: Brazilian Journal of Strategy and International Relations* 2 (3): 101–124.

White, Lyal (2010), 'Understanding Brazil's New Drive for Africa', *South African Journal of International Affairs* (17) 2: 221–242.

Wikileaks (2006), 'Brazilian Firms Samba all the Way to the Bank', drafted by deputy chief of mission Kevin Whitaker, DOC ID: 06CARACAS3561_a (7 December): https://wikileaks.org/plusd/cables/06CARACAS3561_a.html [accessed 17 November 2015].

Wikileaks (2007), 'Brazil Expresses Reservations About Signing the Globe MOU', drafted by ambassador Clifford Sobel, DOC ID: 07BRASILIA834_a (10 May): https://search.wikileaks.org/plusd/cables/07BRASILIA834_a.html [accessed 17 November 2015].

Wikileaks (2008a), 'Scenesetter for the Visit of Minister of Defense Nelson Jobim to Washington', drafted by ambassador Clifford Sobel, Doc ID: 08BRASILIA351_a (13 March): https://search.wikileaks.org/plusd/cables/08BRASILIA351_a.html [accessed 17 November 2015].

Wikileaks (2008b), 'Brazilians Highlight Positive Bilateral Relations for Unders Sectretary Burns', drafted by ambassador Clifford Sobel, Doc ID: BRASILIA1405_1 (24 October): https://search.wikileaks.org/plusd/cables/08BRASILIA1405_a.html [accessed 17 November 2015].

Wikileaks (2008c), 'Brazil's Latin America/Caribbean Summit: Concentric Circles or Circling the Wagons?' Drafted by deputy chief of mission Lisa Kubiske, Doc ID: 08BRASILIA1301_a (1 October): https://search.wikileaks.org/plusd/cables/08BRASILIA1405_a.html [accessed 17 November 2015].

Wikileaks (2008d), 'S/P Director Gordon Holds First Strategic Talks With Brazil', drafted by ambassador Clifford Sobel, DOC ID: 08BRASILIA756_a (4 June): https://search.wikileaks.org/plusd/cables/08BRASILIA756_a.html [accessed 17 November 2015].

Wikileaks (2008e), 'Brazil: Lula Takes on the Fourth Fleet', drafted by ambassador Clifford Sobel, DOC ID: 08BRASILIA943_a (10 July): https://search.wikileaks.org/plusd/cables/08BRASILIA943_a.html [accessed 20 November 2015].

Wikileaks (2009a), 'Brazil: Presidential Foreign Policy Advisor Sees Possibilities for Cooperation with the U.S.', drafted by ambassador Clifford Sobel, Doc ID: 09BRASILIA388_a (27 March): https://search.wikileaks.org/plusd/cables/09BRASILIA388_a.html [accessed 17 November 2015].

Wikileaks (2009b), 'New Brazilian Deputy FM Sees Need to Step Up Bilateral Relations', drafted by charge d'affaires Lisa Kubiske (20 November): https://search.wikileaks.org/plusd/cables/09BRASILIA1342_a.html [accessed 17 November 2015].

Wikileaks (2009c), 'Brazil: Scenesetter for the December 13–14 Visit of WHA Assistant Secretary Arturo Valenzuela', Drafted by charge d'affaires Lisa Kubiske, Doc ID: 09BRASILIA1411_a (10 December): https://search.wikileaks.org/plusd/cables/09BRASILIA1411_a.html [accessed 17 November 2015].

Wikileaks (2009d), 'WHA DAS McMullen Clears the Air on the US-Colombia DCA, Opens Dialog on Regional Issues', drafted by charge d'affaires Lisa

Kubiske, Doc ID: 09BRASILIA1076_1 (27 August): https://wikileaks.org/plusd/cables/09BRASILIA1076_a.html [accessed 22 November 2015].

Zirin, Dave (2014), *Brazil's Dance with the Devil: The World Cup, the Olympics, and the Fight for Democracy* (Chicago: Haymarket Books).

Zoellick, Robert (2003), 'Confrontations Doomed WTO Cancun Meeting, Zoellick Says', *Financial Times* (22 September).

Index

Abdenur, R. 40–41, 213–214
Africa 41–42, 45, 57, 82, 132–133,
    141–142, 184, 188–191, 194
  Brazilian FDI 125–126
  South Atlantic 146–147
  South–South Cooperation 123, 183
Agência Brasileira de Cooperação
    (ABC) 189–191, 194
agro-industry 37–38, 95–97, 102
ALADI (Asociación Latinoamericana de
    Integración) 34
Amazon 51, 143–144
  Cooperation Treaty 145
Amorim, C. 135, 141–142, 149, 188,
    218
Angola 77, 79, 122–127, 146, 178,
    184–185
Argentina 31–32, 70, 94–95, 106–109,
    156–157
auto-estima 60, 68, 183
autonomy, quest for 9–10

Banco do Sul 165–66
BASIC 235
BNDES (Banco Nacional de
    Desenvolvimento Econômico e
    Social) 44, 112–113, 118–119,
    125, 131, 159, 164
Bolivia 43
  gas nationalization 130–131, 165
Boliviarian movement 164–166
BRICS (Brazil, Russia, India, China,
    South Africa) 78, 236–237
business-government relations 115

Cardoso, F. H. 75
  China 224–225
  economic crisis 202–204
  Mercosul 158–159
  presidential diplomacy 32–33
  South America 158, 179–80
CELAC (Comunidade de Estados
    Latino-Americanos e Caribenhos)
    71–73, 169
Chávez, H. 43, 116, 164–165
China
  market economy status 231
  trade with 226–227
  Vale 232
Clinton, W. J. 203
Collor de Mello, F. 89–90
commodity boom 101–102
Community of Portuguese Speaking
    Nations (CPLP) 42, 181,
    187–188
congress 18, 28
consensual hegemony 10–11, 49, 62,
    136, 170–172
constitution and foreign policy 28
Cotton-Four 104

Defence
  expenditure 136–137
  ministry of 214–215
  national development policy
    139–140
  South Atlantic 142
democracy promotion 60–61, 81–82,
    179–180

Dilma 45, 180, 244–245, 247
  Africa 184, 194
  China 238

Ecuador 171
Ecuador–Peru border war 148
Embrear 138, 233
empreiteiras 44, 78, 121–125

Fanon, F. 20
fighter jets 138
foreign direct investment (FDI) 15,
    33, 44, 90, 112–113, 121–122,
    207–210
  Africa 123–125, 129
  corruption 132
  financing of 125–126
  Lula 127
  outward Brazilian 119–121
Fourth Fleet 216
Free Trade Area of the Americas
    (FTAA) 53, 55, 69–70, 91–92
Furlan, L. F. 37

G-20 (WTO) 55–56, 103, 234–235,
    242
Garcia, M. A. 36–37, 43, 131
geopolitics 139–140, 154
global governance 52, 67–68, 177
Guimarães, S. P. 36, 42
Guinea 132
Guinea Bissau 194

Haiti 148–149
Helibras 138
HIV/AIDS 56
human rights 60

IBSA (India-Brazil-South Africa
    Dialogue Forum) 58, 76, 184
ICONE (Instituto de Estudos do
    Comércio e Negociações
    Internacioanais) 38–39, 98, 100
IIRSA (Iniciativa para la Integración
    de la Infraestructura Regional
    Suramericana) 70–71, 160–161
IMF (International Monetary Fund) 51,
    202–204
infrastructure integration 94, 160–161
international organizations 193
  debts to 84
  leadership of 67

Iran 80–81, 217–218
Itamaraty
  Africa 185, 187
  budget 42, 45, 246
  Dilma 45, 186
  diplomatic training 29–30
  ideology 42
  institution 28–29
  policy review 66–68, 176–178
  trade policy 100–101
  white paper 46

Jank, M. 38, 98–99
Jobim, N 140–141

Libya 82–83
Li Jinzhang 237
Li Keqiang 238
Lula
  Africa 141, 182, 188–189, 195
  Bush, G. W. 204
  Chavez, H. 165
  China 225, 233–234
  empreiteiras 182–183
  FDI 128–129
  foreign policy team 36, 75
  Mozambique 129
  South America 163–167, 179–180

MDIC (Ministry of Development,
    Industry and Foreign Trade) 30,
    39, 45, 98–99, 194
media and foreign policy 2, 35
Mercosul (Mercado Comum do Sul)
    89–95
  critiques of 106
  expansion 160
  formation 89, 157
  institutionalization 69
  trade disputes 107
  trade growth 90, 157–158
  Venezuela 169
Mexico 155–156
middle power 80, 176, 240
MINUSTAH 148–149
MOMEP 148
Monroe Doctrine 134, 199
Morales, E. 43
Mozambique 122, 180–181, 188

NAFTA (North American Free Trade
    Agreement) 156

Namibia 146–147
national development policy 111–112
National Security Agency (NSA)
    218–219
Nuclear Non-Proliferation Treaty
    (NPT) 62, 80

Odebrecht 122–125, 131, 185

Pacific Alliance 171
peace-keeping 148–150
Petrobras 116
    Angola 184–185
    Bolivia 130–131, 135
presidential diplomacy 31–32, 45–47,
    195, 255
    Cardoso, F. H. 32–33
    Dilma 45, 184, 194
    Lula 168–171, 184
    FDI 128–129
privatization 111, 113–114

R2P (Responsibility to Protect) 82–83,
    141
real plan 202–203
Rio Branco, Baron of 199–200
Rodrigues, R. 37
RWP (Responsibility While Protecting)
    83

security community 140
Serra, J. 246, 248
SIVAM 144–145
social policy 43, 77
South Africa 146
South America 158
    Brazilian FDI 127
    free trade area (SAFTA) 92–93
    infrastructure integration 160–161
    presidential summits 34, 185
South American Defence Council 142

South Atlantic 145–147
    Treaty Organization 142–143
South–South Cooperation (SSC) 20–21,
    40–42, 45, 76–77, 123, 132, 182,
    183, 187, 189–192
sovereignty 50–51
structural power 10–13, 182
submarines 139

trade policy
    agriculture 97
    geopolitics 102
    Itamaraty 100–101
    MDIC 97–98
    technical advice 100

Unasul (União de Nações Sul-
    Americanas) 69, 71, 164, 169
United Nations 51, 62, 139, 145
United Nations Security Council 148

Vale 185, 188
    Africa 128, 132, 194
    Argentina 128
    China
    Dilma 116
    government equity 115
    Mozambique 122–123, 129
    ownership of 114
Vargas, Getulio 200
Venezuela 169
Vieira, M. 249

War on Terror 212
WTO (World Trade Organization)
    38–39, 53, 55–56, 103–104,
    192–193

ZOPACAS (Zona de Paz e Cooperação
    do Atlântico Sul) 142–143,
    146–147